Hadassah National Convention,
Philadelphia, Pennsylvania, 1957.
Photo by G.D. Hackett.

IT TAKES A DREAM
THE STORY OF HADASSAH

By Marlin Levin

Abridged by Esther Kustanowitz

gefen גפן
publishing house בית הוצאה לאור
JERUSALEM ♦ NEW YORK

www.hadassah.org

Typesetting: Marzel A.S. – Jerusalem
Cover Illustration: Brooke Hunyady

1 3 5 7 9 8 6 4 2

Gefen Publishing House
POB 36004, Jerusalem 91360, Israel
972-2-538-0247 • orders@gefenpublishing.com

Gefen Books
12 New Street Hewlett, NY 11557, USA
516-295-2805 • gefenbooks@cs.com

www.israelbooks.com

Printed in Israel

ISBN 965-229-300-8

Library of Congress Cataloging-in-Publication Data:
Levin, Marlin
It takes a dream—: the story of Hadassah / Marlin Levin:
foreword by Elle Wiesel: afterword by Teddy Kollek.
Includes Index.

1. Hadassah, the Women's Zionist Organization of America. I. Title.

DS150.H4L49 1997 • 320.54'095694—dc21 • CIP Number: 97-19184

Contents

for my parents
ISADORE AND ROSE

FOREWORD

by Elie Wiesel

It is a given in the Jewish world: if you want a project to come to fruition, if you want an initiative to have a follow-up, you think of Hadassah.

Hadassah is more than an organization; it's a family — a family that loves and is loved. It loves to help those in need, the weak, the ill; in short, those who need help. And it is a family that is loved because it does these things with as much devotion as competence. Is it because Hadassah is made up of and run by women? And is it because these women are more dynamic, endowed with a more pragmatic sensibility than men? Far be it from me to even think of hiding behind the "Fifth Amendment." In the case of Hadassah, I am sorely tempted to answer "yes." The women of Hadassah have always been successful in guarding against the scatter-shot approach and the piling up of activities and goals. They know what they want to do, and they do it well.

As for Hadassah's history, it can be found meticulously and, of course, warmly recounted in Marlin Levin's narrative — the beginnings of the dream, the challenges, the apparently insurmountable obstacles, the victories won on Mount Scopus, overlooking Jerusalem. Who is not acquainted with Hadassah's Hospital, which attracts researchers, physicians and patients from the whole world?

The originality of Hadassah stems from its preoccupation with the education of its members, teaching them that it's not enough just to collect money, that it's just as important to be cognizant of the meaning of what they've undertaken.

Several times, I have had occasion to be a participant in their regional and national meetings. Each time I was pleasantly surprised by their organizational talents as well as by the thoughtfulness of their discussions.

Do I idealize Hadassah? Let's just say that I propose the romantic view. That's because, even today, one can still find in Hadassah the inspiring devotion and enthusiasm that were the hallmarks of the early Zionist movements.

A memory: Moscow, 1966. It's my second visit. The holiday of Simhat Torah. My impressions, I have given them elsewhere. The singing, the dancing, the courage of our Jews who, before anyone else, had defiantly dared to confront the Kremlin's terror. Suddenly, I heard some familiar voices: some one hundred Hadassah women had had the very same idea as I did — to come celebrate, with those admirable Russian Jews, the most beautiful of Jewish holidays. Like myself, they would go over to talk to the young people there, they would slip a few siddurim to the aged, they would establish relationships, they would deliver a few words of encouragement; — they were everywhere.

Back in America, I happened to mention to one of Hadassah's leaders how happy I had been to see so many of her associates in Moscow. "How many of us were there?" she asked. I answered: "More than a hundred." She burst out laughing: "There were twenty five of us there." It was my turn to laugh: "You were involved in so many activities that there appeared to be four times as many of you as there were."

I was grateful to them. Hadassah had been among the first Jewish organizations to work for the Jews of the Soviet Union. As for the others, it was impossible to motivate them, to make them take action. May I remind you that, in those days, in the sixties, "the Jews of Silence" were not the ones who were living in fear in the Soviet Union, but rather their brothers who were living in security, if not in happiness, in the West.

Does that mean that Hadassah's past, however glorious, is without fault? That would be an exaggeration. There is no human endeavor without a blemish. For example, I am not convinced that even Hadassah did enough for the Jews of Europe during the Holocaust. Nor, of course, did anyone else. But let's leave that for another time. Today, it is incumbent on us to recount simply all the pride that Hadassah inspires in the hearts of so many Jews in Israel, in America and around the world.

Today, let us say to Hadassah, to its leaders and to its members: thank you for existing, thank you for all the honor you bestow on Jewish womanhood.

Elie Wiesel
Translated from the French by Joseph Lowin

PREFACE

by Golda Meir

Looking back at the changes in American Jewish life, which I myself witnessed, I would put the growth and influence of Hadassah high on the list. Out of a little volunteer group of Zionist women organized some sixty years ago has come a force of great dimensions, a force for health, education and the salvation of human beings. Hadassah has been making a contribution of basic importance to the development of the State of Israel and — clearly because of this — to the survival and enhancement of the Jewish community in the United States. Notably it has, at the same time, developed in thousands of women skills and talents unknown even to themselves.

All this emerges in rich detail from the pages of *Balm in Gilead*. Interweaving the story of Hadassah with the unbelievable, often tragic, political struggle of Jews in Palestine, the book shows Hadassah's efforts in true perspective, not as philanthropy but as nation-building in the face of great odds. Beginning at the turn of this century, Mr. Levin makes us see and feel the filth, poverty and disease of Turkish-ruled Jerusalem. This was the distress that inspired Henrietta Szold to make of American Jewish women "the healing of the daughter of my people."

Those American women were to bring the neglected land modern medicine at its most advanced — hospitals, the training of doctors and nurses, university medical research. It is a great and daring story, from 1913 when the first two nurses came, to 1918 when the Medical Unit arrived in the war-stricken, starving country, to vital aid in successive outbreaks of anti-Jewish rioting. Medicine was supplemented by vocational education and the magnificent Youth Aliyah program that saved thousands of Jewish children from the extermination camps, which snuffed out the lives of a million of their young brothers and sisters in Europe.

I cannot forget the meeting I participated in during the siege of Jerusalem in 1948, when Hadassah's representatives decided to hold on to their hospital on Mount Scopus as long as possible and, in doing so, helped to divert the brunt of Arab attack from the Jewish Quarter of Jerusalem. Until the liberation of Jerusalem in 1967, we were cut off from Mount Scopus where so many Arabs had been healed by Hadassah. Having lost Scopus, Hadassah energetically planned and built its hospital complex in Ein Kerem. Later, many of its medical staff were lent to Asian and African developing countries, as I know very well from my days as Israel's foreign minister. And sadly, though gloriously, the Hadassah Hospital at Ein Kerem is known to so many of us in Israel as the place that cared for hundreds upon hundreds of wounded soldiers during the Six-Day War and thereafter.

This is the record of an extraordinary alliance between Jewish women in the United States and their people come to life again in the Land of Israel — one of the great chapters in the integral relationship between the State of Israel and Jews throughout the world.

Golda Meir
Reprinted from *It Takes A Dream…The Story of Hadassah* (1997)

INTRODUCTION

This is an abridged version of *It Takes A Dream*, an epic that spans two centuries and relates the exploits of generations of fearless women — and men — as they heal, enlighten, and save lives in nearly every corner of the globe. This, then, is the story of Hadassah.

The first slim volume documenting Hadassah's story appeared in 1973 as *Balm in Gilead*. After three printings, it disappeared from bookshelves and demand for it went unanswered. Within a quarter of a century, a younger generation of Hadassah members had appeared, knowing woefully little about their colorful heritage. To fill the need for a guide, the leadership requested that the author update *Balm*.

So much had occurred in the interim that it took more than a year of intensive research and interviewing, under the wise direction of former president Bernice Tannenbaum, to complete the task. And when the update was published, the book was fully twice the size as the original. It made a triumphant appearance at the 1997 Hadassah convention in Chicago under a new title: *It Takes A Dream...The Story of Hadassah*.

The book has had an active career. For the jubilee celebration of the State of Israel in 1998, Hadassah published its first Hebrew edition entitled

Darush Rak Halom. Both English and Hebrew editions are required reading for students in social work courses.

In the US, a study guide for *It Takes A Dream* was prepared by Danielle J. Lewis, then published as a basic text in Hadassah's three-year Leadership Academy curriculum and for use by study groups throughout the country. And the Jewish Braille Institute of America recorded the book on seventeen tapes for use by the visually impaired. By the year 2000, the English edition was nearly out of print and a new version was needed.

To accommodate a generation with a high percentage of full-time professional women, single mothers and part-time volunteers, Hadassah has issued this abridged version of the second edition, edited by author Esther D. Kustanowitz. Some of the most recent changes and achievements since *It Takes A Dream* came out are cited in this introduction.

In the introduction to the second edition, I depicted the life of a Hadassah president as she carried out her responsibilities. At that time the president — Hadassah's twenty-first — was Marlene Edith Post. Since Marlene's routine was quite typical of most of the organization's leaders — in intensity if not in detail — herewith is a portion of that narrative:

> "She rises weekdays at 5:15 AM to avoid rush hour traffic from her home in Manhasset, and after a small breakfast, dashes into her car for the ride to Manhattan, reaching her seventh-floor office in Hadassah House on West 58th Street in forty-five minutes.
>
> "The President of Hadassah carries with her a mountain of paperwork that she gives to her secretary, with whom she goes over the day's heavy schedule. There are sessions with leaders of other organizations and National Board members. There are budgets to study, requests for funding, new projects, a convention in preparation, Hadassah Medical Organization department heads visiting from Israel,

preparation for a visit to the White House and, as always, correspondence to answer.

"Lunch is on her desk or in Hadassah's lunchroom, if at all. Consultations with national or regional leaders can run into dinner. If she manages to leave the office by 9:00 PM she will drive home. Otherwise, there is a Hadassah apartment at her disposal close by. Every year she travels tens of thousands of miles visiting chapters in each of the fifty states. Every six weeks on average she is in Israel to attend to Hadassah matters."

At the 1999 National Hadassah Convention in Washington, DC, Marlene completed her four-year term and went on to chair the highly successful Birthright Israel project that sends thousands of youth to Israel on introductory educational visits. She handed her presidential baton over to Bonnie Lipton, a woman of eminent courage and one of the most successful fundraisers in Hadassah's history.

Being president of one of America's largest women's organizations, with more than 300,000 members, places an enormous responsibility on Bonnie, a former Spanish student and teacher. It elevates her to one of the most formidable positions in American and Jewish life. Following her inauguration on July 27, 1999, she received a direct invitation from President Clinton to join a few other Jewish leaders in the Oval Office. In a private conversation with Bonnie, he inquired about Hillary's appearance before the Washington convention. (Hillary, who was awarded Hadassah's highest honor, the Henrietta Szold Award, received an ovation following her address.)

Bonnie rose to the presidency well prepared. She had already raised more funds for Hadassah than any other individual in the organization's history, having brought into Hadassah's treasury some $50 million. Some of those funds paid for the construction of the new Mother and Child

Center on the Ein Kerem campus in Jerusalem. As HMO chair at the time, Bonnie was involved in every facet of the Center's construction.

Bonnie brings to the top Hadassah position a warm, open personality that has been tempered by the fires of tragedy and triumph. On January 11, 1998, she was in the midst of radiation therapy for breast cancer when she was told that her husband of nearly forty years had been severely injured in a major accident while skiing, not far from their home in Pittsfield, Massachusetts.

"Not knowing whether he would live or die, I still had to undergo [radiation]," she sadly recalls. Alan Lipton, a leader in Jewish affairs, did not die but he was impaired for life with incurable brain damage.

Born in Chicago, Bonnie and Alan met as students in Purdue University where each served consecutively as president of the Hillel Foundation, and then later as president of two other organizations. After marriage, Bonnie's mother-in-law gifted her with a Life Membership in Hadassah.

After Bonnie and Alan moved from Chicago to Pittsfield, she became an active member. But not until their first trip to Israel did she become totally involved, embracing Hadassah's Zionist mission as an expression of her love for Zion. "That trip was the turning point in my life. When I reached Jerusalem I felt as if I was returning home in a way I'd never felt."

"Bonnie brings tremendous knowledge of Hadassah and Israel to the organization. She has a vision for the future," comments Past President Deborah Kaplan. Bonnie makes no secret about what that might be and how she sees herself in the role. "I stand before you," she told the 2,100 delegates crowding the national convention in Washington, DC, "as a professional volunteer."

"…Working for Hadassah means an opportunity for creativity and an awareness of our heritage, duties and privileges that are essential to the existence of the Jewish State. My goal is to move Hadassah into the next century as the premier women's Zionist volunteer organization. Education is the heart of Hadassah; volunteerism is the soul. By promoting Jewish life, and providing education and emotional support for maintaining a Jewish identity, Hadassah will strengthen the Jewish people. This is the legacy of Henrietta Szold.

"But first Hadassah must face the challenge of bringing others into our membership and leadership ranks. We want to attract career women, college graduates and returnees, the staunch feminists, the former Young Judaeans, the widows, the single women by choice or by chance, young couples, families — by definition, every segment of our changing Jewish population. We can do it. We will do it," Bonnie pledged.

"We will educate them. We will involve them. We will show them that Hadassah is an instrument which will help to interpret the life of today while connecting the inseparable links in the chain of the Jewish heritage. We will take them to Israel to see our projects firsthand and to understand the decades of service that Hadassah has given not only to building the Jewish State, but also to building the Jewish people."

Bonnie's style is embracing, informative and informal — uncharacteristic for any organization president. Her style is reflected in her conduct of National Board meetings. The heads of less important committees are called upon more often than previously; reports of the meetings are e-mailed around the country. "I want everyone to feel a part of the action and thinking of today's Hadassah," Bonnie says.

If there were any doubts about Hadassah's Zionist character today, Bonnie decisively dispelled them. "We are Zionists. The issues we take on as American Jewish women are part of our Zionism. I am going to do everything to strengthen our connection to Israel. In my administration, Israel will be one of the dominant issues."

Volunteerism has also become one of those issues. Says the president:

> "The philosophy, direction and strength of this organization
> is derived from the volunteers. There is a place for the
> creative skills of the professional. But when the professional

comes to work for Hadassah, she must understand that it is
the volunteer who decides policy."

The intensive search for an Executive Director led to Dr. Ellen Marson, an academic with an exceptional array of qualifications who had recently joined Hadassah's staff in another position. Ellen had served for thirty years as an educator and administrator at the John Jay College of the City University of New York. She held chairs in Women's Studies and on the Academic Review Committee, and was adviser to the Jewish Students Society. Ellen is also an activist in Jewish and Israel affairs.

As she assumed Hadassah's top professional position, she commented, "I feel that I have come home."

Major personnel changes have also taken place in Israel. In 1999, Prof. Avi Israeli, specialist in internal medicine and administration, deputy to Prof. Shmuel Penchas, was appointed Director-General of HMO, Hadassah's flagship project, but resigned at the end of the following year. He continues teaching and research as a university professor and heads a department in the Hebrew University-Hadassah Braun School of Public Health and Community Medicine.

On January 1, 2001, Prof. Shlomo Mor-Yosef assumed the post of Director-General of HMO. A graduate of the Hebrew University-Hadassah Medical School in Jerusalem, he returns to Hadassah-Ein Kerem where he was deputy director in the early 1990s, before heading Beersheba's Soroka Hospital. At Soroka, the leading health institution in the south of the country, Mor-Yosef instituted new projects that led to significant growth for the hospital and won him great respect among the professional community. A native of Jerusalem and a specialist in obstetrics and gynecology, he also has a master's degree in administration from Harvard University.

At Hadassah's College of Technology (HCT), Prof. Ya'acov Amidi, who had been director since 1977, retired in 1999. Dr. Nava Ben-Zvi, a longtime professor at the Hebrew University in Jerusalem, was appointed

President of the College. She is eminently suited for the position by virtue of her twenty-five years of experience in science, technology and education. She has already introduced the College to new ways to reach and educate the present student body — 1,500 young men and women of diverse backgrounds and learning styles.

Perhaps Hadassah's most significant political and prestigious triumph of the last decade was to achieve consultative status as a non-governmental organization (NGO) in the UN Economic and Social Council (ECOSOC). Next in importance to the Security Council, ECOSOC consists of fifty-four members elected by the General Assembly. It is responsible for carrying out UN functions in non-military, non-political affairs — education, health and the like. Hadassah had made several previous attempts to gain consultative status in this body, but only in 2001 did it win acceptance despite opposition from representatives of several Arab states. The international dimension of its humanitarian contributions to society was finally recognized by this world body.

On the American scene, Hadassah has undertaken a remarkable variety of activities and subjects.

Positive work is being carried out in the nation's capital. During the 1999 convention, 1,800 delegates descended on the halls of Congress for a "Day on the Hill." As members of state delegations they met with thirty senators and ninety representatives, and they had much to say.

Reacting to the many high-profile acts of gun violence — most notably the shooting at the Jewish Community Center in Grenada Hills, California — they strongly advocated for Congress to pass a Hate Crimes Bill. Hadassah joined other organizations in sponsoring the Million Mom March for tighter gun control on Mother's Day, 2000. Five hundred members took part in the march.

Hadassah also actively advocates for legislation on these and other issues:

- Preventing discrimination by health insurance companies on the basis of genetic information.
- Stronger protections for survivors of domestic abuse.
- Continued separation of church and state as stated in the First Amendment.
- Continued foreign aid to Israel.
- The American Schools and Hospitals Abroad program (ASHA).

Few organizations in the US, if any, have been as energetic and as innovative in improving the image and status of women. Abortion was one of the hot issues in the election of 2000. Hadassah was not silent, letting its voice be heard at the Republican and Democratic national conventions by joining pro-choice rallies with the Religious Coalition for Reproductive Choice.

In 1997, the Hadassah Leadership Academy (HLA) was established, offering a curriculum with the aim of creating new leaders for Hadassah and the American Jewish community. In the spring of 1998, the first candidates began studying at eleven sites around the country. HLA members are committed to meet four hours a month for two years to study Jewish education and leadership techniques. The first year focuses on American Jewish communal issues and small group leadership skills, culminating with a trip to Washington, DC to advocate for issues of concern to Hadassah. The second year, focusing on Israel and leadership methods in large organizations, climaxes with a trip to Israel to visit Hadassah sites and explore contemporary issues.

Students for the HLA are chosen on a regional basis and usually take leadership positions in their regions. With these courses Hadassah hopes to assure its future with leaders of the caliber traditionally associated with the organization.

Impetus for the HLA came from the National Commission on American Jewish Women, established in 1994 by Hadassah and Brandeis

University. Some of the recommendations included in the report of the Commission were also included in Hadassah's 1996-2000 strategic plan. One was to set up a program to educate new leadership in the local community. Another recommendation was to create a unique institute specializing in research on women's issues. This institute, established in January 1997 at Brandeis University in Waltham, Massachusetts with a multimillion dollar grant from Hadassah, is the Hadassah International Research Institute on Jewish Women (HIRIJW). Most of the research grants given by the Institute pertain to Jewish women's history and biography. Research is diversified, from a dissertation on the education of Jewish women in America between 1870 and 1920, to a project on women's education in New Zealand.

For a research institute, its activities extend well beyond the usual funding of projects to conferences and symposia. Its publication of *Nashim* ("Women") is devoted to pluralistic reflections of Jewish women. There is a working paper series, a bibliography series and other projects aimed at providing information about Jewish women.

Probably no new Hadassah project of the last decade has been as visionary as the Hadassah Foundation, set up with a multimillion dollar fund by Hadassah. First introduced by Bernice Tannenbaum and Barbara Tirschwell at a National Board meeting at January 1997, it was adopted at the Mid-Winter Conference one year later.

The wellspring of the Foundation flows from a prophetic statement from Henrietta Szold:

> "The new world ahead will require an intensification of every strength and every fitness — intellectual vigor, purity of soul, fervent spirit — but also the addition of new outlooks and new vistas."

The Foundation provides grants for organizations establishing innovative programs that impact women and girls in Israel and the US. The first eight grants — five in Israel and three in the US — were awarded in the summer of 2000.

The mission of the Foundation states:

> "The Hadassah Foundation is dedicated to refocusing the priorities of the Jewish community, through innovative and creative funding for women and girls in the United States and Israel. Its mission is to: improve the status, health and well-being of women and girls; bring their contributions, issues and needs from the margins to the center of Jewish concern; and encourage and facilitate their active participation in decision-making and in leadership in all spheres of life."

No greater tribute could have been made to Henrietta Szold's life and work, and no greater compliment could be made to the noble purpose of Hadassah's *raison d'être* than that.

Hadassah is and always has been about people and their needs — a child in Jerusalem who needs a bone marrow transplant; a youth in Tiberias who wants to learn the complexities of computers; relief for earthquake victims of Armenia or war victims of Sarajevo; Jews in Beijing or Hong Kong searching for their identity; Israeli immigrants from Ethiopia and Russia; and the list goes on.

Hadassah has funded projects that have saved countless lives regardless of nationality, race, religion or gender. It has honed the skills of physicians from many areas, prepared young women and men to meet the demands of high technology and made arid land fruitful by building dams, draining swamps and building reservoirs for possible future water shortages.

It has made American Jewish women more conscious of their heritage while offering curbside mammography tests to them. It is doubtful whether any Nobel laureate organization has done more in so many diversified fields for the benefit of man — and woman — kind.

This abridgement of *It Takes A Dream* attempts to highlight the salient features of Hadassah's whirlwind of activity and its often death-defying adventures in Israel and elsewhere over the last nine decades against the background of political revolution, social upheaval and natural disaster.

The research, writing and editing of the two full editions, which served as the basis for this condensed form, could not have been accomplished without the assistance of many in the US and Israel. Space permits only a mention of their names, but to all I am deeply indebted.

To: Bernice Tannenbaum, Rose Goldman *z"l*, Susan Woodland, Zvia Nardi, Shulamith Nardi, Jean Max and Jerusalem's *Time* office, Alex Auswaks, Henrietta Wolinsky, Marian Lewin-Epstein, Annabelle Yuval, Rhoda Cohen, Hinda Gross, Ethel Carmel, numerous Hadassah staff members in Jerusalem and several score Hadassah veterans who were generous in giving me hours of time to reveal their stories that in some cases went back to well before the First World War.

I am appreciative as well of those visionary and valiant Hadassah leaders who were responsible for generating the first edition. Among them: Rebecca Shulman, Judith Epstein, Esther Gottesman and Rose Halprin — may their memories be for a blessing. And to Marlene Post for giving the green light to bring out the second edition and to Bonnie Lipton for supporting the creation of this new abridged edition.

I am indebted most of all to my wife of fifty-three years, Betty Schoffman Levin, whose critique of the English text was unerring and who, working as a volunteer long nights for three months, helped preserve the accuracy of the Hebrew translation. In so doing she prepared it for Zvia Nardi whose Hebrew expertise brought it to a standard worthy of publication.

Here then is the abridged version of an adventure story that makes the most exciting work of fiction pale by comparison.

Marlin Levin
Jerusalem, July 2001

ACKNOWLEDGMENTS

With deep appreciation, we acknowledge those who enthusiastically offered their talents, expertise and wisdom to help bring to fruition this abridged edition of *"It Takes a Dream...The Story of Hadassah."* We are most grateful to:

Marlin Levin, author of the original manuscript, who brilliantly interpreted the dramatic story of Hadassah against the canvas of history in the making.

Bonnie Lipton, National President of Hadassah, a courageous explorer of new directions for Hadassah, whose tenacity and drive inspire and strengthen us.

Esther Kustanowitz, editor, who sensitively abridged the original text, preserving its quality and integrity.

Danielle Lewis, for her resourceful and meticulous editorial and logistical assistance.

Susan Woodland, for her exceptional archival and analytical skills, which were of inestimable value.

Edith Zamost and Shirley Blumberg, who accepted the challenge of reviewing the abridged text, and then offered penetrating and thoughtful suggestions.

The Communications Division, by Sue Mizrahi, Pamela Vassil, Roberta Elliott, Carol Winer, Julie Farkas and JeriAnn Geller, who provided creativity and guidance during the pre-publication process.

It is our hope that this edition will offer new insights to the old but ever-new story of the extraordinary Hadassah pioneers of yesterday and today.

Bernice S. Tannenbaum
New York, June 2002

MISSION: JERUSALEM

Jerusalem entered the nineteenth century with the eyes of the Western world focused upon it. In 1799, Napoleon Bonaparte stormed the gates of Acre and Jaffa, pushed inland and reached Nazareth where he spent a night in prayer. But his conquest was short-lived. The Ottomans on land and the British at sea defeated his overextended troops, preventing his triumphal entry into the Holy City. Bonaparte's presence in the Holy Land nevertheless electrified Europe and by the first half of the nineteenth century, pilgrims were on a new crusade.

Over the centuries, Jerusalem has been called by a hundred names: City of Heaven, City of Peace, Navel of the World. To Europeans it was more than a city of flesh and blood; it was not really of this earth, but a gleaming golden, fantasy city of sun-burnished castles guarded by hovering angels. The first pilgrims who followed Bonaparte found Jerusalem sublime in its natural beauty, but hardly the glittering capital of some celestial realm. To their dismay they found that the God who reigned over its indolent residents from beneath a golden dome on the Temple Mount was Allah. Except for some shrines, Jerusalem was in fact a neglected city — its venerated streets defiled by heaps of sewage and feces and built upon layers of refuse that had accumulated to a height of over fifty feet since the days of the Second Temple. The sanitary condition of the City of God was such that anyone who sought to spend his last days on earth there could look forward to fulfilling that ideal with dispatch.

The word of Jerusalem's degradation soon spread to the religious councils of Europe. Missionaries and emissaries rushed to the scene from Russia, Britain, Prussia and France. These self-sacrificing souls, unaccustomed to either the ways or the filth of the Middle East, nonetheless attacked disease and ignorance with fervor. But their primary aim was spiritual salvation. By 1840, the local population of 7,000 Jews and 5,000 Moslems looked upon the rapidly increasing number of Christians in Jerusalem (3,000 in 1840) as a threat of conversion much more real than the danger from vermin or microbes. Just as disturbed by the missionary menace were the medicine men who balmed the sick and dying with amulets and talismans. As missionary schools, hospices and clinics began to appear in the walled city, bitter murmurings spread through the marketplaces and the houses of worship:

> Ha! Christians, you say? Not with names like Gershtman and
> Bergheim. Converts! May their names be erased!
> At the English Mission a Jew will step inside with a fever
> and come out cured of both his fever and his Judaism.

The physician Gershtman and the pharmacist Bergheim arrived in 1838. By the early 1840s, the sick and the lame — Jew and Moslem alike — were trooping regularly to mission clinics and getting quicker cures than they could ever expect from the quacks. As conversions multiplied, the rabbis sent frantic messages to Jewish notables in Europe. One of the first to reply was the Italian-born, British philanthropist Sir Moses Montefiore, who made many visits to Jerusalem, the first in 1827. Sir Moses sent a Chelsea physician, with medical supplies, but he did not stay. The missionaries did, and the Jews of Jerusalem wrote more urgent warnings to their brethren on the continent. What was in reality the forerunner of a European invasion of the Holy Land was to them a Christian conquest of the Holy City. The crisis for the Jews reached its peak by 1853 when the Crimean War between Russia and Turkey erupted. As a result, *halukah* (charity) from Russia, on which half the city's Jewish population depended, came to a halt. The alternative to starvation was to take the free food, medicine, and clothing dispensed by the missionaries. The situation was similar in Tiberias, Safed and Hebron. It seemed only a question of time and pills before Jewry in Eretz Israel would silently disappear.

In 1853 there appeared at the gates of Jerusalem a distinguished, bearded French-speaking gentleman who introduced himself as Baron Gustav de Rothschild. To the spiritual leaders of the community he was one of the city's hovering angels in disguise. Baron Gustav was appalled by the conditions in which the Jews lived. He recognized the threat from the missions and sent his father, Baron James, an urgent message in Paris: "All that our brethren in Jerusalem say is true. Their needs call for the most urgent action." In the French capital, Baron James summoned one of his most trusted friends, Albert Cohn, a scholar and a devoted Jew who directed the educational work of the Rothschild family. He gave Dr. Cohn a simple mandate: save the Jewish community of Jerusalem.

In June 1854, Albert Cohn left Paris for Vienna en route to Jerusalem. In the Austrian capital he called on Emperor Franz Josef I, who five years earlier had granted his Jewish subjects full civil rights. Dr. Cohn faced the emperor with this proposal: if Franz Josef agreed to be the patron, a hospital would be built in Jerusalem with Rothschild funds that would serve all, regardless of race or creed, in the spirit of the empire's liberal new constitution. The Catholic Franz Josef assented, and with an empire firmly behind him, Dr. Cohn set sail for the Holy Land with a traveling companion. They landed at Jaffa on July 7, and two days later stood at Jerusalem's Jaffa Gate. There the entire Jewish community awaited them. Dr. Cohn wept both out of joy and grief, and paraphrasing the words of the prophet, he asked, "Is this the city that is more beautiful than the whole land and now is sighing?" Refusing to rest, he went directly to the Western Wall to pray for the success of his venture. Every Jew in the city, Ashkenazi and Sephardi, infant and aged, man and woman, followed reverently in his footsteps.

Negotiations for the purchase of a hospital building began immediately. The most suitable structure in the Jewish Quarter was a religious school belonging to the Sephardi community. It was located on the slope facing the Wall and the Al Aqsa Mosque. With £1,000 in gold available, the negotiations were not unnecessarily protracted, but there was a fly in the ointment. Under Ottoman law, a European was not permitted to own property in Palestine. Dr. Cohn suggested that he take a lease on the building on condition that when the Rothschild Hospital moved to other quarters, the premises would be returned to the Sephardi community. Thirty-four years later, in 1888, that is actually what happened. The Rothschild Hospital moved outside the walled city and the Sephardi community replaced it with its own Misgav Ladach Hospital.

Only seventeen days after Cohn arrived, the conversion of the Sephardi yeshiva into a hospital of eighteen beds (nine for men, nine for women) was completed. It was Rosh Hodesh Menahem Av, July 26. The dedication on that hot, dry summer day was done in the typical Rothschild manner. Turkish and Arab dignitaries of the city attended. So did the consuls of Austria, England, France and Prussia. So did the tailors and the rabbis, the beggars and the carpenters, the scribes and the yeshiva boys. Cohn spoke in faultless Hebrew, Arabic, French and German. He gave notice that the hospital was under the protection of Franz Josef's flag and that it would be open to the sick of all faiths. The Talmud Torah children, proud to appear before so distinguished an audience, lustily sang Psalm 119 (the longest in the Psalter) and the equally proud rabbis besought the Divine to pour his blessings on the sultan, the kings of Europe and the Rothschild family.

The hospital was a declaration of status, a symbol to the non-Jewish residents of the city of Jewish determination to survive. Just as important, it was an assurance to the Jews that they had not been forgotten by their fellow Jews in the Diaspora. In turn there was little doubt they would ever forget the Rothschilds. On the courtyard gate, they put up a Hebrew sign transliterated in Latin characters which read: "For Mayer Rothschild from his sons Amschel, Solomon, Nathan, Karl, James Barrane von Rothschild." From each of the eighteen beds in the green-walled wards hung a plaque bearing the names of members of the family plus those of Sir Moses Montefiore and Lady Judith, Cohn and his wife, Mathilde.

Before leaving Jerusalem later that month, Dr. Cohn provided funds for the establishment of a boys' vocational school and a girls' school. (The latter, named for Evelina de Rothschild, still exists in western Jerusalem.) On his way home he called on the Turkish minister for foreign affairs in Constantinople and received an unusual letter assuring the Rothschilds that all rights accorded to the Gentiles of Jerusalem would likewise be accorded to the Jews. He stopped in Vienna to report to Franz Josef and invited him to visit the hospital, which, in fact, the emperor did sixteen years later. Back in Paris he arranged for a steady flow to the Rothschild Hospital of pharmaceuticals, surgical equipment and a substantial supply of hernia belts. To the schools he shipped libraries in five languages.

The hospital itself was always crowded. Medical care was free. Anyone could visit the outpatient clinic three times a week and obtain all medicines without charge. The Rothschild Hospital doctor was permitted to take a fee only for house visits: two francs during the day and four francs at night. Administration of the hospital was turned over to a mixed Ashkenazi-Sephardi committee, but such were the intercommunal squabbles that the committee was finally disbanded and the hospital was turned over to Dr. Bernard Neumann, who had been resident in Jerusalem for seven years. In Paris, Dr. Cohn received regular reports of the institution's progress. At the end of the first year he happily informed Baron James that of the 542 patients served by the hospital, 502 walked out cured.

In that first year, men of many faiths and nations were served. The meticulously kept records include among the patients "33 Moldavians, 21 Italians and 2 Americans." A glance at the occupations of some Jewish patients is revealing: "1 painter, 2 watchmakers, 5 bakers, 6 laundrywomen and 83 scribes," among others. Expenses were listed down to the last sou:

of the 14,510 francs expended the first year, 9,490 were spent on food and administration. Albert Cohn returned in 1856 and went away heartened. A year later Alphonse de Rothschild (brother of Gustav) paid a visit and took back to Paris a stirring report that both the death and conversion rates of Jews had fallen. Baron Alphonse set up a fund of 250,000 francs from which the annual interest of 14,000 francs would keep the hospital operating on a permanent basis. In gratitude, the *yishuv* (as the Jewish community in pre-State Palestine was known) promised that the memorial prayer for the dead would be recited annually in the synagogue hospital for all Rothschilds.

The Rothschilds' word being as sound as their checks, the hospital never lacked means of support. Obligations were kept, sometimes in bizarre ways. During the Franco-Prussian War, for example, Paris was cut off by siege. In September 1870, Dr. Cohn wrote the following letter to the hospital's administrator in Jerusalem:

> This letter will reach you by means of a balloon, if it reaches you at all. We are under siege this Sunday, September 18. Today is the 33rd day of the siege but we are well, thank God.
>
> Just now I have written by balloon post to London and I have asked Mrs. Lionel de Rothschild to send by way of the London branch to Mr. Valero in Jerusalem 5,000 francs that we will repay, God willing, after the siege is lifted.

In the same year that the Rothschild Hospital was opened, a will was probated in New Orleans, Louisiana, that had a decisive effect on the fortunes of Jerusalem's Jewish community and its hospital. It was the will of the shipowner and philanthropist Judah Touro. He, too, had heard the agonizing cries that came from the Holy City and provided $60,000 from his $1.5 million estate for settling the Jews outside the walls of Jerusalem so that they would be assured "the inestimable privilege of worshiping the Almighty according to our religion, without molestation." Except for monks who lived in seclusion in fortress monasteries, no one lived beyond the walls of Jerusalem nor dared to venture beyond them at night. But life within the walls had become so intolerable that a break finally had to be made. Touro's bequest was given to Sir Moses Montefiore who directed the construction of "almshouses" across the Valley of Hinnom, which in Biblical times was used by the Canaanites for human sacrifice. There, only a few hundred yards away, the walled city was close enough for comfort, yet sufficiently distant to escape the ministrations of missionaries and the fevers of plagues. Named Mishkenot Sha'ananim (tranquil dwellings), they were beautiful homes for their times; so well built, in fact, that a century-and-a-half later they were still being used. Touro's money soon ran out but Sir Moses kept them going. Later, another neighborhood was added with a windmill that became a landmark. As a tribute to Montefiore the new project was named Yemin Moshe (right hand of Moses). Sir Moses, knighted by Queen Victoria for his philanthropy to Jews, placed an illustration of the Mishkenot Sha'ananim-Yemin Moshe site on his family seal.

In 1875, with money for the almshouses gone, the poor moved back to the Old City. The wealthy Jews of Jerusalem leased their own homes within the overcrowded walled city and moved into the almshouses, living in them rent-free and paying only for their upkeep. In that same year the new head of the hospital began to press the Rothschilds to move the institution outside the walls. Recurrent epidemics made administration difficult and the more well-to-do Jews were leaving the Old City to build new homes beyond the ramparts. The hospital, the pioneer director reasoned, should be in the vanguard of Jewish settlement. The argument made sense to Alphonse de Rothschild, who got the necessary *firman* (edict or permit issued by an Ottoman ruler) from Sultan Abdul Hamid II and work soon began on a one-and-a-half acre plot not far from the Russian Orthodox Church compound. One week before Rosh Hashanah in 1888, the hospital — a dignified, three-story edifice costing 211,000 francs and described by a diarist as "the nicest building in our city" was ready. Originally, the hospital was fitted out with eighteen beds but was quickly enlarged to twenty-four. Later, a children's ward was opened, which permitted mothers to live with their infants.

By the turn of the century, the hospital could boast of the city's first maternity ward and its own ophthalmologist who was taken on to combat the rocketing incidence of trachoma. Baron Alphonse increased the capital fund for the hospital from 250,000 francs to a round one million and the income increased accordingly. In 1904, Alphonse began receiving reports of budget "irregularities" — money for the hospital was ending up in private pockets — and ordered the physician in charge to turn over the administration to a special committee "appointed from among the best Ashkenazim and Sephardim." He sent a physician from Paris to assume control of the medical organization, but such were the antagonisms between the communities that the committee could not function effectively. The baron, by now old and ill, threw up his hands and turned over the hospital administration to Kol Israel Haverim (better known as the *Alliance Israèlite Universelle*), the Jewish communal organization in Paris. Within a year the books were straightened out and in 1905 the hospital boasted thirty-three beds, two physicians and an administrator, as well as separate quarters for the three men and their families.

To most Diaspora Jews, as to the Gentiles, Jerusalem had become a mystical, dreamlike place. For the Jews the city's glories were in its history — in the chronicles of the kingdoms of David and Solomon, in the heroism of the Maccabees, in the magnificence of the Second Temple. *Yerushalayim* was a holy word to repeat in prayers; and its rebirth in this world would be a gift brought by the Messiah. Then in the mid-nineteenth century, Cohn's crucial mission changed Jewry's view of Jerusalem. He had come to save a remnant and as a result the city again stirred for Jews everywhere. With the passage of time ordinary Jews began to acknowledge the fact that on top of the weather-beaten, treeless Judean hills, at the end of an aimless road, Jerusalem breathed.

It would be ludicrous to imply that Jerusalem of the Jews was restored only because the Rothschild Hospital of eighteen beds was established. However, it was a significant beginning. Later on, other hospitals were established, but in the first fifty years none of them managed to prevent epidemics or even undertook large-scale public health campaigns. Jerusalem still suffered from malaria, trachoma, cholera, typhus, typhoid, ringworm, malnutrition and pox. But at least the city's Jewish population could receive good care without paying for it either with money or with their consciences. Mothers began going to hospital to have their babies and infant mortality dropped.

The Rothschild Hospital helped lift Jerusalem out of the Middle Ages, brought it into contact with the medical sciences of the Western world and, perhaps as important as anything else, provided the focus from which Jerusalem would be catapulted into the best that medicine of the twentieth century could offer. But that would not take place until after World War I, when a few brave pioneers in skirts came to Jerusalem and looked into the sad, sick eyes of its children.

FLIES IN NOVEMBER

November, 1909. On the uneven stone pavement outside the Old City wall on Jaffa Road, three women stood chatting in a foreign tongue. From where the barefooted beggar woman sat, up against the wall of the apothecary, she could see that the eldest of the three had tears in her eyes. These were definitely Ashkenazim from a foreign land, judging by their clothes. The beggar woman adjusted the scrawny dozing infant in the crook of her arm, extended her hand a bit farther and pleaded, "*Matliq, matliq.*"

The old Ashkenazi matron sent one of the younger women over with a coin. The beggar looked up as the Ashkenazi lady said, in a strange Hebrew accent: "Why don't you brush the flies from the child's eyes?" As the lady deposited the coin she swooshed her hand past the baby's fly-infested eyes. The baby jerked its head as though something familiar were being snatched from it. The beggar woman's own watery, squinting eyes lost some of their vapidity for a moment as she began to explain, "They will only come back." They were part of her abysmal life, like begging and like her chronically ill husband who had to stop work in the carpentry shop because of his consumption. "May God bless you and keep you well and give you a safe return home," the beggar murmured. The matron called out, "Come on now, we have only a few hours to the Sabbath, Henrietta, and we want to make it to the Wailing Wall." Henrietta Szold, then only a month from her forty-ninth birthday, turned and, lost in thought, walked off mechanically to join her mother and friend. Soon they were lost in the crowds of the marketplace.

Not far from the beggar woman a haughty, elderly doctor was receiving patients from the back of his ragged brown mule. "What is *your* complaint?" he asked with a touch of annoyance in his voice.

"Doctor, doctor," half-cried the young man holding his hand to his brow. "My brains feel like they are boiling."

The doctor bent low to probe for the patient's spleen and stated the diagnosis, "ague," in the tone of a magistrate fining a hungry thief for stealing bread. He scribbled a prescription on a piece of notepad paper, took the *grush* that was extended to him and looking at his watch, shouted, "Next!" An elderly man complained of loose bowels and terrible cramps. "Bismuth for you. Next! Hurry up! The Sabbath is approaching."

Prescriptions in hand, the sick turned and stepped past the beggar woman into the pharmacy. In the opening years of the twentieth century in Jerusalem, quinine and bismuth were the magic cure-alls. Physicians took up their stations outside pharmacies because it was both practical and profitable. Doctors and the druggists cooperated as partners-in-trade.

In the first years of the century not more than a dozen Jewish doctors with fairly good training practiced in Jerusalem. Because there was no medical association or effective health department to control standards, quackery and medicine existed side by side. Even physicians who had genuine diplomas scoffed at new methods of diagnosis and treatment. A thorough medical examination was unknown. When one young physician arrived with a lab microscope from Europe as late as 1914, the resident doctors laughed in ridicule. What kind of doctor has to examine blood specimens before he diagnoses malaria?

As for the pharmacists, not all, to put it mildly, had academic training. A large number learned the rudiments of the profession as apprentices.

Turkish law did require a certificate showing professional competence before issuing a license to open a drugstore, but this regulation was easily circumvented. All one had to do was to pay a practicing pharmacist to open another shop in his own name. He would then permit his young apprentice to run the apothecary. Working together with a physician or a quack, they made a good living by splitting the profits.

Jerusalem had four Jewish hospitals. But many Jewish mothers placed their faith primarily in traditional preventive measures and remedies. For example, if a baby's sleep is disturbed at night because of stomach pains, burn white herbs of the field under the cradle. The fragrance, seductive as a lullaby, will caress the child back to sleep. If the pains continue, then drive them away with a burning stick applied to the chest or stomach.

Basically, all ills had their root in the evil eye and there was no safer, better guardian than a well-prepared amulet. Going into hospitals was so risky! Is it not a fact that many who go in never come out alive? If you are going to die, then what better place than in your own bed, among your own sympathetic family. It is better to die peacefully than to take your chance in the French, German, Greek, Russian or British mission hospitals. The government hospital? Who would ever think of putting his life into the hands of the Turks! Jewish hospitals? They were probably the safest of the lot, but better wear the *kame'a* and stay well.

A relatively small community of enlightened souls took advantage of the few reasonably good doctors and hospitals in Jerusalem. They went to the excellent eye hospital established by the Order of St. John of Malta. They entered the Jewish institutions which, for all their administrative problems, gave exceptional medical care. But the best of medicine in Jerusalem was only palliative in the face of enormous problems. When Henrietta Szold and her seventy-seven-year-old mother stared at the flies in children's eyes in Tiberias, Jaffa and Jerusalem — a scene that invariably brought tears to the eyes of Mrs. Szold — they were looking at a problem whose dimensions were social and educational as much as medical. The need for a vast public health program screamed out. Sophie Szold and

Henrietta heard the cry. Throughout their month-long trip to the Holy Land in November 1909, as they visited schools and religious sites and saw beggars in squalid streets, it was a tearful Sophie who prodded Henrietta, "Here is work for you. This is what your group ought to be doing."

Henrietta's group was a study circle that was formed as the Daughters of Zion by Emma Gottheil in 1898. Emma had accompanied her husband, Semitics Professor Richard Gottheil, to Basel where he was a delegate to the Second Zionist Congress. While there, Emma met Theodor Herzl, who encouraged her to organize American women in the cause of Zionism. On her return home she invited young women from New York's East Side to study Zionist and Jewish subjects at her elegant Fifth Avenue home. A few years later, at the suggestion of some of the participants in the group, the name was changed from Daughters of Zion to Hadassah in memory of Hadassah Gottheil, Emma's mother. Similar study groups sprang up in Harlem, then a center of Jewish life in New York City. Most of them were called Daughters of Zion and a few, Hadassah. They were small and met sporadically. The young women, who were in their late teens or early twenties and had some Hebrew education, were concerned about their identity as Jews. In their discussions they eagerly sought Judaism's answers to such problems as social inequality and militarism.

One of the better known group leaders was the brilliant but complex Jessie Sampter, a pacifist and intellectual who traveled to Zionism and back to Judaism by a devious route, through the Ethical Culture movement, Unitarianism, and socialism. She influenced a number of young women who later were to become leaders on the American Zionist scene. One of the more successful study circles called Hadassah was formed by Lotta Levensohn at the encouragement of Rabbi Judah Leib Magnes of Temple Emanu-El, for whom she worked in his capacity as honorary secretary of the Federation of American Zionists (later the Zionist Organization of America). In discussing prospective members for the group, whose primary purpose was to acquaint Jewish women with Zionism and Palestine, Rabbi Magnes suggested to Lotta that his prestigious pacifist friend Henrietta

Szold be asked to join — in an honorary capacity, of course. Lotta later recalled that she was reticent to approach so eminent a scholar and editor as Henrietta Szold and asked Rabbi Magnes to make the approach. He did and Henrietta replied that she would be happy to join, but as an active participant not as an honorary do-nothing member. That assured the success of this particular study group, which met in the YMHA on Lexington Avenue in New York City.

Henrietta was twice the age of most of the young women, so it was natural that she should be their leader. Later, she brought in a few older women ("They will keep me company," she told a friend), among them Emma Gottheil and Mathilde Schechter, wife of the president of the Jewish Theological Seminary. Henrietta set the tone of these meetings. "Wherever she sat," Lotta Levensohn recalled years later, "Henrietta Szold became the head of the table."

On returning from her Palestine adventure in January 1910, Henrietta lost herself more and more in Zionist work. She served as honorary secretary of the predominantly male Federation of American Zionists. But after eight months of trying to straighten out the organization's hopelessly desperate financial affairs, she gave up. That experience, coupled with her mother's urging to "do something" and her own poignant recollections of life in Palestine, quickened within her the idea that a national women's Zionist organization must be formed to carry out practical projects. She arrived upon the scene at the right moment.

Women from the former study groups of Harlem created the nucleus. There was Emma Gottheil, the third woman of the triumvirate that toured Jerusalem. There was Gertrude Goldsmith, with whom Henrietta worked closely on the early plans of a national organization. And there were Mathilde Schechter, Lotta Levensohn, Sophia Berger and Rosalie Philips. "I would be ashamed to attend another Zionist Congress," Emma would say, "and report that we did nothing but talk." That was the sentiment of the hour and it was embodied by these seven Zionist women in the brief invitations sent out to prospective members in the second week of February

1912. "The time is ripe for a large organization of women Zionists," their invitation read. Their purpose? "The promotion of Jewish institutions and enterprises in Palestine and the fostering of Jewish ideals."

Sometime after 8:00 pm on February 24, 1912, in the vestry of Rabbi Magnes's Temple Emanu-El, a group of fewer than twenty (the precise number is not known) met for what was to become the founding session of Hadassah as a national Zionist organization. Henrietta Szold spoke of her trip to Palestine and of the need for a "definite project." Eva Leon, who had been to Palestine more recently and was Emma Gottheil's sister, brought home the need for wider maternity service in the Holy Land. One such service, she reported, was run by the Christian missionary London Jews' Society whose price of admission to the hospital was the agreement of mothers to baptize their babies upon departure.

At the first meeting there was a discussion on numerous projects that the Daughters of Zion might initiate in the *yishuv*: a day nursery, a girls' workshop to make lace, a maternity hospital, a school to train midwives, a district nursing scheme, sending nurses to Palestine.

At a subsequent meeting, a constitution was drawn up. Article I gave the old familiar name Daughters of Zion to the projected national organization. Henrietta held that the organization could not really be considered national in scope until more chapters were established. This constitution, then, was really the by-laws of the New York chapter called Hadassah. The name was a natural if only because the founding meeting was held during the season of Purim and Hadassah was the Hebrew name of the Biblical heroine Queen Esther. In the spirit of the holiday the opening session decided that all future chapters would likewise take on the names of Jewish heroines. (It was historic justice that in later years Henrietta Szold would be among the most popular of all Hadassah chapter names.) Other articles in the constitution spelled out the purpose of the organization and provided that associate membership be given to women who did not consider themselves Zionists. Later, associate membership was dropped when the constitution was amended to foster Zionist ideals in

America. Finally, Henrietta Szold was elected president and nineteen members were made either officers or members of the board. Altogether, thirty-eight women were listed as founding members.

At the first board meeting, held at the home of Mathilde Schechter on April 4 and chaired by Henrietta, the ten members present agreed that if practical projects were not to be mere flights of fancy, the organization would need a membership of three hundred. By the end of the first year, that goal had not been reached: there were 157 regulars and 37 associates, and the cash box had $542.00 from dues. But the chapter did have a motto taken from Jeremiah 8:22, *Aruḥat Bat Ami* — "The Healing of the Daughter of My People"[1]), which was suggested by the Jewish Theological Seminary's Israel Friedlaender. And it had an emblem — a Star of David — on which the motto and "Hadassah" in Hebrew were superimposed. That was the work of Victor Brenner who gave the United States the design for the Lincoln penny. In February 1913, Hadassah Chapter finally had sufficient money — "tribute" as Henrietta Szold described it sarcastically — to affiliate with the Federation of American Zionists. In June of 1914 the first and last Daughters of Zion national convention was held in Rochester, New York, where seven of the eight chapters were represented (Boston's Deborah chapter was missing). At that convention Rabbi Magnes took an active part. His lasting contribution was to urge the delegates to adopt the more concise Hadassah as the name of the national organization. It was done and Daughters of Zion became a footnote in Zionist history.

Apart from its founding day, there is no date in Hadassah's first years that was so significant and hopeful for the organization as January 1, 1913. On that day an extraordinary meeting of the board was called at the home of Emma Gottheil. There, Henrietta Szold brought the exciting news that the department store magnate and philanthropist, Nathan Straus, had

---

1   Although this standard translation is especially appropriate for Hadassah, the phrase is more accurately translated "Healing of My People."

agreed to help finance both traveling expenses and four months' salary for a trained nurse, to be chosen by Hadassah, to open a health station in Palestine. But he set two conditions: that after the first four months Hadassah would have to pay the nurse's salary — that would mean $2,500 for two years — and that she would be ready to leave for Palestine with Mr. and Mrs. Straus by January 18.

Henrietta was sold on the idea of establishing in Jerusalem, for a start, a district home-nursing system. She wanted to model it after Lillian Wald's Settlement House and District Visiting Nurses, then being tried with success in New York City. Nathan Straus, too, was aware of the need. He visited Jerusalem in 1912 and on the spot set up a soup kitchen and a health bureau. The latter was run by a German-Jewish doctor, Wilhelm Bruenn, who on his own had been fighting malaria, trachoma and blackwater fever.

There was a political side to the quick opening of the Hadassah health bureau. When Straus arrived in Palestine, he found that the German government, expecting a war in Europe, was sending doctors and sanitary engineers to Jerusalem. The Kaiser considered Palestine strategic because it protected the flank of the Berlin-Constantinople-Baghdad railroad line. It was therefore necessary to clean up the area for the German soldiers who might have to be stationed there. The Kaiser ordered the Hamburg Tropical Institute to send the doctors and sanitary engineers, one of whom was known to the Jews of Jerusalem as a dangerous and rabid anti-Semite, to close cisterns and give quinine prophylaxis. It was this added factor — to provide a counterweight to the German activity — that convinced Straus to answer the urgent call of Dr. Bruenn and the Jewish community.

When Straus returned from Jerusalem, he told Henrietta Szold in explanation of opening a soup kitchen, "Once long ago, I suffered the pangs of hunger. I was starving; I had no money for even a single meal. I have never forgotten the sensation. In so far as lies within my power, no man that crosses my path shall go hungry." He then told Henrietta that he had heard about her desire to initiate a nursing project in Jerusalem.

"Why don't you do it?" the philanthropist asked Henrietta.

"But we have only $283 in our treasury," she replied.

"That doesn't matter," Mr. and Mrs. Straus said in unison. "Start!" Nathan Straus commanded.

Henrietta insisted there was no money, and Nathan Straus repeated, "That has nothing to do with it!" Henrietta was befuddled for a moment. Then her eye caught Lina Straus standing behind her husband's chair nodding frantically as if to say, Henrietta later recalled, "The Lord will provide." Henrietta was encouraged although doubt still lingered.

The day after that confrontation took place, the Strauses called at Henrietta's apartment. They went through the same "start work — no money" routine until Nathan Straus finally broke it off with the offer that Henrietta somewhat breathlessly reported to her board on January 1. The Lord had indeed provided.

Hadassah was facing its first crisis. "When I heard the proposal, I was terrified," board member Alice Seligsberg wrote many years later. With only a few hundred dollars in the till these women were about to undertake a major responsibility that could make them the laughing stock of the Jewish community. Already, male Zionist leaders were grousing that the women were dividing the movement. An undercurrent of feeling grew among board members that it was too big a challenge for so young an organization. But Henrietta and Emma were insistent. Their self-confidence swung the other members and when a vote to underwrite the mission was taken, all ten hands went up in favor. Everyone was aware that should they fail, the organization would be badly crippled. But should they make a success of it, chances were good of winning over large numbers of American Jewish women.

In the following weeks, hectic interviewing took place. Henrietta talked to twenty-one applicants. In the midst of the search for a suitable nurse came a bombshell message from Eva Leon. Non-Zionist friends in Chicago, she reported, offered to grant $2,000 a year for five years to send a nurse to Palestine and they insisted that Hadassah choose and supervise the nurse. The crisis was over. It was now possible to send two nurses with the Strauses and possibly a third and fourth later on.

On January 18, as planned, the Strauses sailed again for Palestine taking with them Eva Leon and two trailblazing Hadassah nurses — Rose Kaplan and Rachel Landy. Little more than two months later, on March 23, 1913, Hadassah for the first time brought healing to Jerusalem.

WAR, DISEASE, STARVATION, DEATH

T he four horsemen of the Apocalypse had already begun their long, wild ride in the Balkans when the first two Hadassah nurses set sail for Palestine in the bitter cold winter of January 1913. Highly skilled as the nurses were, they were not prepared for the hardships ahead.

Short and stocky, Russian-born Rose Kaplan was the older of the two and had a long, distinguished career in nursing at Mount Sinai Hospital in New York. Tall and blonde, Cleveland-born Rachel Landy was a light-hearted, fun-loving woman who had supervised nurses at Harlem Hospital Dispensary in New York. Rose signed up for two years, Ray for two-and-a-half. The nurses' personalities were complementary and they got along well. The plan was to introduce a district nursing system under the guidance of Dr. Bruenn, head of the Straus Health Bureau. Things turned out differently.

When the nurses, together with the Strauses and Eva Leon, arrived in Jerusalem, public health work was being done by a number of independent organizations. An eye clinic, Lema'an Zion, was functioning under a popular young German-Jewish physician, Albert Ticho. Anti-trachoma clinics were operating under the Austrian-Jewish doctor, Arieh Feigenbaum. Dr. Bruenn had gone to Tiberias to fight a cholera epidemic. Rose and Ray hardly knew where or with whom to begin. With more financial aid from the Strauses, they furnished a stone house located in the ghetto-like, ultra-orthodox quarter of Mea Shearim, opposite the Hungarian Houses. A fragrant lemon tree grew in the courtyard. On the iron gate entrance a sign was hung: "American Daughters of Zion Nurses Settlement HADASSAH," and — as fate would decree — at Purim time, on March 23, 1913, they accepted their first patients.

In the beginning they took maternity cases, but trachoma was so rampant that under the guidance of their neighbor, Dr. Ticho, they began to care for the sick eyes of Jerusalem. One year later, they reported to Hadassah that they had treated five thousand children for eye disease, 20 percent of them trachoma cases.

The Strauses and Eva Leon soon left. Hard work and loneliness took a double toll of the nurses' spirits. They had hoped they would be accepted with open arms by the community. Instead, they were greeted with suspicion and skepticism by both residents and professionals. In those days nurses who went to Jerusalem were nuns; rumors spread that Rose and Ray were spies who had come to infiltrate the Jewish community. They plugged away nevertheless against Jerusalem's spiritual and bodily malignancies. Their monthly reports contained an encyclopedia of illnesses: enteritis, dysentery, typhoid, paratyphoid, trachoma and starvation. What disturbed them most was the high maternal mortality rate. It seemed that at least every other mother died while giving birth. Ray and Rose were horrified to discover that "midwives" would supervise births without even washing their hands. To ease difficult labor the ignorant attendants would pour impure oil into the womb and unintentionally induce septicemia which was usually fatal.

The nurses immediately scoured Jerusalem for Jewish women who had received some training abroad in obstetrics. They discovered four, all graduates of Viennese and Constantinople schools, and employed them to pay regular visits to pregnant Jewish women in the city. Rose and Ray also formed a class for "big sisters" to whom they taught personal hygiene and child care.

When not tending to patients, the two nurses helped destitute families with a little money or food, sometimes giving them linen or a layette, and generally building confidence and faith in genuine medical practices. Where they could not help with medicines or money, they would ease social problems with sympathy and understanding. Gradually a feeling of kinship grew between the nurses and the Jewish community. Their warm, gentle manner and easy Yiddish talk had won out. Where once they were called spies, they were now called angels. In schools, where teachers had refused to permit the nurses to examine the children's eyes, they now eagerly greeted them. (Ray always had an added inducement in her pockets for the children: hard candies.)

When they diagnosed serious eye trouble, their most difficult task was to convince the patients, or the parents in the case of children, to enter Dr. Ticho's eye clinic for treatment. Once the patients did risk it, they found the cure well worth the treatment. Fear and prejudice gradually declined and the queues outside the settlement house grew longer from week to week. One of Ray's favorite stories was about a Bedouin who brought his young wife to Dr. Ticho's clinic. The Arab asked the doctor whether he could restore the sight of his bride's one bad eye. Ticho found that her sight had been impaired by tissue that had grown over an old inflammation and he operated. A short time later the woman could see well again. Her proud husband, profuse in his gratitude, said to Dr. Ticho, "I bought this woman cheaply because she had one bad eye. Now she is worth twice as much."

Jerusalem had a deep effect on the nurses. Rose was no Zionist when she left for Palestine and she never seemed to have considered the possibility of settling in the Holy Land. But in her letters home she wrote of the joy she felt when she visited schools, particularly the secular Gymnasium, where she saw hundreds of bright and alert children who had emigrated with their parents from Eastern Europe. She also wrote despairingly of the poor children she treated in Jerusalem's Tin Quarter, so-named because the hovels in which they lived were made from discarded Standard Oil Company tin cans. So bad were conditions of other Jewish families living in cramped, underground cavelike rooms, she said, that even a little bit of sunlight would have made an immense difference in preventing and curing illnesses. She reported back to Hadassah that social hygiene conditions were the prime factors influencing the health of the Jewish community, but the problems were so enormous that a large-scale public health effort would be needed to change the picture.

A few months before World War I erupted, noted Baltimore eye physician Harry Friedenwald spent two months' volunteer service in Jerusalem. He saw that the nurses were doing fine work, but that health institutions were duplicating each other. Besides four Jewish hospitals there were the Straus Health Bureau and Pasteur Institute, Dr. Ticho's Lema'an Zion, Dr. Feigenbaum's clinics and Hadassah. Competition among them caused animosity and friction. Ray and Rose worked around the clock — in the schools, at the settlement house, in Dr. Ticho's clinic, with pregnant women, teaching midwives. In the United States it was impossible for Hadassah leaders to get a clear picture of what was taking place. Frantic correspondence went back and forth between New York and Jerusalem. Hadassah was troubled that the nurses were fighting trachoma in schools when they should have been setting up a district nursing system. Besides, why wasn't the Straus Health Bureau doing the anti-trachoma work? So much had to be done by so few competent people that everything was being done on an emergency basis. It was clear even before Dr. Friedenwald arrived in Jerusalem that two more nurses were urgently required. Eva Leon reported to Hadassah that the nurses needed help to get their district visiting system underway. She said she planned to return to help them. After hearing Eva's report in January 1914, Hadassah's central committee in New York adopted two principles that fixed the guideposts for its future work in Palestine. In agreeing to Eva's return, it requested frequent reports and to consult with the home office on essential matters, "even at the risk of delay." Even then, Hadassah was thinking in terms of a permanent presence in Palestine and that final responsibility for all the work overseas had to reside with the home organization. Hadassah was to be no mere fundraiser but a dynamic American-based Zionist movement.

The war exploded in August 1914. Communications with Palestine were broken. Eva Leon did not return as planned. The additional nurses could not sail. Dr. Friedenwald reported his experiences to Henrietta Szold and suggested that Hadassah establish a lying-in hospital in Jerusalem, the first serious suggestion that Hadassah build a hospital. Henrietta reported this to the central committee in October. The committee decided to ask Rose Kaplan to consider remaining until a replacement could be sent. Ray Landy's contract was to expire in July 1915, and by then, it was felt, the war would be over. The request never reached Rose and her letters pleading for instructions never arrived in New York.

Conditions in Jerusalem were fast deteriorating. The city's Jews were panic-stricken at the thought of being trapped on a potential battlefield, but even more so that sons and fathers would be drafted into the sultan's army. Hundreds of families packed their bags, preparing to flee to Egypt. The Turks expelled all non-Turkish citizens. The French physician heading the Rothschild Hospital, Jacob Segal, returned to Paris and joined the army. Dr. Bruenn, of the Straus Health Bureau, sailed for Germany to enlist. Bruenn's successor, Abraham Goldberg, was inducted into the Turkish forces. Later on, Ticho and Feigenbaum would have to leave the city on perilous adventures. The prospects were not bright for the American nurses. The Jewish agronomist, Aaron Aaronsohn, famous for discovering the original species of wheat in eastern Galilee, warned the nurses to return home. Rose was in a dilemma. The last ship was about to sail from Haifa. She was not aware that Hadassah urgently wanted her to remain. Her contract was expiring. Refugees were pouring out of Jerusalem. She had little money left and no prospects for getting more. Aaronsohn, aware of the international political situation, pleaded with her to go. Rose bent to the pressures, but with a purpose. She sailed with the Jewish refugees, meaning to care for them in three camps set up in Alexandria. Then, while Hadassah's central committee was meeting in New York on February 15, Rose walked in. The committee members were startled. They soon learned that Rose could not stay on in Egypt because she needed urgent medical care. After an operation, she insisted on returning to the refugee camps in Alexandria. She set sail in November 1915, but the Greek steamer she had taken sank in the Atlantic as a result of a fire in the engine room. She was rescued and finally got to Egypt in early 1916. There she served in the camps until, later that year, she died of cancer.

Ray kept on with the maternity and anti-trachoma work in Jerusalem after Rose's departure. "Although it is not very pleasant living here alone, especially just now," she wrote to Alice Seligsberg in January 1915, "I am perfectly willing and satisfied to keep up the Hadassah work, as long as I have funds."

Brave but lonely, in an unpredictable situation where the Turks were daily becoming more anti-American, Ray tried to maintain a normal regimen of work. Every Thursday morning she continued to give classes in what she called her "School of Home Nursing." She wrote:

> We have taken bed-making with and without a patient in
> bed. I gave one of the children a bed sponge bath. We have
> made linseed poultices, mustard pastes and foot baths. The
> girls are very clever and enjoy the classes very much. The last
> few weeks I have been teaching bandaging, so as to be up-
> to-date. We all find it very fascinating. I just give practical
> work and then give them notes. The girls are from 15 to 17
> years of age — only seven of them — but small classes are
> always better…

Around Ray's island of normalcy the whirlwind of terror grew daily. Jews in Jerusalem were a suspect alien element. They were liable to sudden arrest, banishment and torture at the will and whim of Jamal Pasha, a tyrant who answered exclusively to the sultan and, on occasion, only to Allah. Little wonder that anyone who could escape the city did so. So many left that midway through the war only three Jewish physicians remained. Hard as they worked, they were helpless in the face of chain-reaction epidemics. Malnutrition set in on a large scale soon after the hostilities began. Day in, day out, families lived on *tzibile mit shires* (onions dipped in sesame seed oil), a few spoiled vegetables that were brought to market by the Bedouins, a bit of bread and a little goat's milk. Children suffered from a lack of vitamins, and as the war continued their stomachs became bloated. They were a pathetic picture, walking the streets of Jerusalem, searching garbage cans for scraps of food. Ray never forgot the scene:

> They are perfect studies of pain, misery and starvation. I never saw such faces. You can imagine how it feels to meet people who you can see are hungry, yet you don't like to approach them and they are ashamed to approach you. The Straus soup kitchen is open. What a blessing it is…You can imagine the number of applicants — such screaming and pushing — women fainting… I was watching some children of the Sepharad Talmud Torah eat their midday meal yesterday. Some had a piece of bread and the green leaves and stalks which come off a head of cauliflower. I have often wondered how these children can be happy — for they really seem to be. They are very amusing — perfect little devils. I have a right jolly time with them once in a while…

Two weeks later: "The children seem to be getting smaller and thinner every day. They…are such pitiful sights."

Then the locusts came. Voraciously, as though they too were victims of the famine, they ate fabrics, curtains, rugs. Infants had to be protected with heavy clothing. They fastened on to the garments — even the underwear — of adults.

Debilitating diseases became widespread — diarrhea and intestinal ailments were common, spread by unattended cesspits that poured rivers of sewage into the streets. Few residents boiled their water. Paratyphoid, typhoid, typhus swept across the city in waves. In summer, water in the cisterns sank low. The Old City of Jerusalem swarmed with mosquitoes and few residents escaped malaria. Trachoma cases multiplied and Jerusalem became known, along with its traditional names, as the City of the Blind. Spotted fever made an appearance, then cholera. On and on rolled the list of diseases and the registers of the dead.

Jerusalem was a ghostly city. In mid-morning, Jaffa Road was deserted except for the movement of military traffic. A few old people, who seemed immune to death, showed up regularly to sweep the streets. Men of military age dared not go out lest they be pulled into the sultan's forces by Jamal Pasha's police. And that was worse than a thousand plagues.

The situation might have been somewhat relieved if sources of money had not dried up. But Jerusalem was as poor as it was sick. Soon after the war began, families sold furniture, pillows, bedsheets and rugs to buy food. They would barter it to the Bedouin who came in out of the wilderness with vegetables. As the war went on, families were left living in bare houses, sleeping on stone and tile floors with nothing but the clothes they wore.

At this time, Ray wrote in one of her letters, "There is a lady physician here, an obstetrician and I have asked her to help us in our maternity work."

Helena Kagan was her name. Spurned and scorned by professional colleagues when she first arrived in Jerusalem from Switzerland the year before, she was later to carry on the Hadassah nurses' work when they left, and to treat Jerusalem single-handedly when the last two Jewish male physicians were forced out of the city. She was to become a legend in her own time.

In those days Helena Kagan kept a cow in her backyard just to provide milk for the children who visited her clinic. But it was only a drop in an ocean of need. To save the Jews of Jerusalem, transfusions of money and supplies were needed on a grand scale. They arrived in a most dramatic way.

Young as it was, Hadassah was making urgent inquiries at top political levels in Washington to send relief to the Jews of Palestine. Acting on its behalf was Louis Levin, a noted social service worker and brother-in-law of Henrietta Szold. Levin knew that a Navy collier, the *Vulcan*, was about to sail for the Middle East. He asked the Navy Department whether Hadassah could send along a physician and supplies. Inexplicably, the *Vulcan* was not permitted to take a physician but space was made for 900 tons of food and medicines sent by Mary Fels, wife of the founder of the Fels-Naphtha soap company, an active Zionist until she died, at age ninety, in 1953. Levin and a young dentist, Samuel Lewin-Epstein, were authorized to travel along with the relief.

The *Vulcan* put into Jaffa port four days after Passover in 1915, too late for its supplies of *matzot* to grace holiday tables. Awaiting the *Vulcan* were the Turkish police with orders to arrest Levin and Lewin-Epstein the moment they set foot on shore. The charge was that they were agents of the Allies who had come to incite a revolt against the Turkish regime. But the Turks were stymied by the American consul in Jerusalem, Otto Glazebrook, an Episcopalian minister who went aboard and announced that the two men had the diplomatic protection of the neutral US government. The two men turned over to Glazebrook $100,000 in gold which they had brought from American Zionist organizations for the Jews of Palestine. The consul returned immediately to Jerusalem with Lewin-Epstein who later checked into a Jerusalem hotel. Levin remained with the *Vulcan*.

One day, Jamal Pasha called on Lewin-Epstein, and in the presence of the consul invited him to dinner. Suspecting that the Pasha intended a plot against the American, Ellis Gillette, the interpreter, stepped on the foot of the consul and said, "But Dr. Glazebrook, you already have asked our guest for dinner." With that Lewin-Epstein was rushed to the safety of the consulate. In a few days, the *Vulcan* was to sail for home. Lewin-Epstein had to make the ship, but the consul had been warned that Jamal Pasha was not going to let him leave the country alive. It was suggested that he leave in disguise, but the proud Glazebrook would have none of it. "He arrived here as an American. He will leave as an American."

Telegraphs passed urgently between Jerusalem, American Ambassador Henry Morgenthau in Istanbul and the State Department. Finally, Glazebrook was authorized to inform Jamal Pasha that if Lewin-Epstein was harmed before he reached the *Vulcan*, the US cruiser *Tennessee*, steaming off the coast of Palestine, would fire its guns on the port of Jaffa. Jamal Pasha quickly indicated that the man need not worry about traveling to Jaffa. The ride to port went off without incident.

Back in Jerusalem, Jamal Pasha's agents began searching for the gold. Glazebrook had handed it over to David Yellin, then chairman of the Va'ad ha-Kehila (the committee of the Jewish community), whose headquarters were located in the Street of the Prophets not far from the Rothschild Hospital. One night, Yellin raced across the street to Helena Kagan, hauling the hot gold. He pleaded with her to hide it, arguing that the Turks would not search the premises of a single, young woman. Years later, Dr. Kagan recalled, "I almost fainted when I saw all that gold, because I knew that if I were ever found with it, I would have been hanged." Working at night, she and Yellin dug a hole next to a palm in her backyard and buried the money there. As they needed it, Dr. Kagan would dig it up and turn as much as was needed over to a special committee of the community. The treasure did not last too long. Nor did the relief supplies, half of which were confiscated by the Turks.

Through the summer of 1915, Ray Landy worked together with Helena Kagan. Her own money was down to practically nothing. Hadassah sent messages through Ambassador Morgenthau to Glazebrook to find out how she fared. Ray replied that even though her contract had run out, she was willing to stay on if everyone at home agreed. But Ray's parents in Cleveland were terrified by news reports from Palestine and implored Hadassah to recall their daughter. Finally, the central committee cabled:

"Come home." Ray could hardly believe that she was to seal the doors of the settlement house. She wrote to Hadassah, "I don't know whether I had malaria or whether my fever was due to your telegram, but my temperature went up to 39 degrees C. (101.6 F.) and stayed there off and on until I sent you a reply."

Ray settled her affairs, distributed supplies that she had received from the *Vulcan* and closed the settlement house. But she remained in Jerusalem until the very last moment. She disliked Jaffa so much that she asked Consul Glazebrook to telegraph her from the port precisely when the ship was to leave. As she sat for several days waiting, she wrote, "I still wish I would be obliged to stay until you could send nurses. I don't know whether it is Jerusalem or these trying times, but I have become so attached to everything and everybody that it gives me a sinking feeling when I think of leaving it all at this stage, especially since I have been through the worst. It upsets me very much to break up the Settlement. I had looked forward to leaving it in a different fashion."

Ray's last words from Jerusalem in September were to ask Hadassah to raise the salaries of the two local "probationers." Wrote Ray, "No matter what or how much I asked them to do, they always did it cheerfully." At the specific request of Hadassah, Dr. Kagan and Dr. Ticho continued the medical work. Glazebrook took fond leave of Ray. He had written Hadassah, "Miss Landy is one of the most useful people in Jerusalem. She is a splendid woman and is accomplishing most excellent work. I congratulate your society on having such a representative."

In New York, Hadassah had no word after it sent the "Come home" cable. It sent more cables to Glazebrook. Finally, on October 8 a telegram arrived from Ray in Naples. Two words: SAILING *CRETIC*. Ray was home two weeks later. The following day she reported to a meeting of the Central Committee. The gathering was full of emotion, pride and some disappointment, too. Ray reported that Albert Ticho was continuing with the anti-trachoma work. In one school she visited, she said, trachoma had been eradicated, but it would return. Helena Kagan was caring for the maternity cases. Ray pulled a letter out of her purse. Written by Dr. Kagan, the letter asked that a small polyclinic for female diseases be established. At a later meeting the committee accepted the suggestion on condition that the work be done in the name of Hadassah and in Dr. Kagan's office, and that she submit monthly reports.

But back in Palestine there was little hope of setting up such a clinic. Through 1916 and 1917 the community of Jerusalem dwindled. Corpses lying in the street were becoming a common sight. The new Jaffa suburb of Tel Aviv, begun with great hope and spirit in 1909 on the sands north of the port, was inhabited by ghosts. When the war broke out, Jamal Pasha ordered the evacuation of all Jews. Some ran back into Jaffa, others fled north, but most sought refuge in Alexandria. Tel Aviv, then consisting of nothing more than four main streets, was left without population. By the beginning of 1917 it looked like a deserted set of a Western film. Papers and packing materials were whisked up and down the sand-covered streets by the winds blowing in from the sea. Doors banged and echoed through the hollow town. Empty windows looked out on empty streets. Occasionally a guard from Jaffa shuffled through the quarter, coming and going like a mirage out of the dunes.

In November 1917, the Balfour Declaration was issued, promising a Jewish National Home in Palestine. But the Jews of Palestine knew nothing about it, and even had they known, they would have despaired that the only Jews left by the time the British could arrive would be dead ones. The Turkish authorities were aware, of course, of the declaration. General Edmund Allenby (known as "the Bull") was on his way from the south at the head of the British forces. It would be a month until he entered Jerusalem.

Of a prewar population of over 50,000 Jews, fewer than 25,000 remained, most of them women and children, old men and some frightened young men, many of them in hiding. The Turks became increasingly suspicious of the Jews who remained in Jerusalem. As Allenby's men took El Arish and were on their way to Beersheba, Jamal

Pasha insisted that every Jewish male of Jerusalem be called into service. Turkish police rounded up any man who could walk. A few young Americans studying in yeshivas were told to report to a police station to register as aliens. When they found they had been tricked into the Turkish army, they protested and waved their American passports. That brought sneers of contempt. They were corralled with all the rest.

Rothschild Hospital was taken over by the Turks and was then closed altogether. Three other Jewish hospitals remained open but had no funds or nurses and could do little for patients.

Shortly before the British entered Jerusalem, Jamal Pasha arrested the heads of the Jewish community. Consul Glazebrook used his influence to have them released on the pretext that they had to hand over the affairs of the Va'ad ha-Kehila to others. Once out of prison they needed a place to hide. They remembered the refuge they had used for the gold — Helena Kagan's house.

A sharp rap on the door scared the wits out of Dr. Kagan, that cold, rainy night of December 7. At first she refused to reply, fearing the Turkish army had decided to conscript women as well. The knock came harder and harder, again and again. Helena opened the door slightly to prevent it from breaking. Through the crack she could make out two figures: Rachel Feigenbaum and her father, Yosef Baran Meyouhas, a leader of the Jewish community.

Said Meyouhas, "Helena, I must hide here. They won't look for me in your house. I must stay the night."

Helena reluctantly agreed. She went to her kerosene stove to warm food for the drenched, shivering Meyouhas. Then, another brisk knock at the door. Meyouhas ran for cover inside the house.

Helena opened nervously. Another member of the Va'ad, Siegfried Hoofien, was looking for refuge.

"I'm coming from Glazebrook," whispered Hoofien. "He said he could not keep me another minute. Let me in." He told her that Ya'acov

Thon, then head of the Palestine office of the World Zionist Organization, was at Hadassah House (as the clinic was popularly known).

Helena ordered Hoofien to take cover with Meyouhas, wrapped a shawl around her shoulders and ran over to Hadassah House. She slipped through lines of Turkish soldiers moving out of the city. She banged violently on the door, but the frightened Thon refused to open. She continued knocking until he finally relented.

Thon followed her back through the storm. Helena gave refuge to one of the men in her clinic, put another in an empty house next door, and a third in a neighbor's flat. She asked Meyouhas for news of Arieh Feigenbaum, the eye specialist. Meyouhas said he heard Feigenbaum had been taken prisoner and was being held with hundreds of others in the Dominican monastery near Damascus Gate.

At dawn the next day, December 8, Helena headed for the monastery. Her plan was to bribe the guards to release the ophthalmologist. But the place was empty when she arrived. She found a deaf-mute and, in writing, instructed him to take one hundred pieces of gold to Feigenbaum. Since the messenger could not talk, he would not be questioned. If the deaf-mute brought back a note from Feigenbaum saying that the doctor had received the money, he would receive a reward of ten gold sovereigns. Two days later, the honest messenger was back, with a receipt from Feigenbaum, whom he had met on the road to Jericho.

Dr. Feigenbaum had been arrested while making his rounds of the Old City. When asked why he was being taken to the *nookta* (police station), the policeman replied, "Doctor Feigenbaum, you are a Zionist. The British have promised Palestine to the Jews. Therefore, you Jews are the enemy of the sultan." It was the first inkling that any Jew of Jerusalem had of the Balfour Declaration.

On the way to Jericho, the miserable group of men — Moslem Arabs, American Jews, Palestinian professionals and beggars — were strafed by British planes. They walked all the way to Jericho, a distance of twenty miles. En route one night they were held in an empty cistern. From Jericho

they were taken across the Jordan River in German lorries to e-Salt. Then
they marched to Dera'a and boarded a train to Damascus. In all, it was an
eight-day trip. They found chaos in Damascus and many escaped, among
them Feigenbaum. He moved south, walking, hitching rides, and got as far
as Kfar Saba where he waited for the British advance. But it was long in
coming. He saw horrible scenes of men and women dying of starvation.
The fleas were incredible. People dropped dead everywhere from typhus.

In the meantime, Dr. and Mrs. Ticho had fled via Damascus to
Istanbul, returning to Jerusalem after the war on a refugee ship.

On December 9, 1917, Allenby took the surrender of Jerusalem in
what is today the Romema Quarter of the city and signed the peace terms in
Sha'arei Tzedek Hospital, Jerusalem's oldest existing hospital. For the Jews
of the city the war was over, but it still raged farther north, and it would be
yet another year before the Armistice stopped all fighting. An American
Red Cross unit moved in with the British forces, but it was woefully
inadequate to deal with the dreadful health problems of Jerusalem. What
the *yishuv* needed was radical and complete medical rehabilitation, not just
supplies and pills.

It would be another eight months and a long hard winter before that
kind of aid would arrive. Unknown to the survivors, it was on the way.

THE UNIT

Broadway, "the Gay White Way," as it was then known, was neither gay nor white that second week of June 1918. Fourteen months previously, President Woodrow Wilson had asked Congress for a declaration of war. Now twenty-five American divisions were already in France and fresh ones were leaving weekly. In Belleau Wood, the green American Marines were stopping the massive German thrust toward Paris. Mightier, bloodier battles were still ahead, but the Marines were welcome relief to the growing numbers of casualties that would total more than 100,000 American dead and twice that number wounded before armistice five months hence.

The group of Hadassah doctors and nurses who gathered on 42nd Street in the early evening of June 11 were making an effort to be happy and carefree their last day on home soil. At midnight they would report at the pier for duty overseas.

Three thousand American men and women moved into the ship. Most were soldiers in khaki. Others were Red Cross and social welfare personnel. Forty-four, most of them doctors and nurses, wore a badge that no one had ever seen before: a red Star of David encircled by the words "American Zionist Medical Unit." At 4:00 am on June 12, the ship known as "number

19" joined eleven other ships in the predawn haze and sailed in convoy into the U-boat-infested Atlantic.

The AZMU — as the Unit was popularly known — was long overdue. It was conceived in June 1916, after the World Zionist Organization (WZO) in Copenhagen cabled an urgent appeal to the Provisional Executive Committee for General Zionist Affairs in New York City to send a medical force to Palestine. The committee passed the request on to the Federation of American Zionists, which in turn fielded the ball to Hadassah. That July, Hadassah was holding its third national convention in Philadelphia. The treasurer reported that the organization was in the black to the tune of $2,880.65, and membership was at a record high of 1,937. The goal of 2,000 members would certainly be reached before the end of the year. Henrietta Szold, who was also Hadassah's representative on the Provisional Executive Committee of WZO, disclosed that money had been raised to send two more nurses to Palestine. But in the name of Hadassah's central committee, she announced that what was really needed from Hadassah was to organize and contribute to the dispatch of an entire medical unit. The Federation of American Zionists had set a budget of $265,000, of which Hadassah would be required to raise only $25,000. "Only!" whispered a horrified delegate from Boston. "Only eleven times more than we have in the bank!" Henrietta made it sound simple. If every member saved on carfares, each could certainly donate up to fifteen dollars. And that would do it. Henrietta's leadership won the day. The project was endorsed.

Across the nation, as far as Kansas City and Galveston, then Hadassah's westernmost and southernmost chapters, Hadassah women saved nickels and dimes for the project. Henrietta had once said to her New York chapter, "The emergency should be used as an opportunity." It was. The AZMU became a cause to believe in and work for. Membership rose. And so did costs. By the end of 1917, Hadassah sent out word that its share in the project was now $30,000.

But money was only one of the problems in forming the AZMU.

Transport was another. Trans-Atlantic shipping was scarce for all but the military; the AZMU was to aid Palestine — a low priority — when, for America, the war was in Europe. Visas were a problem because the Turks held Palestine. Then, when the British issued the Balfour Declaration in November 1917, an entry permit from the Turks was unthinkable. In December, after Jerusalem was conquered by the British, the Unit's organizing committee began to negotiate with the British ambassador in Washington. By March 1918, authorization for the Unit had been received from Washington and London through the personal intervention of Supreme Court Justice Louis Brandeis, a leading Zionist. At first, the plan was to send the AZMU to Palestine via the Cape of Good Hope, but finally sanction was given for the medical team to sail directly to Europe on an American troopship.

Originally, the Unit was planned for two doctors, two nurses and a half-ton of supplies. By the time it got underway, there were twenty nurses, a dermatologist, obstetricians and gynecologists, an orthopedist, a pathologist, pediatricians, dentists, a pharmacist, eye and ear-nose-and-throat specialists, a sanitary engineer and five administrators. The manager, white-goateed Eliahu Lewin-Epstein who was secretary of the Provisional Executive, had sailed on ahead.

Henrietta Szold wanted to go but stayed behind to help raise funds, choosing Alice Seligsberg, a Central Committee member and children's welfare leader in New York, to replace her. Henrietta described Alice as "a rare human being, wise, devoted to duty to the point of self-effacement." However, Henrietta refused the pleas of another friend, Jessie Sampter, to join the mission. To Jessie, a poet, she wrote, "What your pen could add would not, to my mind, be so valuable as to justify changing what I conceive the character of the Unit should be — a strictly professional undertaking."

The pharmacopoeia and supplies that were shipped separately included 2,000 cases of medicines, two ambulances, eight vehicles, uncounted gallons of anti-louse fluid, medical instruments, blankets, linen and clothing — all told, enough to open a fifty-bed hospital. A great deal of thought went into the choice of summer and winter uniforms. The women had light cotton greys with panama hats and veils (to protect sensitive skin) for summer wear, dark grey woolens and velour hats for winter. According to prevailing fashion the hemline was just above the ankles. The men wore khaki cottons or woolens. For shipboard emergency, each member was given an outlandish life-saving unit that, when inflated, would have blocked the ship's companionways. When the commanding officer of the troopship saw the lifesaver, he exploded, "Anyone who inflates one of those tents in an emergency will be shot on the spot."

For all Henrietta Szold's meticulous preparation, the Unit went off without a medical director. Dr. Isaac Max Rubinow, a medical statistician from Washington who had accepted the post, suddenly backed out at the beginning of June at the insistence of his family. Szold appealed to Adolph Hubbard to go as an administrator in charge of equipment, personnel and finances. He agreed.

Thirty thousand Americans sailed in convoy that day, but only the AZMU and a group of American Judeans (who volunteered to fight with the Jewish Legion in Palestine) sailed through three submarine zones — the Atlantic, the English Channel and the Mediterranean. The two-week crossing of the Atlantic was hard from the outset. Homesickness was aggravated by seasickness, which was brought on by violent storms. Anxiety over submarines was so great that most Unit members climbed into their berths with boots and overcoats on and kept lifebelts at arms' length. Lifeboat drills two and three times daily did nothing to reassure them.

At 4:00 one morning, close to Scotland's shore, sirens sounded the submarine alert. Members of the Unit hurried to their lifeboat stations.

> We waited in silence. It was dark except for a thin glow of
> light on the horizon to the east. The minutes passed by in
> agony. Three thousand men and women thinking a single

thought. Most of them were soldiers who had to be there...But we were volunteers. We could have remained home. We nurses were all about 25 years old. Most of us never ventured beyond our home states. Some of us had gone for the adventure...we were scared. Some were here because they simply got bored at home doing not much of anything and this was one way of serving both our country and our fellow Jews. The pay was certainly good. One hundred dollars a month and maintenance for nurses. For the doctors, two hundred and twenty-five dollars. But at four o'clock in the morning, standing on top of a hunted ship, the pay was not so good as it first seemed...We heard muffled explosions off in the distance. Our escort cruiser, the San Diego, spotted the sub and sank it. The eternity was over. All-clear sounded. Later, when we learned that the San Diego went down in the Atlantic while returning home, we all cried a little.

Blacked-out Liverpool was a blessed sight. The night of June 24, the nurses marched down the gangplank waving tiny British and American flags. Two women, one with pneumonia and one with Spanish flu, were taken to the hospital on stretchers.

In London the Unit split, some bedding down at the Regent Palace in Piccadilly, the others at the Strand. With Vera Weizmann, Chaim Weizmann's wife, and WIZO founder Rebecca Sieff as their hosts, the nurses quickly got their fill of sightseeing, theaters, parties and teas. Wherever they went they were greeted as the AZMU's.

But the most remarkable welcome of all took place in the regal London Opera House on the afternoon of July 14. Posters all over London proclaimed: "A Public Meeting to Welcome the American Zionist Medical Unit on its Way to Palestine."

Zionists packed the opera house in high spirits. The previous

November, the British government had sent Lord Rothschild a short note saying that it looked with favor on the establishment of a Jewish home in Palestine. As a follow-up, Chaim Weizmann had gone off to Palestine in March as head of the British section of the Zionist Commission to survey conditions in preparation for implementation of the Balfour Declaration. In June, Weizmann had his first meeting with Emir Feisal, leader of the Arab world, with whom he was to come to an understanding on Arab acceptance of a Jewish State. In two weeks, the cornerstone of the Hebrew University would be laid on Mount Scopus in Jerusalem. The Zionist program was rolling forward rapidly; the AZMU's presence in London added vigor to the momentum.

Lord Rothschild, who chaired the meeting, was interrupted nine times by applause and cheers during a five-minute opening welcome address. "I consider the sending out of a fully-equipped Jewish Medical Unit as a very great tribute to the progressive means by which modern Zionists are seeking to solve the problems of the new Palestine."

The most rousing speech of the day, however, was made by a non-Jew, Member of Parliament George Barnes who represented the war cabinet. In a long-forgotten, but nevertheless highly significant address, he said to mounting crescendos of hand clapping:

> The British Government proclaimed its policy of Zionism because it believed that Zionism was identified with the ideals for which good men and women are struggling everywhere. That policy is the policy of the Allies with us in this war. It is the policy to which we are pledged. It is the policy which we believe accords with the wishes of vast numbers of the Jewish people. They are taking help and hope and succor to people long-oppressed and down-trodden...They are taking to a liberated East the knowledge and science of the modern West.

Another cabinet member, Sir Alfred Mond (later to become Lord

Melchett) followed: "What we have been promised in a declaration of policy made on November 2nd by the British Government, and which has since been gladly endorsed by the Governments of our gallant allies, France and Italy, is the establishment in Palestine of a Jewish national center, to which Jews from all over the world, who wish to unite in spreading the influence of Jewish thought, Jewish industry and Jewish energy throughout Palestine and the adjacent countries, can do so in complete harmony with the other people living in that territory." Then Nahum Sokolow, the great Hebrew writer and early Zionist leader, referred to the Balfour Declaration as the "Magna Carta of the Jewish people" and declared that the AZMU was the "beginning of the result of that Declaration."

Among the greeters was the highly popular and good-humored Colonel Josiah Wedgwood: "You are going to lay a foundation stone that will convert a race into a nation," and David Lloyd George who later became prime minister and had just come back from Palestine: "I have been working alongside the Arab Army and I want to say there is plenty of room in that country for the Jewish people, for the Arab people and for all the peoples that are in it."

The last to speak was Sergeant Gershon Agronsky (Agron) on behalf of the American Judeans. In the forthright manner that was later to make Agron a popular Zionist speaker and a fine editor of *The Palestine Post*, which he founded, he told the audience, "Bid us, if you will, good-bye or farewell but for a very short time, because we shall see you all in Palestine. In these circumstances, you cannot speak to us of homecoming in the sense of returning or of seeing us on a return when we shall pass through England again, because it is not our intention to come back."

Originally scheduled to remain ten days, the Unit had now been in England three weeks. The meeting in the Opera House had been arranged partly to keep up morale. It would still be another week before they could continue. Adolph Hubbard and a few others spent the time digging out as much information as they could on the conditions in Palestine. Having learned something of the terrifying situation awaiting them, they thanked heaven that they had the foresight to take along half a ton of medical supplies; the four hundred tons being shipped separately would most certainly be delayed en route. Now they could begin work the minute they stepped off the ship.

Finally, on July 22, the Unit was on the train to Southampton.

The group arrived in Paris past midnight to find a dozen army-requisitioned taxicabs waiting to take them in a grand convoy to their hotel near the Place de l'Opera. Only the next morning did Hubbard learn that the AZMU had been given the status of official guests by the French government because Baron Edmond de Rothschild had assumed "sponsorship" of the group. The war-bankrupted government, eager to maintain good relations with the financier, had laid out the red carpet. Hubbard, Alice and engineer Louis Cantor called on the baron. Impressed by their mission, he agreed to turn over the Rothschild Hospital in Jerusalem to the Unit and to help maintain it financially. The baron authorized James de Rothschild, then serving with the Zionist Commission in Palestine, to draw up a contract. Addressed to Eliahu Lewin-Epstein on October 17, 1918, the agreement provided that while the Unit would be responsible for managing the hospital, it would always carry the Rothschild name. The three-year contract likewise provided that the furnishings and equipment would be returned to the Rothschilds on its expiration. But that provision was never invoked. After three years the accord was not renewed, but the hospital remained in Hadassah's hands and subventions from the House of Rothschild were continued until 1940 — 300,000 francs in the first three years and 2,000 Egyptian pounds thereafter.

Paris was bubbly, even in wartime. French food made up for the grey, hard weeks of scarcities in London. On July 26, the much happier contingent went to the railroad station. But on the train there were no washing, dining or sleeping facilities. Hubbard recalled later: "Most of our two days in Rome I spent getting our papers in order. Were it not for the aid of the British naval attaché, we would have had even more delays. And to prove that nothing could go right, when it came to getting the final papers a clerk told us that he had orders for us to remain in Rome until the camp at Taranto, our next stop, was prepared to take us."

When Hubbard figured that it would cost about $350 more daily to remain in Rome, he charged ahead to Taranto, despite the orders. "I decided to go on, trusting to be able to talk us out of trouble, if trouble came."

Taranto, located on the burning sands of a gulf on Italy's heel, was the principal reception center for Allied troops and supplies moving from Europe to the Middle and Far East. The heat hovered around 120 degrees, but nothing was so fierce as the British commanding officer's temper on hearing that Hubbard's contingent had arrived against orders. The Unit remained only because no transport was available to take them back to Rome. According to Hubbard's itinerary, the Unit was to ship out to Alexandria within forty-eight hours. But a submarine raid in the Mediterranean delayed them for ten days. From botanist Aaron Aaronsohn and Major Ormsby-Gore (later to be colonial secretary), who had been hunting for the Unit high and low in his capacity as British military liaison officer to the Zionist Commission then in Palestine, the Unit received a sobering picture of raped Palestine. The war was still in a critical stage; Jerusalem was in British hands but northern Palestine was not. The American Red Cross unit, headquartered in Jerusalem, was not equipped to cope with Palestine's basic medical and rehabilitation problems. The Unit was desperately needed.

On August 9, the AZMU shipped out on an Indian transport convoyed by three Japanese destroyers and an Italian hydroplane. As the ship slipped out of Taranto, the nurses and doctors glumly stared at the hulks of sunken vessels. Several hours before the ship's arrival in Alexandria, all hands were told to put on life belts and stand by at lifeboat stations; submarines were lurking about at the entrance to the harbor, but the danger passed without incident. On hand for their welcome to the Middle East was Chaim

Weizmann, who regretted the delay in the Unit's arrival and said that departure for Palestine would be given top priority although most transport was then being used by the military.

The doctors and nurses spent four days in Alexandria and two in Cairo. The Unit put up at Cairo's Shepeard's Hotel and the wealthy Mosseri family who dominated the Jewish community was their host. They dutifully visited the sixty-bed Israelite Hospital where the director told them, "If it were not for the Jews of Palestine who came to Egypt during the war, we would not have had this hospital. It was they who infused us with a new spirit and it was with that spirit that we built this institution."

There was just time enough for the group to see something of Egypt before leaving. The impressions never left them. They were horrified by the mud villages along the Nile, the oxen yoked to the waterwheel, the sickly peasants ploughing the earth with scraggy camels. They tasted and smelled misery wherever they went. Poverty, filth, dirty naked children, blind beggars and everywhere flies — billions of flies spreading an invisible germ canopy over the teeming metropolis. What made the experience grotesque was that, amid the destitution, a small ruling clique enjoyed fabulous wealth, luxuriant living and high culture. The region, illiterate, indigent, a diamond on a garbage heap, intoxicating in its tawdriness, frustratingly inconsistent, magnetically enigmatic, a mosaic of contradictions that no Westerner could understand.

By Saturday evening, August 17, 1918, the British had cleared space on troop trains to send the AZMU on the last leg of its voyage to Palestine. Leaving one nurse behind to take charge of the camp of Palestine Jewish refugees in Alexandria, the group boarded double-decker berthed trains — according to one scholarly version, traveling the route into the Holy Land chosen by Moses to take the Israelites out of bondage. Across the horizon, they could discern long caravans of camels. By early morning they crossed the Suez Canal and were in Qantara. A sandstorm swirled up out of the desert and all views were lost in the gritty winds.

Eighteen hours after they started out, the train finally arrived in Lydda

(Lod), a sandy tent town where the railroad terminal was a rickety shed. Sitting on valises for two hours waiting for someone to greet them depressed the unit. Several nurses fainted from the oppressive heat and fatigue.

Their presence in Palestine was a source of contention between the Zionist Commission and the British authorities. The British had decided that the AZMU would not be quartered in Jerusalem. But Chaim Weizmann put their case before General Allenby who, while not overly sympathetic toward Zionist aims, was fair. Since the American Red Cross had already pitched its tents in Jerusalem, Allenby argued, there was no need for a second mission there. In the end, Weizmann's persuasive arguments won. As a compromise the two agreed that the Unit would split up, with the AZMU establishing its base in Tel Aviv and a detachment working in Jerusalem. But both certainly knew what would happen in the end. There was an air of permanence about the AZMU and only Jerusalem could be headquarters for any Zionist organization.

Despite the agreement, the largest number of AZMU members boarded a train for Jerusalem. The others — Executive Headquarters — set out in vehicles over the limestone road through the citrus groves for Tel Aviv. In Tel Aviv, the Unit occupied the only three houses located on what is now Allenby Street. These houses marked the limit of the town. Beyond, all was sand dunes. With the emergency supplies, squads began work immediately. In Jaffa, a unit sprang into action, supervising garbage collection, food inspection, cattle examination at slaughter houses, malaria control. In a short time an emergency hospital of ten beds was operating.

Not long after the Unit was functioning, Tel Aviv stirred with military activity. Moving at night in long shadowy columns, British troops tramped through toward Petah Tikva. On the evening of September 18, two members of the Unit were returning from Lydda when they reported an extraordinary sight — an unending line of 25,000 camels loping northward, each animal carrying two tanks of water. On a nearby road, trucks and ambulances moved in the same direction. The next day muffled booming of heavy artillery could be heard in the streets of Tel Aviv. Allenby's offensive to capture northern Palestine had begun. Later, trains and ambulances brought in the wounded. Several of the AZMU's physicians were put into service at a casualty clearing station set up in the Gymnasium on Herzl Street.

Soon the Turks were routed and the north of the country was open. All of Palestine waited to be cared for and only the American doctors and nurses were prepared to cope with the long, bitter task.

PANTIES IN THE GAS TANK

Jamal Pasha, the Turkish tyrant, could not have cared less about the miseries of Jerusalem when he retreated from the British in December 1917. He told an aide, "There is enough bichloride of mercury (mercurochrome) in the drug shops for all of them." Nine months later, the Holy City seemed like a terminal patient suffering its last agonies. Rarely had microbes grown in such favorable conditions. Apart from the usual endemic ailments, cases of typhoid and meningitis were common. The men and women who could still walk were shells. Well did the Wailing Wall live up to its name. There, mothers lay on the stone pavement weeping, praying, beseeching the Lord to save their children.

The Unit sought out the sick. As they visited Jewish homes, one picture emerged. In unlit hovels, humans writhed on rag-covered floors. Their furniture was gone, sold to the Bedouins for vegetables. Sunken-eyed, bearded men shook violently from chills. Disheveled women held scrawny infants at dried-out breasts. Even the houseflies were skinny. The stench was overpowering. One nurse commented at the time that living quarters were so bad it would have been necessary to fumigate to turn them into dog kennels.

The moral climate of the city was in raucous tune with the general war atmosphere. The army was an intoxicated troop. Off duty, the men's cry was, "Here today, gone tomorrow — so let's have a time, lads." Girls and women stayed alive by turning to prostitution.

Jerusalem's most pitiful sight was its little army of orphans and abandoned children. Their mothers were either dead or too feeble to care for them and their fathers were behind Turkish lines. An estimated four thousand waifs roamed the streets of Palestine, most of them in Jerusalem. Alice Seligsberg, who had dedicated her adult life to solving the problems of neglected children in the United States, went about the country establishing orphanages and foster homes, and searching for parents.

From August until November 1918, the AZMU handled Palestine's unfortunates on a basis of emergency care. Before it could do more basic work, the Unit had to settle in and acclimatize. Their first few days were hectic. On the first morning after their arrival, the nurses awoke to find their faces dotted with red spots. Most thought it was a dread tropical infection. Others diagnosed it as measles. A doctor hurried over and announced his diagnosis to the women: "Sand flies! They haven't had the pleasure of such well-fed animals in years." Three days later a more serious affliction gripped the Unit: enteritis. What made the affliction particularly unpleasant was the lack of a modern plumbing system in Jerusalem. The Bedouin carried water to the nurses' quarters in goatskins. More fortunate householders had cisterns. Cooking was done on smelly kerosene stoves. Kerosene was likewise the fuel for lighting. Daily, the Unit had to take quinine against malaria.

Language was a problem. Few AZMU members spoke Hebrew or Yiddish sufficiently to make themselves understood. There was friction between the Unit's doctors and the few Jerusalem doctors who survived the war, the latter believing that the newcomers had no experience to handle the medical problems peculiar to the Middle East. At night there was no entertainment except for one cinema which played the same film for a solid year. In winter the unpaved streets turned into quagmires. In summer the air was polluted by clouds of gagging dust.

By September 1918, the Turks were on the run. Nablus, Nazareth and Haifa were all yielding to British forces. Refugees streamed southward into Jerusalem as they did to Jaffa and Tel Aviv. Then, Tiberias fell to the Allies and the flow of refugees to Jerusalem was even greater.

Friday, September 27, 1918, was a memorable day in Jerusalem. It brought the season's first rain. Those who escaped the Turks up north and had recently returned were in better physical condition than the people who had remained in the city. Elated, they walked through the muddy streets of the city observing the festival of Sukkot. They were a mixed crowd of Yemenites and Bokharans, Hasidim wearing their holiday *shtreymlach*, North African Jews in fezzes — all singing and dancing lustily. The Sephardim carried their white-bearded *hakham* (rabbinical leader) on their shoulders; Jewish soldiers of the British army whipped through the streets on horseback. It was bittersweet merrymaking because Jerusalem was a ghost city and the holiday jollity resembled a wake. In between the Sukkot processions, bands of ragged Turkish prisoners, starved and gaunt, interspersed with the better-fed, straight-backed Germans, ambled along to POW camps under the wary eyes of victorious Australian soldiers and bearded Sikhs in white turbans.

The more areas that were liberated from the Turks, the more the Unit was called upon to do. Its members traveled south to Hebron, the most orthodox Moslem town in all Palestine.

In the Jewish schools of Hebron about 40 percent of the two hundred pupils were suffering terribly from malaria. That same September, the Sea of Galilee area was liberated. One day, the Unit's manager, Eliahu Lewin-Epstein, got an urgent call from Allenby's headquarters in Tiberias: a cholera epidemic had broken out in the wake of the Turkish retreat. Lewin-Epstein hired a droshka, fitted it with supplies and sent two doctors, a sanitary engineer and three nurses. The evidence of the war was everywhere. The rotting bodies of Germans and Turks were a common roadside sight.

On the desolate road the team was stopped by a British officer and an escort with rifles at the ready. "And where are you going at this time of night?" the officer asked with his pistol drawn. He suspected that the doctors and nurses were disguised German spies returning from a behind-the-lines foray. The forgetful doctors had left their passports behind, but fortunately one of the nurses had hers. After sharing coffee from a Thermos with the reassured Tommies, they got a good send-off on the last lap of the trip. As it turned out, the route they were traveling was taking them directly into the German-Turkish lines. The British officer set them straight.

It was dawn when they arrived on top of the hills overlooking Tiberias and the Sea of Galilee. The trip had taken them forty-eight hours. The sun was just rising over the Golan Heights and the vast panorama below made them gasp. Never had they seen a picture so sublime, so full of nature's wonders. But even more surprising was the welcome they received. All night long scores of Jews had waited on the road in expectation of the "Amerikanim." Some were crying, some were laughing. All chanted in unison a single prayer: *Sheheḥeyanu, vekiyemanu, vehigi'anu, lazman hazeh.*

The team was horror-stricken to discover that before burial, corpses were being washed in the Sea of Galilee at the same spot where women were filling water jugs. Most of the Jews in Tiberias were so weak that they could not dig graves deep enough to bury the dead properly. Dogs and jackals scratched open the shallow graves and pulled out the corpses.

The Unit found that 75 percent of the town had cholera, a disease transmitted by bad water, and usually fatal if not checked within a few days. Hadassah's doctors immediately ordered the populace to stop using Sea of Galilee water and the British army fenced off the most frequented sites. The entire town was placed under quarantine. Truckloads of food and medical supplies were sent by Hadassah from Jerusalem. Inoculations were given to hundreds. Most cholera patients were treated at home, but the Unit opened an emergency ward in a private house for forty of the most seriously ill.

One day as Madeline Epstein[1] stood on the balcony of the Tiberias Hotel where members of the unit were housed, she noticed a long line of army trucks and cars parked outside. It dawned on her that they held the solution to the lice problem. Asking no one's permission she picked up a stick, hammered a nail into it, furtively headed for the trucks, opened the cap of a gas tank and then proceeded to dunk her underclothes in the gasoline. The solution was effective although somewhat irritating to the skin, but it was better than the vagrant vermin. The daily rinsing of clothes in military gas tanks went along smoothly until one day Madeline carelessly let a pair of pink panties slip off a nail.

Early next morning, Nurse Epstein stopped short on her way to the dunking ritual. She saw a British officer severely reprimanding one of the army drivers. The soldier was pleading that he knew nothing "about it." Later that day, Madeline was ordered to report to the headquarters of the commanding officer. As she entered the staff room, she faced the granite faces of the C/O, his aide-de-camp and officers in charge of military transport. The C/O was direct.

"Sister, do *these* belong to you?"

He held high a pair of pink panties, now bleached white.

"I suppose so," mumbled Madeline, pink-faced.

"Sister, can you explain this act of sabotage?"

The C/O listened patiently, drumming his fingers on the desk. When she concluded, he remonstrated icily, "Do you realize that you put four Staff HQ vehicles out of commission. *Four*!" Only later that day did Madeline understand: the lice that she had killed in the gas tanks had clogged the feed lines of the vehicles. Next morning, a tin of petrol was placed at the door of her room marked "For Personal Use ONLY!"

---

1. Madeline married dentist Samuel Lewin-Epstein, son of the Unit manager, and lived the rest of her years in Jerusalem. Her second son, Ya'acov (Jack), a prominent oral surgeon, was dean of the Hebrew University-Hadassah School of Dentistry. He died in 1988. His widow, Marian, active in Hadassah affairs for over 50 years, lives in Jerusalem.

Tiberias's off-limits status posed a problem as the British military machine pushed on toward Damascus and Constantinople. As it went, the conquering army freed more Palestinian Jewish refugees and the road home for the war victims led through Tiberias. One morning a group of five hundred riding on hay wagons suddenly appeared at the city's gates. In the city, the health risk was great. The weather had turned stormy and the frail refugees could not continue to Jaffa and Jerusalem in their wagons. At the intercession of Nurse Epstein, the British agreed to send them to their homes in a military convoy. After being fed and housed by the Unit, the refugees trudged up Tiberias's hills to the takeoff point, which they reached by midnight. At 2:00 am, a message was received by the Unit at the Tiberias Hotel that the convoy was nowhere to be seen. Enraged, Nurse Epstein dressed, jumped on an unsaddled horse and dashed after the truant convoy. She found the British officer-in-charge several miles beyond the appointed place, calmly shaving. He explained airily that he did not intend to take the civilians because they were not the responsibility of the British army. A fierce argument ensued, with Nurse Epstein doing most of the arguing and gesticulating. When she threatened to report him to army HQ in Jerusalem, he finally gave in, turned the convoy around and picked up the refugees. It occurred to Nurse Epstein only after she returned to the hotel at dawn that she had rarely ridden a horse and never bareback. Frightened, she pulled the covers over her head and went to sleep.

As Hadassah made it a rule never to distinguish between Arab and Jew, so did its doctors not distinguish between British, German and Turk in Tiberias. The British kept a large number of ill POW's in an administration building behind the Scottish Mission Hospital, which had been turned into a general hospital. Hadassah treated the prisoners — as it later would Arab terrorists — with the same professional care given to Jews.

Members of the Unit soon moved north from Tiberias into the Hills of Canaan where lay the mystic town of Safed, venerated home of sages and kabbalists. No more charming site existed in the Middle East. But the war had left its scars. When a Hadassah doctor arrived in the winter of 1918-19, he headed straight for a Jewish elementary boys' school. After the physician finished examining the pupils, none more than ten years old, the teacher addressed them softly: "Children, it's now time for *minhah* (the afternoon prayers). Those of you who must go to synagogue to recite *kaddish* (prayer for the dead) may now leave."

The doctor looked up from putting his stethoscope in his bag. He was shocked to see half the class leaving to say *kaddish*.

A typhoid epidemic hit Safed early in 1919. The AZMU provided the town with three physicians, five trained nurses and 12 student nurses, who took over a 50-bed hospital built by the Rothschild family. The American Red Cross unit which was then disbanding sold the AZMU its equipment and by June 1919, a five-ward hospital was formally opened. It provided free outpatient service to all of Galilee and surgical work for the entire north of Palestine. Because of Safed's long dry season it was a favorite site for tubercular patients. By June 1926, Hadassah Hospital had opened a ward for 28 consumptives.

At the western gateway to Galilee, in the little port town of Haifa, the AZMU opened a clinic and introduced school hygiene services after the war. But immigration so heavily taxed the city's resources that by 1922 Hadassah established a small hospital which it continued to subsidize until the late 1930s. Between Safed and Haifa, the Jewish settlers of north Palestine were cared for fairly well. Tiberias was not to have a hospital until May 1930, although money for the construction of an institution had been contributed by Mr. and Mrs. Peter Schweitzer as early as 1921. Maintenance funds were not available for nine years when finally Hadassah assumed responsibility.

In 1919, an epidemic of relapsing fever and bubonic plague broke out in Jaffa. The AZMU opened an emergency ten-bed hospital in Mordecai Ben-Hillel Hacohen's two-story house. In the summer of 1920 an out-patient clinic and forty-five beds were added. Eight years later, the Tel Aviv area had its first modern, fully-equipped hospital. In the late 1930s

Hadassah transferred it to the Tel Aviv municipality, but for more than 50 years the name Hadassah Hospital would linger on.

Jerusalem was still Hadassah's capital, however, and the immediate need in Jerusalem was to open the Rothschild Hospital which had been entrusted to the AZMU. "I shall never forget the first day we saw the hospital," said one nurse. "We walked right in and we walked right out." Jewish community leaders, expecting the Unit, had done their best to clean up the worst of the mess left behind by the Turkish Army, which had stabled its horses there. Charwomen were not available, so the nurses assaulted the building. The cleaning took nearly a week, and hundreds of cases of medicines, instruments and food were unpacked. Hadassah had forgotten nothing. The only item that was in oversupply was toilet paper; it was several years before the original inventory was depleted.

The ceremonial opening of the Rothschild Hospital took place eight days before the end of the war — on November 3, 1918 — as part of the celebrations marking the first anniversary of the Balfour Declaration. In retrospect, the presentation of the hospital to the AZMU was a milestone in Palestine's medical history. Present at the ceremonies, held on the steps of the building, was the Grand Mufti of Jerusalem, who blessed the project in Arabic, as well as the highest ranking British officers in Jerusalem at the time headed by General Arthur Money, and diplomatic and ecclesiastical representatives of France, Italy, Spain and Armenia. The United States was represented by the Spanish consul. For the occasion, Jerusalem's Bezalel Art School fashioned a silver key which Eliahu Lewin-Epstein, looking like King George V, accepted from the monocled Major James de Rothschild.

At the official opening the Rothschild Hospital had ninety beds, six departments with outpatient clinics and three laboratories. The two largest departments of twenty-four beds were set aside for internal medicine and pediatric patients. The others were obstetrics, ophthalmology, dermatology and general surgery. An isolation hut, morgue, machine shop, garage and laundry were soon constructed and bacteriological and pathological labs were installed. The demand for beds was so great that within a short time twenty-two were added.

By the end of 1918 the hospital had received 255 patients, but conditions were far from ideal; the atmosphere was more that of a field hospital. In the operating theater, kerosene lamps provided light. During the operation the task of an unfortunate nurse was to hold the lamp high over the anesthetized patient.

The AZMU's most valuable innovation was the introduction of an X-ray institute. At first it was poorly equipped and could provide only emergency services, but by 1921 the institute had a specialist and new equipment provided by the American Jewish Physicians Committee. It helped make Rothschild the most important medical institution in Palestine. From September 1918 to end of that year, Hadassah treated 15,000 ambulatory patients who made 59,000 visits. In the first full year of the AZMU's work in Jerusalem, twenty out of every 100 patients were Arab.

The foundation was now established for the Hadassah Medical Organization (HMO), which would run all medical services, usually under the chairmanship of Hadassah's retiring National President.

Hospitals had been activated up and down the country — probably a unique undertaking in medical history for a foreign, private volunteer women's organization. Twenty years later, when Palestine's first medical center was opened on Mount Scopus in Jerusalem by Hadassah, over 200,000 patients were being treated in Hadassah's institutions annually. That amounted to nearly 60 percent of all Jewish patients treated in Palestine hospitals. By the end of the century, the number of annual visits, including hospitalization, to all Hadassah institutions would grow to nearly one million.

Hadassah was rooting itself deeply into the life of the country. A sanitary commission made up of Hadassah doctors was on a six-week tour of the settlements to determine the health situation of the "colonies." Hospitals were fine institutions to build, but the *yishuv* also needed a network of preventive and educational services, which only the AZMU was in a position to create. This, the commission later recommended, led to the beginning of the nurses' training, school hygiene and mother and child care initiatives. The commission was deeply moved when it stopped at seven-year-old Degania, mother of kibbutzim, and heard one of the settlers speak:

> To work in such heat requires superhuman effort. To sleep is well nigh impossible. We are constantly drenched with perspiration and we drink gallons of water. This pouring water into our systems while we are overheated [and] the poor quality of the food and the irregular hours of work and sleep have made everyone here a confirmed dyspeptic...Are we fighting a losing battle? We believe that we cannot carry on here much longer unless conditions are made more endurable...We are trying to hold a front which is unsanitary, unhealthful, unlivable. You must remedy these evils for us.

The commission found that blackwater fever, a pernicious type of malaria, had already claimed a number of Degania pioneers. All the settlers had malaria, including the infants, and most suffered from anemia. One of the commission members observed, "The colonists are all intelligent-looking but have a yellowish pallor. They are our most promising forces. We must establish a system of public health and hygiene and harness the Jordan River to drive every labor-saving motor in every farm and homestead in Palestine."

The commission continued its investigation and Dr. Joseph Shapiro noted in his diary:

> At Rosh Pina, 40 settlers, 100 hired laborers. Sephardim, Persian, Ashkenazi Jews dressed in rags. Homes are one and two rooms in which five to 10 humans huddle. Diet: durrha

bread, tea, green vegetables. No medical help except the local druggist who dispenses quinine and eye applications.

Mishmar Hayarden: An old greybeard tells this heart-breaking story…'Turks, Arabs, Germans, Arabs, British, Arabs followed one after the other and each contributed something to our destruction. Horses, cattle, food. All are gone. We are sick. We have no medicines.'

Metulla: With adequate sanitation and mosquito control, this could be the health resort of Palestine.

Zichron Ya'acov: Pop. 1,000 of whom 100 are Yemenites. Hospital built by Baron de Rothschild is neglected. They're waiting for him to come up with money to repair it…Colonists are apathetic, indifferent, nursed on charity.

Hadera: Turks destroyed 1,000 eucalyptus trees. Seven years ago, 300 enthusiastic Yemenites arrived. 200 died, some returned home, 70 left. Filth, poverty, overcrowding, low wages, malaria, trachoma, tuberculosis.

The six-week tour of the colony mapped the *yishuv's* needs. The commission found that if the land was ever to be turned into a Jewish home as the Balfour Declaration had promised, more than curative and preventive medicine was required. Solutions and remedies had to be found for neglected children, ignorance and indolence, communal and intercommunal strife. As the war ended, there was nobody on the scene capable of coming to grips with these problems except the AZMU, which was fast becoming known to everyone in Palestine as, simply, Hadassah. The Unit itself was beset by enormous internal administrative, personnel and financial problems at the time. Financially, the Joint Distribution Committee played a life-saving role in keeping the venture going. Between 1919 and 1923, it provided over $800,000 — first to the AZMU and then to Hadassah when the name of the Unit was changed to the 'Hadassah

Medical Organization' in the 1920s. But, more than anything else, Hadassah was kept alive by the *yishuv's* need to survive. And Henrietta Szold would admit in 1929 that she had been wrong about Hadassah's name disappearing. "The Hadassah Medical Organization came into the country as a war relief organization and remained in the land as a peace organization."

"JEW! SPEAK HEBREW!"

At nineteen, beautiful Shulamit Yedid-Halevy could be excused for having more nerve than sense. But her father, well-known and well-to-do in the Jewish community of Beirut, Lebanon, was at the point of exasperation. Girls of traditional families simply did not go in for nursing careers. That was a job for nuns, not for good Jewish daughters. But Shulamit inherited a healthy portion of her father's willpower, and threatened that if he did not let her become a nurse, she would run away to some foreign school to study. So, as most loving fathers do, he compromised. She would remain at home in Beirut and study nursing at the American University Hospital.

The same determination that overcame her father's objections also helped Shulamit through a strange, even hostile, new environment while training. She was pained to be obliged to attend Christian prayer services in the university chapel on Sunday mornings. The curriculum was based on church mission ideology, because nurses were expected to heal bodies and souls alike. In this foreign world she dreamt of going to Palestine where one day she would help organize a Jewish nursing school. As she studied late into the night her thoughts would meander — Jerusalem was so close — only 150 miles to the south — and yet so far.

In September 1918, word reached Beirut that the Hadassah Unit had arrived in Palestine. By then, Shulamit was a registered nurse. She satisfied her longings for Jerusalem by joining the Maccabee Zionist Organization. One day in December, the coastal vessel *Geula* (Redemption) called at Beirut. On board were war refugees returning to Palestine from Constantinople. Only males were permitted on board. The exception was the wife of a prominent eye specialist. Shulamit's cousin was emigrating to Palestine and Shulamit pleaded with him to take her along as a stowaway. In a moment of weakness he agreed and hid her on deck behind a stack of camp beds. He warned her to remain there for the overnight voyage to Jaffa. But when the returning Palestinians gathered on deck to sing and to dance, the temptation was too much for her. Shulamit came out of hiding to join the joyous men. Almost at once the captain roared, "Who's this young woman?" Discovering that she was taking a free trip, he ordered the helmsman to return to Beirut.

Shulamit ran to the doctor, a Jewish physician returning to Jerusalem. He was Albert Ticho.

"Dr. Ticho," she pleaded. "I am a registered nurse. I know that the Zionists have come to Palestine from America to help and I want to join them. Please influence the captain to let me go on."

The famed physician was at first dubious. How could he know that she was telling the truth?

"My cousin is on board. You can ask him."

Dr. Ticho was still skeptical.

Members of the Maccabee organization came to Shulamit's aid, pleading with Mrs. Ticho, who convinced her husband to vouch for the girl and her fare. The captain grudgingly ordered another turnabout.

On landing in Jaffa her joy was unbounded. She noticed signs everywhere addressed to immigrants. "Jew! Speak Hebrew!" Thanks to her father, she had been given a good Hebrew education and could read easily. But Shulamit's joy was quickly eclipsed. When she applied to join the AZMU, the doctor in charge told her abruptly, "We don't need nurses."

Shulamit could not know then how wrong he was. She had the choice of returning to Beirut or of taking a post as an operating nurse in the Catholic St. Louis Hospital and once again working under the sign of the cross. She chose the latter. About six weeks later, she noticed a doctor wearing a Star of David on his military uniform. He had come to St. Louis Hospital to observe operations and to seek out a Jewish nurse who he had heard was working there. He was pathologist Benjamin Roman, acting medical director of the AZMU.

"We are in a predicament in Jerusalem, Shulamit. We have taken in students who want to be taught nursing — but only in Hebrew. The girls are refusing to attend classes if they are taught in any other language. Do you by any chance know Hebrew?"

Her heart pounding hard, Shulamit barely managed to say, "I do."

In February 1919, Shulamit reported to Dr. Roman at the Hotel de France, Hadassah's headquarters in Jerusalem. She moved into the Hughes Hotel across the street where the nurses now lived. The following day she began teaching.

Shulamit's Hebrew was classical rather than colloquial, and she read better than she spoke. At first she would write out lectures in English, then with the help of two Palestinian-born members of the staff, she would translate them, always keeping two lessons ahead of the class. Shulamit would even write down replies to a long list of questions she was sure the students would ask. They rarely did ask the ones she prepared.

Halting as her spoken Hebrew was, it was much better than that of the other nurses. Even the students themselves were not too good at the language, most of them Russian and Polish immigrants. Their Hebrew was fractured, but thanks to their tenacity, the Hadassah school became the first anywhere to instruct nurses in the language of the Book. It did present difficulties. No texts were available in Hebrew nor were there Hebrew typewriters to prepare them. So a scribe was engaged to transcribe the lectures and these were given to the students. Most members of the Unit not only had no knowledge of Hebrew, but they had no readily available translations of scientific words. On occasion the father of modern Hebrew, Eliezer Ben-Yehuda, would sit up long nights with members of the staff creating Hebrew medical terms. Some words, such as "vitamin", defied translation and remained unchanged.

Professional standards were high and the curriculum was wholly American. In charge at the beginning was Russian-born, American-educated Rose Klombers. Shulamit took charge for a short time. She was relieved by Anna Kaplan. Anna, a nurse with long experience in New York hospitals, started out with the Unit, but remained behind in a London hospital gravely ill with flu. During her tenure as head of the Nursing School she broadened the curriculum, introduced textbooks and established a permanent staff of instructors. But not without periodic crises.

To begin with, the Americans on the staff and the others, like Shulamit, were worlds apart in outlook. The Americans were high-and-mighty about their superior training. This often expressed itself in a supercilious attitude toward non-Americans. Many picayune, personal battles were fought with non-American staff members. Objection was raised, for example, to Shulamit's wearing the same uniform and pin as the Unit's nurses or even eating at the same table. Acting Director Roman did much to calm tempers, but new irritations constantly erupted.

The European physicians at Rothschild had their own idiosyncrasies. They objected strongly to a three-year period of training for nurses, which they thought was far too long. They considered theoretical classroom work a waste of time. On the Continent, nurses learned all they knew in the wards. But Hadassah was teaching them all sorts of preventive work that was the private preserve of the physician. The German-born Jewish doctors, who had always worked with nuns, thought that regular hours for nurses was madness. They could not quite accustom themselves to the fact that nurses were human. The Russian-born doctors objected particularly to nurses who had something to say about the condition of the patient. One European-trained doctor cried out in exasperation, "Nurses should have feet, hands and eyes! They are not supposed to think! They should *do, see,* and *rush. That's all!*"

Working and teaching conditions for nurses always leave something to be desired. But in Jerusalem in the early years after the war they were downright primitive. Anna Kaplan recalled:

> We had no classrooms. We taught wherever we could find an empty room, even in the laundry. The nurses' home was some distance from the hospital. We had no transport and the students had no suitable wearing apparel. When I opened the Surgical Department, the plumbing was not yet completed. Equipment came from America but not furniture. We saved the shipping cases from the Palestine Supply Department and from these made bedside tables, chairs and cabinets. Electricity was only a dream in those days. Ice was unheard of.

The first class of student nurses was assembled on November 3, 1918, the same occasion at which the Rothschild Hospital was formally opened. Most came from rural areas. Some had been employed in menial jobs at the hospital. Few of them had as many as eight years of formal schooling. A number of the girls had sneaked through Turkish lines in northern Palestine after they heard a nursing school was being organized. They were a ragged, sickly group of refugees. But what they lacked in physical appearance they made up in high spirits. Matured by war and hardship, they were highly independent. On one occasion, one of the girls took off without permission for an overnight trip to Tel Aviv together with a doctor of the Unit. She was temporarily suspended on her return. Her enraged fellow students, claiming that the Don Juan physician was at fault, went on strike. They won. Strikes were frequent among the nurses, but they did not always succeed. Their most successful protests opposed the use of Yiddish, English and all languages other than Hebrew.

With it all, Hadassah upheld its high, if martinet, standards: "You are expected to give respectful attention to your superiors," read the rules, "to obey orders promptly and unquestioningly, to refrain from carrying on conversations while on duty, to speak in a low voice, to move about gently, not to indulge in familiarities with patients or discuss their illness with them."

The school soon developed a strong feeling of responsibility among the students. Once the question arose before the five-member governing committee whether a nurse should be punished for giving a patient the wrong medicine.

"Definitely not!" replied Anna Kaplan, to the shock of the committee members. "Nurses must not be afraid to report such errors. On the other hand, failure to report should be severely punished."

As the first year passed, the school insisted on more stringent screening of students. After Henrietta Szold arrived in 1920 to head Hadassah's work in Palestine, she personally scoured the country for candidates.

"Do you owe any debts to your parents or to anyone else, and how much do they amount to? Do you suffer from rheumatism, headaches, emotional upsets?"

These and twenty other questions were routinely asked. If the students' debts were too large they were disqualified, because they would then have to take on outside work to repay the loans. They had to be twenty-one years old (now nineteen), had to know Hebrew, the Latin alphabet, and remain on probation for six months. They were not permitted to treat sick relatives at home or in the hospital, except in the line of duty. They received a small allowance for the first six months. The working day was twelve hours with three hours off for homework and recreation. The students got one afternoon off a week and had a two-week annual vacation. Lights-out was 10:00 pm with late leave until 11:30 pm once a week. (Today student nurses do not reside on campus.) On graduation, nurses were assured of work and a starting salary of the equivalent of $50 a month. And yet they did have a measure of self-rule. The girls had their own committee, which dealt with complaints against both students and nurses, and could mete out

light punishment for disciplinary infractions. The committee later grew
into a national students organization.

Twenty-two nurses made it through the first three years. But those who
graduated did well. Six became principals of schools or supervisors in
hospitals. Several made excellent reputations in public health nursing. Later
on, Shulamit Yedid-Halevy Cantor, the stowaway from Beirut, would
succeed Anna Kaplan and serve a long and distinguished career as
Hadassah's supervisor of nurses and director of the school.

Graduation exercises are set and staid affairs. But the rites of the first
class of Hadassah nurses were an exception. Since the school's dedication
coincided with the first anniversary of the Balfour Declaration, the
graduation ceremonies were set for Balfour Day, November 2, 1921. In the
last week of October, the Hebrew-English invitations were about to be
dispatched by two Yemenite runners (more reliable than the local mail
service) when a representative of the Zionist Executive asked Henrietta
Szold to postpone the festivities. Rumors were wild that the Arabs would
observe this anniversary as they had in 1920 and again at Passover 1921: by
shooting and stabbing Jews.

The rumors turned out to be true. Fortunately, Henrietta took the
advice to delay the ceremonies for one week. On Balfour Day 1921,
bloodthirsty Arab mobs ran out of the Old City of Jerusalem. They burned
and pillaged. Before the day was out, five Jews were dead and twenty
wounded. British Governor Ronald Storrs's police neglected to intervene
energetically, though Storrs himself, whom Henrietta described as "an evil
genius", had taken refuge in Hadassah Hospital during the Passover riots
under the pretense of "protecting" the Jewish community. Zionist officials
demanded his removal. But Storrs remained and riots continued
periodically through the 1920s and 1930s. On November 4, 1921, a
massive funeral procession left the Rothschild Hospital compound. More
than 1,000 persons marched in silence behind the stretchers on which the
tallit-draped bodies were borne. When a month of mourning was declared,
the graduation exercises were postponed again to December 2. But the

graduation certificate still bore the date November 2. Henrietta insisted the date be left unchanged as a sign "of unquenchable hope for the future of the Jewish people."

Dressed in crisp white uniforms and caps, on which was emblazoned a blue Star of David, the graduating class of 1921 was led into the hall of Bet Aminoff on Jaffa Road, the new nurses' home, by Anna Kaplan. Henrietta Szold presided and Lady Samuel, wife of the British Mandate's first high commissioner, handed out the diplomas. Szold commented in her address:

> For this day you have waited three years, and across the ocean (in the United States) there are thousands of women who have waited for it nearly ten years. When they sent two pioneer nurses over here to inaugurate District Visiting Nursing, they thought of this evening. When the summons came to enlarge the number of nurses from two to twenty, they rejoiced for the sake of this evening.

Now, as if in payment for the loan of the twenty-two nurses that America had sent before and after the war, the *yishuv* was contributing twenty-two of its own. And none too soon. Only two of the original AZMU nurses were still on duty at Rothschild Hospital by the time of graduation.

Immediately after the exercises were over, six-month courses began in midwifery, operating-theater nursing and public health. Later, these would be integrated into the undergraduate studies.

By the end of its first decade, 135 registered nurses were graduated by the school. The standards of the profession were fixed. In its eleventh year, the Hadassah School of Nursing was adjudged by the International Association of Graduate Nurses to be the finest in the Middle East.

Hadassah was the main source of highly qualified registered nurses until 1935 when Kupat Holim Clalit, the health fund of the Jewish Federation of Labor (Histadrut), opened a school. A municipal school was opened in 1940 in Tel Aviv. Both these institutions drew heavily on Hadassah's experience and personnel. Still, the demand for graduates was insatiable. Hadassah started courses for male orderlies, partly to make up for the lack and partly to care for those Arab and Jewish Orthodox patients who refused to be tended by women.

In 1952, Hadassah transferred to the Israeli Government the responsibility for nursing care in the public schools as well as for other public services. The need for even more qualified nurses became apparent during the war of June 1967 when the medical center at Ein Kerem treated nearly one thousand cases in seventy-two hours. It could do so not only because of the dedication of its staff but because medicine had become more specialized, its tools the products of a revolution in technology.

Higher education was obviously needed if nurses were to cope. Besides, a better education would attract talented candidates who at the time were moving to more lucrative professions. In 1975, Hadassah initiated the first basic academic nursing education program. It awarded a Bachelor of Nursing Science (BNS) to graduates after four years' study, creating a new generation of highly-educated nurses for Israel's hospitals.

In 1987, Sara Levi, daughter of Holocaust survivors in Romania, became the first at Hadassah to earn a doctorate in nursing (at the University of Pennsylvania).[1]

The nursing school, nearly eighty years old, had taught 3,000 nurses but only now after years of inequities the sisters in white were coming into their own as women and as professionals. By 1996, 35 percent of

---

1 In 1982, the program created a need for nurses with master's degrees and doctorates to teach the new courses. Muriel and Philip Berman of Allentown, Pennsylvania, major contributors to projects at Hadassah College of Technology and both campuses of Hadassah Hospital, set up a scholarship fund to help train nurses in a specifically designed three-to-five-year program at the University of Pennsylvania. Sara Levi was one of the scholarship awardees. Three years later, she was appointed head of the school. Says Dr. Levi, "An academic education has enabled the nurse to function in today's technologically sophisticated health system."

Hadassah's nurses held academic degrees, with the percentage growing annually, and some RN's were returning to the classroom to earn a BNS.[2]

Israel today has twenty-nine nursing schools, most of them offering academic degrees. With so many, competition for students increased to the point where the old taboo against married women had been abandoned. Still, Hadassah manages to fill its quota of fifty students a year. Of these, an average of forty graduate.

All told, Israel now has nearly 21,000 registered nurses and 17,700 practical nurses, providing the country with one nurse for about every 130 citizens (vs. 63 in the US). At Hadassah, 1,600 nurses (75 percent RNs) were not nearly enough.

Even with the introduction of an academic program, the profession had still not attained the dignified status it deserved. Part of the roadblock was a conservative medical profession that anticipated a challenge from academically-trained nurses. Some MDs held to the old belief that nursing was at best a semi-skilled job, arguing that academic studies were not needed to carry a bedpan or to follow orders. What need had nurses for academic literature or post-graduate study? These doctors rationalized with some justice that higher education would make the nurses loath to carry out menial jobs — making a bed or emptying a patient's urinal. Even worse, they might no longer take orders unquestioningly.

In practice, both fears came true, but not only because the nurses were better educated. More specialized medicine was making heavier demands on nurses' time and on their skills. They were no longer mere ward maids. Many were overworked; they claimed they had little time to carry out menial tasks.

Inevitably, members of families complained that their kin were being

---

2 Muriel and Philip Berman demonstrated special interest in Hadassah's nursing programs. Their gifts made possible a nurses' residence, and an academic program in nursing became a reality through the Berman Scholarship program at the University of Pennsylvania. Hadassah's nursing students received support during their years of study for advanced academic degrees.

neglected in emergency rooms and in the wards. Mothers and fathers, husbands, wives and children felt compelled to spend long hours at bedside. What the nurses had little time to do, the family did.

In an address to nurses in 1996, former nursing services director Ahuva Regev-Michel aptly defined nursing as "caring." But she complained that nurses were being required to ensure quality in "an ever more demanding environment."

Challenges from conservatives in the medical community and the public led some Hadassah leaders in the US to take unprecedented steps. They mobilized thousands of American nurses to form Nurses' Councils, sparking a radical change in the profession.[3]

To at least one veteran nurse, however, there was in all this a sense of *déjà vu*. As a girl of 16 in 1922, nurse-to-be Hava Shohat-Karlin was admitted to a Hadassah hospital suffering from exhaustion. "Then as now, there was a severe nursing shortage, so I got out of bed and began bringing other patients glasses of water and bedpans," she recalled years later.

With budgets growing tighter there seemed to be no ideal way out, but nursing was not the only profession where women faced an uphill battle. Nor was this new to Hadassah. Long before Israel was born, Hadassah women who tried to break new ground and old habits remembered how they were told, plainly, that they were wasting their time.

---

3   Hadassah Nurses' Councils were founded in 1991 for American women in the nursing profession. 3,400 women were on the membership rolls in 2002.

"YOU'RE WASTING OUR TIME, DOCTOR!"

A year after World War I ended, the third great wave of Jewish immigration (the "Third Aliyah") began to hit the shores of Palestine. It also brought a small number of immigrants from the United States, among them Henrietta Szold and Golda Meir. Nearly 10,000 Jews from Central and Eastern Europe arrived in a single year. They left their homelands for many reasons, but essentially they had taken the Balfour Declaration literally and yearned to be in Eretz Israel for the founding of a Jewish State. The immigrants were rugged idealists. They trooped off to the marshes of northern Palestine, joined the colonists in building roads and draining swamps. By the end of 1920 more than 60 labor centers were organized throughout Galilee. Living conditions for the pioneers were primitive. The region was a morass that spawned malaria, typhus and typhoid. Roving doctors and nurses from Hadassah provided the only medical aid. Hadassah's public health teams from Jerusalem tried to teach elementary rules of hygiene, but the workers soon found that if they wanted to subdue the louse, the fly and the mosquito, they would first have to overcome the mulish, senseless opposition of the *halutzim*, the pioneers. As a matter of course, the laborers refused typhoid inoculations. Not even the offer of an American cigarette could entice them to submit to the needle. Some spurned an injection even when they were lying flat on their backs with soaring fevers.

The largest of the labor centers was located at Migdal on the western shore of the Sea of Galilee.

"Your toilets are lousy," the enraged Hadassah public health doctor Joseph Shapiro spluttered in a mixture of weak Hebrew and Yiddish. "Besides that, you men have just got to stop taking your drinking water out of the Sea of Galilee because that's where your sewage is being dumped. You'll all soon be dead if you keep going on like this and then what good will your Zionism be to anybody?"

The camp foreman gave a half smile. "We had worse conditions when we first came and we've survived."

Of the 500 men and women at Migdal, nearly every one had malaria. Yet the foreman insisted that they were willing to struggle — and to die. Let the shopkeepers of Jerusalem and Jaffa worry about things like chlorinating water or building toilets. *Halutzim* had to do just as well as the Arabs and under the same conditions.

Defying the *halutzim*, Dr. Shapiro put in a filtration plant to purify the water at Migdal. The workers boycotted it and kept taking their water from the lake. The foreman told his men: "The Arabs don't drink antiseptic water. We've got to live as they do." And to Shapiro he said, "You're wasting our time, Doctor."

The men realized only later that the mortality rate among the Arabs was calamitous and only their enormous birth rate saved them from extinction. As they would later find out, the Arabs were glad to accept aid from the Hadassah teams.

What Dr. Shapiro could not do, nature did. Soon a typhoid epidemic struck with terrible swiftness and stopped work in the labor centers. Common sense finally won out and in answer to an urgent appeal, Hadassah set up a 38-bed field hospital at Migdal.

But there was a point beyond which one could not reasonably ask a pioneer to go. He would now grudgingly agree to take a shot in the arm, but to demand that he eat oatmeal for breakfast? "What are you giving us?" the Russian Jew with the heavy beard demanded. He looked at the bowl of porridge as though it were poisoned mud.

The pretty, young nutritionist, Yehudit Aaronson (who would later become Mrs. Alex Dushkin), fresh from the United States, stammered, "You *must* eat it. You and all the other men are eating the wrong kind of food. You need a good diet to keep you going." She had put the bowls of steaming, enriched oatmeal on the mess tables as a surprise one morning and watched from the kitchen as one worker after the other stared at it, sniffed it and passed it down to the end of the table where the bowls were now piled, untouched. The Russian glowered at Yehudit, "All our lives we men have done without this. We like herring and we will continue to eat herring. Don't throw this stuff at us again."

Yehudit was one of the few graduate Jewish nutritionists of her time. Highly successful in her field, she became a staff dietician of the American Red Cross and agreed at Henrietta Szold's request to serve with the AZMU. In fact, she accompanied Henrietta to Palestine early in 1920. The Unit's new medical director, Isadore Rubinow, had cabled an urgent plea for a nutrition expert because there was not one qualified dietician in the country. Soon after their arrival, Henrietta, Yehudit and Rubinow toured Galilee, and Yehudit agreed to try to solve the nutrition problems at Migdal.

No one spoke to her when she arrived. She went to the kitchen and began peeling onions. At the end of work on the second night, Jennie Landsberg, who was in charge of the kitchen, took Yehudit aside.

"You must be wondering why we ignore you," said Jennie. "We could not tell our people we were bringing in a nutritionist. As it is, you are suspect. You come from America where everything must be sterile and everyone must be healthy or life cannot go on. But here, these people are followers of Tolstoy. They deny the importance of the body. To them the power of the spirit of ideals is everything. I know you mean well. But go slowly."

Yehudit did not realize how slowly. She began by doing a hated job — washing pebbles out of the rice. Eight girls normally spent a full day at it, griping because they were not out on the road working with the men. The water for rinsing the rice was carried in buckets from the lake. After a few days on the job, Yehudit suggested that she might save the campers the bother of rice-washing if they could get her a donkey and the use of a tinsmith for one day. In no time, Yehudit had an ass and an artisan. Outside the kitchen wall she built a heap of stones. On the stones she placed a barrel to which the tinsmith attached a pipe. The pipe led into the kitchen through an opening made in the wall. A spigot was fitted to the end of the pipe. Yehudit hired a boy to fill the barrels with water and transport them on the donkey. The result: running water. It cut the rice-washing crew in half and Yehudit could now move on.

The basic diet in the camp was bully beef, herring, mushy rice and jam. The heavily spiced, British army tinned beef and the salty herring burned the scurvied settlers' bleeding, spongy gums. The bread was badly baked. Actually, as Yehudit found out, it was cooked. Yehudit solved this problem by making friends with a British officer who gave her a field oven from military stores in Afula. Better bread won her additional merit.

Slowly, at spaced intervals, she introduced peanuts, fresh vegetables and dried milk to the tables. The supplies had to come all the way from Haifa and for that purpose a marketing agency was set up by Yitzhak Sadeh, who became famous as commander-in-chief of the Haganah in 1945, while the marketing agency that he set up later became Hamashbir Hamerkazi, the Histadrut's giant retail outlet. From vegetables, Yehudit went on to a highly nutritious, somewhat sophisticated dessert, which she convinced the men was a delicacy from America. The dessert was Jell-O, sent to Palestine by American Zionist leader Justice Louis Brandeis.

Yehudit had now been at Migdal nearly six weeks and she was ready for her greatest triumph. One day, a delicious pudding reached the tables. It was dark brown in color and it was served in bowls. By now the men had learned to trust Yehudit and they dug in. After the first mouthful, there was some hesitation, but a burly, bearded Russian Jew shouted, "All right men! This we eat for the sake of *havera* Yehudit!" And with true Tolstoyan sacrifice they licked their bowls clean of pudding-disguised oatmeal. That night Yehudit held a party for some of the men and women and she served herring. By now, all the malnutrition symptoms had disappeared.

Yehudit's oatmeal victory was far-reaching. By the time she left the camp, the leaders of the women's liberation movement at Migdal were convinced that they also had a role to play in the kitchen. When one of the camp's fifty girls was found to have a defective heart she was forced off the road. "Food conquered our health problems, so it certainly isn't a disgrace to cook," she rationalized to the other girls. In a noble act of comradeship they all decided to join a permanent corps of cooks.

Malaria was a more difficult problem to beat. The pioneers took quinine, but the bitter pill was only a repressor. When the pill was not taken, the symptoms resurfaced. The only effective control was to drain the swamps and to rid the country of its mosquito-breeding grounds. Malaria was endemic; it fevered the cities as well as the farms. The work against the blight in the urban areas was the exclusive domain of the Mandatory government's health department, which began to function in the latter part of 1920. Hadassah was initially forbidden to do any sanitary work in the cities and towns, most probably for political reasons. Recent arrival Henrietta Szold was furious: "The prohibition would be just and proper provided the Government fulfilled its functions. It has a corps of Arabs, low-class inspectors, who are charged with practicing graft. They sell the petrol entrusted to them for (pouring into) wells, cisterns and puddles, and accept *baksheesh* (bribery) from householders who desire not to drink petrolized water."

The Mandate government, under its first high commissioner, Sir Herbert Samuel, soon saw the error and authorized Hadassah's sanitary engineer Louis Cantor to direct squads of inspectors in an all-embracing anti-malaria campaign. Hadassah was, after all, killing mosquitoes that were biting both Arabs and Jews and even an occasional Englishman. Cantor's efforts were long remembered by all sections of the community. He introduced toilets and garbage disposal units in Arab villages. He drew up the first plan for draining quarters in Jerusalem that were avenues of running sewage. He gave the first course of instruction on how to install plumbing ("installators," as plumbers are still known in Hebrew). And some distinguished Zionist leaders long remembered him for the hot shower installation that he introduced into the Hotel de France, Hadassah's headquarters. It soon became a regular Friday afternoon rite for the *yishuv's* captains to wash themselves under Lou Cantor's showers.

Work with pioneers in the marshes of Galilee led Hadassah to participate in the healing of the land through reclamation projects undertaken by the Jewish National Fund. Founded on December 29, 1901 at the Fifth Zionist Congress in Basel, the JNF was created for one purpose: "...to buy lands in Palestine." Such lands, according to the founding declaration, would be "the inalienable property of the Jewish people." But reality decreed otherwise. Within a short time the JNF, known worldwide for the little blue-and-white coin boxes that still grace Jewish homes, was not only buying land but draining swamps, rehabilitating river beds, cutting new roads, planting forests, creating picnic areas and parks, and making desert soil fertile.

At the end of its first century, the JNF has planted more than 200 million trees and owns 17 percent of the land on which Israel exists. The annual budget has reached one-quarter of a billion dollars and Israelis now have more than half a million acres of forest.

Having extended far beyond its mandate, no other institution could boast at having fulfilled Zionist aspirations as could the JNF. It was to this star in Jewish life that Hadassah firmly hitched its Zionist mission. Killing mosquitoes in the Galilee had given this healing society a hearty appetite for more projects to revive a land that, after centuries of neglect and rape, was nearly dead.

From 1926 to 1996 Hadassah would spend fifty million dollars to finance twenty-five diverse schemes through JNF. These programs would include, among others: redeem 4,000 acres in the Haifa Bay area, 10,000 acres in Galilee, drain the Huleh Lake to create 33 villages and, in the 1990s, participate in recreating part of the Huleh to preserve its ecological balance. It created a grassy shore that the western side of the Kinneret (Sea of Galilee) never had. In 1949, Hadassah set up a hospital in Beersheba when the village consisted only of two dirty streets. Four decades later through the JNF, Hadassah would replace the scrub and sand of Beersheba (population 153,000 in 1995) with a park and playground at the entrance to the city.

For all their ingenuity none of Hadassah's founders could have imagined their members would one day build dams in a desert. But in 1986 that is just what they did. One of the largest soil barriers in Israel — 56 feet high — was partially financed by Hadassah. The Hadassah-Eshet dam has spawned a 10 million cubic meter blue, freshwater lake in the Arava along the border with Jordan. Floodwaters that formerly ran to the Dead Sea or Jordan now recharge depleted aquifers and provide water for 3,000 settlers in ten villages. Where once there were only snakes, scorpions and tumbleweed, water has produced winter crops of melons, mango, persimmon and avocado that feed the markets of Israel and Europe.

Not far away, near Kibbutz Sde Boker, another Hadassah dam blocks winter's flash floods, providing water for flocks of sheep and orchards of acacia, pistachio and tamarisk.

But all this was yet to come. Back in the early 1920s relations between the Zionists and the new British Mandate government were testy. The fact that Sir Herbert Samuel was a Jew and pro-Zionist made little difference to Colonial Office bureaucrats many of whom, like Heron, had transferred from the army or the Occupied Enemy Territory Administration to what they hoped would be adventurous, well-paid, easy jobs in Palestine. Many had served in Cairo and knew how to "handle" Arabs. Jews, ideologically motivated and anxious to establish a state, were another cup of tea.

In Haifa, for example, the anti-Zionist military governor had remarked that the overcrowded and unsanitary conditions in which Jewish immigrants were living endangered the health of the Arab population. This, despite a dispensary that was being run for Jews and Arabs by Hadassah.

In reply to the military governor's challenge, Hadassah rushed Joseph Shapiro to the port town. His public health survey concluded, even to the satisfaction of the British governor, that the Arabs were less likely to fall ill from the Jews than from the drinking water from shallow wells or from the garbage they were spilling into the streets or from the sewage running by their houses or from the open barrels of water which they used to wash clothes — which bred mosquitoes. Shapiro proved that the health and sanitation conditions of the Jews were as good as, and in many cases better than, those of their Arab neighbors.

By mid-1920, immigrants were entering Haifa and Jaffa ports en masse, bringing with them an unprecedented plague of East European lice. Delousing of their bodies was not much of a problem since there was plenty of chlorine at hand. The problem was how to deal with the clothes. The British had invented an apparatus called a Serbian Barrel to sterilize clothes, but it was not yet available in Palestine. Shapiro improvised by taking empty alcohol barrels and making them air-tight. He then fitted them with false bottoms which were filled with water. Placed over a fire, the barrels became giant pressure cookers. In a short time the clothes placed in the Shapiro Barrels, as they became known throughout the country, were free of lice.

By mid-1922, Hadassah asked the Mandate government to take over rural sanitation along with malaria control. In any case, inspection of newcomers ceased to be a great problem since immigration had been curbed. Thus relieved of preventive medical work, Hadassah could expand its medical services throughout the country. From the Jordan to the Mediterranean, from Galilee to Judea, a string of sixty Hadassah clinics soon functioned in towns and villages. Clinics serviced nearly all the *moshavim* (cooperative villages). In 1931, the rural medical service was turned over to Kupat Holim Amamit, a health maintenance organization founded by Hadassah. It thrives today as Kupat Holim Meuchedet, now one of the largest in Israel.

Throughout the 1920s the Hadassah horse-and-buggy doctors and nurses who traveled the dirt paths into remote settlements were familiar figures. At the beginning of the 1930s they worked under different auspices, but Hadassah was still the first to send them on their appointed rounds. Henrietta Szold later paid them the ultimate tribute when she said, "The itinerant doctors had become the lineal successor to the priest in the camps of ancient Israel."

Few people living today have a full understanding of the extent to which Hadassah — young, poor and inexperienced — fashioned the future of the *yishuv's* medical history in the third decade of the century. When Americans were only beginning to dream of national health insurance, Hadassah in Palestine was forcing an amalgamation of the health funds that were started by the two existing political labor parties. Both parties were serving as contractors on the road-building and swamp-clearing projects in Galilee; each demanded separate field hospital services from Hadassah. The Unit's acting director at the time was Henrietta Szold. She put her foot down and issued an ultimatum for the two to amalgamate. That decided the issue. The result was Kupat Holim Clalit of the Histadrut, Israel's Federation of Labor. Until 1931, Hadassah institutions at first took on all Kupat Holim cases free of charge. With financial help from Hadassah, Kupat Holim built its first hospital in the Jezreel Valley in 1929. A second, Beilinson, was constructed in Petah Tikvah seven years later. These two institutions took considerable pressure off Hadassah and permitted Hadassah to reach for new horizons. Kupat Holim Clalit covered nearly the entire Jewish population. In time the others would be cared for by three private health funds. In 1995, the Knesset decreed that all Israelis be covered by one of the four. Fees set by the government were deducted from salaries like social security payments in return for which residents received blanket coverage. Hadassah had the satisfaction that its good medical care was helping give Israelis longer lives than nearly all other peoples.

As in the Galilee, where Hadassah pioneers were being told that they were wasting time, they were similarly rebuffed in Jerusalem. And, as in the Galilee, the Americans refused to accept "no" for an answer. In the Holy City they persisted until the population accepted them. No single Hadassah worker was more persevering than a dynamic mite of a public health nurse by the name of Bertha Landsman. Her charges would relate how in the summer of 1921 she issued orders with the cadence of a top sergeant marching into battle against a dangerous enemy. "If they don't let you in the front door, go in the back door. And if they don't let you in the back door, go through the window. But get in!" It was a battle cry no one believed could possibly emerge from pink-cheeked, blue-eyed Bertha.

In some ways Bertha's story was much like that of Shulamit Yedid-Halevy Cantor. At about the same time that Shulamit was threatening her father that she would run away from Beirut to go to nursing school, Bertha was doing the same. She told her father that nursing was definitely for her and if she could not study in her native New York City, she would flee to Washington, DC. The poor man agreed, providing she remained near home. So Bertha trained at Mount Lebanon Hospital, in New York, the source of many of the AZMU's first nurses. After graduation she served in mother and infant welfare stations established by philanthropist Nathan Straus in New York City's underprivileged neighborhoods. But her heart was in Palestine and in 1921 she followed it there.

To the newcomer, Eretz Israel has always been seductively rich in challenges; Henrietta Szold would say, "Where everything is needed, everything needs to be done." Bertha saw that in Jaffa-Tel Aviv four out of every ten babies never lived to celebrate their first birthday. In Haifa, the mortality rate was 30 percent and in Jerusalem 20 percent. To keep babies alive, then, was her challenge. She reached into her experience and pulled out a plan to adapt the Straus mother and infant stations to Palestine. She organized a platoon of nurses, opened the first center in the ancient walled city of Jerusalem and then went out to drag in the reluctant mothers. In the beginning, the male members of the Jewish families beat off the nurses, sometimes physically. Most of the nurses did not wear wedding bands, so they would be taunted with: "Hah! You are not even married and you are going to tell us how to take care of our babies!"

The nurses were caught in a crossfire. From one flank they were being driven on by Bertha's exhortations; from the other they were being pushed away by irate husbands. At times they took Bertha's orders literally and climbed through back windows to plead, to cajole, to tempt mothers to come to the stations. Inside, they found dark, dank rooms where babies lay bundled like mummies, their hands and feet tightly tied "to give them good postures." Their eyes were watery from the smoke of charcoal cooking fires. Windows were kept closed even in temperate weather because the families believed it was the only way to keep out unseen germs — and the evil spirit. For extra protection, a *hamsa* (brass hand) was hung in every room. Flies and vermin plagued the tots, but they were disregarded because they were "too small" to do harm. When mothers had insufficient milk to nurse, they gave the infants unpasteurized goat's milk.

Bertha broke the opposition by offering free layettes and pasteurized formula milk to parents on condition they give birth in Rothschild Hospital. Once the mothers were in the hospital Bertha would exhort each one, "Bring your babies to our station regularly and I promise you they will live to bless you with many grandchildren."

The "Drop of Milk" (*Tipat Halav*) station, as it was known, had a kitchen and two rooms. Each day in the kitchen hermetically-sealed vats of milk would be lifted on to a three-headed kerosene stove. When the milk reached close to boiling point, the vat would be hurriedly shifted into a bathtub filled with ice where it would be quickly cooled. The result was the first pasteurized milk in all of Palestine, probably in the Middle East. Nurses and volunteers, headed by the wife of the director of customs, Mrs. Harold Solomon, would then prepare formulas, fill bottles and wait for the mothers to appear. Those who came for the first time would receive a free tin container to carry the bottles home. The word quickly passed from mouth to mouth in the Jewish quarter of the Old City that Hadassah was giving out a new type of milk that did not turn rancid quickly. That appealed to mothers and their numbers at the Drop of Milk station grew. Some began coming from outside the walled city, but many were still hesitant.

Bertha was impatient. If mothers did not come for milk, she would bring the milk to them. And so was established the Donkey Milk Express. Each bottle was labeled with the baby's name, packed in ice and put on a donkey cart whose sides carried the name "Tipat Halav" in Hebrew, Arabic and English. Each weekday morning, the Donkey Milk Express began its journey from the David Street station, joined the raucous traffic of horses, camels, carriages and tin-lizzies on its life-giving mission to the Rothschild Hospital, which was the New City's milk distribution point. There, volunteer women of the Hebrew Women's Federation (*Histadrut Nashim Ivriot*) handed the sterilized bottles to waiting mothers.

So popular was the Donkey Milk Express and its cargo that housewives from Western countries who had no infants clamored for pasteurized milk. One well-to-do American mother once approached Bertha to provide her with pasteurized milk because her daughter disliked drinking boiled milk. Bertha's reply was in character: "Of course we will provide you with our product. Just send someone each morning to pick up a pint. And send along 50 cents for each bottle." Hadassah's Robin Hood explained that she was charging the outlandish price to cover the cost of the milk for several children whose parents could not pay one cent. Actually few got it free. Except for the destitute, mothers were required to pay something, even though it be a pittance, teaching the lesson that mothers and fathers must care for their own children, that charity should not replace responsibility. Bertha and her nurses struggled with this problem as they had struggled to get the mothers to visit the station in the first place. Mostly, the fathers were the ones who objected. For this kind of luxury they expected the Americans or Europeans to pay. Mothers cried on Bertha's slim shoulders begging her to help convince their husbands. For those with more generous spouses, Bertha kept precise accounts of the pennies the women paid and made out individual receipts which they could show their husbands. At times, exhausted, Bertha was tempted to give up the idea, be done with the accountancy and hand out the milk free. Then one day a pretty, young Orthodox mother came to her, smiling coyly, and told a story that convinced Bertha the battle was won.

The mother had always complained that she could not get milk money from her stubborn husband. This day she showed up with the coins clenched in her fist and a promise that she would no longer have to plead for milk money.

Bertha was surprised. "How did you do it?" she asked.

The mother's cheeks turned pink and she dropped her eyes. She wanted to talk to Bertha privately. They stepped aside and the mother whispered, "It was very hard, but my husband does not like sleeping on the floor."

Bertha's eyes opened wide with an unspoken question.

"It was the day I was supposed to go to the *mikvah* (ritual bath). I absolutely *refused* to go until he gave me the money for milk. He won't refuse again," she said with a twinkle.

Forty years later, Bertha recalled the story and said that it was the turning point in her personal battle. Never again did she waver.

With the milk program running smoothly, Bertha now felt sufficiently sure of herself to move into related fields. She sent her nurses into homes to advise mothers how to prepare cereal, how to refrigerate, how to nurse. And by mid-1923 they were all going through the front door. At the station, Bertha insisted that babies be weighed regularly. Some mothers objected because they said it would invite the evil eye, so they fed their children before they took them to the station and then insisted that there was no need to weigh them. The nurses overcame that obstacle by forcing the mothers to leave the children at the center for three hours before going ahead with a test feeding and a weighing-in. Periodically, the children were examined and fortunately for everyone concerned, Jerusalem's first pediatrician was Helena Kagan, whose understanding and kindliness earned her the respect and gratitude of generations of parents.[1]

So popular was the station after a time that the non-Jewish mothers in the neighborhood began to ask for aid. Everyone was accepted, Jew and non-Jew alike. In 1923, with a gift from Nathan Straus, another station was opened in the lower Musrara Quarter near the Damascus Gate where the population was predominantly Arab. Even during the bitter Arab riots of the 1920s and 1930s, a Jewish and an Arab physician would remain on duty at the station. Veteran nurses in Jerusalem still remember with a smile the diminutive Dr. Abu Saud, who had to stand on a bench to examine the taller children's eyes and throats and whose favorite — and effective — treatments for many ailments were barley water or castor oil. The nurses, too, courageously carried on through the bloodletting, keeping to their rounds in both Arab and Jewish quarters.

One of those nurses, Hanna Elkayam, was sent into the village of Siloam (Silwan) in the southern environs of Jerusalem to open a station. The village was mainly Arab, but about 100 Yemenite Jewish families lived there peacefully. From 1925, Hanna lived in Siloam and served the community as nurse, confidante, pharmacist, social worker. All problems came to Hanna for resolution: how much to spend on a bar mitzvah party, what clothes to buy for the children, how to reunite a separated couple. Hanna was the mother of the village.

One night the leading Sheikh of Siloam, Haj Ghuslan, did Hanna the unique honor of calling upon her. After the usual formalities were ended, he asked whether she would go to his house to deliver his wife's child. Not a little tremulous, Hanna agreed. She found the woman in difficult labor, but Hanna delivered the baby after a few tense hours. As the Sheikh's son uttered its first cry, the grandmother threatened the nurse, "That child you

---

1   On July 31, 1958, Mayor Gershon Agron and the city fathers bestowed upon Dr. Kagan the coveted Freedom of Jerusalem, the first woman to be so honored.

have brought into the world will grow up one day to throw a rock at you at the Wall." Sheikh Ghuslan never forgot Hanna's kindness. During the riots of 1929 he placed guards over the property of all the Jews of the village and nothing was stolen or touched during their temporary absence.

The lone milk station that was opened by Bertha Landsman in 1921 had by the end of the decade multiplied to twenty-two, not counting numerous sub-stations throughout the country. One result was that the Mandate government's slow-moving health department was obliged to emulate Hadassah, opening its first infant welfare center for Arabs in 1925. By the end of the decade it had fourteen going. The idea spread beyond the borders of Palestine. In Cairo, WIZO (Women's International Zionist Organization) asked for the loan of a Hadassah-trained nurse to run a center. Nurses from Iraq were sent to Jerusalem to observe Hadassah's work and returned to Baghdad to organize similar operations. A center based on the Hadassah pattern was likewise opened in Amman.

Fruits of the infant welfare work were quick and sweet. Mortality dropped dramatically. In 1922, 144 Jewish children out of every 1,000 throughout the country died before their first birthday. By 1930, the rate had dropped by more than half to sixty-nine.

By the end of the decade Hadassah closed the Drop of Milk kitchens. In nine years the Jewish population had accepted the necessity of proper milk preparation. In the 1960s, the Jerusalem health stations were transferred to the municipality and in the rest of the country to the Ministry of Health. Although now officially known as "Well-Baby Clinics," the original name Tipat Halav has endured.

The pulse of every undertaking in preventive medicine and in education initiated by Hadassah in Palestine came from the heartbeat of the child. When the generation of Yitzhak Rabin, Shimon Peres and Moshe Dayan was in its infancy, Hadassah was there doing its best to protect and nurture it. When the AZMU arrived in Palestine, trachoma afflicted the eyes of upward of forty of every 100 Jewish school children. A similar number had scalp and skin ailments. Home inspection was tried, but Hadassah soon learned that the most efficient way to attack these maladies was through strict control in the schools where one child was more apt to infect another. No agencies existed to carry out inspections in schools in 1918 and 1919. So, as Henrietta Szold reported back to New York in finger-snapping prose, "A School Hygiene Department was organized."

To beat trachoma, Hadassah doctors and inspectors dispersed throughout the country. Itinerant ophthalmologists made regular calls at remote settlements. One of the first eye specialists who traveled the trachoma circuit on the back of a donkey was Haim Yassky, then on the threshold of a brilliant career that would end in tragedy. Hadassah took responsibility for children in the regular school system but also went into the homes of youngsters who studied at private schools. At one time thirty specially trained nurses were treating children under doctors' supervision. The results were spectacular. By 1930, trachoma was practically beaten; by 1938 only four out of every 100 children had the disease.

Hadassah's service to Jewish students was the most comprehensive in the world. At the start of each term the child was weighed, measured, tested for tuberculosis, examined for defective eyesight and hearing, and periodically vaccinated and inoculated. A child absent from school for more than two days was visited at home by a school nurse and treated before being permitted to return. In an average year 80 percent of all Jewish public school pupils received some kind of medical help.

Under the energetic direction of department chief Mordecai Brachyahu, pioneering work was carried out in mental hygiene. Kindergarten teachers reported emotionally unstable or mentally disabled children to Dr. Brachyahu, who ran guidance clinics in Jerusalem and Tel Aviv.

At the end of the first ten years — by which time the Straus Health Centers provided the roof for all of Hadassah's preventive medical work — the School Hygiene Department was supervising more than 250 schools in eight urban areas and sixty-four rural settlements. Altogether, 25,000 children were being examined yearly. And in that decade Hadassah dispensed to school pupils alone more than 10 million individual treatments.

By 1927, Hadassah wove its network of infant welfare stations and school hygiene services into a countrywide child welfare program that was years ahead of its time. By the latter part of the 1920s Hadassah was not only bringing children into the world, feeding them and making them disease resistant, but it was also attempting to supervise their recreation. This came about after the first playground in Palestine was opened in 1925 at the edge of the Jewish Quarter inside the Old City of Jerusalem. The money for the playground came from a $100,000 fund set up by Bertha Guggenheimer, of Lynchburg, Virginia, aunt of former Hadassah President Irma Lindheim. Until the lot was opened, the slum children's favorite games were playing cards, throwing dice or scrounging in ash cans. In February 1928, the trustees of the fund under which the playground was established turned over responsibility to Hadassah. A teacher in the Old City, Rachel Shwarz, wife of a noted Jerusalem attorney, whose two daughters later married Moshe Dayan and Ezer Weizman, was placed in charge. She moved to a larger area outside the city walls and brought in a Hadassah doctor to examine all the children who registered to play. The playground was beautifully equipped and so successful that this program quickly spread to all parts of the country.

But when a plot was opened in the Mahane Yehuda section of the New City of Jerusalem opposite the Etz Hayim Yeshiva, the principal of the school was enraged. He complained bitterly that his children were not paying attention to their Torah and Talmud lessons and instead were gazing out the windows at the boys and girls playing below. Repeatedly he implored Rachel Shwarz to close the field, using the argument that it was sinful according to Jewish law to permit boys and girls to romp together. The principal was all the more disturbed because his own granddaughter was playing there. Rachel stubbornly stood her ground, countering with the argument that his pupils might study better if they had time off daily to kick a ball around. But he would not be moved and applied to the

Jerusalem rabbinical court to issue a summons calling on Rachel to give good reason why the playground should not be closed.

Rachel had no choice but to appeal to the rabbinical eminence of the day, Chief Rabbi Abraham Isaac Hakohen Kook. Rachel stood before the saintly mortal and pleaded, "Our children have a natural instinct to play. How can a rabbi deny it to them?"

"My daughter," he said reassuringly without committing himself, "go back to your work and all will be well."

Objections evaporated as fog before the sun. The summons application was withdrawn, the playground flourished and municipal authorities all over the country made increasing demands on Hadassah's experience in helping establish them. Hadassah reasoned that playgrounds were more than sites for idle frolicking; when run Hadassah's way with a properly trained staff, they were educational instruments that sharpened leadership qualities and molded good bodies and minds.

The British authorities looked upon the project with benevolent grace. In 1934, they even went as far as to turn over to Hadassah a one-half acre plot in Jerusalem and then at the end of the year cited that act of charity in a report to the League of Nations as a major contribution to the Jewish population of Palestine.

By 1950, nearly 50 playgrounds had been set up by Hadassah while numerous others profited from Hadassah's expertise. That year all the grounds were turned over to the Israeli government.

BUTTER FOR THE PARSNIPS

O ne miserably cold day in December 1922, a tall, gaunt figure with
sad, bespectacled eyes and a finely-trimmed goatee stood before
Henrietta Szold in her Jerusalem office. He was beloved as a
teacher and principal of a girls' school in the Old City.

"Not a day goes by," sighed Yeshaya Press, "that one of our children
does not faint in the classroom. They come to school with nothing in their
stomachs. When they go home, they are lucky if they find bread and a few
vegetables to eat. I have found some of them raiding garbage pails. How
can I expect them to do their lessons? Can't your American organization
help us get some warm food into their bellies?"

Press would not admit it, but Henrietta knew that his teachers were just
as hungry as the pupils and there were instances where they had collapsed as
well. Palestine was then paralyzed by economic stagnation. Imports far
outpaced exports, there was little industry and many of the plants that had
opened soon went bankrupt for lack of working capital. Fifty years later in
Jerusalem, Prime Minister Golda Meir would smilingly recall those days to
an economic conference of millionaires: "I remember when I first came in
1921. The only 'heavy' industry was chocolate. But the chocolate it

produced was full of sand and when I asked why, I was told that sand was the country's only natural resource."

So poor was the country that in the struggling kibbutzim and villages farmers had nothing more to eat than the vegetables they grew. Their patron, the World Zionist Organization, was having trouble finding money to carry both them and the Unit over their initial period of development. The AZMU got some support, as we have seen, from the Joint Distribution Committee, the Rothschilds and from the young Hadassah organization in the United States. Partly because of a severe economic depression, membership in Hadassah in 1921 was little more than 10,000 and so was not big enough to bear single-handedly the burgeoning burdens of the pioneers in Palestine. Hadassah's weakness was also partly organizational. From 1918 to 1921, it was affiliated and subordinate to the male-dominated Federation of American Zionists. Full independence came only in 1933 when Hadassah stopped paying affiliation dues to the Federation's successor, the Zionist Organization of America (ZOA). Growth was slowed as well by the intellectual and political climate in the United States. The Jewish masses, engrossed in sopping up American culture, were practically untouched by Zionism. After some initial enthusiasm over the Balfour Declaration, apathy quickly set in when the British pledge failed to instantly produce a Jewish nation. Hadassah's problem was a small reflection of the general American lack of interest in the Zionist movement.

In the early 1920s the largest fundraiser on the American scene was the Joint Distribution Committee which, in the main, channeled funds to the poverty-stricken Jewish communities in Europe. So it was that Palestine's requirements far exceeded Zionism's ability to meet them. In Jerusalem, Zionist headquarters was so badly off that electricity and telephone services were shut down periodically for nonpayment of bills. The World Zionist Organization cut its budget for Hadassah's work by two-thirds, forcing it to the brink of bankruptcy. Grocery bills piled up. Pharmaceuticals suppliers pounded on Henrietta Szold's desk. Hadassah employees went for months without salaries; once they were paid in linen. Medical Director

Rubinow had to close a clinic in the Old City and the hospital in Tiberias and reduce the number of beds in the Tel Aviv hospital. The pressure was so great that Rubinow repeatedly threatened to quit. Into Henrietta's lap fell the whole sorry mess. She was then sixty-two years old and ailing. She knew that the only logical thing to do would be to disband the Unit but even that was impossible because there was no money to pay off the doctors. She wrote her sister Rachel, "If the Unit and I survive the winter, it will be a miracle."

Early in October 1922, Henrietta Szold desperately fought to keep the Unit alive by calling on Baron Rothschild in Paris. As she walked past great works of art in his ornate mansion in the Rue de Faubourg Saint-Honoré, she daydreamed that the old man would say: "Over there is a little thing of the school of Leonardo da Vinci — take it." But he did not. Rather, he used the occasion to berate American Jews in general and Zionists in particular for not supporting what they started. The only constructive part of their meeting was the lavish praise that the baron voiced for Hadassah's work. Bitterly, she later commented, "I have heard that too often now to be flattered. Fine words butter no parsnips and keep no hospitals going."

The baron's advice was to go to America to raise the money. She would have done so even though she detested the idea, but poor Rubinow in Jerusalem had frantically cabled he was about to leave for good.

Henrietta was not back in Jerusalem very long when her old friend Nathan Straus, having heard of her distress, cabled $20,000. As much as it was appreciated, the dollars covered only one-fourth of the Unit's debts. Should she use it to pay salaries or to pay the baker or the drug manufacturers? "I know the agony of an honest bankruptcy," Henrietta said. "Hour by hour I sit in the office and count and calculate." Happily, the Unit's administrative staff and even a few of the doctors were prepared to forgo their back pay to allow the work to continue, accepting Henrietta's promise that one day they would receive their money in full.

It was at that gray hour that Yeshaya Press stood before Henrietta Szold. She told him that she had no money for even a piece of chalk, but ever optimistic, she repeated to him her overworked slogan, "Where everything is needed, everything needs to be done. And it will be done." Press walked out of her office empty-handed, but buoyed by Henrietta's faith that help would come. Shortly after, tourist Rabbi Maurice Harris of New York burst into Henrietta's office. As a religious educator, he was appalled to see how badly nourished the school children of Jerusalem were. He had brought a small sum of Hanukkah money with him, contributed by his school, and he thought Miss Szold could put it to use to feed the unfortunate pupils. It was not nearly enough to help everyone, but what if he started a campaign in the United States to provide lunches for Jerusalem's needy pupils? Would Miss Szold ask Hadassah in New York to help him?

Henrietta could hardly encourage Rabbi Harris enough. And Yeshaya Press was, of course, the first to be told. Rabbi Harris did go back and together with Leon Lang organized a school lunch program committee on which Hadassah was represented. Soon thereafter the project was transferred to Hadassah. At first, appeals for lunch money were made almost exclusively to pupils of religious schools throughout the United States. The slogan was simple: "Give a penny so a child in Jerusalem can eat." Pennies rolled in by the basketful. Hadassah women organized thrift luncheons whereby they would cook and serve the same meal that was served to the Jerusalem pupils. But they would charge each guest from five to ten times more than the cost of the meal given in Palestine. A typical lunch was oatmeal, soup, coleslaw and date and raisin compote. On Fridays the children got free cocoa and bread at 10:00 am recess because mothers gave them no solid food for breakfast in anticipation of the Sabbath evening meal. With a healthy donation from Hadassah the first hot lunches were served in Yeshaya Press's school in September 1923. A small kitchen and dining room were equipped. At first, only some of the girls could afford the one-half piaster (2.5 cents) for a meal. When the Hadassah committee under Nellie Straus Mochenson saw other girls standing "in tears at the door of the dining room looking on the feast," it was decided to include every child in the school. No one but Press knew who paid and who did not.

But that was only the beginning. It was Henrietta's policy that each endeavor must serve wider educational aims. A cook was hired to supervise the six weekly meals, but pupils in the higher grades were taught not only how to cook but how to serve and clean up, and most important, the fundamentals of nutrition. Henrietta's ultimate goal was to introduce domestic science into the school's curriculum. In 1923 as the lunch program started, that goal was remote. Among the girls of Press's school, there were some who were not accustomed to sitting on a chair or at a table to eat. Before they could learn to plan a balanced meal, they had to be taught how to use a knife and fork. At the end of the first year Henrietta reported, "Eventually the school luncheon program will be the means of teaching the food values of the rich variety of cereals and vegetables obtainable in Palestine which are largely disregarded now, particularly by the newer arrivals."

Teaching dietetics was not exactly new. Yehudit Aaronson Dushkin introduced the idea in the labor centers of Galilee. Student nurses in Jerusalem took cooking lessons for three hours every morning in a converted stable at Rothschild Hospital. On the whole, the cadet nurses liked their lessons and the more proficient were chosen to cook part of the lunches served to the 120 patients and 105 staff members in the basement dining hall — originally built as a mammoth cistern.

Hard times in Palestine grew harder in 1927 and 1928 and the penny lunches were extended to kindergarten children, but even they did not get away with merely filling their little stomachs. The five-year-olds were also taught how to use cutlery, how to set a table and how to ask politely for the bread. By the turn of the decade 1,000 children were being fed from eight centrally-located kitchens in Jerusalem, Haifa, Safed and Tiberias. So extensive had the project grown that Hadassah set up a Nutrition Department in the newly-opened Straus Health Center in Jerusalem.

In charge was a Dutch-born nutritionist, Sara Bavli, who opened the first course to train domestic science teachers in December 1930. As the teachers became available, the lunch programs broadened. By the time Israel was founded in 1948, 28,000 children were being fed daily in 300 schools and when Israel was ten years old, the number increased to 130,000 children. That was more than 25 percent of the entire school population of the country. By now the government was carrying most of the budget and parents were only paying 10 percent of the bill. Meanwhile in 1953, Mrs. Bavli had opened the College of Nutrition and Home Economics in Jerusalem.

Sara Bavli's college trained nutritionists for hospitals, clinics, schools and senior citizens' homes until 1981. It was then split: part formed the basis of a school for Nutritional Sciences in the Hebrew University's Agriculture Faculty, the only source in the country on worldwide nutrition research, and part introduced nutrition to the curriculum of the David Yellin Teachers College in Jerusalem. Sara Bavli died in 1993.

What had started out as a frantic measure to ease the hunger pangs of a few score children and teachers in the Old City of Jerusalem had, within 25 years, grown into a ramified educational effort. Girls were being taught everything from child development and child guidance to interior decorating and stain removal. Hadassah's School Luncheon Committee made inroads into the kibbutzim where the science of food preparation was generally ignored in favor of the business of food production. Teachers in a number of kibbutzim asked Hadassah to set up cooking lessons even though, oddly enough, kibbutz parents objected. After an experimental lesson in one collective succeeded, the idea caught on and many set up kitchen committees. Hadassah knew it had succeeded when one kibbutz finally put hated spinach on the menu in the children's dining room. The kids ate it because they themselves had prepared it.

THE BLOOD OF AUGUST

Tired and tense, close to midnight on Friday, August 23, 1929, administrative director of Hadassah Hospital in Jerusalem, Reuven Katznelson scrawled a cable to Hadassah in New York, "We have eleven dead and twenty-five wounded. Arabs attacking several Jewish hospitals."

On Saturday night, August 24, he wired:

> Another seven dead and eight of yesterday's wounded have died also. More than thirty wounded. The Arabs are attacking Mekor Haim, Talpiot and Motza. New surgery departments have been opened. We are calling all doctors we can. Babies Home has been transferred into town. Need money badly.

Arab rioting lasted eight days, spanning the whole of settled Palestine from Safed in the northern Galilee to Hebron, city of the Patriarchs, south of Jerusalem. The violence was the bloodiest since the end of World War I: Arabs killed 133 Jews and wounded 330; British police killed 110 Arabs and wounded 232 and the Jews killed six Arabs. The riots illuminated the inadequacies of the British police and the need for a better Jewish system of defense. Zionist leaders in Jerusalem took immediate remedial measures that transformed the underground Haganah, forerunner of the Israel Defense Forces, into a skilled fighting unit.

The Arab riots of 1929 were the outgrowth of a quarter of a century of political struggle and intrigue. Throughout, Hadassah had a unique role to play, particularly during the height of the bloodletting. And everything that Hadassah accomplished in the Land of Israel from the arrival of the two nurses in 1913 seemed in retrospect to have been fated as preparation for those eight bloody days in August 1929.

The seeds of the riots, a turning point in Middle East history, were watered by the turbulent political crosscurrents of the late nineteenth and early twentieth centuries. Jewish nationalism in the form of Herzlian Zionism, dramatized by the formation of a political movement at the First Zionist Congress in Basel in 1897, was only a hop, skip and jump ahead of a similar movement then forming in the Arab world. In 1904, Herzl was dead only a year and the Zionist platform was just beginning to sweep over the Jewish communities of Europe when the first serious call was heard for Arab secession from the Ottoman Empire. In 1905, Christian Arab publisher Neguib Zaouri envisioned an Arab empire stretching "from the Tigris and the Euphrates to Suez, and from the Mediterranean to the Arabian Sea." Interestingly, he excluded Egypt, writing, "The Egyptians do not belong to the Arab race; they are of the African Berber family."

During World War I in the Sykes-Picot agreement, the British and the French secretly arranged to divide the spoils of war and to establish two protectorates over lands the Ottoman Empire had held for four centuries; the French were to rule Syria and Lebanon and the British would control Iraq and Palestine. No provision was made for Jewish or Arab autonomy.

In Cairo, the British high commissioner was goading the Bedouin tribes of the Arabian peninsula to join the war on the side of the Allies. Toward that end Sir Henry McMahon made contact with Sharif Hussein Ibn Ali of Mecca. Writing from Cairo, McMahon pledged British support for Hussein's dream to place the Arab world under one caliphate. That convinced him to fight the Turks.

By June 1916, Hussein got the Arab revolt under way against Ottoman rule. T. E. Lawrence (Lawrence of Arabia), a British agent who was assigned to assist Hussein's forces, added glamor to the revolt. But as things turned out the Arab contribution to the overall war effort was not so effective as either the British or the Arabs had hoped it would be. Sharif Hussein boldly planned to drive straight north and capture Syria. Once that was done he would install the commander of his troops, his son Feisal, as the king of a united Arab monarchy in Damascus, but the power behind the throne would remain in Mecca with Sharif himself.

While this scheme was being hatched, noted chemist Chaim Weizmann, unaware of the Sykes-Picot agreement, was organizing a Zionist lobby to encourage the British government to establish a Jewish nation in Palestine once the Turks had been defeated.

Feisal's forces, together with the British, did not reach Damascus until October 1918 and did not take all of Syria until a fortnight before World War I ended. What the Arabs tried to do in battle, Weizmann had already succeeded in doing on paper. He had helped the British war effort by inventing a cheap method to produce explosives and had convinced the British to support the establishment of a national home for Jews in Palestine. The Balfour Declaration was issued on November 2, 1917, a month before General Allenby reached Jerusalem and nearly a year before Feisal got to Damascus. Arabia was stunned by the Zionist victory. In June 1918, the British tried to allay Arab fears and at the same time urged them to fight on by promising to work for Arab independence as well.

Little more than a month after World War I ended on November 11, 1918, the Allies solemnly gathered in Versailles for a peace conference. Zionist and Arab leaders were present too, among them Chaim Weizmann and Emir Feisal, who were no strangers to each other. In June 1918, they had met in Feisal's tent on the shores of the Gulf of Aqaba in an attempt to pave a path to Arab and Jewish co-existence. Later that year they met again in London where, with the assistance of T. E. Lawrence, they drafted an accord which was to have tied the destiny of their two peoples. But the agreement came to nothing. Poor Feisal fell victim to British-French power politics and the extremists among his own people. The latter pressed him to lead a revolt against the French who had taken over from the British in Syria. Forced to renege on his pledges to Weizmann, he began to mouth vicious anti-Zionist propaganda.

Feisal was at the mercy of an extremist group called the General Syrian Congress. The congress was created by Arab nationalists in July 1919, with the aim of creating an independent Syria that would include Lebanon and Palestine. Once the French took over Syria and Lebanon, as laid down by Sykes-Picot, the congress shifted to violence. On March 1, 1920, it instigated an attack on two Jewish farm settlements in Galilee — at Tel Hai and at Metulla — in which seven pioneers died, including noted Russian-born Zionist Captain Joseph Trumpeldor. One week later, the congress crowned Feisal king of United Syria and sent gangs into Galilee. During Passover, April 4 and 5, Arab mobs ran amok in Jerusalem, killing six Jews and wounding 211.

The Allies counterattacked, dealing a mortal blow to the congress. Toward the end of April, the Allied powers met a few miles east of Monaco in the Italian town of San Remo. They had still not concluded a treaty with Turkey and since the situation in the Middle East was fast deteriorating, they gathered to work out a permanent settlement for the peoples of the area. Three mandates were set up: two went to Britain to administer Palestine and Iraq and one went to France to govern Syria and Lebanon. Most important for the Zionist cause was a rider on the Palestine mandate that obligated the British to implement the provisions of the Balfour Declaration.

Little more than two months after the San Remo conference ended, the French sent King Feisal packing into comfortable exile (on the shores of Lake Maggiore, Italy) and brought independent United Syria to an ignominious and abrupt end. In that same month of July, the British appointed a prominent, pro-Zionist Jew, Sir Herbert Samuel, to be the first high commissioner of the Mandate government of Palestine.

As Jewish and pro-Zionist as Sir Herbert may have been, he was still committed to British colonial policy, then called "the equality of obligation." Today, it might be known as "even-handedness." Eight months after he took office, in the worst decision of his career, Sir Herbert appointed Haj Amin el-Husseini to be Grand Mufti of Jerusalem. Husseini was a rabid anti-Zionist and was regarded as one of the leaders of the Passover riots in Jerusalem. Sir Herbert mistakenly believed that the Arabs would now be mollified.

In March 1921, Winston Churchill appeared on the scene. As British colonial secretary, he was responsible for the Mandate. New to the area's problems, he was determined to clean up the mess that had been created by contradictory British promises to Jews and Arabs. His ultimate aim was to pacify the area so that he could remove all British military forces. In his view the Arabs were the injured party; in characteristic Churchillian style he moved boldly. He called Emir Feisal out of Italian exile and rigged an election that made him king of Iraq. Churchill then sliced off that portion of Palestine that lay east of the Jordan River, including the hills of Moab from where Moses saw the Land of Israel, and put Feisal's brother, Abdullah, on a separate throne. Abdullah was to rule an area to be called Trans-Jordan, later renamed the Hashemite Kingdom of Jordan.

Zionist leaders did not kick up much dust at Churchill's handing half of Palestine to Abdullah. But the Arab dream was shattered. Arab nationalists despaired of uniting their peoples under the Syrian flag. So they united their energies — and found unity in — fighting Zionism in Palestine. To Churchill's credit, he did not renege on promises to Zionists even while he championed the cause of Arab independence. When a delegation of Moslem and Christian Arabs asked him in Jerusalem to rescind the Balfour Declaration and to stop Jewish immigration, Churchill replied, "That is not in my power and it is not my wish."

In retrospect, Churchill did not succeed, but unlike others who tried to solve the problem of Palestine, he executed his failure with brilliance and flair. He did not achieve a rapprochement between Zionists and Arabs. He fractured the idea of a single Arab state, apportioning slices to the favorite sons of Sharif Hussein. (Hussein himself would in short time be overthrown as the ruler of Hedjaz by Ibn Saud, who would give his name to the kingdom of Saudi Arabia.) Arab nationalists remained dissatisfied and the Jews grew apprehensive.

Churchill was gone from the scene little more than a month when violence again erupted. In Tel Aviv, now twelve years old, members of the socialist Zionist Ahdut Avodah party held a May Day parade. A rival parade was staged at the same place by the Trotskyite party. The two met head on with banners flying. Being an all-Jewish riot, there were no serious casualties. Arabs, watching from Jaffa, picked up arms and while the Jews were scuffling, went on a rampage of killing. Martial law was declared, but the "disturbances" continued sporadically for a full week. The Arabs had been provoked with rumors that atheist, Bolshevik immigrant Jews who recently arrived in Palestine were going to raze the mosques.

The first Arab target was an immigrant hostel in Jaffa. Twelve men and one woman who had just arrived from Russia were hacked to pieces. The Arabs raced on toward the center of Tel Aviv where they were held off by Jewish veterans of the World War. It was the first successful defense of the all-Jewish city. But farther north, Petah Tikvah was sacked by hundreds of angry Arab peasants. Hadera, Kfar Saba and Rehovot were invaded by Arabs who destroyed crops and vineyards and made off with farm equipment and livestock. Henrietta Szold happened to be at lunch in Jaffa on the day of the riot. Halfway through the meal she rushed to the Hadassah dispensary. The 300 dead and wounded lined the floors and crowded neighboring buildings. She immediately phoned to Jerusalem for additional medical personnel and supplies. Then she went about talking to eyewitnesses and residents. She concluded that the riot had been well-planned.

Faint-hearted Herbert Samuel tried appeasement again, this time by suspending Jewish immigration. It was another major *faux pas*, for the Jewish community of Palestine never trusted him wholeheartedly after that. In London, attempting to mediate the problem, the Colonial Office met separately with a Moslem-Christian Arab delegation and with Zionists. Talks began in 1922 and continued for a year, but the Arabs would not accept anything remotely like the Balfour Declaration and the Jews would not accept anything that diluted it. Winston Churchill tried to mollify both groups by issuing a White Paper in which he defined the declaration as giving the Jews a national home in Palestine but not over all of Palestine. He thus laid the groundwork for eventual partition. He candied the pill for the Jews by adding that they were in the Holy Land by right and not on sufferance. Weizmann wisely convinced his colleagues to accept the White Paper, although with some reservations. The Arabs rejected Churchill's formulation totally. They also rejected a plan to set up a legislative assembly in Palestine in which they would hold a majority.

The immediate effect of all the Arab "no's" was to hamstring some of their firmest supporters in England. In 1923, the outcome was a decision by the British that effective administration of the Mandate was feasible only if the Balfour Declaration and the Zionist cause were given full support. The deadlock between Arabs and Jews had become so hardened during the discussions that the British even considered giving up the Mandate altogether. But they held on to Palestine because the area might be needed at some future time to protect the Suez Canal.

A lull of almost five years then prevailed in Palestine affairs. Strangely, Zionism suffered thereby despite some progress. In Palestine, Hebrew was fast catching on. The Histadrut had taken roots as a powerful trade union and out of the road-building projects in the north had sprung the first major construction company, Solel Boneh. But the kibbutzim were still struggling. Land was hard to come by and Arab landowners demanded steep prices; even when a transaction was completed, Mandate officials often interfered. The brightest star of the mid-1920s was the opening of the Hebrew University on Mount Scopus in Jerusalem. Arthur Balfour, architect of the controversial 1917 declaration, was present. Wherever the white-haired, white-moustached diplomat traveled, cheers rang out — but only from the Jews.

Quietly, Haj Amin el-Husseini, the Grand Mufti, organized his forces against the Zionist settlers. On the surface it almost seemed that co-existence between Arabs and Jews was possible, so much so that Zionist land developer Arthur Ruppin founded an organization called Brith Shalom (Peace Covenant or Peace Alliance). This group, in which Henrietta Szold and Hebrew University Chancellor Judah Magnes were active, advocated a bi-national state in Palestine where Jews and Arabs would coexist peacefully, enjoying equal rights and equal duties. Chaim Weizmann himself was likewise lulled into thinking that peace was really possible. At the Fourteenth Zionist Congress, held in Vienna in 1925, he said: "Palestine must be built up without violating the legitimate interests of the Arabs — not a hair of their heads shall be touched...Palestine is not Rhodesia."

The tranquility that enveloped the land can be explained in a number of ways. In these years a general malaise gripped the Zionist movement. The Arabs, seeing that the idea of a national home was not taking hold among the Jewish masses, decided to wait patiently for Zionism's collapse. There was good reason to believe that might happen. In the years following the establishment of the Mandate, American and European Zionists fought bitterly over two contradictory philosophies. Most American Jews prioritized raising money for special projects in Palestine that would establish facts on which future political decisions could be based, while the Europeans saw Palestine as the last stop on the way home for millions of Jews living abroad in "exile." To the Americans, Palestine was for the philanthropist and the investor; to the Europeans, Palestine was the site for the fulfillment of the prayers of generations to rebuild the third Jewish commonwealth by settling the land through a universal ingathering.

In the United States, Zionist ranks were strongly influenced by Louis

D. Brandeis, a justice of the Supreme Court.[1] Still Weizmann and the Europeans had their supporters in the US, most notably Louis Lipsky, a maverick within the establishment. The differences between the American and European approaches came to a head with the establishment by Weizmann of the Keren Hayesod (the Foundation Fund) as the principal fund-raising arm of the World Zionist Organization. The Brandeis group insisted that money raised in America by the fund be used mainly for economic and industrial projects in Palestine. The Weizmann-Lipsky group urged that the money be used for settling immigrants on the land. These differences split the Federation of American Zionists. When Weizmann's view finally prevailed, the Brandeis group resigned from the American Zionist leadership. The dispute had a decisive effect on the future of Hadassah, most of whose leaders sided with Brandeis. The organization felt a growing need for complete autonomy. At Hadassah's 1921 national convention in Pittsburgh, delegates voted to break the amalgamation with the Federation of American Zionists, which it had voluntarily accepted three years earlier.

Because immigration to Palestine was less than a roaring success, the Arabs suspected that Zionism was a flash in the pan. The Jewish multitudes in the Diaspora did not rush to enter the gates of the Holy Land. Palestine's only good year was 1925 when about 35,000 Jews immigrated, most of them prodded by economic depression and raging anti-Semitism in Poland. Toward the end of the decade the numbers fell to a point where by 1929 more Jews were leaving the country than settling in it. Palestine was not particularly attractive to many Jews. A devastating earthquake struck in July 1927. A severe financial crisis hit the Jewish economy; Tel Aviv, the much-touted all-Jewish city, was bankrupt.

---

1 Brandeis, a fervent Zionist and champion of liberal causes, was appointed to America's highest court by President Woodrow Wilson. The first Jew to sit on the Court, he served with distinction for twenty-three years. President Franklin D. Roosevelt compared him with Isaiah.

Fortunately for Palestine, the British appointed a fine, high commissioner, Field Marshal Lord Plumer, one of the most brilliant officers of World War I. He replaced Herbert Samuel in August 1925, and quickly built a reputation for fairness and firmness. Plummer created an air of goodwill by reducing the security forces of the country. But his tenure was all too brief. He left in July 1928 and about six weeks later the peace of Palestine was ended.

When the Jews did not sink from the weight of their woes, Arab patience ran out. Only a small spark was needed to set the two communities on fire. On the eve of Yom Kippur in 1928, Jews gathered for Kol Nidre prayers at the Western Wall. Hemmed in by a warren of Arab hovels, only several hundred worshipers could crowd into the narrow alleyway in front of the Wall. But a few thousand always tried to crush in during the Holy Days. To separate men and women, the rabbi at the Wall put up a screen. Although the screen had been there on Rosh Hashanah, a British official now declared its presence to be a major violation of the status quo in Jerusalem.

On the morning of Yom Kippur, as the Jews were reciting the sacred *Amidah* prayer, British police arrived to remove the menacing divider. The aforewarned Arabs were right behind. Fortunately, no one was killed in the melee that followed, but the tempers of Jerusalem immediately began simmering.

A countdown on the inevitable blow-up began far from the scene, in Zurich on July 28, 1929, when Zionists gathered for their Sixteenth Congress. There, Chaim Weizmann formally established the broadly-based Jewish Agency, composed of both Zionists and non-Zionists. The establishment of the Agency was authorized by the British Mandate government, decided upon at San Remo and later ratified by the League of Nations. The Jewish Agency was now the executive arm of the World Zionist Organization, and was designed to work with the British for the implementation of a Jewish national home. As it turned out, the Agency developed into a shadow government of the incipient Jewish State.

At that same congress, firebrand Vladimir Zev Jabotinsky spoke passionately about the borders of the national home. In a widely reported oration, he pronounced, "The Jordan River does not mark its frontier but flows through its center."

To the Arabs of Palestine the Zurich congress was clear evidence that the Zionists planned a takeover in Palestine. This, coming on top of all the frustrations that had built up since the World War, primed the bomb of mob violence.

One day in August a Jewish boy, who ran after his ball into an Arab courtyard in Jerusalem, was knifed to death. Zionists turned his funeral into a protest march. Tishah b'Av, the yearly fast day when Jews mourn the destruction of the Temple, occurred shortly thereafter on Friday, August 22, and it was then that the Arabs struck.

Crowds gathered to worship at the Al-Aqsa Mosque on the Temple Mount above the Western Wall on this Muslim sabbath day. The Grand Mufti, leader of the Supreme Moslem Council, chose to address the congregants. British police officers noticed that many of the worshipers were carrying weapons. When they made inquiries, the Grand Mufti assured them they only wanted to protect themselves from possible Jewish revenge for the murder of the boy. The assurance was accepted. Shortly after the noon hour, a single shout was heard. Then several more. Someone began running in the direction of the Jewish Quarter opposite the Wall. The mob followed.

The Arabs' timing was good. British forces had been moved to Egypt and only a few hundred policemen were available. The new high commissioner, Sir John Chancellor, who had been at his post eight months, was out of the country. All the important members of the Jewish Agency were abroad at the Zionist Congress. The violence spread like wildfire beyond Jerusalem. Jewish settlements were laid waste. Wholesale murder and pillage struck Safed, Tel Aviv, Haifa and Hebron. In the course of eight days, 820 Jews and Arabs were either killed or wounded.

Hadassah in Jerusalem faced its own crisis. Henrietta Szold was attending the Zionist Congress. HMO Director Ephraim Michael Bluestone had resigned and the responsibilities for supervising the medical services were left in the hands of the one-time itinerant ophthalmologist Haim Yassky. Administration was under Reuven Katznelson. Yassky, too, was in Europe. When the storm hit, it was Katznelson aided by Chief Nurse Bertha Landsman and Mrs. Katznelson who ran the show. Fortunately, they had prepared for trouble. A week before the riots began, fifty extra surgical beds were made ready in Hadassah-Rothschild Hospital. In the Old City, an emergency first-aid station was opened. The spanking new Straus Health Center was set to house and feed refugees; it finally catered to 3,700.

Newspapers ceased publication. For eight days in August, Hadassah in Jerusalem became an operations center, simply because it alone had telephone contact with its units throughout the country. Telegrams arriving from abroad asking for information about relatives were delivered to Hadassah. Medical communiqués were issued not by the Mandate's department of health but by Hadassah.

The man who controlled communications was Haim Shalom Halevy, who began at Hadassah in 1927 as the keeper of statistics and went on later to develop the first modern hospital record department in the Middle East.

Edward Joseph, a massive man with massive hands, arrived in Palestine from his native New Zealand in 1928. He had fought at Gallipoli in 1915, studied medicine and came to Israel after three years at Rochester's Mayo Clinic. A follower of Jabotinsky, Dr. Joseph was convinced that Israel was the place for him after he read a boast of the Grand Mufti of Jerusalem: "The Jews want to make a National Home in Palestine. We Arabs will turn it into a Jewish national graveyard." He arrived at Hadassah to find himself in charge of the small surgery unit. The chief was on three months' leave. Sooner than he expected, Joseph was saving riot victims, working day and night in the stifling August heat, bare to the waist. He later recalled:

They suffered mostly dagger wounds. We had no

antibiotics. Surgical treatment was rather primitive. If there was active bleeding into the lung, we would go in and try to find the source and control it. Otherwise we would let things alone.

We had no plasma but I remember introducing blood transfusions. That was the citrate method. Problem was we had no saline for the people. We used the saline as an anti-shock treatment but even so everybody got reactions. Today it is routine. Nobody gets a reaction. In those days it was so dangerous we were afraid to use it.

During the riots the hospital was fired at by Arabs passing in the streets, but no one was hurt. We had no security. So, our orthopedic surgeon, Dr. Treu, and I decided to barricade the hospital to keep out the invaders. Treu was a little man but very courageous. He would venture out into the night to call on his patients. I warned him against it. He held up a huge Arab key and said, 'This is enough for me. If anyone comes near me, I'll slug him with this.'

In Jerusalem, Hadassah was not the only hospital that took in the wounded. But in other cities Hadassah was the sole source of medical care and supply.

News of the riots in Jerusalem reached Tel Aviv on the afternoon of August 23. There, twelve girls at Hadassah prepared bandages. Weekend leave was canceled for everyone. On August 25, three operating tables were made ready with a surgical team for each. First-aid corpsmen stood alert at the hospital doors with stretchers. Jewish policemen were given 300 bandages cut from diapers. By noon, the first sixteen wounded, attacked near a mosque, were brought in. Their names were posted outside the hospital. The hospital could not get to its laundry so improvised one in the yard. The municipality was in charge of the 700 refugees who sought shelter in the Ahad Ha'am School, but in fact Hadassah nurses looked after them.

In Haifa, Hadassah received all wounded from the Galilee. Expecting riots to break out, Hadassah prepared the Technion (Israel Institute for Technology) to take in refugees. August 26 was the worst day. Arabs used firearms as well as knives, stones and clubs. Thirty-eight wounded flooded the hospital. Medical personnel accompanied by British escorts went into the thick of the fighting to drag out the victims, among them Arabs whom British authorities asked Hadassah to treat. By nightfall of August 26, 3,000 Jews were evacuated from their homes by the British.

The Galilee town of Safed was alerted by Jerusalem on the 23rd. The next morning, Arabs gathered at the Safed mosque. At noon, they raced from the mosque screaming hysterically and throwing stones at Jews. Only one person was hurt that day: an Arab had been hit on the head by a stone thrown by another Arab. He was treated at Hadassah. The situation remained tense until August 29 when at the hour for the afternoon prayer, Arabs attacked the Sephardi quarter, started fires that kept the city illuminated all night, killed twenty and destroyed over 100 Jewish dwellings. The first wounded was an Arab policeman. The first dead was a Hadassah worker, Yitzhak Maman. A second victim was Hadassah physician Haim Israeli who died defending his home in Be'er Tuvia. Three hundred refugees filled the Safed hospital. On September 2, Dr. Yassky, home from Europe, organized relief work and ordered expansion of medical facilities in the town and reported:

> When we arrived many of the ruins were still smoking and it was impossible to attempt to remove corpses. The stench was unbearable. Whole streets were razed as though they had been bombarded and the city presents a picture of desolation and suffering that cannot be described...The people are in a state of extreme hysteria. The city and the roads leading to it present a picture of war times — armored

cars, automobiles with armed escorts bringing medical supplies from Haifa and returning with refugees.

The most macabre orgy of killing took place in Hebron where Jews had lived for centuries side by side with their Moslem neighbors. Life with the Arabs was amicable, although the Jews there were always second-class citizens: no Jew was permitted into the tombs of the Patriarchs because a grand mosque had been built over them. For the seven hundred Jews of Hebron it was sufficient to be able to live and to study the Law close by. Haganah men were sent to the yeshiva, but were summarily dismissed by the rabbis who said that their presence in the town was a provocation.

On August 24, the Sabbath, armed Arabs reached Hebron. Arab policemen watched them race through the town, enter an inn and hack twenty-three Jewish inhabitants to death. The mob then marched to the yeshiva where about forty Jews were massacred, their bodies butchered as though they were cattle.

All Hadassah services were suddenly integrated into a smooth-functioning life-saving machine. Refugees were shepherded to the Straus Health Center, newly opened to house Hadassah's preventive health-care work. The homeless were fed by the school lunch service. Meals were cooked and diets prepared by Hadassah's nutritionists. Tots were cared for in the infant welfare stations. Even the school playground project became vital as it set up special recreation activities for children separated from their parents.

In 1929, Hadassah was in its eighteenth year. One Hadassah eyewitness to the riots, an American tourist from Pittsburgh, returned home a month later and reported the words of an unidentified Haifa resident. "If Hadassah had done nothing else in the land during its years here, this one week of its activities would be worth all the money it has spent."

Chaim Weizmann later wrote, "If the riots were intended, whatever their effect on our nerves, to overthrow the structure of the National Home, they came too late. We had built too solidly and too well."

The British government fumed and fumbled in the years that followed the 1929 disturbances. High Commissioner Chancellor issued a caustic statement blaming the Arabs for "savage murders." But for balance — and to soften Arab protest — he announced that a commission would investigate "Arab and Jewish responsibility." The commission, headed by jurist Sir Walter Shaw, concluded that the attack on the Jews had not been premeditated. This august commission was immediately followed by another, chaired by Sir John Hope Simpson. His task was to investigate land sales to Jews. He concluded that Palestine could economically hold only 100,000 more immigrants — Jews and Arabs.

On October 21, 1930, the colonial secretary, socialist leader Sydney Webb (Lord Passfield) issued a White Paper based on the reports of the commissions. The White Paper in effect restricted Jewish immigration into Palestine and land sales to Jews.

One outcome of the riots was to rally world Jewry behind the Zionists, and the Zionists made the most of it. In the United States, Hadassah joined the men's Zionist organizations in a political demonstration. Hadassah's President was then Zip Szold, Savannah-born wife of attorney Robert Szold, a cousin of Henrietta. Zip remembered:

> We went to Washington with Rabbi Israel Goldstein as our spokesman. We wanted our government to stop the riots in Palestine. I don't believe we were very effective but we did speak to many Congressmen, Senators and one or two Cabinet members. This was probably the first time that Hadassah had taken part in a political act.

Arab extremists emerged from the crisis stronger than ever. The Grand Mufti lost his battle to throttle the Zionist effort in Palestine, but he became a national hero nevertheless because he had won strong British support for the cause of Arab nationalism.

As Palestine entered the 1930s, the stage was set for a drama in which three motifs would play simultaneously: Arab against Jew, Jew against Arab and both against the British. These were cruel years. America was agonizing in economic depression. Germany was watering the weeds of Hitlerism. Russia, suffering under Communist dictatorship, was actualizing George Orwell's *Animal Farm*.

In Palestine, oddly enough, economic recovery was quicker than almost anywhere else. Investment in Zionist projects ran relatively high. Construction picked up and despite the restrictions, Jewish immigration was heavy. There would be a brief eruption of violence in 1933 as the Arabs, having failed to frustrate the Zionists, would suddenly turn against the British. Beginning in 1936, the Grand Mufti would try to rid the country of the infidel Jew, and would buddy up to Hitler toward that end.

In the new storm that was gathering, Hadassah would brave the winds along with the rest of the *yishuv* and emerge from the decade strengthened many times over, for it was in these years that membership would mushroom, new and vigorous leadership would rise and genuine independence would send Hadassah into a Zionist orbit of its own. In short, Hadassah was on its way to becoming the most forceful single Zionist organization in the world. All this could be traced in part to Hadassah's efforts to save children from the Nazi inferno.

Hadassah in Photographs

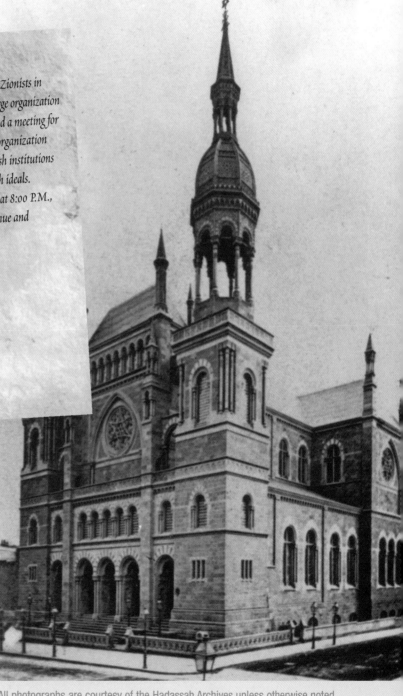

February 24th, 1912

The undersigned, in consultation with other women Zionists in New York City, have decided that the time is ripe for a large organization of women Zionists, and they desire to invite you to attend a meeting for the purpose of discussing the feasibility of forming an organization which shall have for its purpose the promotion of Jewish institutions and enterprises in Palestine, and the fostering of Jewish ideals.

The meeting will be held Saturday, February 24th, at 8:00 P.M., in the Vestry Rooms of Temple Emanu-El, Fifth Avenue and Forty-Third Street.

Sophia Berger
Emma Gottheil (Mrs. Richard)
Rosalie S. Phillips (Mrs. N. Taylor)
Henrietta Szold
Gertrude Goldsmith
Lotta Levinson
Mathilde Schechter (Mrs. S.)

**February 24, 1912.
Temple Emanu-El, meeting place of
Daughters of Zion. There, during
the Purim season, Henrietta Szold
proposed the creation of Hadassah.**
*Courtesy of Congregation Emanu-El
of the City of New York.*

First American nurses sent by Hadassah to Jerusalem: Rachel Landy left, and Rose Kaplan right, with Eva Leon, a member of the New York chapter, outside original Hadassah infant welfare station. 1913.

Sign on the "Drop of Milk" infant welfare station, Jerusalem. 1920's.

Hadassah's "Drop of Milk" campaign brought pasteurized milk to Palestine for the first time and was delivered to mothers via donkey "express." 1920's.

Arab families come to Hadassah infant welfare station to pick up daily ration of fresh milk, Jerusalem. 1920's.

British Army hands over the keys to the Rothschild Hospital in Jerusalem to the American Zionist Medical Unit (AZMU), whose 44 members became the "founding fathers and mothers" of the Hadassah Medical Organization. Standing, center, James de Rothschild. In 1939, when the new Rothschild-Hadassah Hospital opened on Mount Scopus, the original Rothschild building remained in Hadassah's hands and later housed the Alice L. Seligsberg Vocational School for Girls. (Today, it is the home of the Hadassah College of Technology.) November 3, 1918.

Nurses in the American Zionist Medical Unit (AZMU) on the eve of departure for Jerusalem, pictured with the members of the Central Committee of Hadassah, who are seated in front row: right to left: Henrietta Szold, Alice L. Seligsberg, Dora Lefkowitz, Ruth Fromenson, Emma Gottheil, Bertha Weinheim, Ida Danziger, Libby Oppenheimer. 1918.

Doctors, sanitarians and other medical personnel in the AZMU photographed on the eve of departure for Jerusalem. 1918.

Henrietta Szold with the first graduating class of the Nurses Training School, 1921, (today, the Henrietta Szold-Hadassah Hebrew University School of Nursing is located at Hadassah Ein Kerem).

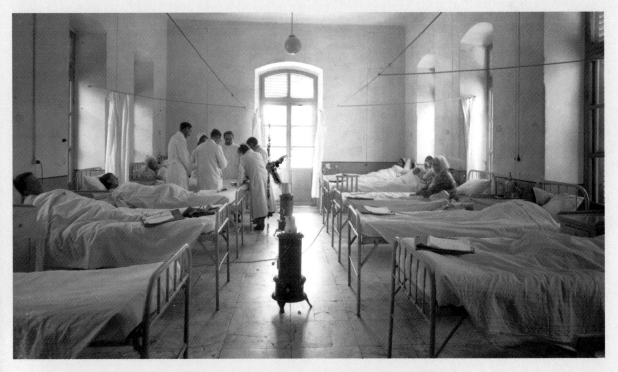

Doctors on their rounds in the women's ward in the old Rothschild-Hadassah Hospital. 1920's.

Henrietta Szold speaking at the opening of the Nathan and Lina Straus Health Center in Jerusalem, 1927. (Today the building houses Hadassah-Israel, Hadassah International, Hadassah Career Counseling Institute, HMO Complementary Medicine clinics, HMO AIDS Testing Clinic, HMO Eye Clinic, and HMO Breast Cancer Diagnostic Clinic.)

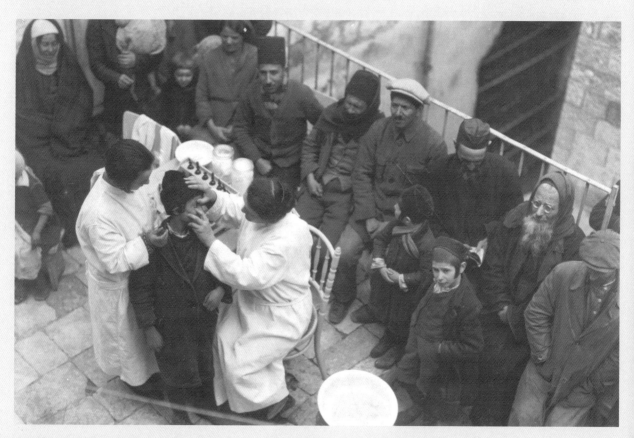

Hadassah Eye Clinic, Old City of Jerusalem. Parents watch as nurses treat children for trachoma. 1928.

Henrietta Szold with members of Junior Hadassah, which merged with Young Judaea in 1967. Hadassah assumed sole sponsorship for the expanded American Zionist youth movement Hashachar, comprising young, intermediate and senior Judaea, and college-level Hamagshimim. 1930.

The Hadassah School Lunch Program taught hygiene and good nutrition to thousands of children who, in turn, helped change the eating habits in their homes. 1930. Photo by Alfred Bernheim.

Henrietta Szold participating in groundbreaking ceremony for
the Rothschild-Hadassah University Hospital on Mount Scopus. 1936.
Photo by H. Orushkes.

Henrietta Szold, first director of Youth Aliyah,
dancing with Youth Aliyah teenagers. 1941.
Photo by Nahum Gidal

Feeding infants and toddlers under the supervision of
a Hadassah nurse at the Infant Welfare Station. 1940.

Malnourished "Teheran Children" arrive in Palestine after wandering for years across war-torn Europe and Asia. 1943.
Photo by Keren Hayesod.

Rothschild-Hadassah University Hospital on Mount Scopus, 1947. From 1948 to 1967 the road to Mount Scopus was in Jordanian hands. Hadassah continued its work in five scattered buildings in Jerusalem. After the Six-Day War in 1967, Scopus was restored to Israel and Hadassah received the keys to its hospital on Mount Scopus.

Hadassah convoy with supplies and medical personnel is ambushed in the Sheikh Jarrah Quarter on the road to its Mount Scopus Hospital. Seventy-seven doctors, nurses, Hebrew University and Hadassah Hospital staff were killed, including Dr. Haim Yassky, Director. April 13, 1948.

Chaim Weizmann is inaugurated as first President of the newly proclaimed State of Israel. May 14, 1948.

Rose Halprin speaking at dedication of the new Hebrew University-Hadassah Medical School. Seated, from right, David Ben-Gurion, Prime Minister of Israel, and James G. McDonald, first American Ambassador to Israel. May 17, 1949. Photo by Hazel Greenwald.

Dr. Kalman J. Mann, Director-General of HMO, speaking at groundbreaking ceremony for the Hadassah-Hebrew University Medical Center at Ein Kerem. Left Dr. Miriam Freund Rosenthal; right Etta Rosensohn, Prime Minister David Ben-Gurion and Rebecca Shulman. 1952. Photo by Studio M. Huttman.

Hebrew classes for National Board members. Clockwise from left: Dora Inselbuch, Esta Ellis, Ray Meiselman, Florence Perlman, Faye Schenk, Miriam Fierst (in glasses), Bertha Hamerman (Standing at right), Shirley Weisgal (sitting forward on right). 1954. Photo by G. D. Hachett.

Eleanor Roosevelt, World Patron of Youth Aliyah, made several visits to Youth Aliyah children's villages in Israel. She is pictured here during a visit to the Youth Aliyah Herbert H. Lehman Home in France. 1955.

Moving Day. Patients on stretchers were loaded into ambulances in move from temporary hospitals in town to new Medical Center at Ein Kerem. June 6, 1961.

Nurses and nursing students say farewell and thank the nuns of St. Joseph's Convent, where the Hadassah nursing school had been housed for 13 years. They are in process of moving into the new nursing school at Ein Kerem. June 6, 1961.

Marc Chagall, left, studies installation of his 12 world-famous stained glass windows in the hospital synagogue. Joseph Neufeld, the Medical Center's architect, is by his side. 1962. Photo by Dr. K. Meyorowitz.

Hadassah's staff is overjoyed when they learn that Mount Scopus has been liberated in the Six-Day War. 1967.

Hadassah participates in Solidarity Day March in New York City. April 13, 1975. Photo by Alexander Archer.

Hadassah participates in Soviet Jewry Vigil in New York City. From left: Charlotte Jacobson, Bernice S. Tannenbaum, Rose E. Matzkin, Rose L. Halprin, Dorothy Brill, Bess Katz and Miriam Siegel. May 31, 1977.

"Youth Rally for Truth" — Young Judea and other youth movements rally in support of Israel and in protest of the media's biased portrayal of events in the Middle East. October 29, 2000.

Hadassah International Congress in Jerusalem. "March of the Flags" by Young Hadassah members. Each flag represents a country in which Hadassah International has a presence. 2000.

Youth Aliyah students from Ramat Hadassah Szold participate in Hadassah's "joy of Judaism" bar mitzvah programs, celebrated annually at the Western Wall. Photo by Shlomy Ben-Ami. 2000.

Hadassah members at the Salute to Israel Rally in Washington D.C. April 15, 2002.

Hadassah-Keren Kayemeth L'Israel Park in Beer Sheva, a joint project of Hadassah, Jewish National Fund, and the Beer Sheva Municipality. 1997.

The Jewish National Fund (JNF) has been building dams and reservoirs with the help of its partners, and researching innovative recycling techniques to help Israel alleviate its water crisis. Hadassah committed $3 million towards the construction of the Tirzah reservoir. 2000.

Hadassah University Hospital, Mount Scopus. "Our Tree of Life," monumental sculpture by Jacques Lipchitz in foreground.

Aerial view, Hadassah-Hebrew University Medical Center, Ein Kerem. 2002.

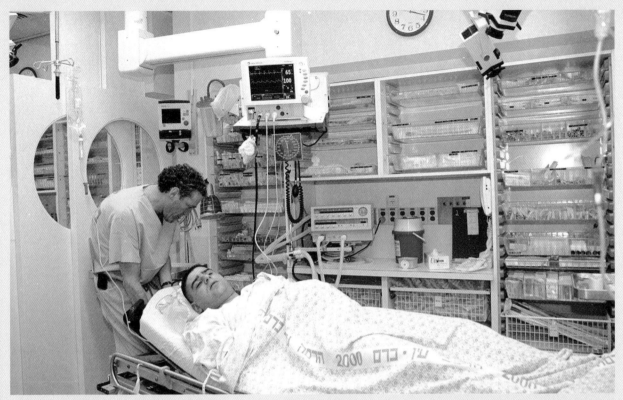

Professor Avi Rifkind, Head of Trauma Center, tending to a patient. 2002.

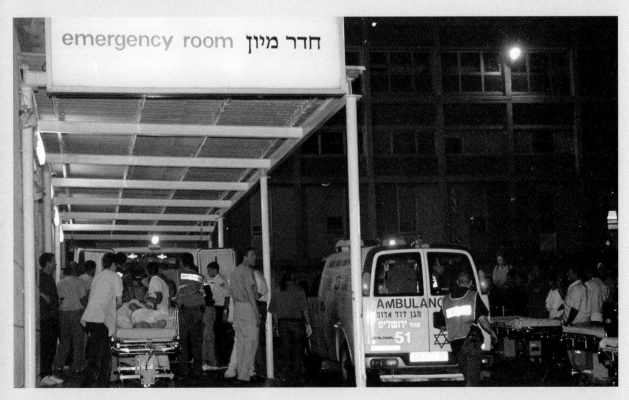

Entrance to the Emergency Room, Ein Kerem. 2002.

The entrance to the
Mother and Child Center,
Hadassah-Hebrew
University Medical Center,
Ein Kerem. 2002.

Child-friendly elevators move young patients swiftly. Neon animals identify each floor. 2002.

Patient with nurse. Pediatric Oncology, Mother and Child Center, Hadassah-Hebrew University Medical Center, Ein Kerem. 2002.

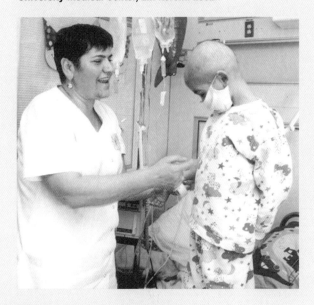

Lobby of Mother and Child Center. 2002.

Executive Committee. December 6, 2001.

Seated left to right: Judith L. Palkovitz, Secretary; Marlene E. Post, Honorary Vice President;
Deborah B. Kaplan, Honorary Vice President; Bonnie Lipton, President; Bernice S. Tannenbaum, Honorary Vice President;
Ruth W. Popkin, Honorary Vice President; Barbara Tirschwell, elected member of Executive.

Middle Row: Joyce Rabin, Vice President; Marcie Natan, Vice President; Barbara Levin, Vice President;
Janice L. Greenwald, Vice President; Elizabeth L. Fox, Vice President; Dr. Fran Fettman, Vice President;
Nancy Falchuk, Vice President.

Top Row: Elected members of Executive – Ruth G. Cole, Ellen Hershkin, Ruth B Hurwitz, Eddyse Kessler, Annette Meskin,
Sue Mizrahi, Annette Sondock, Jane Zolot.

Absent: Honorary Vice Presidents – Charlotte Jacobson, Carmela E. Kalmanson, Rose E. Matzkin; Barbara Spack, Vice President;
June Walker, Treasurer; elected members of Executive — Diane Issenberg, Maureen Schulman, Belle H. Simon, Karen G. Venezky.

THE CONTRACT

One cold February afternoon in 1932, Recha Freier was musing in the study of her home near Berlin's Alexanderplatz. She was the wife of a prominent Orthodox rabbi, the mother of three sons and an author of fairy and folk tales for children. Writing fantasies helped Recha escape the wretched world rising around her. The Weimar Republic of Chancellor Heinrich Bruening was collapsing under the twin sledgehammer blows of an economic blizzard and Hitler's hypnotizing cry for a new order. Across the frontier, dictator Benito Mussolini held Italy in the vise of Fascism and was about to undertake a reckless escapade into Ethiopia. Fickle France's Third Republic was changing governments as fast as fashions. England languished under an austerity economy led by ailing Prime Minister Ramsay MacDonald. Across the seas, mighty America agonized under a depression that put millions out of work. Militaristic Japan, having subdued Manchuria, was on its imperial march into China. What was there for a poetic soul like Recha to do but to write and dream and call up memories of her early childhood in Norden on the North Sea at the turn of the century, of Sabbath afternoon strolls into town with the family. Recha recalled one special Sabbath when they came upon a white paper with a black border posted on a gate:

We stop to read it. I am only four and cannot understand but I hear what the others are saying. They say the sign reads "Entrance Forbidden To Dogs And Jews." Soon we move to another town and there I am the only Jewish girl in the class and the pupils ridicule me when I say that my religion does not permit me to ride on the Sabbath…how homesick I am for a town I can really call home. In my childhood I know of the Land of Israel but I believe that it is unreachable because it is in heaven.

A knock on the door roused Recha. Her caller was a pale, thin sixteen-year-old boy who introduced himself as Nathan Höxter, son of the late Rabbi Höxter. "I thought that you might be able to help us," he said.

"Us?"

"Yes, my five friends and me. We are members of the Brit Ha-Olim, a group of Zionists. We have been thrown out of our jobs. They said they no longer wanted Jews. Maybe we can find work in the mines in the Rhineland. We don't know where to turn."

"Bring your friends to me and let us discuss it. We will work something out," replied Recha.

Next day she ran to the office of the Jewish Labor Exchange of the Zionist movement. Yes, the secretary knew the problem, but insisted with a shrug that it was only temporary. The Norden memory strongly in her mind, Recha could not be reassured. She sat in her study at night and pondered:

How I always dreamed of an exodus of Jewish youth to Palestine! But this was only a dream that was never practical. Maybe, just maybe, now is the time. How helpless that boy made me feel. And how joyous, too. This certainly must be the hour. I must dream no longer. I must make reality my partner. Palestine is their home. They must go to it. It is my home too.

Recha called on Enzo Sereni, an Italian-born Zionist living in Palestine, who was in Germany as the representative of a kibbutz movement. (During World War II, Sereni would be killed by the Nazis after he parachuted into Italy to organize underground rescue operations.) She explained to him that she would like to organize large groups of German youth to live in the kibbutzim.

"Do it. Do it at once and you will revolutionize the entire German Zionist movement," Sereni explained excitedly.

When Nathan Höxter returned with his five friends Recha said, "There is no future for Jewish youth in Germany. Eretz Israel is your home. You must go there. You can work in a kibbutz. And if you so decide, I shall help you."

The boys immediately agreed. At Sereni's suggestion, Recha wrote the Histadrut in Tel Aviv for assistance to arrange places in kibbutzim. The Histadrut was encouraging but Berlin's established Zionist leadership was not supportive. Several Zionist leaders told her to send the boys to German farms where, as one advised, "They'll really learn to work and to spend money properly."

In the spring of 1932, Recha was ready to give up the idea when the Histadrut's education and cultural chairman in Tel Aviv, Yaacov Sandbank, wrote that three agricultural settlements, Geva, Ein Harod and Nahalal, were ready to accept the boys. Recha went back to the German Zionist Organization, to WIZO (the Women's International Zionist Organization) and to EZRA, a Jewish agricultural society. All rebuffed her.

"In the kibbutzim they will become Communists."

"You cannot separate adolescents from their parents."

"The kibbutzim are not kosher."

Only the young Zionists showed enthusiasm. "In them I kindled a spark that burst into a flame," Recha later recalled. The excitement of the youth moved Georg Landauer, a member of the Zionist Executive in Berlin, to agree reluctantly to Recha's plan on condition that the Va'ad Leumi (National Council of Jews in Palestine) arrange for the care of the young immigrants. The head of the Social Welfare Department of Va'ad Leumi was then Henrietta Szold. Recha wrote to Henrietta. Henrietta replied that no funds were available in Palestine for the poor children already there; a large influx of parentless children from Germany might strain the limited resources of the *yishuv*. The memory of Norden and the exuberance of the youth around her pushed Recha on.

In June 1932, still unable to mobilize sufficient aid, Recha was visited by Siegfried Lehmann, founder of the Ben Shemen youth village in Palestine. He liked Recha's idea and was ready to arrange twelve entry permits for her boys if they would agree to study farming with him. Recha's ideal was the kibbutz, but she agreed. Forty teenagers applied and twelve were chosen. She now worked feverishly to raise money for their care at Ben Shemen. Recha fought stiff opposition from parents and peers. But she had a few friends who helped. One raised 4,000 marks by pawning her jewelry.

On October 12, 1932, Nathan Höxter and his friends left Berlin by train for Ben Shemen. When they landed in Jaffa on December 2, they became the vanguard of the mass movement of children who traveled to Palestine under the banner of an organization, unique in history, that was soon to be known in Germany as *Jugendaliyah*, or Youth Aliyah.

Among the Jewish youth of Berlin, Recha became known as "the dreaming woman." She did not mind: "I happen to come from the world of fairy tales. There as you know, everything is anonymous. So I would like to remain anonymous, too. It's the youth, not me, that want help. I only want to turn dreams and fairy tales into reality."

Recha spoke incessantly, at times obsessively, about sending 10,000 German youth to Palestine. That only enhanced her image as a dreamer, for even her closest colleagues thought in terms of fifty or sixty. Time and genocide would vindicate her vision.

Early in January 1933, the Histadrut's Sandbank wrote Recha that she must come to Tel Aviv to further her cause. That same month, Henrietta Szold decided to retire. It wasn't for the first time. After retiring in 1931 she returned to Palestine from the United States only at the urgent insistence of *yishuv* leaders to organize the haphazard social services of the incipient Jewish nation. Now, she wanted, at last, to finish out her years with her family in Baltimore.

Back in Berlin, Recha prepared to go to Palestine. On the last day of January she gathered together in the office of notary Hugo Fuerth seven young Zionist leaders, some of whom were not yet twenty-one. They called themselves the Aid Committee for Jewish Youth, carefully avoiding any hint that their real purpose was emigration to Palestine. But among themselves they referred to the project as Youth Aliyah. At nightfall they left Fuerth's office and as they turned into Berlin's broad Unter den Linden boulevard, they saw masses of jack-booted Brownshirts marching in a mammoth torchlight parade in celebration of the coming to power, earlier that day, of Adolf Hitler.

Persecution of the Jews became a major function of the new German government and even with primitive international communication it was not long before the Jews of Palestine felt the foul winds blowing in from Europe. By April 1933, Berlin decreed a boycott on all Jewish enterprises, but at the last minute canceled it when Mussolini convinced Hitler the time was not ripe. Chaim Arlosoroff, head of the Political Department of the Jewish Agency in Jerusalem, went to Berlin to try to convince the German Zionist organizations to prepare for the emigration of Jews to Palestine. They knew he was right. The Zionist opponents of Youth Aliyah formed one joint committee to prepare youth and to raise money.

Henrietta Szold's personal plans were complete. She invited sister Bertha to Palestine to show her all the sights, after which they would return home together to America. But, yet again, the Jewish leadership in Palestine pressured Henrietta to give up the notion of retirement. They were now forming a committee to do something about German-Jewish refugees and they insisted that she head it. Bertha went home alone.

In Tel Aviv at the end of May, Recha attended a Histadrut rally at the Jascha Heifetz Hall where a large audience heard labor and kibbutz leaders call for the immigration of German youth. One even mentioned the number 10,000. The meeting passed a resolution opening the settlements to the youth. After the rally, Recha rode to Jerusalem for her first meeting with Henrietta Szold. No two more dissimilar personalities ever faced each other. Recha failed to convince Henrietta that it was urgent to flood the gates of Palestine immediately with German youth; Henrietta could not convince Recha that the *yishuv* was not prepared for mass immigration. What, asked Henrietta, would happen to German youth left unattended on the wharves of Jaffa and Haifa unless homes were waiting for them? Recha remembered the frightening torchlight parade on the night of January 31 and all that it foretold.

Recha went home that summer only slightly encouraged by Palestine's noted land developer and pioneer of the kibbutz movement, Arthur Ruppin. He promised to try to convince Henrietta of the worth of Recha's idea. In Berlin, Recha pestered Zionist groups to organize training camps for the youth. Already entire German-Jewish families were beginning to leave. In 1932, total Jewish immigration into Palestine was 9,553. In 1933, the year Hitler came to power, immigration of Jews into Palestine was 30,327, two-thirds of whom were Germans. But Recha was interested in the youth and especially in those whose naive parents had faith that Hitler was a passing fantasy.

In Jerusalem, the committee that Henrietta headed had no guidelines. Housing was short. So many refugees had already arrived that they slept underneath the sky on Tel Aviv's beaches. That made Henrietta all the more dubious about the idea of encouraging large numbers of German youth to immigrate. Then the kibbutzim agreed to accept one thousand children. Recha was jubilant. Henrietta insisted on inspecting kibbutz housing facilities. Finding that they were not up to her high standard, she suggested a compromise whereby some youth would go to the settlements. But when she went to the British authorities for certificates, they refused, saying that none of the facilities were ready. Immigration in those days was limited to "capitalists" (those with the equivalent of $5,000) and to those youth for whom two years' sustenance was available. Henrietta personally urged the settlements to begin building for the youth she now knew would come.

The Eighteenth World Zionist Congress met in free-but-threatened Prague on August 21, 1933. While Hitler's shadow grew darker over Germany, political debate at the Congress was marred by the deep rift between the Labor and Revisionist parties. The Congress took up the German question and established what became known popularly as the "German Bureau" under the chairmanship of Chaim Weizmann in London. Henrietta did not attend the Congress, but Arthur Ruppin, who chaired the Jerusalem section of the German Bureau, implored her to take over as head of a new *ad hoc* office of the Jewish Agency devoted to Youth Aliyah affairs. That October in London, at a worldwide meeting of Jewish organizations called to declare a boycott on all German goods, Henrietta heard more of the disaster that was overtaking the Jews of Germany, so off she sped to Berlin. There, she deliberated day and night with Zionist leaders, expressing dismay at their lack of understanding of life in Palestine and at the absence of an organized effort to raise funds and prepare youth for their new life.

Any doubts that the youth must leave were now dispelled. Before departing, Henrietta succeeded in arranging for the early "conditioning" and transfer of sixty-three boys and girls, aged fifteen to seventeen, under the leadership of Hanoch Reinhold. Henrietta did not meet Recha Freier in Berlin and Recha resented it. But Henrietta did appreciate Recha's role. At the Nineteenth World Zionist Congress held in Lucerne in 1935, Henrietta Szold said: "I would like to say a word of thanks to the organizer of this movement [Youth Aliyah], Mrs. Recha Freier. It was she who conceived the ingenious idea and carried it through despite all difficulties and obstacles. We are grateful that she held with such devotion to her idea, which in the beginning found little support." Recha herself reached Palestine only in 1941 after a harrowing journey through Eastern Europe.

By the time Henrietta returned to Palestine the British government offered Youth Aliyah 350 permits for German-Jewish children.

Immediately, she left for Kibbutz Ein Harod where she personally oversaw the kibbutzniks' building of housing for the expected newcomers.

In mid-February 1934, the winter's worst gale hit the shores of Palestine. On the high seas opposite Jaffa was the *S.S. Martha Washington*. On February 18, the ship tried to drop anchor off Jaffa, but the weather was so bad she headed north to the recently opened port of Haifa. There on Monday, February 19, the first organized group of Youth Aliyah children walked down the gangplank — precisely two years after Recha Freier met Nathan Höxter in her Berlin apartment. Henrietta smiled as she watched the German youngsters standing on the quay with their mandolins and their skis and rucksacks on their backs. Some had brought along bicycles and even flagpoles. No one seemed to mind the pelting rain. Henrietta greeted each child by name, a custom she was to follow for the rest of her days. She escorted them to Ein Harod, spent the first day with them, even joined them in a *hora* in the kibbutz dining hall.

From that day on Henrietta's life was devoted to the affairs of Youth Aliyah. All the vitality that she could mobilize went into raising funds, supervising training, struggling for permits. By the end of 1934, a dozen groups totalling about five hundred arrived. Henrietta wrote: "This great constructive movement has only begun. Five hundred young people are not more than 5 percent of the number that should be drawn out of Germany into the productive, promising life of Palestine."

Her toughest problem was always money. But now, money meant young lives. The Joint Distribution Committee had practically nothing to give. Raising cash in Palestine was difficult. Henrietta appealed to one wealthy Jerusalem landowner and came away with a paltry fifty pounds. In one letter home she wrote, "The public does not like the German Jews." Cash was being collected in Germany by a joint committee, the *Arbeitsgemeinschaft*. The first appreciable sum that flowed into the organization's coffers grew out of a pageant, "The Romance of a People," that was produced by Meyer Weisgal in Chicago at the Century of Progress Fair. The pageant took place on "Jewish Day," July 3, 1933, before

130,000 people jammed into Soldiers' Field. At Weisgal's insistence, Chaim Weizmann traveled 8,000 miles to make an appearance and received $25,000 on the spot for refugee relief. Another $75,000 was presented a few months later in London by Weisgal to the director of the German Bureau, Martin Rosenbluth, with the words, "Here is money you can use for Youth Aliyah. Now you're in business."

In New York City during 1934 there was a woman who in some respects was the counterpart of Recha Freier. Tamar de Sola Pool, Hadassah's National President from 1939 to 1943, was also a visionary and a treasure-trove of madcap ideas. She had charm and megatons of energy. Despite any opposition, Tamar's resilience always kept her afloat. Then president of the New York City Chapter of Hadassah, she had been abroad many times with her husband, the courtly Rabbi David de Sola Pool. She knew Palestine well. Her most recent trip planted a "bug" in her head that an immigration project was essential to maintain a high level of involvement in Hadassah at the grassroots level. Many National Board members agreed, but the responsibility was a tremendous one and the leadership, while moving in that direction, decided to move cautiously. Many years later, Tamar would remark with justification, "The National Board had no confidence in me. They thought I was scatterbrained, that I was not a good organizer. But I must admit I do have a talent for creative thinking."

In line with the principle established by Henrietta Szold, Hadassah was then in the midst of a devolutionary program, turning over its projects to municipal or other local public authorities as soon as they were ready to maintain them. The transfer of hospitals, preventive medical stations, school hygiene programs and tuberculosis care outside Jerusalem was hastened in the early 1930s because of the financial squeeze caused by the Depression and because of Hadassah's eagerness to move ahead on Mount Scopus with the construction of the most modern medical center in the Middle East. In October 1934, Henrietta Szold laid the cornerstone of that center. Hadassah was 50,000-strong, but National Board member Judith

Epstein, a great champion of the center, would later recall: "We suddenly found that our world could not be bound by Palestine and the medical work we were doing. Nobody saw clearly in 1934 in what direction an expanded program would go."

To find new direction and purpose, Hadassah President Rose Jacobs left for Palestine in the summer of 1935. An intimate friend of Henrietta Szold, Rose was a powerhouse armed with an iron will. Some found her schoolmarmish and criticized her for expecting to be followed blindly into the unknown. But few faulted her on her decisiveness. During Henrietta's presidency, Rose often served for long periods as acting president. She wore Henrietta's mantle and had her confidence.

Over the next two months in Palestine, Rose drove herself to exhaustion pondering two non-medical projects for Hadassah, Youth Aliyah and vocational education. Henrietta was her mentor, but at this time Henrietta did not suggest that Hadassah assume the responsibility of funding Youth Aliyah.

What Rose saw confirmed Tamar de Sola Pool's earlier observations. She wrote vividly of meeting the ships bringing Youth Aliyah children, of following them together with Henrietta to the kibbutzim. In Merhavia, one frightened youth fresh from Berlin suggested that the windows be closed so that their conversations would not be overheard. In a kibbutz near Haifa, the children arrived with books by Schiller, Goethe and Heine. The kibbutz children jeered when they saw the German writings. Reported Rose:

> I shall never forget Miss Szold. She turned to the German children and said, "It is wonderful what you have brought; you have brought prize possessions from Germany which Germany itself does not value. Don't forget the cultural things, the fine part of Germany that you have learned. Try to forget the other things." The children of the kibbutz bowed their heads, ashamed. Thus did Henrietta Szold lay

the basis for mutual respect in the relationship of German
and Palestinian youth.

Rose also saw the need for vocational training, although her interest leaned
toward Youth Aliyah. But she planned to take both proposals back to New
York and let the National Board decide. In August, Henrietta and Rose
traveled to Lucerne, Switzerland, where the Nineteenth Zionist Congress
convened. Chaim Weizmann returned to the presidency after four years out
of office and Henrietta reported on two years of Youth Aliyah. To a hushed
hall she said:

> Before I left Palestine last week I took a trip through all the
> *kvutzot* [settlements] where our young boys and girls are
> placed, in order to see at close hand the full extent of my
> responsibility. I was gripped by the thought of the children
> whom we have lost during the course of generations. I
> thought of the children who were sent to the Island of St.
> Thomas by the Inquisition, of the cantonists in Russia. I
> thought also of the crimes we are committing against our
> own children — that we have not gathered the funds which
> Palestine needs to solve the most important problem — the
> problem of the Jewish child.

Seventy-five-year-old Henrietta was the star attraction of the congress.
Rose Jacobs was as proud as though she were Henrietta's own daughter.
There was no doubt that the National Board would accept Youth Aliyah as
its own project in America. Attending the Congress, too, was Georg
Landauer, director of the German Settlement Bureau in Jerusalem. With
Henrietta's acquiescence, Rose and Georg drew up a confidential letter on
August 27, 1935. The five-paragraph statement, addressed to Rose as
president of Hadassah and signed by Georg, specified that Hadassah would
be the sole representative of Youth Aliyah in the United States for an
experimental two years during which Hadassah would cover $60,000

worth of expenses for 100 German and Polish youths at the rate of $500 each.

In the annals of American Zionist history, it would be difficult to find a document that raised more dust. The Zionist Congress had just passed a resolution prohibiting separate fund-raising appeals apart from those which were already established. Yet Georg Landauer committed the Zionist Organization to doing just that and would suffer great embarrassment for his sin. With Henrietta's support, Rose was confident that Hadassah would prevail, but she too had certainly gone far beyond her terms of reference.

By the end of September, Rose was back in New York, convening a meeting of the National Board. "The saving of European Jewry is the crying need of the hour," she said with deep emotion. "Hadassah is that channel through which the appeal for the rescue of our youth can be made effective. We can help convert the Youth Aliyah project into a great movement." With the still-secret contract in hand, Rose obtained the Board's unanimous consent to accept Youth Aliyah as Hadassah's newest major project. Immediately after the meeting, Rose rushed off to Atlanta to be at the bedside of her ailing father. Acting for her, Judith Epstein wrote Landauer in Jerusalem of the Board's unanimous decision to recommend the resolution to the convention opening in Cleveland on November 28. No one was more jubilant than irrepressible Tamar de Sola Pool. She wrote a letter to Henrietta in Jerusalem saying how happy she was that Hadassah had accepted Youth Aliyah and that she was sure Hadassah would raise not only the $60,000 promised but at least $100,000. Hadassah raised $250,766.76 in the first two years.

On October 29, one month before the convention was to meet to approve the Youth Aliyah project, the Jewish Agency Executive in Jerusalem annulled the Landauer-Jacobs contract.

When Louis Lipsky, the chairman of the board of the American Palestine Campaign, first heard of the agreement — six weeks after it had been signed — he immediately wrote indignantly to Rose Jacobs that a separate campaign for Youth Aliyah run by Hadassah "would inevitably lead to the disintegration of the Zionist Movement of the United States." The Jewish community was conflicted. To whom did control of Youth Aliyah belong?

Lipsky self-righteously thought that Hadassah "thought as always only of their own Hadassah fund-raising without seeming to care for one moment what the effect would be on the rest of the Zionist fund-raising in America. They would hear of no arrangement other than the one which they *think* [Lipsky's emphasis] they have concluded with Landauer." Lipsky protested against the Jewish Agency Executive's entering into the contract "without our consultation, communication or advice." He obviously had a point.

Two days later, on October 29, the Zionist Executive met in Jerusalem. Treasurer Eliezer Kaplan was the chair. Also present were Moshe Shertok, Jewish National Fund President Menachem Ussishkin, David Werner Senator, Rabbi Yehuda Leib Fishman and Georg Landauer. On the agenda was an urgent item: "Special Campaigns."

With Lipsky's cable of protest before him and obviously angry, Kaplan said it was obvious that American Jews would not contribute twice in the same year to a Zionist appeal. Therefore, the Congress had wisely forbidden separate fund campaigns. Landauer pragmatically pointed out that Youth Aliyah needed about $200,000 for those children already registered to emigrate from Germany and Poland. The Keren Hayesod could not provide that kind of money. "Hadassah has informed us that it has the capability to carry out a separate campaign and has guaranteed to care for 100 children. I would favor a United Zionist Campaign if it would guarantee to raise the money Hadassah is willing to raise. But if it won't, then I suggest that Hadassah do it."

"The money must be found," Shertok responded, supporting Landauer. "Hadassah conducts campaigns for other projects and I see no sin committed if this year it includes Youth Aliyah in its general appeal." Senator supported Shertok. But they were in the minority. The stern-eyed Rabbi Fishman, supporting Ussishkin and Kaplan, said that unity of the

Jewish people and its campaigns overrode all other considerations. Landauer was outnumbered.

At the end of the debate Kaplan said that Hadassah could raise funds for Youth Aliyah but only within the framework of the overall united appeal, in effect, abrogating the contract. His strictly conservative stand won a majority.

Trying to forestall a fraternal war, Kaplan instructed Berl Locker, his colleague stationed in London, to hurry to the United States. "Bring back an agreement between Hadassah and the American Palestine Campaign that will satisfy the just demands of Hadassah, that will assure the participation of the American Palestine Campaign and will safeguard the interests of Keren Hayesod."

On October 30, Kaplan ordered Lipsky to go ahead with his plans for a united Palestine drive and to "include youth immigration in the slogan" and cabled Hadassah an official repudiation of the Landauer-Jacobs contract. The Hadassah board went into emergency session. On Friday, November 1, Hadassah cabled back to the Jewish Agency that "repudiation of the contract would hurt the Youth Aliyah project and Hadassah's effectiveness in Palestine."

Hadassah's cable explained that its year-round, day-to-day way of running a campaign was much more effective than the united campaign's one-shot drives, run for a short period. "Your failure to honor the contract will stunt Youth Aliyah's future development in America and force Hadassah to adopt a substitute specific project," the cable ended.

With that cable, Hadassah, now twenty-three years old, entered the major league of Zionist politics, challenging the Jewish Agency and therefore the World Zionist Organization, as well as the organized, male-dominated Zionist Organization of America.

Two days later, Kaplan in Jerusalem cabled Lipsky in New York: "Hadassah has cabled a demand for revision on the basis of the agreement with Rothenberg in Lucerne," referring to an oral agreement made at the

Zionist Congress between Rose Jacobs and Morris Rothenberg, President of the ZOA, to permit Hadassah to run Youth Aliyah.

That same day a livid Lipsky replied: "Neither Rothenberg nor myself in Lucerne knew of Hadassah's intention of taking exclusive possession of children's aliyah in America. Would not have agreed then. Cannot agree now."

The Hadassah board exploded and continued preparing its campaign to sell Youth Aliyah to its membership, which by now had reached 60,000. The American Palestine Campaign was becoming edgy. Executive Director Robert Silverman cabled Jerusalem on November 13, two weeks before the Hadassah convention: "Despite Jewish Agency Executive rescinding exclusive contract, Hadassah insists continuing the children's campaign, threatening a serious conflict."

Hadassah received support from outside the Zionist fold. Maurice Hexter, non-Zionist member of the Jewish Agency Executive and key figure in American-Jewish philanthropic work, cabled the Jewish Agency: "Strongly urge revision in favor of Hadassah."

On November 18, the Agency Executive wired Hadassah: "Executive anxious to settle conflict by agreement without resorting to the imposition of our decision. Therefore deputizing Locker with the approval of Szold and Halprin for mediation with instructions to safeguard the interests of Hadassah, American Palestine Campaign (Ampalc) and the integrity of the Zionist Organization."

Into the war of cables now entered a heavy caliber gun. David Ben-Gurion, chairman of the Zionist Executive, thought the situation sufficiently serious to force a solution. His message to Rose Jacobs: "Conflict liable to endanger the integrity of the Zionist Organization. Object to the intervention of non-Zionists in internal Zionist affairs. After consultation with Szold, advise settlement by agreement through the intervention of Locker as an impartial deputy."

Ben-Gurion's reference to "non-Zionists" meant Hexter and others such as the *Arbeitsgemeinschaft* who were solidly behind Hadassah. The final cable that arrived on that climactic November 19 was from Henrietta Szold and Rose Halprin, then Hadassah board representative in Jerusalem, and was addressed to Rose Jacobs: "We've been shown your cable to the Executive. Advise acceptance of the intervention of Locker whatever else you may do."

Locker left on November 20 and arrived six days later in time for the opening of the Cleveland convention. The Hadassah board had been in continual negotiations with Lipsky and Rothenberg, even carrying the debate to an all-night beanery opposite Hadassah's New York office at 111 Fifth Avenue. In Cleveland, the sessions between the National Board and Locker went on throughout the night before the convention formally opened. He pleaded with Hadassah leaders to let go of their exclusive right to Youth Aliyah. They held on like tigers, informing Locker that the entire issue would be put before the delegates. Forlorn, frustrated, alone on foreign soil, Locker retired for what was left of the night.

The following day Rose Jacobs addressed the delegates at a session lasting from 10:00 pm to 2:00 am. Marian Greenberg followed with an exposé of the cable war, the acid messages, the acrimonious negotiations. The delegates gave both women an ovation. Locker knew his mission was lost and gallantly seconded Rose Jacobs's resolution affirming Hadassah's role as the sole agency in America for Youth Aliyah.

Recalling the convention fight in 1957, Rose said Berl Locker was no match for Hadassah's women who proved they could stay up all night, if necessary, to win their right to a project. In the end, Youth Aliyah was a great success, the United Palestine Appeal was not destroyed, a Jewish State was established and Hadassah gave Lipsky a citation.

In January 1936, a peacemaking formula was worked out whereby Hadassah could begin its toil in earnest, still satisfying the needs of the United Palestine Appeal and the Jewish Agency Executive in Jerusalem. In exchange for exclusive rights to Youth Aliyah, Hadassah agreed to confine its campaign to women (a pledge made to be broken) and to credit the Palestine Appeal with the money it raised. Thus, the UPA reported that during its first drive from January 1 to October 15, 1936, it raised $1,779,454, *including* the $125,000 raised by Hadassah for Youth Aliyah.

In December, Henrietta Szold arrived to a hero's welcome. The night was cold and wet when her ship arrived at Hoboken, but reporters were there for interviews. She was rushed to a newsreel studio for a statement that appeared on screens across the nation. Later, Mayor Fiorello LaGuardia handed her the key to New York City. She spoke at a mass rally. "I come to you not only from Palestine, but from Germany, Austria and Holland," she began. There was hardly a dry eye in the crowd when she finished. Her trip netted thousands of dollars for Youth Aliyah. She was the pampered guest at the luxurious home of Mrs. Felix Warburg, where the first National Youth Aliyah Committee was set up.

Hadassah's "massed motherhood," as Marian Greenberg phrased it, fought for the children with every gimmick it could devise, approached Zionist and non-Zionist, Christian as well as Jew, to fulfill its contract. Thousands of Hadassah workers were in the field rousing America to the need. They mobilized the most prominent women in America, among them the wives of Secretary of the Treasury Morgenthau, Senator Robert Wagner, Supreme Court Justice Louis Brandeis and Governor Herbert Lehman. Elinor Morgenthau, a close friend of Eleanor Roosevelt, brought Youth Aliyah to the attention of the First Lady. Later at a meeting in the Blue Room of the White House with Hadassah representatives, Mrs. Roosevelt accepted an honorary post with Youth Aliyah and, on the death of South African Field Marshal Jan Smuts, became the second World Patron of Youth Aliyah.[1]

With the campaign now officially on, Tamar de Sola Pool went into a state of perpetual motion. In February, she raced off to the Hollywood Beach Hotel in Florida where comedian Eddie Cantor was staying. Eddie

---

1   Smuts accepted the titular post of World Patron at the behest of active Youth Aliyah worker Vera Weizmann, a leader of WIZO and later First Lady of Israel. Following Mrs. Roosevelt's death, the title went to Baroness Alix de Rothschild.

was having his breakfast when Tamar bounced in. She showed him an article written by right-wing columnist Westbrook Pegler, in which he denounced Hitler's war on children. Tamar asked him to work for Youth Aliyah. "For this cause," the pop-eyed father of five girls said, "I'm ready to give my life." One month later, in March 1936, when Hadassah ran the first donor lunch in New York for Youth Aliyah, Eddie appeared, surprising everyone with the announcement that he had already collected $44,000 — then a tremendous sum — for Youth Aliyah. Of all the star-studded names that went on the official letterhead and on the posters, none worked more conscientiously for Youth Aliyah than Eddie Cantor.

In Madison, Wisconsin, the local Hadassah president found that it was too much to ask the members to raise $360 each to take care of a child in Palestine. For some, that was four months' salary. She got the idea of holding a *minyan*: ten women would gather weekly or monthly for teas or parlor meetings and each would ante-up a few dollars until the $360 sum was reached. The *minyan* idea spread throughout the country.

Junior Hadassah, Hadassah's exuberant young women's group organized in 1920, carried out its own campaign. At their convention in Washington, DC in December 1936, 1,000 delegates pledged to expand the youth village of Meier Shfeyah to care for 150 young refugees. Junior Hadassah had adopted Meier Shfeyah in 1925, supporting it financially until 1923 when it was transferred to the Israel Ministry of Agriculture.[2]

In Palestine, Henrietta was unbelievably active. Nearly eighty years old, she awoke at 5:00 every morning and, after her usual calisthenics, dived headlong into a long day on behalf of Youth Aliyah. In June 1936 she wrote Rose Jacobs, "Three days a week I get to bed at two and rise at five; the rest

---

2   Sadly, Junior Hadassah did not last as an individual organization, but Hadassah gave the Zionist youth movement a massive infusion of new blood when it merged Junior Hadassah and Young Judaea into a single youth organization called Hashachar (the Dawn), and created Hamagshimim (the Fulfillers) for college-aged young men and women, all in 1967.

of the week I have from four to five hours' sleep, including the nap. I never, never relax. I never read unless it is a memo. I am inhuman."

The Arab Riots of 1936-1939 had now broken out. The British government, trying to ease tension, started by handing out fewer immigration certificates to Jews. In December 1936, Henrietta appeared before a royal commission, set up to hear Arab and Jewish grievances. Her appeal for more Youth Aliyah immigration certificates was rejected. When she persisted, she was again cut off. The situation looked desperate. In October 1937, Henrietta attended Hadassah's Jubilee Convention in Atlantic City, where Judith Epstein was elected president and retiring Rose Jacobs became the first woman to be named a member of the Jewish Agency Executive. With more than 2,500 delegates present, it was the largest Zionist gathering held in the United States up to that time. Henrietta told the delegates, "My office is the center of a cobweb; threads run out of Germany to the youth in Palestine."

On March 10, 1938, the British government suddenly changed course, notifying the Jewish Agency that it was establishing a new category of immigrant — students. Certificates would be unlimited on condition that housing was made available for the students. On the following day, March 11, when Germany marched into Vienna and annexed Austria, 200,000 Jews sought to leave. Most wanted to go to Palestine, but in Palestine there were places — in the kibbutzim primarily — for only 1,000 youths. In New York, Youth Aliyah Chairman Marian Greenberg called a meeting at the home of Mrs. Roger Straus. An emergency committee of 1,000 was organized with the aim of raising enough money to pay for 1,000 youths in Palestine by September 30, 1938.

Responding to Hadassah's urgent pleas to step up his work, Eddie Cantor cabled Hadassah: "Except for Sundays and Mondays, Hadassah's time is my time."[3] Cantor became Youth Aliyah's single biggest fund-raiser. Eleanor Roosevelt came to Hadassah's aid with endorsements of the rescue

---

3   "My Time Is Your Time" was the theme song of Cantor's popular radio program.

movement in her "My Day" column. When the September 30 deadline arrived, 903 of the 1,000 were already in Palestine and the remainder were on the way. Hadassah had managed to triple its Youth Aliyah income during that period.

1939 was a year of frantic effort. Hadassah organized meetings featuring noted British women, among them the wives of Foreign Secretary Lord Halifax and the Marquis of Reading. They told poignant stories of refugees arriving in England. In Washington, Hadassah board member and first Hadassah Washington representative Denise Tourover pounded the sidewalks between the White House and Congress, even appealing to foreign diplomats to pressure the Germans about Youth Aliyah. In June, Marian Greenberg flew to England to meet leaders of the *Arbeitsgemeinschaft* at a Youth Aliyah conference (the Nazis had closed the Berlin office of Youth Aliyah the year before and headquarters were now located in London).

On September 1, the Luftwaffe bombed Warsaw. Two days later Britain and France declared war on Nazi Germany. Trapped behind the iron gates now closing on the Continent were nine million Jews.

The war marked the end of Youth Aliyah's first phase. Between February 1934 and September 1939, Youth Aliyah rescued 4,886 children. By the war's end, 7,446 children would be moved to Palestine from Europe by Youth Aliyah. The total saved from Nazi Europe would thus number 12,332, not including about four thousand additional children from Asian and African countries. During that period more than two million young Jews were murdered in Hitler's extermination and concentration camps.

Youth Aliyah was a success. "I have always felt that Youth Aliyah is one of the most creative accomplishments in history and that its importance is reaching far beyond the borders of Israel," Eleanor Roosevelt said. On its twenty-fifth anniversary in 1959, Youth Aliyah won the coveted Israel Prize. Education Minister Zalman Aranne said, "There seems to be no similar exodus of children and youngsters of this scope in the annals of mankind." As the fourth decade of the organization's work closed, it could be justly proud; 350,000 young people had benefited from its pathfinding education and human reconstruction.

The few years that it took for normally sensitive Jewry to interpret in full the signals emanating from Berlin were precious years lost that only now can be counted in numbers of dead. It was not until 1943 when the war was half over that the Jewish Agency Executive accepted full authority and established the Department for Child and Youth Immigration.

Henrietta Szold, a woman of impeccable character and boundless energy, was, as David Ben-Gurion has said, the most outstanding Jewish woman of the twentieth century. When she was asked to manage the affairs of Youth Aliyah, she was already in her seventies. She did the work that should have been done by a legion of imaginative younger men and women. She applied good principles to the rescue operation. Her demand for perfection provided those who did escape assurance of proper housing and upbringing. Henrietta met every single ward that came off the boat. But the tragic fact is that Jewish steps toward rescue were a classic World War II case of "too little too late."

And what of the British? A nation that had the courage to snatch 360,000 men from the bombed beaches of Dunkirk in eight days grudgingly permitted Henrietta Szold to save less than 5 percent of that number in eleven years because of its fear of Arab retribution. As Josef Mengele decided the fate of a Jew at Auschwitz with the wave of his hand to the right or left, a British civil servant in Jerusalem decided the fate of a Jew destined for Auschwitz by accepting or rejecting the request for a visa. But the lack of permits cannot completely absolve world Jewry from dragging its feet. When, in March 1938, the Mandate government announced it would give "unrestricted" immigration certificates to students, Henrietta wrote, "Unrestricted! On second thought — restricted not by Government, but by our limitations: available places and available funds."

And American Jewry? They held the richest pocketbook in the Jewish world. Millions of dollars were urgently needed but only thousands were given — hesitantly. In December 1936, when Hadassah petitioned the

British to grant Youth Aliyah permits for young Jews from Poland, in addition to those from Germany, protests were heard from American Jews. At best, American Jews were out of touch with the scene in Europe.

Hadassah never claimed perpetual control of Youth Aliyah in America. Finally, when Jewish Agency leaders thought of *aliyah* of youth in terms of 50,000 rather than 10,000 youths and budgets soared beyond the capacity of one organization, Hadassah took the initiative in relinquishing its monopoly. On November 29, 1943, Henrietta together with Kaplan and Landauer confirmed (in a cable, of course) that a coordinating committee suggested by Hadassah would now operate to collect money in America. Joining Hadassah in the fund-raising effort on an equal footing were the United Palestine Appeal, Mizrachi Women and Pioneer Women. Hadassah was permitted to retain the title of official agent for Youth Aliyah in America.

Hadassah's noteworthy achievement in the early years of the Hitler menace was to awaken masses of Americans to the needs of Europe's children. No other organization was sufficiently broad or more intrinsically suited to the task. There are no measurements to judge the accomplishment in human terms. In terms of money, the results achieved were impressive. The original contracted sum for Youth Aliyah's first two years was actually quadrupled. In the first eight years, Hadassah alone covered 75 percent of Youth Aliyah's requirements. At the beginning of 1960 when Hadassah's accumulated contribution was close to $40 million, Israel's director of Youth Aliyah, Moshe Kol said, "Were it not for Hadassah, Youth Aliyah would have ceased to exist."

By the same token Hadassah benefited enormously from its involvement. Saving children worked like magic to attract members. Within one year after assuming responsibility for Youth Aliyah, the number of chapters rose from 272 to 375. Former National President Judith Epstein remarked that Youth Aliyah was a "turning point" in Hadassah's development. Bertha Schoolman, Henrietta's successor as mother of Youth Aliyah, regarded the association as "a humanizing force" in Hadassah's work in America. Gisela Warburg Wyzanski, a "lonely refugee" from Germany who guided Youth Aliyah work for Hadassah during the war years said, "it forged the 'maternal tie' between Hadassah and Israel."

However one characterizes the effect of the Hadassah — Youth Aliyah union, in practical terms the results were long-lasting. After World War II tens of thousands of Jewish children were saved. Not all were Holocaust victims. During the 1950s and 60s orphans from Asian and Middle Eastern countries were cared for. When immigration slumped in the late 1970s, Youth Aliyah changed course, focusing on culturally-deprived children of large immigrant families who were doing badly both in school and in a western society in which they could not compete. Youth Aliyah came to the rescue. In the early 1980s there were 18,000 wards in its residential youth villages, schools and programs, nearly all Israeli-born. Its thrust was to fit them into the jigsaw of Israeli life.

A two-year-obligation became a life-long partnership. Youth Aliyah saved lives; Hadassah paid most of the bill — to the tune of $135,000,000 by the end of the twentieth century. More than sixty years old, the contract has been honored many times over.

NAILS ON THE ROAD

After the Arab riots of 1929, with few exceptions Palestine enjoyed seven years of truce. Then, in 1936, began the worst reign of Arab terror in living memory.

Exasperated by the flood of Jewish immigrants and frustrated because the British had not blocked the tide, extremist Arab nationalists demanded armed action. More moderate Arab leaders, meanwhile, were engaged in confidential but futile talks with David Ben-Gurion and other Zionists to seek an understanding. In one such conversation in August 1934, Ben-Gurion was asked to agree to restrict immigration so that in ten years the Jewish population would not top one million. Ben-Gurion replied negatively, even though the Jews in Palestine then numbered only 400,000. By 1936, Arab right-wingers had gained the upper hand; their three demands: stop Jewish immigration, stop land sales to Jews, make Palestine an Arab state now.

The British tried to coax both sides to accept a single, bi-national state and invited Arab leaders to confer on the subject. When the divided Arabs failed to agree on the makeup of their delegation, the British finally despaired of the proposal. That undermined the moderates further and by mid-April the Arab fanatics, riding high in the saddle, flashed the signal for a rebellion that flared intermittently until the eve of World War II and ended in a major, if short-lived, political victory for the Arab nationalist cause.

On the evening of April 15, 1936 outside Nablus, the eye of the Arab nationalist hurricane hit. Ten trucks and cars were stalled in front of a barrier of barrels and rocks. An eyewitness recalled:

> We were proceeding from Haifa to Tel Aviv. Yehoshua Napchi, of Tel Aviv, stopped his car. Two Arabs appeared from the side of the road. They took Napchi to a lorry standing in front of us and they shot him, but he was only wounded. The shots killed Israel Khazan, 61, a Salonica Jew who was taking a load of chickens to the poultry market. They also wounded Zvi Tannenburg. A bullet went through his spine and he died later. One Jew identified himself as a German and he was not touched.

The leader of the gang was a feared highwayman, Sheikh Izz e-Din, who had marauded in the Samarian hills for years. Now he was mixing business with politics. He informed his victims before he shot them, "I am taking your money to buy arms for the holy cause."

Friday, April 17, was a day of public bereavement for the *yishuv*. Thousands attended Khazan's funeral and Tel Aviv Mayor Israel Rokach addressed the mourners, "Our innocent brother was murdered by people who wish to frighten us and stop our work. But the world will know that terrorist acts will not stop our work."

But the Jewish crowd marched to Magen David Square where they scuffled with British police. Flying stones, the traditional weapon in Palestine since the days of David, injured a few constables who finally dispersed the demonstrators with shots in the air.

Arab violence mounted geometrically. After a false rumor spread in Arab Jaffa that Tel Aviv Jews had murdered several Arabs, Arab gangs, some dressed in Boy Scout uniforms, smashed, knifed and clubbed their way through the Jewish Quarter on the border between the twin cities. Elsewhere, Jewish movie houses, clinics and shops were broken into and their occupants shot. At Kibbutz Ein Harod, Arabs uprooted five hundred citrus trees. Houses, barns, machinery and forests were scorched. Arabs returned eight times to burn groves near Mishmar Ha-Emek. A children's home was set afire. Crude bombs were thrown in market places. Snipers shot at cars on the road and at Jewish pedestrians. The terrorists poured lysol and kerosene on vegetables being delivered to Jewish markets. By the end of April, half of Jaffa's 18,000 Jews were refugees in Tel Aviv. Refugees filled synagogues in Jerusalem and Tiberias. As a result of the general strike called by the Supreme Arab Council, hundreds of Jews were unemployed because they feared to cross picket lines. The toll between April and October of 1936 is estimated at 700 persons dead, thousands wounded, 2,000 Jewish communities attacked, 100,000 trees destroyed and $15 million in property damaged.

In an attempt to tame the tempest, the British dispatched an army to Palestine and promised to establish a Royal Commission that would probe the causes of the disturbances. After a long hot summer, the Arabs finally called off the strike in October, and in November a six-member commission arrived.

The people of Palestine were cynical about commissions. Moderates on both sides of the fence were doubtful that any third party could possibly solve Palestine's problems; left alone, Arabs and Jews might possibly work out a modus vivendi, whether through arms or negotiations. But this was never to be; foreign noses would always be stuck, and stung, in the Palestine beehive. Even so, this latest commission, led by Lord Robert Peel, managed to raise faint hopes that Jews, Arabs and British could together pave a new road to peace. In the end, the Peel Commission failed in its immediate mission, but it did succeed in introducing a new concept in the tiresome search for a settlement. From the Commission's sessions came the first concrete proposal to carve Jewish and Arab states out of Palestine. It was an idea that would be partly realized precisely eleven years later.

On their arrival in Jerusalem on November 11, 1936, the Commission members checked into the five-year-old King David Hotel and then drove straight to the British War Cemetery on Mount Scopus for Armistice Day services. In Jerusalem, the Anglican bishop and the chief rabbi of the non-Zionist Agudat Israel issued appeals to pray for the success of the commission. But the Grand Mufti of Jerusalem did not consider such an appeal appropriate. The Arab leadership decided on a boycott and dramatized it in a bizarre fashion. On the day after their arrival in Jerusalem the Commission members were the guests of High Commissioner Sir Arthur Wauchope at a gala reception held at the official residence on the Hill of Evil Counsel. On the way one car after another was put out of action. The Arabs had strewn nails on the road. Lord Peel got through unscathed, but one of his colleagues was immobilized three times by flats.

The Peel Commission opened its hearing at the Palace Hotel on November 16. Sir Arthur was the first of many witnesses who would testify in 66 sessions over the coming two months and two days. The third witness was of special interest to Hadassah. He was Colonel George Heron, the director of Palestine's medical services, who told the commission: "The Arabs must rely on government health services whereas the Jews have their own organizations." He noted that the government spent £180,000 a year on health work, while Jewish organizations spent nearly twice that much. He boasted that Palestine had one physician for every six hundred persons, compared with one for every eight hundred in the United States. That was one of the highest — if not the highest — ratio in the world. Nearly all the doctors were Jews, many of them newcomers.

The most poignant moment in the Commission's hearings was the appearance of Chaim Weizmann. Speaking in deep, measured tones, he traveled the history, hopes and fortunes of the Jewish people for more than two hours. He spoke prophetically and tragically of Jews in Europe "pent up in places where they are not wanted and for whom the world is divided into places where they cannot live and places which they may not enter." He flayed at the bugaboo of Palestine's "absorptive capacity" — the specious argument used by anti-Zionists to keep Jews out. Lord Passfield had once told him, "But Dr. Weizmann, do you realize that there is not room to swing a cat in Palestine?" Weizmann could now tell the Commission, "Many a cat has been swung since then and the population of Palestine has increased...by something like 200,000." The Zionists presented forty more witnesses, among them David Ben-Gurion and Henrietta Szold.

So strong was the evidence on behalf of a Jewish State that the Arabs broke their boycott and testified. The Grand Mufti went first with a counter-balancing review of Arab history, hopes and broken promises, and of fears that the Jews were immigrating with the intention of reconstructing the Temple on the mount where now stood two of Islam's sacred shrines. Fourteen more Arab leaders followed and finally on January 19, 1937, the Commission members started for home to determine the fate of Palestine.

Of all the sessions, the most fateful was a closed meeting with Chaim Weizmann on January 8, 1937. One member of the group, Oxford University historian Reginald Coupland, asked Weizmann to comment on the possibility of partitioning Palestine into independent states. Within the British government the idea of establishing a Swiss-like cantonal system under a British federal government was being mooted at the time, but this was the first occasion that the idea of two independent states was broached officially to the Zionist leadership. Weizmann believed that he had finally arrived at the threshold of the Jewish State. Aloud, he asked the members of the Commission for time to consult his colleagues. He spoke with high enthusiasm to intimates; he was aware that the road ahead was burdened with obstacles, but he intuitively realized that somewhere at the end of the maze partition was the only way out. The story is told — although it may be apocryphal — that a few days later Weizmann met secretly with Professor Coupland in the cooperative farm village of Nahalal. There they stooped over maps to try to determine rational borders for the two new states. And when they emerged from their meeting place in a wooden shack Weizmann exclaimed to a group of inquisitive Jewish farmers, "Today, here in this place, we have laid the foundation for a Jewish State!"

Lord Peel published his report in July 1937, and died days later. He complimented the Zionists for their constructive work in Palestine and presciently noted that "there is no common ground" between Jews and Arabs. "Neither Arab nor Jew," he wrote, "has any sense of service to a *single* state." Partition alone would allow for the parallel development of national goals and cultures. Having come to that sensible conclusion and having noted that the country's 400,000 Jews made up 40 percent of the population, the Commission went on to recommend the creation of a Jewish State with only 20 percent of Mandate Palestine's territory. The much larger Arab state was to be united with Trans-Jordan. Jerusalem was to remain British — a captivating jewel in the imperial crown. These recommendations appeared in a White Paper issued by the British government almost simultaneously with the appearance of the Peel Report.

The White Paper of 1937 angered the British administrators in Palestine who wanted to retain more control over the land and its people through a federated system. The Arabs, horrified that Jews were about to be given a part of the Arab domain, reached again for their guns. The Jewish leadership, meeting at the Twentieth Zionist Congress on August 3, fought bitterly over the Peel Report. The partition principle itself was acceptable to most, but the size of the proposed state was not. Favoring the map were Weizmann, Ben-Gurion and most Palestinian Jewish leaders. Opposed were the Americans, led by Stephen Wise and Robert Szold, who were supported by Hadassah. Among the militant "maximalists," surprisingly, was Henrietta Szold who opposed Peel partly because he severed Jerusalem from the Jewish body. "How can one be with a Jewish State from which Jerusalem is excised," she wrote. "I don't like it." In whole or in part, neither did most Zionists.

Those in favor, however, made a strong argument that any small bit of sovereign territory was welcome now to provide a haven for masses of European refugees who had nowhere to go. "Territorial adjustments" could be made later, Weizmann said. "The Negev will not run away." Opponents argued that a state the size suggested by Peel was not viable. One speaker ridiculed, "We will call the new Jewish state 'England' because it is so small." The Arabs would not resist the temptation to declare war on the state; it would be quickly overrun, destroying forever the dream of Jewish national renascence, they argued.

In the end, the Congress rejected Peel's proposals. The overwhelming majority of Hadassah's eighteen delegates, elected as a separate political entity for the first time, rejected partition on any terms. This stand was confirmed by a large vote at the Hadassah convention in Atlantic City two months later. But the Congress, bearing in mind the refugees and the first practical offer of Jewish sovereignty, did not close the door completely. It accepted the partition principle as a basis for negotiation.

As it turned out, the fight was academic — the Arabs were not ready to tolerate even a microscopic Jewish state in Palestine and the British were in no mood to buck Arab opposition. The Arab response to Peel was murder. After a congress of four hundred Arabs held at Bloudan, Syria, rejected the surrender of even an inch of Palestine to the Jews, the Arab revolt intensified. In October, one of the first victims was the popular district commissioner in Nazareth; that was enough to tame the British lion. In November the British government pacified the Arabs, declaring that it was not bound to partition. But within three months the government formed a new commission, presided over by old India hand Sir John Woodhead. He was assigned the task of drawing up new partition borders. Woodhead presented two maps, both of which whittled down Peel's Jewish State to 400 square miles — the size of Hong Kong — twenty times smaller than the state that came into being in 1948. No Jew could possibly have accepted such "a useless little ghetto," as it was described by historian Christopher Sykes. In November 1938, in the face of this new absurdity, Britain froze the idea altogether, announced that it was renewing its hold on the Mandate, called the Jews and Arabs to attend a negotiating conference in London and warned them that if they did not reach a settlement, one would be imposed upon them.

February 1939. The mood of western Europe was appeasement. In March, Prime Minister Neville Chamberlain spoke foolhardily of "peace in our time" as Hitler devoured Czechoslovakia. The Arab delegation arrived at St. James's Palace in London for talks and promptly announced its refusal to sit in the same room with the Jews. As a consequence, Prime Minister Chamberlain ordered two ceremonial openings for the conference and gave the same speech twice.

The London negotiations were stillborn. The Jews said that the Peel Report was their basic minimum; the Arabs pushed their demands to stop immigration, stop land sales and declare an Arab state in all of Palestine. True to their ultimatum, the British tried to enforce a solution. Weizmann had some forewarning of what was coming after a long conversation with Lord Halifax, the British foreign secretary, who suggested to Weizmann that he forget about the creation of an independent state. "Renounce your rights under the Mandate," Lord Halifax advised. On May 17, 1939, the Nazis took Prague. On that same day, the Chamberlain government issued a White Paper that will live in infamy in Zionist annals. With only four months before war would trap millions of Jews inside Hitler's bastion, the White Paper decreed a drastic reduction of Jewish immigration into Palestine; only 15,000 yearly for five years — then none. It also placed heavy restrictions on land sales to Jews, and called for the establishment of a bi-national state within ten years. The limitation on immigration made it certain that the Arabs would rule Palestine. But even this proposal was utterly rejected by the Arabs; they demanded a state immediately, an absolute stop to Jewish immigration and a review of the status of all Jews who had immigrated to Palestine since 1918.

Nullification! That word became the branding iron of enraged Zionist leaders, for with the White Paper of 1939 the British government nullified the Balfour Declaration. By their intransigence, the Arabs had won a major political victory.

Dejected and disheartened, Chaim Weizmann could only call the White Paper exactly what it was — "a sellout." But it was for a younger man of action, David Ben-Gurion, to utter a rallying cry. As chairman of the Jewish Agency he characteristically set a course of defiance: "This cruel blow will not subdue the Jewish people." But after the war against Hitler began, it did present a dilemma. Should Jews in Palestine fight a weakened, preoccupied Britain for a Jewish State, or should they join Britain to fight the greater evil, Hitler? Ben-Gurion's reply was Solomonic. At a public gathering he declared the words that would be quoted for years to come: "We will fight together with Great Britain in this war as if there is no White Paper, and we will fight the White Paper as if there is no war."

Ben-Gurion sensed that the British had papered over the Balfour Declaration for reasons of expediency. With war imminent, Britain could not anger millions of Arabs into firing up the revolt again. But Ben-Gurion knew also that the Jews would pay a heavy price for that expediency: the lives of those masses who could not pass the locked gates of Palestine. For Ben-Gurion, there were now two supreme tasks: to build a Jewish army that would help fight Hitler and to build an organization that would bring in Europe's refugees despite the British lion and the German werewolf.

The Jewish people were facing their darkest hour. Everyone seemed to be against them — Germans, British, Arabs. An unholy combination of forces had dashed their sweetest dreams. Isolated, the Jews of Palestine steeled to meet all comers.

Dark as the hour was, the *yishuv* did not give up faith. The Jews of Palestine continued to build, to train and to prepare. The concrete mixers churned and the hammers swung. In Jerusalem, morale lifted considerably only eight days before the White Paper was issued, when Hadassah opened, for all creeds, the Middle East's most modern healing, research and medical education center. The glistening hospital on Mount Scopus dominated much of the city. Not overlooked at the time was that this accomplishment of Zionist endeavor stood on the site from which the Roman Emperor Titus launched his attack on the Holy City nearly 1,900 years before.

MOUNT SCOPUS

For several days in October 1934, sound engineers of the Palestine Broadcasting System bustled in the turret office of the Hebrew University's chancellor on Mount Scopus. They had a thousand problems. Not the least of them were the heavy echoes in the room and the field mice that nibbled away at the tangles of wire lying twisted on the floor. In preparation was the first live broadcast from the Middle East to New York through relay stations in Cairo and London. From the Manhattan studios of the National Broadcasting Company, the program was to be transmitted from coast to coast and piped specially into the grand ballroom of the Wardman Park Hotel in Washington, DC where 1,500 Hadassah delegates were assembled for their national convention.

H-Hour was 4:00 pm on Mount Scopus, 9:00 am in Washington, on Tuesday, October 16, 1934. Seated uncomfortably in the office of Hebrew University President Judah Magnes with a grand view of ancient Jerusalem were Henrietta Szold, Nahum Sokolow, Menachem Ussishkin, HMO Director Haim Yassky and Magnes. Groundbreaking ceremonies on Mount Scopus, attended by 500, were over. In the Washington auditorium the delegates had been in their seats for many hours; some had gone without breakfast to make sure they were close to the loudspeakers. Across the hall was a banner: "We Will Build."

A few minutes after nine, Rose Jacobs read a cable from Jerusalem into a battery of NBC microphones that relayed the proceedings over a national hookup. The cable described the ceremonies that had just taken place on Mount Scopus. At 9:28 a crackle of static filled the hall. The first words were those of Magnes's assistant Julian Meltzer: "This is Jerusalem calling from the Hebrew University on Mount Scopus."

Then came Nahum Sokolow's voice: "...world Jewry celebrates..." The static allowed only a few words to get through. Magnes was heard to say, "it is but a few minutes' walk to the laboratories of the Hebrew University..." Third was Henrietta. The delegates were on the edge of their seats: "we celebrate today the culmination of an idea... the Healing of My People." Dr. Yassky followed: "coordination and united effort will bridge the distance between us..." Radio was not sufficiently developed at that early stage for such broadcasts but that did not matter. The "Hadassah Newsletter" reporter wrote:

> The words are not clear. But that does not matter. Hadassah's founder is speaking to thousands of her colleagues and it was enough to hear her voice. On the platform and scattered throughout the hall are some who toiled with Miss Szold in the early days. Before them, in these seconds, must have flashed a quick kaleidoscope of those pioneer days. They could not restrain their tears. The audience is tense, electric, trying to catch every syllable. And when the 20-minute broadcast is ended the whole assembly rises to its feet, applauds and cheers and breaks into singing Hatikva. Women weep for joy and kiss and embrace one another.

The same exuberance burst forth at the Hadassah convention in Chicago the previous October when, the Depression be damned, the delegates voted to raise $200,000 from Hadassah's thirty thousand members to build a hospital in Jerusalem. But it was on October 15, 1934, in Washington, that Hadassah formally voted to join the American Jewish Physicians Committee in the construction of a medical center on Mount Scopus. With that act, Hadassah moved from an age of pioneering into an age of sophistication and voted itself a physical permanence in Palestine. It thus gave full expression to the idea that medicine — healing, teaching and research — was inextricably bound to the ultimate goals of the political Zionist movement.

The idea itself was not new. In 1920, the Zionist Organization in London probed the possibility of establishing medical and scientific institutes in Palestine. As a follow-up, Albert Einstein and Chaim Weizmann, on behalf of the Zionist Organization, sailed to America in 1921 to drum up support for the Hebrew University. Their trip inspired the founding of the American Jewish Physicians Committee under Nathan Ratnoff, which raised $500,000 and in 1924 bought land on Mount Scopus for a projected medical school. Later, more land was to be donated by the JNF and Mary Fels, the Philadelphia Zionist and soap heiress. That same year — one year before the Hebrew University was to open — the first medical institute in microbiology was created by Saul Adler, world-famous parasitologist.

In 1926, malaria fighter Israel Kligler, director of Hadassah laboratories and head of the University's Hygiene Department, urged the establishment of a medical center in Jerusalem. Henrietta Szold supported Kligler and drew in Chancellor Magnes. The first formal discussion of the joint project was held on April 23, 1927, with the American Jewish Physicians Committee acting as marriage-broker.

The medical center proposal took seven years to blossom and another five years to ripen. Countless meetings were held in New York and Jerusalem to clear the many obstacles posed by financing, planning, division of authority and Hadassah's budget. In 1930 the budget had been cut for the first time owing to the Depression. However, with immigration beginning to soar, hospital space rapidly became inadequate. At times, some departments of Hadassah's 150-bed institution were running at 120 percent capacity. Magnes spoke of the eighty-year-old Rothschild building as "that rickety, dangerous structure." Finally in 1934, Hadassah and the Hebrew University reached an agreement on the running of the medical center: the former would oversee its medical work while the latter would supervise its teaching aspects. A monumental debate, however, broke out over the location. Magnes insisted that a medical center should be located close to a university; the only plausible site was Mount Scopus. But Hadassah was split. Dr. Ephraim Bluestone, who resigned as director in 1928, but continued as chief consultant in New York, fought to put the center where potential patients could get to it quickly. It was folly to site a vulnerable medical complex where it would be isolated from the Jewish population and surrounded by hostile Arab quarters and villages, Bluestone claimed. Although Scopus had the most beautiful view in the Jerusalem area, he answered, "It is more important for a patient to see a doctor than to see the landscape. Never place an obstacle between the patient and his doctor and remember that distance is an obstacle."

The primary difference between Bluestone and Magnes was in outlook: Magnes, a pacifist and humanitarian, believed whole-heartedly that the medical center would hasten the peace process, Jews and Arabs would soon live in peace and would jointly enjoy the fruits of the university and center. Bluestone, a coldly analytical scientist and realist, was just as sure that the medical center would be a sitting duck for vengeful Arabs.

Hadassah failed to support its chief consultant. Instead it sought more advice and sent to Palestine the director of New York's Hospital for Joint Diseases, Jacob Golub, with Dr. Nathan Ratnoff to examine all the possibilities. Hadassah agreed in advance that their decision on siting the center would be irrevocable. On July 23, 1934, Golub and Ratnoff cabled, "conclusively determined Scopus most suitable site." In 1947, Golub wrote that the clinching argument for Mount Scopus was that a medical school would one day be established there and it was only logical that it should be near the University: "The hilly landscape of Mount Scopus will increasingly become a university and hospital campus for students and faculty."

But Golub wrote too soon. In 1948, a convoy of physicians, nurses, teachers and workers of Hadassah and the University would be ambushed by Arabs while passing through the Sheikh Jarrah Quarter of Jerusalem on its way up to Scopus and most would perish. Not long after the ambush, Scopus was abandoned for 19 years; for most of that time Jerusalem was to be without proper hospital and university facilities. It was a crippling blow and an immense price to pay.

What went wrong? "Two mistakes were made," recalled former President Rose Halprin, who served as Hadassah's liaison in Jerusalem in the 1930s. "The minute that our hospital went up, there should have been a Jewish community started near Scopus. That was our mistake. The second error was that of the Jewish Agency. They should, as they promised, have built settlements to close the gaps in the road."

In mid-1935, Golub reported to Hadassah that during the first half of the decade the number of physicians in the Jewish population had doubled. One out of every 225 Jews in the country was an MD. Because of the immigration from Central Europe, there were proportionately four times more physicians in the Jewish area of Palestine than in the entire United States. Hadassah, in an attempt to cope with the integration problem, took in as many as 35 doctors at one time to prepare them for medical work in Palestine. But the organization soon realized that it must get on with the medical center if for no other reason than to build a bigger roof to house this vast treasury of brain power.

Ludwig Halberstaedter from the University of Berlin, one of the world's greatest authorities in cancer therapy, was now at Hadassah. Refugee Halberstaedter arrived carrying one-fifth of a gram of radium, worth $15,000. With it he opened the first radium and X-ray institute in Palestine, under Hadassah's auspices. So badly quartered was Hadassah at the time that Halberstaedter worked in a converted stable. With him came an equally noted Berlin cytologist, Leonid Doljansky. Their work provided Palestine with its first effective treatment of cancer. Gynecologist Bernhard Zondek, a co-developer of the first quick, reliable test for pregnancy (the A-Z test), was also an immigrant. Viennese surgeon Felix Mandel opened a second surgery department in Hadassah. Pediatrician Benno Gruenfelder and physiologist Ernst Wertheimer were also respected Old World physicians. But young men would soon also make their mark, and most of them would work as volunteers. The volunteer doctor is a strange phenomenon in the annals of medicine, and in Palestine — rich in talent, poor in everything else — the profession was to bear voluntarism for years to come.

Some doctors had escaped Europe by the skin of their teeth. Aharon Yehuda Beller, born in a small town in Galicia, was twenty-four when he was arrested in Vienna by the Nazis in November 1938. "The [Vienna] Rothschild Hospital was closed. I was taken. My head was shaved and I was put on a bus to Dachau. En route we were turned around. There were no places left for us in the death camp and for some unexplainable reason I was released." Via Romania, Beller reached Palestine:

> I started working under Dr. Joseph as a volunteer in the Department of Surgery. I was the seventeenth doctor — only one was paid. Dr. Yassky gave me a job as a translator. The German physicians had to lecture in Hebrew and they did not know the language so I translated their papers from German to Hebrew in Latin characters.

Professor Beller later served as Hadassah's chief neurosurgeon for many years. He died in March, 1996.

Hanoch Milwidsky, born in Berlin, arrived in Palestine in 1932:

> I saw there were sufficient doctors here so I started working for a fruit jobber. I also knew some car mechanics and found that helpful. In those days it was more of a *mitzvah* to go

into agriculture and the trades than take up a profession. But my father insisted I return to Germany to complete my medical studies. When the Nazis came, I went to Strasbourg because I did not want a diploma with a Nazi signature. Then I returned to work in the only Jewish hospital in Berlin. When the Germans got wind that I was also helping Jews leave the country illegally, I had to run away. In Jerusalem, there was no possibility of getting a job as a surgeon at Hadassah because the hospital was so small. I worked in pathology and as an anesthetist. I started as a volunteer but later received a salary of £1 a month. Dr. Yehuda Bromberg, the Hospital's red-headed administrator, told us volunteers when we asked for a proper salary, "It is a buyers' market. I am an economist and I work according to market conditions. If I can get doctors like oranges, why should I pay high salaries?"

Milwidsky was the first to perform a heart operation in the Middle East. The operation, carried out against the opposition of hospital authorities, was successful. He had been warned by senior hospital officials not to go through with the operation because it would reflect upon the medical reputation of Hadassah. It did, but in a positive way. The elderly patient's stenotic valves had become obstructed by scar tissue due to rheumatic heart disease and his only chance to live was through the radical new surgery that Milwidsky learned under the tutelage of American heart surgeon Charles Bailey. The procedure later became commonplace. Hanoch Milwidsky perished when a Swissair plane exploded in midair en route to Israel on February 21, 1970. The Arab Popular Front for the Liberation of Palestine proudly claimed responsibility.

Ino Sciaky was born in Salonika, spent his childhood in Turkey and studied dentistry in Switzerland when his parents moved to Bulgaria:

When I came to Jerusalem as a tourist in 1937, I declared

my desire to settle but the British refused me permission. They said I could remain only if I were a capitalist. I went to Egypt, borrowed £1,000 — the minimum needed to be regarded as a capitalist — sent it to Palestine and followed soon thereafter. After I was accepted as an immigrant, I returned the money to my cousin. I was then a bona fide capitalist but without capital.

Professor of Oral Medicine Ino Sciaky was appointed the first dean of the School of Dentistry. He died in 1982.

One young doctor who received his education in Odessa left for Palestine before earning his degree. The closest job to medicine he could get from the British health authorities was that of sanitation inspector in Tel Aviv, for which he received £6 monthly in 1919. After tiring of running after garbage men, he left for Geneva with his wife to continue his studies in eye diseases and public health. In 1921, with his framed degree on the wall, he joined Hadassah in Haifa as an assistant in the ophthalmology department. Three years later he headed that Hadassah department in Tel Aviv. It was there that this six-foot idealist caught the eye of Henrietta Szold. "Trachoma in the villages and settlements is appalling," he insisted. "I want to go out there." She agreed. And the lanky eye doctor, often traveling bareback on a donkey, his shoes scraping the ground, went as far as the Galilee, treating and operating on Arab and Jew alike. In 1927, that "lanky eye doctor", Haim Yassky, was called to Jerusalem to take over the department of ophthalmology.

After much soul-searching, Henrietta Szold named Yassky acting director of the Hadassah Medical Organization. In 1931, likewise after much soul-searching, the Hadassah National Board made the post permanent. Haim Yassky held his post until he was murdered in the Scopus convoy on April 13, 1948.

Yassky did not rise easily to the custodianship of Hadassah medicine in Palestine because he was not an American. Understandably, the Hadassah board in New York kept its faith with American medicine and administration and during the first decades its man in Jerusalem was an American citizen. In the early years of the twentieth century, American medicine was avant-garde, lacking the tradition of Vienna, Berlin or Geneva. The New World's doctors were much more informal and its hospital administration was much less bureaucratic than that of the autocratic, status-conscious Old World. New Zealand surgeon Edward Joseph would soon find that "the German doctors considered themselves the top people. They looked upon American-trained physicians as being beneath contempt. A director coming from America would also be considered beneath contempt and so there was always hostility between them." Russian-born Moshe Rachmilewitz, the noted heart specialist who arrived at Hadassah in 1931, was critical of "the German approach" even though he himself was trained in Germany. Not long after his arrival he went off to New York for eighteen months of advanced study at Mount Sinai Hospital where, he recalled later in life, "I was reborn medically. There had been a shifting of centers for me from the European Continent to America." The American approach was direct, simple, natural. Status did not decide which medical opinion should be accepted. An opinion was judged solely on its merits. A young man — or a young woman — was free to speak up. This was distinctly different from the European approach.

The clashes of approach and the mixtures of nationalities had made it impossible for American directors to work in Jerusalem with the same efficiency as they had back home. Because of Hadassah's requirement that policy and budget be controlled from New York, much time was lost as telegrams bounced across the seas. In the end, medical work suffered. Often, even Henrietta Szold found herself locking horns with Hadassah's centralized authority. As she focused her interests increasingly on local problems of social welfare, she began to urge Hadassah to become increasingly subservient to local Palestine Zionist authority. But Hadassah in New York understandably insisted on making its own policy to ensure maintenance of high American scientific standards in Palestine. The problem was to be a constant irritant. In time, the Hadassah Medical Organization would grow to undreamed-of proportions with a budget comparable to that of a large American corporation. With medicine itself becoming so complex, the lay leadership in New York could no longer cope. Too much power in the hands of the Israel leadership became self-serving and did not always meet American Hadassah's needs. In 1996 a dramatic solution was attempted: HMO would be run by a twenty-one-member Management Board consisting in equal numbers of independent experts, National Board members and Israeli professionals.[1] How it would work out was the question that might not be answered for a considerable period.

Henrietta's headaches with Hadassah directors began the moment she moved to Jerusalem in 1920. The first formally appointed medical director, Dr. Isaac Max Rubinow, gave up after two attempts to juggle budgets and staff. Henrietta took over for a time, then asked Judah Magnes to step in while she returned briefly to the United States. In November 1923, Simon Meshullam Tannenbaum of New York's Beth David Hospital went to Jerusalem, but left in October 1924. Henrietta then asked Alexander Salkind, chief of the department of Internal Diseases, to assume charge, but he had to quit after falling ill. The search for a permanent director ended, so it was thought, with the appointment of the assistant director of Mount Sinai Hospital in New York, Ephraim Michael Bluestone. Young, talented, idealistic and determined, Bluestone was regarded by the Hadassah Board as the answer to their prayers. From a well-known Zionist family, he graduated with distinction from Columbia University's College of Physicians and Surgeons, served overseas in an American base hospital during the war and by the age of thirty-five was well known in New York City hospital administration. He signed on for three years; Hadassah felt he

---

1   In earlier years HMO had an Advisory Board, but the 1996 Management Board was an entirely new creation.

would remain longer. But Bluestone was back home in America little more than two years after arriving in Jerusalem in March 1926.

This state of affairs could not last. Henrietta concluded that Hadassah must have a director who was ready to cast his lot, physically and spiritually, with the *yishuv*. Bluestone wisely concurred. With Henrietta's acquiescence, he approached Dr. Haim Yassky. Yassky was reluctant but when Henrietta impressed upon him the importance of the task, he agreed. Bluestone left early in September 1928 and continued a long association with Hadassah as a consultant, becoming the first chairman of Hadassah's Medical Reference Board.

Dr. Yassky found that he was not alone at the top. Hadassah retained him as acting medical director because he was still in his early thirties and he had no formal training in hospital administration. Reuven Katznelson was named acting business director. As they shared a stormy stewardship, Henrietta sensed that one permanent Palestine director with overall authority was the only answer to the Hadassah Medical Organization's problem:

> The time has come when the permanent Palestinian and not the elusive American should be considered for the directorship. We cannot go on paying salaries and we cannot go on paying apprenticeship monies to Americans who must adjust themselves, each one in succession, to the conditions of Palestinian life and who, no sooner adjusted, take flight. Whether we approve or disapprove of the conditions of Palestinian life, for better or worse, they are the conditions under which the country is being developed by the forces who are content to throw their lot in with the country.

In New York, Hadassah's board also realized that a co-directorship could only be a stopgap solution. After several reappointments as acting director, Yassky was appointed director-general of the Hadassah Medical Organization in June 1931. And in 1932 under the board's auspices he spent six months in the United States studying administration. On his return, he set his compass in the direction of Mount Scopus. There he was to achieve his greatest dream and meet his tragic end. His objectives were high: "To create a medical institution whose fame will extend far beyond the boundaries of Palestine is our national and human duty." Without Yassky, Scopus would certainly not have been ready for World War II; he was the engine that kept the project moving forward. It was he who created a pre-medical faculty that was to be the forerunner of the medical school he never lived to see. Under his directorship new medical disciplines were introduced into Palestine — neurosurgery, occupational therapy, a medical record system. "The medical center," said Yassky's widow Fanny many years after his death, "was Dr. Yassky's entire life — his whole devotion."

After Mount Scopus was finally agreed upon as the site of the center, Hadassah sent Dr. Golub on several trips abroad in connection with the plans. On one occasion he met in London with the exiled German architect Eric Mendelsohn who had taken up residence in Palestine and was chosen to create the hospital complex on the stony ridge. Mendelsohn dreamed of the simple lines of the Escorial and Assisi: "I want to create monumental austerity even though it will disappoint the layman who expects British baronial splendor or America's imposing verticals." He took as his guide the simple lines of the Arab village because he was seeking local harmony — non-ornamental walls, courtyards with fountains and pergolas. "This," he said, "must be built for the ages."

Mendelsohn had great problems in creating immortal architecture. The location was a narrow, knifelike ridge about one mile long, rising 150 feet above the city of Jerusalem. On the east there was a deep descent toward the Dead Sea, to the west a slope into the Kidron Valley facing the site of the Temple upon which Moslems had built the golden Dome of the Rock. He had cold, rainy, windy winters of four months to cope with and dry, cool summers of eight months with parchment-dry days of spring and autumn sandwiched in between. Mendelsohn laid out three three-story buildings in an east-west pattern: the hospital connected by pergolas to the nurses school and, opposite, the Nathan Ratnoff building for postgraduate studies. Like the surrounding Arab villages, the architect kept the profiles low.

First earth for the hospital and nurses school was turned in mid-November 1936. The buildings were completed in September 1938. Construction of the postgraduate institute began in January 1937 and was finished in April 1939. For the first time in Palestine's construction history, machine-cut white stone slabs were used to face the edifices rather than the traditional hand-fashioned stone. Hadassah planted a grove of 1,500 pine trees in honor of Henrietta. The total cost was over $1 million — the single most expensive project Hadassah had undertaken up to that time. Said Golub, "For the first time there will be an institution which combines teaching and research and the immediate care of the sick. The medical men of Palestine look forward to the new institution as a model not only for the medical work of that country but for the whole Near East."

On May 9, 1939, Chaim Weizmann rushed out of Palestine on a plane bound for London after hearing that the British White Paper was to nullify the Balfour Declaration in eight days. Berlin and Rome agreed on a pact that established the Axis and Japan said it was willing to join. In Germany, a quarter of a million Jews were waiting for visas to leave: ninety percent would never make it. On Mount Scopus, Mendelsohn looked upon the completed work as though it were Shangri-La and said to a colleague, "It has the serenity of the greatest spiritual creations in this part of the world." The dedication was modest because of the security situation. Haim Yassky chaired the ceremony. Rose Jacobs spoke on behalf of 82,000 Hadassah members in America. Dr. Magnes spoke for the American Jewish Physicians Committee. Henrietta Szold, now seventy-eight, opened the ceremonies and accepted a silver key from Yassky. On the key was an inscription: "From Hadassah in Palestine to Hadassah in America with deep appreciation."

The ceremonies were hardly over when the move began from the old Rothschild Hospital on the Street of the Prophets in downtown Jerusalem. Even as the trucks lumbered up to Mount Scopus doubts still lingered about the site. "I remember the morning when we moved to Scopus," Dr. Moshe Rachmilewitz said later. "There was an explosion. There was shooting throughout Jerusalem. There had been much discussion whether it was advisable to move the hospital to Scopus. I was not clear in my own mind about it." The move went on nonetheless and the old Rothschild building was put up for sale. Approval for the sale was given by the Rothschilds on condition that their family name be part of the new Scopus building. But in the end, the building was not sold and continued to serve Hadassah's educational needs into the twenty-first century.

Scopus opened with modern lighting and 200 beds. It was later expanded by eighty and is now officially listed at that number. Nurses could effectively control an entire ward from their central stations. "It was a fine hospital from every point of view," said veteran surgeon Edward Joseph.

By May 14, the Hadassah Medical Organization's offices were on Scopus and on Tuesday (a twice-blessed day, according to Jewish tradition), May 30, 1939, the hospital doors swung open for the public. Happily, the first case was maternity and on that first day two babies were born. In all, 120 patients, aged two to seventy, were moved up to Scopus. The first *brit milah* was held on the second day with Chief Rabbi Isaac Halevy Herzog officiating. The infant was named Meir in honor of the founder of the Rothschild family.

Little more than three months later, the world was at war. Palestine was soon isolated and threatened. Scopus was set for battle.

A WORLD AT WAR

Fighting back tears on a late August night in 1939, Chaim Weizmann bade the 1,500 World Zionist Congress delegates farewell, knowing in his heart that by returning home many were going to their doom. Said Weizmann: "It would need the eloquence of a Jeremiah to picture the horrors of this new destruction of our people. We have none to comfort us."

That was the end of the most melancholy Zionist Congress in the history of the movement — the 21st or, as Weizmann had hopefully named it, the "Coming-of-Age Congress." In the midst of the sessions Berlin and Moscow announced their villainous pact. War was now certain. The general mood was one of frustration and helplessness. President Judith Epstein, heading the Hadassah delegation, observed, "The most horrible feeling in Geneva was that not a sound came out of the magnificent League of Nations building looking at us. I shall never forget the silence coming from those portals."

Most delegates were warned to leave Geneva immediately. Polish delegates were ordered to detour Germany through Yugoslavia and Hungary. German Zionists faced the horrible dilemma of remaining abroad or rejoining their families. Some Palestinian Jews brazenly crossed into Nazi Germany to try to organize escape routes. Having gone through the motions of condemning and rejecting the terms of the British White Paper, the delegates turned out the lights and scattered. Weizmann, who returned to England a few hours before the ceremonial closing, embraced his old colleague, Menachem Ussishkin, and despairingly whispered, "What kind of a world will it be when we meet again, Menachem?" Ussishkin shook his head gravely.

Back in London, Weizmann penned a letter to Neville Chamberlain politely asking the British government to permit Jewish manpower and resources in Palestine to join the war effort. Chamberlain demurred. Then, a few days later Hitler bombed Warsaw. For the next six years most of the world was aflame.

Cut off from the west, Palestine fell into economic chaos. Banks took a three-day holiday to prevent a run. Prices skyrocketed. The depression hit so fast and hard that Jews and Arabs cooperated economically to stave off ruin. Hardest hit was citrus, Palestine's largest export, in which both communities were engaged. As markets closed abroad, however, oranges soon came into demand locally as a source of acetone for making smokeless gunpowder. Soon, Palestine re-geared for a war economy and emerged from its financial doldrums.

The *yishuv* was trapped into simultaneously helping the British fight Hitler and fighting the British to save the refugees from Europe. As Ben-Gurion had anticipated, throughout the war the Mandate administration successfully parried attempts to create an independent Jewish army. The British constantly obstructed Haganah men who trained to meet a Nazi invasion; at the same time, British Intelligence used Haganah agents on dangerous missions behind enemy lines. Arab countries allied with Britain either cooperated with the Nazis or remained neutral until victory was almost in sight.

Amid these conflicting interests the *yishuv*, begging like a neglected child for British recognition, struggled for survival and to achieve its goal of statehood. That it finally achieved national status, considering the odds against it, is one of the most breathtaking dramas in the long history of this ancient land, one in which Hadassah played a key role.

As the war took its toll of European nations, Nazi Field-Marshal Erwin Rommel crunched steadily eastward across the North African sands toward British Middle East Headquarters in Cairo. Anxiety gripped Palestine and the British army hurriedly began training the Haganah's strike force, the Palmach, to make a last-ditch stand on Mount Carmel which was to be a modern version of Masada. It was feared that if Rommel broke through to Cairo, the entire Middle East would fall under the sign of the swastika. In the summer of 1942 it seemed that the world's fate — which was actually more critically at stake at Stalingrad — depended on whether the British could hold Cairo. Weizmann renewed his pleas in London for a Palestine Jewish Army. Winston Churchill, now prime minister, supported the proposal and, in February 1941, even arranged that Weizmann meet the intended commander of the Jewish force, General Leonard Hawes. In the end, a combination of the opposition from anti-Zionist British in Palestine and a dearth of supplies prevented the establishment of the army.

Overnight, Palestine turned into a war camp of Allied soldiers. In light of the peril the British put the country under virtual martial law. Anticipating the worst and hoping that the British would agree to the mobilizing of a Jewish army, the Jewish Agency opened its own national service register ten days after war began. Within two weeks, 135,000 men and women — about 20 percent of the entire *yishuv* — had signed up. In Jerusalem, the recently vacated Rothschild-Hadassah Hospital served as registration headquarters. Haganah men began to drill but the British, fearful of Arab reaction, brought their heels down heavily and on one occasion arrested forty-three men eager to move against the Nazis.

But still the *yishuv* prepared. The Haganah secretly worked up contingency plans for partisan warfare, should the British pull out. Blackouts, air-raid warnings and drills, food rationing and controlled prices were part of the scene. Forty-eight hours before fighting began in Poland, the 19th class of nurses, the first on Scopus, was graduated. Dr. Yassky called it the "Disturbances Class" because the students had studied through three years of Arab riots and terror. Even in August 1939, three months after the Arabs had supposedly been appeased by the White Paper, 87 people died in riots. Yassky cabled New York for emergency funds and immediately the National Board sent a first aid grant of $60,000. The role Hadassah was to play in the war was described to Yassky by Tel Aviv Mayor Rokach: "We turn to Hadassah in our need just as grown children turn to their mother when they are in distress."

Feverishly, the preparations to withstand an onslaught went on. Patients and staff were given air-raid drills. On Mount Scopus, a shelter was built with seven self-contained units for doctors, nurses and patients. By setting up emergency beds, Scopus was ready to care for 500 patients. The 20th class of nurses was accelerated by two months and all graduate nurses were called for refresher courses. Over the Palestine Broadcasting System, Hadassah dietitians gave instructions on how best to use rationed foods. Yassky offered the British Medical Corps and the families of all men in uniform the full use of Scopus's facilities. Henrietta Szold cabled New York from Jerusalem: "Cry Of The Hour To Feed Hungry Children." Hadassah put 25,000 children on an emergency feeding program, in addition to serving 75,000 lunches daily in 600 schools. And apart from free medical services for men in uniform and their families, refugees received free medication and clothing.

In so doing, Hadassah was also on a full war footing at least two years before the United States. In an Order of the Day sent to the national membership, President Tamar de Sola Pool wrote: "Our front line of defense lies in Zion as in Britain." Hadassah's Palestine Chairman Rose Halprin announced at a press conference that "Britain, America and Palestine are one fighting front...The 500,000 Jewish inhabitants of Palestine are banded together as one man to aid England and protect democracy. The aggressor stands for everything which, both as Americans and Jews, we abhor. By helping Palestine defend itself we are helping the

Allies." Zionist objectives were thus immediately aimed at making Palestine part of the Allied war effort.

At the same time, Hadassah did not neglect home front duties — selling War Bonds, mobilizing members for Civil Defense, volunteering for auxiliary services — and, for its work, in December 1944, won the "Big E" (for Excellence) award from the US government. Hadassah could make this contribution to the war effort because of its ability to meet crises as they arose. In responding to the government representative at the presentation ceremony, President Judith Epstein said: "We are proud to receive this award; we would have been ashamed if we had failed to receive it."

As Britain's fortunes worsened on all fronts, the Palestine administration began putting uniforms on Jewish volunteers. A Palestine Battalion was organized under the Union Jack and by March 1940 nearly 2,000 Jews were in action. By June 1941, the number reached 8,900 and already 1,000 were missing in action and 1,200 were Nazi prisoners in the Greek campaign. Jewish soldiers fought in Libya, Greece and Syria. They served in the Royal Air Force. Haganah scouts opened the way for General Maitland Wilson's forces moving into Vichy-held Syria where Company Commander Moshe Dayan lost his left eye. Others parachuted into Europe on British intelligence missions. Bombs crashed into Palestine's cities. Haifa, a principal naval facility, was hit most often from the air, but Tel Aviv suffered too. In September 1940, one air attack took the lives of 122 persons in the Jewish city.

While the Jews of Palestine were understandably jittery, the Arabs seemed sure of their future regardless of who won. In London, Weizmann heard that the Arabs of Palestine were preparing to divide the spoils once Hitler arrived. He noted in his memoirs, "Some of them are going about the streets of Tel Aviv and the colonies marking up the houses they expect to take over: one Arab, it was reported, has been killed in a quarrel over the loot assigned to him."

In June 1942, in one of the major tank battles of World War II,

Rommel shattered the British defense at Tobruk, Libya, and took 33,000 British prisoners, including Palestinians. The fateful breakthrough left Egypt wide open. Churchill sailed secretly to Washington for a conference with Roosevelt. There he received a letter from Weizmann offering to raise three divisions of 32,000 men and a force of 40,000 home guard. "If we go down in Palestine, we are entitled to go down fighting," he pleaded. That and the apparent hopelessness of the situation persuaded the British to enlarge the Palestine Battalion to a regiment of about 2,000 men. It was still not a Jewish army nor could it stop the Nazis. But few as they were, they acquitted themselves well enough to win Churchill's commendation.

For eight months before the fall of Tobruk, the transport company of the Palestine Battalion kept the British at the front supplied and after the defeat, transferred a New Zealand division from Syria to Egypt in a record six days. The engineers kept the bombed roads and ports repaired and paved the way for the fateful battle at El Alamein, where Rommel's advance faltered, one day's ride from Cairo. As the British moved westward pursuing Rommel, the Palestine regiment marched in the vanguard. In Tunis, where the chief rabbi welcomed the battalion as "messengers of peace," their commander, General Fred Kisch, a Jewish Agency Executive member in the 1920s who served as General Montgomery's chief engineer, was killed.

For the Allies in the Mediterranean area, the big headache was lack of supplies. Convoys had to travel mined waters and duck sorties of Axis bombers. Tens of thousands of tons of shipping went to the bottom of the sea. The civilian effort was likewise dependent on a constant supply of goods, medicines and equipment from abroad. Some did get through the Mediterranean; others had to be rerouted around the Cape of Good Hope to Basra on the Persian Gulf, then by truck over the desert to Palestine — a voyage of 18,000 miles. Like clockwork, thirty tons of supplies were shipped every month from Hadassah in New York to Hadassah in Jerusalem. Along with the new wonder sulfa drugs came surgical instruments, serums and vaccines, cod liver oil, clothing and X-ray film. On one ship there was a twelve-ton steel elevator for the Scopus medical center's underground shelter, and an incubator. More than 1,000 Hadassah sewing groups in the United States sent hundreds of thousands of clothing items.

As a result of the need to get these vast quantities of scarce supplies through war zones, Hadassah became a familiar figure in high places in Washington. In 1939, foreseeing the need, the National Board appointed New Orleans-born Denise Tourover to represent the organization in the nation's capital. Having lived in Washington since 1920, Denise soon became as familiar as the Washington Monument to political leaders. She moved among them with an easy informality but could be, if necessary, as determined as a bulldozer in removing bureaucratic roadblocks. At the beginning of the war, it was still possible to move money and supplies abroad since America was not at war. Because shipping was severely restricted, the White House set up a special board — the President's Advisory Committee on Foreign Voluntary Aid[1] — to approve good causes. Recalled Denise:

> We had to clear everything with the Board of Economic Warfare. To do that we had to have export licenses from Washington and import licenses from the British in Cairo. We did a great deal of work with both the British and the American boards. For example, if we needed quinine, which was in short supply, we would put our hands on the drug through various drug associations. Then we had to see the right people in the Board of Economic Warfare to get clearance. Very often we got the licenses, sometimes we did not. If after ten days we did not receive an affirmative reply from the British, we would assume the clearance was lost. We would send the article on and mark on the shipment

---

1   Hadassah became a member in 1949 and its representatives attended meetings for the next 34 years.

"Clearance Lost." Somehow, they worked out the problem
on the other side.

Denise had her own highly developed techniques in snipping red tape. It
helped that she represented a volunteer, humanitarian organization.
Washington was crawling with war profiteers and "ten percenters" —
agents making fortunes on 10 percent commissions. In contrast, Hadassah
was "clean'" and not one major Hadassah item was refused by the board
during the entire war.

Of all the war years none was more crucial for Zionism than 1942.
Annihilation seemed constantly imminent. The scare of invasion did not
pass until November, but there was much more to be dreaded than
Rommel's tanks. On January 20, subordinates of Hitler, meeting at
Wannsee near Berlin, adopted a program of systematic genocide,
euphemistically calling it the "Final Solution." The decision that led to the
extermination of six million Jews would not reach the ears of world Jewry
until autumn.

Even without knowing the specifics of Wannsee, Chaim Weizmann was
sufficiently depressed by the turbulence thrashing world Jewry to call an
extraordinary conference of Jewish leaders in May. He felt that without a
united front in America — the strongest bastion of free Jewry remaining —
the hobbled Zionist effort could collapse. The assembly of about 650
delegates, among them Tamar de Sola Pool and Bertha Schoolman
representing Hadassah, met at the Biltmore Hotel in New York City.
Emerging from the deliberations was the first clear call by Zionists for the
establishment of an independent political state in Palestine, distinct from
the less precise "national home" of the Balfour Declaration. The Biltmore
Program also demanded unlimited Jewish immigration at a time when the
British were limiting it to 15,000 a year. Biltmore put the derelict Zionist
movement on a firm course. But it also served as the scene for a bitter fight
between Chaim Weizmann and David Ben-Gurion. Shortly after the
meeting ended, Ben-Gurion, now the Jews' shadow prime minister in

Palestine, challenged Weizmann's leadership. At a painful meeting in conference chairman Rabbi Stephen Wise's private study, Ben-Gurion accused Weizmann of depending wholly on his own personal prestige to fulfill Zionist goals and thus, of failing to create a Jewish army. No one had ever addressed the eminent Zionist in terms so brutal and so frank. Weizmann could only reply that there was no answer to political assassination. Ben-Gurion went on to claim credit for the Biltmore Program although Weizmann had outlined its principle in an article in the January 1942 issue of *Foreign Affairs.* Whatever the source, the Biltmore Program was a Zionist milestone that brought the movement's blurred aims into sharp focus.

In a negative sense, Biltmore spotlighted the widening gap between Diaspora and Palestine Zionism. Weizmann believed that an irreparable breach with London would be more injurious to the Jews than to Britain, that if America had to choose between Britain or Zionism she would ally herself with London. Ben-Gurion held that only two forces mattered — Palestine Jewry and American Jewry — and Weizmann would get nowhere because non-Jewish politicians would always act in their own national interests. Ben-Gurion's policy was radically new, reflecting a new spirit among the pioneers in Palestine. But at first it was not universally accepted. In 1942, Ben-Gurion was too raw and too brash for the more conservative American and British Zionists. Although both Weizmann and Ben-Gurion agreed on the Biltmore Program, they differed on its implementation.

Populist Ben-Gurion made the most of Biltmore. He used it as a rallying cry — to state forthright aims in simple terms, to excite the people into sounding trumpets and waving flags. But on whichever side one stood, all could acknowledge that he had the pulse of his people at his fingertips and he knew they were ready to march.

The Biltmore Program achieved its goal of rallying American Zionists. At its 1942 convention held in New York City, Hadassah gave the program its wholehearted support. For the National Board of Hadassah, however, a serious problem grew from the fact that the founder of Hadassah,

Henrietta Szold, and chairman of the Hadassah Emergency Committee, Judah Magnes, were among the founding members of *Ichud* (Unity), a new organization proposing the establishment of a bi-national state in which Arabs and Jews would share sovereignty. A bitter debate erupted within the leadership over a proposal to disassociate Hadassah from the stand of Dr. Magnes and Henrietta Szold, both closely identified with Hadassah in the public mind. At this critical stage in Zionist history Hadassah was in no mood for solutions such as bi-nationalism; it was now mature enough to say so and to put the organization four-square behind the concept of a Jewish commonwealth. That was a significant milestone in Hadassah's history for it had taken a firm stand in political affairs. With a membership of around 150,000, Hadassah had grown enormously on the American scene which had been dominated by male leadership. That irreversible growth would make the organization the largest single Zionist group in the world.

In the mid-war years, Hadassah was so active in so many fields in Palestine that it could justifiably throw a little weight around. Scopus was the center of much of that activity. British army physicians took courses on tropical diseases from Saul Adler, a world authority. That led to a series of regular, formal medical conferences attended by British military doctors who were just out of medical school. Hundreds of physicians attended lectures. In the labs, British army X-ray machines were repaired and margarine was regularly tested for vitamin content. Hadassah supplied Britain's Royal Air Force in Egypt with medicines that it could not get from its own medical corps. Hadassah sent vaccines and supplies to the Russians, the Turks, the Free French, the Czechs and the Anglo-Iranian Petroleum Company; trained a lab technician for the Yugoslav partisans; and sent eight nurses to care for war wounded at an Alexandria hospital directed by the personal physician of King Farouk of Egypt.

With the war came the fear of epidemics. By right, the health department of the Mandate government should have commanded the battle. But it was Hadassah that inoculated 70,000 school children against typhoid, furnished the department with anti-typhus vaccines, reduced the incidence of malaria to a point where it no longer posed a risk for troops and even set up small emergency field hospitals.

Then there was the regular regimen of work: combating tuberculosis brought in by immigrants (the anti-TB hospital in Safed maintained a 110 percent occupancy rate and Hadassah was planning a new hospital in Jerusalem when new drugs practically eradicated the disease); establishing a home medical service to relieve overcrowding on Scopus; launching two major vocational education centers in Jerusalem and preparing the groundwork for a medical school; opening a medicine-producing pharmacological institute that would one day be turned into a school of pharmacy; helping found a soldiers welfare committee; setting up more kindergartens and playgrounds and supervising nutrition in seventy-seven summer camps.

With it all, Hadassah's performance in medical work was impressive: 90 percent of all seriously war-wounded treated at Hadassah survived. And in Palestine, largely as a result of Hadassah's care of the young, the *yishuv* had the world's lowest child mortality rate — twenty-seven per thousand (seven per thousand in 1996).

To keep the machinery well-oiled, Hadassah set up an emergency committee. With the onset of war it was clear that the National Board, six thousand miles away, needed an independent field command with powers almost equal to their own. In 1940, Rose Jacobs asked Judah Magnes in Jerusalem to head the committee. The eloquent Magnes accepted the task "to imprint upon the committee a Hadassah personality."

Hadassah always faced the problem of running affairs with its mind in New York and its heart in Jerusalem. Soon after non-medical projects were started in the early 1920s, the Palestine Council, Jerusalem-based women volunteers, coordinated *yishuv* activities. In 1924, Henrietta Szold urged the Central Committee[2] to appoint Nellie Straus Mochenson as its

---

2   The Hadassah Central Committee was predecessor to the National Board.

representative in Palestine. The council's executive secretary, Yugoslav-born Shari Berger, arrived in Jerusalem in 1923 and immediately began helping Henrietta and Jessie Sampter set up the Hebrew Women's Organization (later WIZO). When Shari resigned in 1934, Rose Halprin went to Jerusalem, and remained until 1939. During those years Rose kept reports flowing to New York.

Thus, the Emergency Committee had strong precedents on which to build. It kept firm control over expenditures and it negotiated for Hadassah with the government and the Jewish Agency. Its long-lasting importance was that it broke down the artificial barriers between preventive and curative services. Until 1939, the Hadassah Medical Organization was a power unto itself while the Palestine Council served as a cover for all other services. Now the Emergency Committee was responsible for all.

The Committee could pull down these barriers only because three persons of stature were in command: Magnes, Henrietta, and Julius Simon of the Palestine Economic Corporation. Later, others were co-opted — Ethel Agron, Rose Viteles, Yehuda Bromberg and Haim Yassky himself. When the state was finally established, the Committee's successor, the Hadassah Council in Israel, would become a permanent feature of volunteer service in Jerusalem.[3]

One of the more piquant aspects of Scopus's personality during the war was the improvement of the relationship between Jews and Arabs once the fear of invasion diminished. By 1943, Arabic was being taught in Hebrew schools, the League for Jewish-Arab Relations opened joint youth clubs; schoolchildren exchanged visits. Part of the reason for this era of goodwill was that some of the troublemakers were out of the country.[4] In 1943 and 1944, there were no serious outbreaks between the two communities.

---

3   In 1996, the Hadassah Council in Israel was absorbed into Hadassah-Israel, twelve years after HI's birth as the first unit in the Hadassah International family of organizations.

4   The Mufti of Jerusalem, who fled first to Iraq and then to Iran, consorted with the Nazis in Berlin where he worked out a plan with Hitler for the future of Palestine.

Upon his discharge from Hadassah, the Emir Abdullah — future ruler of the Hashemite Kingdom of Jordan — penned words of praise for Hadassah on the opening page of the medical center's visitors' book and invited Yassky to visit the palace in Amman. "More than half of our patients in the neurosurgery department were Arab," recalled Professor Aharon Beller. Abdullah himself — and King Hussein, his grandson — would keep Scopus a lifeless shell for nineteen years after Israel's War of Independence. Yet they would send Jordanians for treatment at the Hadassah-Hebrew University Medical Center at Ein Kerem when specialists were not available at home.

Hadassah personnel were killed by Arabs in the 1920s while on mercy missions. Yet one of the prize documents in Hadassah's archives is a letter to Joseph Krimsky, dated November 1918, from the British military governor in Beersheba and signed by twenty-seven Bedouin sheikhs, thanking him and his nurse for saving the eyesight of Bedouin patients. No Arab was ever turned away.

During World War II Arab royalty sought out Hadassah's doctors — among them King Feisal of Iraq who had reneged on his agreement with Chaim Weizmann in 1920, and a prince of Saudi Arabia, whose father, King Ibn Saud, would toward the war's end influence President Roosevelt to veer away from a Zionist policy. But in the summer of 1944, shortly before the Roosevelt-Ibn Saud meeting, Saudi Prince Mansour insisted that his brother-in-law Prince Fahd be hospitalized at Hadassah. Ibn Saud objected to a Zionist state but not a Zionist hospital. Said Prince Mansour to Dr. Yassky: "When my brother-in-law fell ill, there was a consultation of some twenty physicians in Cairo and it was suggested that he be flown to London. I said, 'Nonsense! Why should he be taken to London if there is Hadassah in Jerusalem?' Now nobody will go anywhere but to Jerusalem."

During the war years, even as the *yishuv* smoldered because of Britain's immigration policy, formal visits were made by the British high commissioner. On those occasions, the hospital would be on its toes as though an admiral were being brought aboard a naval destroyer. On one such occasion, Esther Passman Epstein, who served as a one-member

Hadassah welcoming committee, took Lord Gort, then the British High Commissioner and a bachelor, into the maternity ward. "He was twirling his walking stick and looking at the infants when a sudden smile crossed his face. He lifted his hand and started waving to the babies. Lord Gort turned to me and said that they were lovely children. Without thinking, I replied, 'Yes, this is our internal immigration department.' He looked at me, his face red and gruff, cleared his throat and said, 'Yes, you have a point there.' Then we looked at each other and broke into laughter. The ice was cracked and after that we were all good friends." During Lord Gort's administration, a measure of peace between Arabs and Jews was possible, but he did not remain in Jerusalem for long.

Immigration was the issue on which the British, the Arabs and the Jews were ready to risk their future. The Arabs feared inundation. The British feared Arab retribution. The Jews feared neither and by a combination of audacity, terror, skill and sanguinity decided the issue. In the end the British would take desperate departure of the land; the Arabs who sought to resolve the problem by arms would be defeated.

Even before Hitler rose to power, the refugees began to accumulate. The first known attempt of a large group to steal into Palestine was carried out successfully in 1934 by 300 Polish Zionists who landed in the night aboard a small hired Greek boat, the *Vellos*. Quickly they dispersed into the collective settlements where they took on new identities. The second attempt of the *Vellos* failed and no large-scale attempts were made for several years. Finally, in 1937 at a clandestine meeting in Tel Aviv, a group of Haganah, labor and kibbutz leaders set up *Mossad l'Aliyah Bet*, "the Institute for Immigration B," a euphemism for uncertified, or, as the British called it, "illegal," immigration. In 1938, Mossad l'Aliyah agents operating in Nazi Germany and Austria made contact with Adolph Eichmann, then head of the Central Bureau for Jewish Emigration, and won his agreement to help them establish training farms for Jews wishing to live in Palestine. Eichmann, the fiend who transported millions of Jews to extermination camps, implementing Hitler's genocidal policy to make Europe *Judenrein* (free of Jewry), was certainly no lover of Jews.[5]

By mid-1939, hundreds had managed to slip by the British. To show they were serious, the British callously returned refugees on three small ships to their ports of departure in Nazi Europe — a virtual verdict of death in each case. The resultant world-wide uproar prevented further repatriations. On the day war was declared in Europe, the Mossad ship *Tiger Hill*, carrying 1,205 refugees, settled in the sands south of Jaffa. As it approached the shore the British opened fire killing two passengers, one a physician. The senseless shooting was ordered by over-anxious officers who suspected that the Gestapo had planted Nazi agents among the immigrants. With the help of the Mossad about 7,000 others set sail but never reached Palestine's shores; leaking, rusted, rotten boats tried weathering heavy seas and, like the *S.S. Salvador* carrying 300 Bulgarian Jews, sank with everyone aboard.

The more the British tried to limit the entry of refugees the more the *yishuv*, directly and indirectly, tried to defy them. Because of the unauthorized immigration, the Mandate government on July 12, 1939 proclaimed a ban on the entry of all Jews to Palestine for six months beginning on October 1. On January 5, 1940, the British decreed that refugees with German or Austrian passports would not be allowed to enter Palestine because they were "enemy aliens." In November 1940, refugees intercepted on their way to Palestine were transferred to the *S.S. Patria* in Haifa harbor. The *Patria* was to deport these 1,771 Jews to the Indian Ocean island of Mauritius where they were to be held for the duration and

---

5   In 1960, Israeli agents captured Eichmann, a fugitive in Argentina, and extradited him to Jerusalem for crimes against the Jews and humanity. In Jerusalem during the nine-month trial that followed, newly-uncovered documents and evidence from Holocaust survivors awakened a horror-stricken world to the enormity and bestiality of Nazi crimes against the Jewish people. After the Israel Supreme Court dismissed his appeal and the president refused clemency, Eichmann was hanged in 1962. He remains the only criminal to be executed by the State of Israel.

presumably repatriated after the war. But the *Patria* never made it out of Haifa harbor. On November 25, an explosion rocked the ship, killing 241 persons. In a misguided attempt to prevent the vessel from leaving port, a Haganah agent attempted to immobilize the engines, but the blast was heavier than planned and lives were lost. The surviving *Patria* refugees were held in detention at Atlit, an internment camp near Haifa, and finally released. But nearly 1,800 others were sent to Mauritius where they languished for the remainder of the war.

While the Jews were restricted, other refugees were permitted entry and colonies of non-Jewish Poles, Serbs, Greeks, Czechs and others began growing in Tel Aviv and Jerusalem. The British were effective to a greater degree than they might have hoped. On April 1, 1944, when the White Paper's quota restrictions on immigrants ran out, about 20,000 certificates were still unused. The British extended their validity, offering a visa to anyone who managed to reach Turkey. By the beginning of 1945 they were finally used up and simultaneously the British withdrew their agreement to automatically grant visas to Jews arriving in Turkey. With that the Turks no longer would grant transit rights to stateless Jews en route to Palestine. Knowing that the war would soon end, the Jewish Agency requested permits for 100,000 survivors in Europe. The reply, in February 1945, was that because of housing difficulties only 1,500 certificates would be available monthly. This was a slight improvement over the previous 15,000 yearly but not nearly enough to absorb the expected deluge.

One effect of relentless British efforts to restrict immigration was the rise of Jewish extremism. In 1942, two such groups appeared on the scene. One was the Fighters for the Freedom of Israel (known by its Hebrew acronym LEHI), or as the British called them, "the Stern Gang." The Sternists, smallest of the underground groups, were led by a young poet, Abraham Stern. One of their most notorious acts was to assassinate Churchill's Minister of State in Cairo, Lord Moyne, on November 2, 1944 (Balfour Day), only two days after Weizmann and Churchill had discussed the partitioning of Palestine. Many believe that Moyne's murder so angered Churchill that he temporarily set aside his pro-Zionist sympathies.

A much larger and older clandestine underground group was the Irgun Tzevai Leumi (National Military Organization), which broke away from the Haganah in 1937. Allied to the Revisionists and to Zev Jabotinsky, it was commanded by Menachem Begin, a Polish soldier who crossed into Palestine from Trans-Jordan in 1942. Although its terrorist character cannot be denied, it respected a truce for most of the war and allied itself with the Haganah in a number of operations toward the end of the war.

In Europe, Jews tried desperately to escape. Few succeeded. There were examples of incredible endurance such as the ill-fated flight of 1,200 Jews from Vienna, Danzig and Czechoslovakia, who sailed down the Danube in three boats, were delayed on the Yugoslav frontier, and were frozen in for three months. The British agreed to release certificates for 200 children on board and they found their way overland to Palestine. The corpses of the 1,000 adults who remained were discovered by the Serbian government after the war, fully dressed, their passports in their pockets.

The most heartening tale was that of the Teheran children. Their saga began in the Russian-occupied part of Poland shortly after the fall of Warsaw in 1939. Hundreds of thousands of Poles, among them thousands of Jews, were deported to Siberia. There they worked in the forests and in labor camps. But when work became scarce, they began to move south toward warmer climes. They spent long days and nights traveling and trudging from village to village. Always their preoccupation was to find food. So scarce were provisions that they took to eating grass, dogs and fruit pits. Thousands died of malnutrition on the back roads of Russia. They trekked onward into the Asiatic republics. Nearly 1,000 children, either orphaned or separated from their parents, were among the ragged contingent of Poles (Christians and Jews, adults and children, civilians and army detachments) who struggled into Teheran in late summer 1942. Henrietta Szold won permits for them and the Jewish Agency negotiated to have the children sent to Palestine through Iraq, but Baghdad refused. Neutral Turkey likewise denied the children passage.

Zionist leaders were incensed, particularly since Iraq was then receiving Allied aid. In Washington, Hadassah's Denise Tourover had been keeping abreast of developments through her contacts in the State Department:

> We called on the Turkish Ambassador but made no progress. We called on companies that had major oil interests in Iraq. That too failed and I was really incensed that a two-by-four government which was getting lend-lease from us should set its will against a humanitarian effort such as this. I went to the White House. The meeting there was arranged through Mrs. Henry Morgenthau [wife of the Secretary of the Treasury]. A few days later the White House said that nothing could move the Iraqis.

Together with Tamar de Sola Pool and Youth Aliyah Chairman Gisela Warburg Wyzansky, Denise then called on British Ambassador Lord Halifax at the British embassy in December 1942. The ambassador told them, "I am most sad that at this time of the year when the world is about to celebrate the birth of Jesus that I have not been able to do something on behalf of Jewish children. But I will make one last effort."

A few days later Denise heard from British War Ministry chief John McClay in Washington that the children were to be shipped out shortly. On January 2, 1943, the first group of 600 with 60 guardians left their refugee camp in Teheran, where some had been waiting ten months, for the Iranian port of Ahwaz. They sailed to Karachi, then to Bombay and after that across the seas to Port Said. On the way, hostile planes scouted their vessel, but did not attack. At Port Said they boarded a train for Palestine and arrived in Atlit outside Haifa on February 18 — a voyage of nearly seven weeks. For Henrietta, who was there to meet them, their safe arrival was one of her most ecstatic moments. The *yishuv* was joyously delirious, for refugees had not been arriving in large numbers and here at last was a large treasure of

Jewish children snatched from certain death. Wherever the train stopped on its way to Atlit, it was mobbed by people seeking their own children or relatives. They threw flowers and pushed food and drink through the windows. The bewildered children looked down wide-eyed and silent from the windows, waving little white and blue flags they had been given in Port Said. At the clearance station in Atlit, one of the women guardians on the train fainted. In the crowd she had recognized her husband, an officer in the Polish army who had been transferred from Russia to the Middle East. Another woman among the greeters found her own child on the train — dazed and sobbing.

"They nearly tore us apart when we landed," recalled one of the children, Yaacov Orr, who later fought Egyptians on the southern front in Israel's War of Independence. Orr was thirteen when he arrived clutching the hands of his eleven-year-old brother Ron and sister Leah. "Everyone fought over us. It was like a war. The *yishuv* thirsted for immigrants. Wherever we went we were showered with gifts. If we took in a movie and said we were from Teheran they refused to take money. If we went to a kiosk to buy a drink it was free."

Thus the story ended happily. None was more elated than Denise Tourover, whose only gripe was that after the children arrived, she received a bill of $57.46 from the State Department for cables made on Hadassah's behalf. It was paid.

About a year after the first group of Teheran children arrived, rumors began reaching Palestine that Jews were walking out of the desert from remote sections of the Arabian Peninsula and appearing in the British Crown Colony of Aden at the confluence of the Red and Arabian seas. The Joint Distribution Committee sent an old hand, Harry Viteles, off to Aden. He reported that about 1,200 people were lying in the streets, in courtyards and in synagogues, waiting for the fulfillment of the prophecy that they would be returned to the Promised Land. Medical help was urgently needed. Immediately Hadassah's malaria expert, Israel Kligler, was sent to do control work. In April 1944, German-born Dr. David

Ullmann, who had worked in a Haifa paint factory before joining Hadassah, was sent to Aden by the Joint Distribution Committee. With nurses Zipporah Friedman, Yehudit Kepara and Rahel Mashat, Professor Ullmann spent six months caring for the refugees:

> They came in groups of fifteen and twenty; it took them weeks, even months to reach Aden. They knew Biblical Hebrew from their religious training, and nurses started modern language instruction in the camp that was set up for them. They had many medical problems — relapsing fever, malaria, dysentery, diseases caused by the intense heat. I was their only doctor and they called me King David. I had brought along a microscope — an unheard of instrument there — and diagnosed relapsing fever. Before that, all fevers were said to be malaria.

In February 1945, the war was drawing to a close. The newly organized Jewish Brigade of several thousand men fighting under their own flag was moved to the front in northern Italy. The brigade tasted only five weeks of battle before V-E Day and had no serious effect on the course of the war. But by war's end, 19,207 Palestinian Jews, including 2,000 women, had fought with the British forces, and 3,000 with other Allied units. In Palestine itself, 7,300 served in police units. By the time the Axis collapsed, 30,000 men and women were in uniform, some of them hardened soldiers and all of them with good basic training, making a fine cadre for more difficult future battles.

That same month, the British halted the five-year internment of Jewish refugees on the Indian Ocean island of Mauritius. In July 1945, a Hadassah medical unit was permitted to go to the island to care for the 1,520 refugees since their return to Palestine was imminent. The Hadassah team shipped back with the refugees and at the end of August, 1,320 refugees landed in Haifa. While on the island, 128 had died, 268 joined the armed forces, and about 60 children were born.

Despite approaching victory, February was also a sad month for Hadassah. The organization was bigger, stronger and more energetic than ever and ready to face a new world of challenges. But in a way Hadassah was now orphaned, for on February 13, 1945, her frail heart no longer able to keep pace with her breathless energies, death came in the Mount Scopus medical center to Henrietta Szold. She was eighty-four.

In her last years, Henrietta was grieved that on arrival in Palestine, children were put into detention camps along with adults. As a gift to her, Hadassah had decided to build a $400,000 reception and screening center that would serve Youth Aliyah exclusively.[6] On February 10, 1949, Ramat Hadassah Szold was opened amid the oak forests in the Hills of Ephraim behind Haifa, not far from Alonim, the first kibbutz founded by Youth Aliyah graduates. It was a site that Henrietta herself had chosen. Ramat Hadassah Szold, its title bearing two names that would live inseparably in the annals of Youth Aliyah, was perhaps the finest tribute she could have. But inevitably there would be others. Hadassah established the Henrietta Szold Award for Humanitarian Service, conferring the first award on Eleanor Roosevelt. The nursing school was named for Henrietta, as was the scenic road that leads to the Ein Kerem medical center which would be dedicated on August 3, 1960. So were a social research institute, a forest, a publishing house, a kibbutz, a Tel Aviv taxi company. Henrietta was buried on the Mount of Olives opposite the Old City of Jerusalem. Later, the Jordanians obliterated the grave and its precise position was lost for nineteen years. But nothing could erase her spirit.

---

6 Although Henrietta did not live to see it completed, she attended its groundbreaking in 1944.

SIEGE!

Hitler was dead. So were most of Europe's Jews. Stateless and penniless, four hundred thousand survivors wandered the face of the continent, finally moving into displaced persons camps while political leaders disputed their fate. Hitler's Holocaust had reaped a dreadful harvest. But it had also begun to generate a terrific creative force among the remnant.

In 1945, Zionists faced a new set of world leaders and a new balance in the power struggle. Britain was shedding its empire; France and Italy, struggling for internal stability, fell to the second echelon in the world order; Germany was prostrate; the United States and the USSR now called the shots. In Britain, Clement Attlee succeeded Winston Churchill as prime minister. Campaigning vigorously, Attlee recklessly promised all things to all peoples. To Jews, his party pledged not only a national home but even an unrealistic exchange of Arab and Jewish populations. In Washington, Harry S. Truman was president and his Congress was strongly pro-Zionist — even though his administration was not.

At the end of July 1945, an exuberant but untutored Truman flew to Potsdam, outside Berlin, for a summit conference. Genuinely concerned over the fate of European Jews, Truman asked Attlee and his boorish foreign secretary, Ernest Bevin, to permit Holocaust survivors to move to Palestine. By making the request, Truman unknowingly drew America, for the first time, into the Palestine question. When Attlee asked him to help Britain by providing troops for Palestine so that Jewish immigration could be facilitated without bloodshed, Truman refused.

On August 1, the day the Potsdam Conference closed, Zionists from around the world gathered in London. The scene could best be described as pathetic. Weizmann's fears of August 1939 had come true. The once great Jewish community of Poland could send only eight delegates, four of them partisan fighters. German Jewry had only the gaunt, noble figure of Rabbi Leo Baeck, a concentration camp survivor. "To be a Jew," he told a stunned conference, "means to be prepared for tragedy. Our people were the objects of a brutally-minded gang which developed cruelty into a system, ferocity into a science and bestiality into a philosophy. The question now is, what is to be done?"

Hadassah had four delegates in London. Two — President Judith Epstein and National Political Chairman Rose Halprin — would lead Hadassah on Zionism's political march in the three bitter years to come. Rose reported, "We did not acclaim the victory of the [British] Labour Party as a Zionist victory...but still everyone looked forward to an improvement over the Churchill administration, which allowed the White Paper to strangle Jewish development."

In the debate, Weizmann and Ben-Gurion disagreed over how to deal with the British. Impulsively, Ben-Gurion sped off to the Colonial Office and demanded 100,000 immigration permits and a Jewish State forthwith. Aghast, the neophyte colonial secretary spluttered that it was too much to expect the ruling Labour Party to change Palestine policy after being in power only two weeks. In Washington, President Truman received a report that most of the Jews in the displaced persons (DP) camps desired no other home than Palestine and pressed openly for the acceptance of 100,000 by the Labour Mandate government. In Britain, the Labour Party split over the next step. One faction, led by Harold Laski, insisted that the pre-election pledges be honored. But the majority, led by Attlee and Bevin, feared an Arab uprising at a time Britain was trying to sign a treaty with Egypt. The Americans, too, were split. While the White House and Congress were squarely behind the Zionists, the State Department and the military pulled in the opposite direction.

In Europe, meanwhile, the Mossad was reactivating its agents to get the stateless Jews out of the camps by hook or by crook, legally or illegally, and on their way to Palestine. So chaotic was the picture at this time that a surreptitious organization like Mossad could work at maximum efficiency. "Aliyah Bet" became a rallying cry that stirred the *yishuv*. After the State was established, when immigration was unrestricted, the Mossad served as an intelligence agency, respected by Israel's allies and feared by its enemies.

In Palestine, both Jewish and Arab leaders knew that the British could not hold on for long. Forces in both camps organized for an underground struggle. As pressures grew for and against mass immigration from Europe, the united Jewish underground struck a first blow. In one coordinated operation the partisans freed 200 Aliyah Bet immigrants from detention, wrecked railroad lines, damaged the British-run Haifa oil refinery and hit British naval craft.

Anxiously, Foreign Secretary Bevin asked America to help him out of a tight spot by undertaking a joint probe of the immigration problem. Washington agreed to participate in a twelve-member Anglo-American commission. Overjoyed, Bevin committed himself to accept the body's findings. The members visited the European refugee camps, Palestine, the Arab countries and Washington. On January 8, 1946, Hadassah President Judith Epstein appeared before the commission. Representing 200,000 American women, but speaking for all Zionists, she said, "The burning need of solving the Jewish problem, of creating a home where those Jews who needed or wanted to rebuild their lives in a Jewish land be given that opportunity, was what moved this large army of Jewish women in America to dedicate their lives to this cause."

After four months, the commission reported in April 1946 that a bi-national state was preferable to partition, that 100,000 immigration certificates be issued to Jews immediately, restrictions on land sales to Jews be dropped and the Mandate continued. A happy Truman applauded the immigration recommendation but a flabbergasted Bevin cried foul. He told Parliament that he would never agree to 100,000 Jews going to Palestine. Now, the magic figure of 100,000 became a *cause célèbre* in the world press.

A series of events then shook Palestine and turned the country into an armed camp. On a moonless night in mid-June 1946, the Haganah blew up eleven bridges, all of them connecting Palestine and the neighboring Arab countries. This was the *yishuv's* reply to Prime Minister Attlee for saying that he, like Bevin, could not go along with the 100,000 figure until all the underground forces disbanded. On "Black Saturday," June 24, the British rounded up the top Jewish Agency and Haganah leaders in Palestine including shadow "Foreign Minister" Moshe Shertok (later, Sharett) and 2,800 young Jews and sent them all to detention camps. Ben-Gurion was then in Paris and for the rest of the year ran the *yishuv's* affairs from the French capital.

Two weeks later, the Irgun, after a forewarning, blew up the southern wing of Jerusalem's King David Hotel, headquarters of the British army. More than 90 Englishmen, Jews and Arabs died in the blast. The commanding officer in Palestine, General Evelyn Barker, ordered a policy of "non-fraternization" with the Jews and said he would punish the Jews "in a way that race dislikes — by striking at their pockets." Barker was subsequently transferred. The *yishuv* now knew that it was fighting not only anti-Zionism in the British administration but anti-Semitism as well.

Despite British opposition, immigrants were pouring on to the shores of Palestine from Mossad ships. Most were caught and sent to the Atlit detention camp south of Haifa but some made it safely inland and "lost" themselves with fake papers in the kibbutzim. In July 1946, to make it a bit easier for the ships to land, a Haganah commando platoon led by a young Yugoslav Jew named Haim Bar-Lev (later an Israel chief of staff) blew up a British radar station that was tracking the ships. The ships began coming so frequently that on August 12, the British announced "Operation Igloo;" immigrants arriving without permits would no longer be sent to Atlit but deported to detention camps on the island of Cyprus, from where they would be released at the rate of 1,500 monthly. That same day a ship with 543 on board arrived from a Greek port. It was the *Henrietta Szold*, one of sixty-three ships to be bought clandestinely for Aliyah Bet with funds quietly collected in the United States. The *Henrietta Szold's* passengers were the first to be sent to Cyprus. Nearly 40,000 more followed until the end of the Mandate.

Only ten days before the *Henrietta Szold* arrived, the Jewish Agency put Hadassah in charge of immigrant health. At that time, 2,500 people were cooped up in Atlit. Within twenty-four hours, Yassky had a sixty-bed emergency hospital staffed round the clock by a doctor and five nurses. After an inspection of immigrant ships in Haifa, Yassky angrily reported, "Beasts are not kept under such conditions."

The Jewish Agency was banned in Cyprus, so Jewish teams went in under the aegis of the American Joint Distribution Committee. To organize this welfare work, the JDC sent American-born Rose Viteles, a member of the Hadassah Council in Palestine who, unknown to most, was one of the early organizers of the Haganah in Jerusalem. Rose was soon followed by units of Hadassah physicians and nurses. Tamar de Sola Pool arranged for an entire educational foundation for children, including teachers and texts, to be moved from the Abraham Ruttenberg Foundation in Haifa to the camps. The last Hadassah team returned with the last immigrant on February 16, 1949, nine months after the birth of the State.

As more ships challenged the British navy and underground pressure increased to lower the gates, the British committed more troops to Palestine, eventually numbering 100,000. But Bevin knew force could not settle anything; out of despair he called for a conference of Jews and Arabs in London in September 1946. Neither Palestinian Arabs nor Jews would attend, so the British met with delegates of the newly-formed Arab League, a loose union of Arab nations formed with British encouragement. The

Zionists stayed away because the British refused to put Ben-Gurion's new plan on the agenda. His plan was visionary, suggesting the partition of Palestine along lines almost identical to those eventually drawn in 1949 following the War of Independence. The British recessed the conference after two months of getting nowhere, but Bevin carried on discussions with both sides nonetheless. Just as he thought he was making some headway, President Truman took the wind out of Bevin's sails by announcing full support of the Ben-Gurion partition plan.

November 1946. Bevin tried again, releasing the imprisoned Jewish leaders and the 2,800 youths in DP camps. In return, the Haganah severed its ties with the more extreme Irgun and Sternists. On December 9, the Zionist Congress returned to Basel for its first postwar meeting. It was to be known as the "Confused Congress," for the leadership was divided on how to move forward to independence. At Hadassah's 32nd national convention in Boston and at the Zionist Congress, Ben-Gurion railed at the British, demanding an autonomous Jewish State. But no one was clear on what to do next or how to do it. Should Zionists encourage a regime of terror to get the British out? Rabbi Abba Hillel Silver, the booming-voiced orator from Cleveland who was to lead Zionism's battles in the United States as the head of the American section of the Zionist Executive, encouraged revolt. The aging Weizmann stuck to the guns of moderation. The Congress had before it the British Morrison-Grady plan to divide Palestine into four cantons and Bevin's call for another Jewish-Arab conference to meet in London in January 1947. The Congress rejected both. The Morrison-Grady plan would have given the Jews only 17 percent of the country. The Congress called for the establishment of a Jewish commonwealth and unlimited immigration, renounced terror as a political weapon and rejected Bevin's suggestion for a five-year trusteeship. Hadassah had its own triumph in Basel. Its "foreign minister," Rose Halprin, was elected to the Jewish Agency Executive's American section and later became its chairman. For much of the next quarter of a century, she would be its sole female representative.

Zionism may have been perplexed about what route to take but it was not confused about where it was going, nor was it hesitant to look to bolder captains to get it there. A depressed Weizmann resigned as President of the World Zionist Organization when the Congress rejected Bevin's proposal for the London conference. As a sign of respect the post of president was left vacant, and by default, leadership of the Zionist Organization fell to the aggressive David Ben-Gurion. Sixteen months hence, out of office, divested of position and a future, Chaim Weizmann would play a fateful role in the birth of the Jewish State. History would then reward him with the task of appealing at the 11th hour to the President of the United States for vital American support.

On February 15, 1947, seeing no possibility for a peaceful settlement, Bevin announced Britain's intention to give up the Palestine Mandate, relinquishing "the Question of Palestine" over to the United Nations, itself created two years earlier. The UN General Assembly met in special session on May 9 and set up an eleven-nation special committee on Palestine (UNSCOP). The Arabs announced their refusal to cooperate with the committee. The British Foreign Ministry showed no interest, expecting that after UNSCOP's failure the General Assembly would call upon Britain to return to make order out of chaos. But both the United States and the Jewish Agency held high hopes for the committee and both backed it fully.

UNSCOP began its work in June 1947, as terrorism and British counterterrorism reached new heights of insanity. The British made one *faux pas* after another. While UNSCOP was in Palestine, Bevin committed the worst blunder when he ordered the 4,554 refugees of the Aliyah Bet ship *Exodus 1947* to return to Germany. That single act brought widespread sympathy for the Zionist cause, for it dramatized the homelessness of the victims of Nazism and the empty-headedness of British policy.

As UNSCOP met in Jerusalem, it heard much the same testimony that had been presented to the British commissions preceding it. The Hadassah Council in Palestine presented a memo on behalf of 218,000 members in forty-seven out of forty-eight US states (only Idaho was not represented among the hundreds of chapters). Hadassah's Zionist effort, said the memo, had transferred twenty-five million dollars to Palestine since 1921. In that time, infant mortality had been reduced dramatically, trachoma was no longer epidemic and all in all, "Palestine is the most healthful area in the Middle East." The memo ended, "The Jewish women represented by Hadassah will continue their unremitting efforts to help re-create Palestine, the Jewish National Home, as a democratic Jewish Commonwealth." UNSCOP visited Scopus on June 27 and heard Dr. Yassky say, "Everyone is welcome here."

Back in New York on September 1, UNSCOP voted seven to three, with one abstention, for partition. Its plan was much less than that suggested to the British by Ben-Gurion, but it was by far the best ever offered the Jews. The UNSCOP map cut the country into six interlocking segments — three Arab and three Jewish — and made Jerusalem an international city.

In Zurich, the Zionist General Council, meeting in place of the Zionist Congress, accepted the plan. The Arabs announced they would go to war to kill the plan. The British said they would leave Palestine so the two sides could fight over the map. As it turned out, UNSCOP not only created two states but unintentionally drew borders that were battle lines for the inevitable war.

For the next two months the UN was a labyrinth of confusion. The battle to win sufficient votes in the UN General Assembly was fought by Jews on all continents. Jewish Agency representatives used every stratagem, every contact, every argument to get the necessary two-thirds majority. In the United States, the head of the Jewish Agency delegation, Moshe Shertok, had the help of a vast array of volunteers. Booming out over all else was the voice of Rabbi Abba Hillel Silver. Working in every single state to turn public opinion were nearly 250,000 Hadassah members. "We had something no one else had — grassroots," President Judith Epstein said. "We were everywhere. I remember one period when I had a midnight call

234 • IT TAKES A DREAM

from the Hadassah president of Philadelphia. 'We are still in the office,' she said. 'What can we do? We don't want to go home if there is something we can do.' They had written personal letters to every member of Congress, phoned, sent telegrams, and still they wanted to know what they could do!"

As if to anticipate the historic events that were now about to occur, Hadassah, meeting at its thirty-third convention in Atlantic City in late October 1947, adopted a record budget — $4,070,000. Speaking to the convention, Guatemala's UNSCOP delegate Dr. Jorge Garcia-Granados compared the opposing positions: "There is a fundamental reason why the Jewish case is stronger than the Arab case. It is not a question of nationalism fighting for a land or a territory. It is a question of giving thousands of human beings hope and a reason for living...The human case is unanswerable."

Retiring President Epstein turned her office over to veteran political fighter Rose Halprin with a simple statement of Hadassah philosophy: "From the very beginning of Hadassah — whether it was the establishment of a playground or the introduction of new hospital methods — we have always had before us the compulsion of a great idea — The Jewish State."

One month later, on Saturday, November 29, 1947, the UN General Assembly firmly implanted the seeds of a Jewish State in Palestine by passing the partition resolution, 33 to 13, five more votes than the required two-thirds majority. Ten states abstained. The news hit Palestine late at night. Unrestrained joy splashed over the *yishuv* and over Jews everywhere. The Arabs called for a day of mourning and the Grand Mufti, appearing on the scene like an evil genie, called a three-day strike.

After the rejoicing over the UN decision, individual survival in Palestine became a matter of fortitude, luck and ingenuity. One Hadassah board member who saw the radical change on partition night was Palestine Committee Chairman Bertha Schoolman who had arrived only a week earlier to help plan a program for educating and settling 6,000 Youth Aliyah children about to be freed from the Cyprus camps.

On November 30 a reign of terror erupted on Mount Scopus. An ambulance on the way to Scopus was fired on at Nashashibi Bend in the Sheikh Jarrah Quarter. Located between the Jewish part of the city and Scopus, a half-mile narrow roadway that wound through this Arab Quarter was to be the scene of high tragedy and to paralyze Scopus as a regional center of healing and education for two decades. The Nashashibi house, a colonnaded manor dwelling of a wealthy Arab family, was to serve as a focal point from which continual attacks were launched on traffic. Several hundred yards farther on, at an L-curve that led down into a valley at the bottom of Scopus, was another manor house that belonged to the Mufti and was set back from the road in a lovely garden. Rented by well-known Arab nationalists George and Kate Antonius, the dwelling was known as the Antonius House and would be another key point for the tragedy to come.

Arab rioting, under the Mufti's orders, broke out elsewhere on that last day in November. Two buses were gunned down near Lydda Airport; one of the six killed was Hadassah pathologist Nehama Zelutovsky. That night Arabs began shooting at buses on the #9 route to Scopus. On the first day of the Arab general strike, frenzied young Arabs stormed out of Jerusalem's Jaffa Gate, targeted their attacks on workshops in the New Commercial Center where they looted, burned, stabbed and stoned, and then headed for the center of the city. British troops did not interfere until the mobs approached downtown. There, Haganah men stood ready to make their first open stand, but the British arrested sixteen Jews and only then moved to stop the mob. Major attacks were launched against Jewish neighborhoods and against isolated settlements in all sections of the country. A torch having struck tinder, the Jewish leadership ordered "a census" of all seventeen- to twenty-five-year-olds for "public service." Eventually, men up to age fifty-five would be mobilized.

For the first five months of the war in Jerusalem, Scopus would remain open but would increasingly assume the role of a military hospital.

Hadassah's local governing bodies — the Council in Palestine and the

Medical Organization Board — met almost daily for the remainder of the crisis. Director Yassky was abroad from November until February to attend the Hadassah national convention and to help plan Palestine's first medical school. That left the direction of Hadassah Hospital activities to British-born Deputy Medical Director Eli Davis and Deputy Administrator Mendel Krupnik. Acting for the National Board, the Council in Palestine was chaired by Hebrew University Chancellor Magnes and in mid-1948 by Ethel Agronsky (Agron). Bertha Schoolman's presence in Jerusalem gave the Board an extra representative.

As fighting became certain, the legislature of the *yishuv* — the Va'ad Leumi — immediately urged Hadassah to prepare for the worst and appointed a national medical board on which Eli Davis was a representative.

Uppermost in the minds of the Hadassah people was the security of the road to Scopus. Within the week following the UN partition vote, Davis reported that all departments in the medical center had augmented emergency services. Although the Hadassah station wagon had a military escort through Sheikh Jarrah, only essential journeys were being made. On matters concerning Scopus, the University (represented by Administrator David Werner Senator) and Hadassah acted in unison. On December 8, Senator and Davis asked the police to station more guards at the hospital and to provide Hadassah's staff with arms. The request for more security was made the day after a bus, jammed with Scopus-bound workers, narrowly missed destruction when a grenade crashed through one window and went out another to explode on the ground. But twenty bullets hit the bus, wounding two doctors. Bus #9's windows were thenceforth screened with steel netting. One hundred staff members bedded down at Scopus rather than risk the ride. Patients went elsewhere for treatment. Despite the increase in war casualties, the number of admissions on Scopus declined in December. Davis judiciously set up an independent operating theater at Hadassah's downtown clinic.

Constant attacks indicated that the Arabs were intent on neutralizing

Scopus to make an assault on Jewish Jerusalem that much easier. Before the year ended five doctors miraculously escaped injury when their car was set on fire on the Scopus road. But fifteen staff members were wounded in an attack on a bus and on December 30, for the first time, the magnificent foyer of the medical center was turned into a clearing station and shock treatment room. In one act of terror, Szold Nursing School professor Hugo Lehrs was murdered by three Arab gunmen at Jerusalem's Hospital for Contagious Diseases while walking in the compound with an Arab doctor and nurse. The Arabs asked them, "Which of you is a Jew?" and when the Arab doctor and nurse stepped aside, Lehrs was slain.

The year ended with another tragedy for Hadassah. On Friday, December 26, Bertha Schoolman and Youth Aliyah director Hans Beyth were returning to Jerusalem from the coast where they observed the arrival of children from camps in Cyprus. The long battle for control of a four-mile stretch of the road from Tel Aviv to Jerusalem was underway. As their convoy headed up the steep Judean Hills past hostile Arab villages, the buses absorbed heavy Arab fire from the crests of the mountains on either side of the serpentine, two-lane highway.

Bertha was riding in a car with Golda Meir and two members of the Jewish Agency. She recalled: "Yitzhak Gruenbaum, one of the Agency men, had a small pistol and he kept shooting back through the window as we drove. Fifteen minutes from Jerusalem the bus ahead of us was hit. Hans was in the bus. He, too, had a gun and shot back. He was a good target when he stood and he was killed." From then on, Bertha shared the management of Youth Aliyah with Moshe Kol, who later joined the Israeli cabinet.

January 1948 began badly. Prospects for a Jewish military victory were dim. Arabs in Palestine outnumbered Jews 1,250,000 to 650,000. Arab armies had a two to one advantage (115,000 to 50,000). Although the Jews had a well-trained core of 20,000 who had fought in World War II, they had only one gun for every four men, no air force and no navy to speak of. The Arabs on the other hand, had planes, ships, tanks and heavy artillery.

They also had defense treaties with Britain and British officers serving in King Abdullah's Arab Legion. The United States clamped an arms embargo on the Middle East in December; in January Britain announced it would supply arms to Egypt, Iraq and Jordan. Secretly, Ben-Gurion sent agents to Prague to buy weapons, but Arab agents were there doing the same and before the arms arrived the fighting could well be finished. The Zionists' position could not have been more grim. Their scattered forces were surrounded on three sides by hostile Arab nations and in the west by an unconcerned sea. Triumph would emerge out of tragedy nevertheless, but at a tremendous price in casualties: 10 percent of the entire Jewish population.

Aware of the looming struggle, Hadassah called an extraordinary meeting of the full National Board on January 4 in New York. Yassky informed the members that all 105 Hadassah doctors in Palestine were at the service of the *yishuv*; in fact, thirty were put into uniform.

In response to the *yishuv*'s request that Hadassah coordinate all medical services for the emergency, the Board voted extra allocations including an immediate grant of $100,000 to help develop the central military hospital at Tel Litwinsky, near Tel Aviv. In so doing, Hadassah became a founder of the Israel Army Medical Corps. By the end of 1948 the extra disbursements would reach nearly $1,000,000.

The first heavy attack against a Jewish settlement outside the Jerusalem area was launched against Kfar Szold, a new kibbutz only 200 yards from the Syrian frontier. Nine hundred Arabs rushed the tiny outpost, but British armor drove off the attackers. Isolated settlements everywhere were pounded.

Battle-hardened by war, riot and plague, Hadassah was on the front lines in two urban areas where the *yishuv* was most vulnerable — Safed and Jerusalem. In the mountain-top town of Safed, center of Jewish mystics for centuries, Hadassah's tuberculosis hospital lay between the Jewish and

Arab quarters. Most of the TB patients were sent home as fighting began and the hospital, the only one in town, was used for casualties. Safed was a key to upper Galilee and the vital waters of the Jordan River. As in Jerusalem, the Arabs began a war of attrition, blowing up houses, firing on traffic, encircling the Jewish area. When the British left in April, they turned over the main forts of the city to the Arabs.

Bitter fighting by the Palmach finally captured Safed on May 11. The hospital cared for 250 casualties.

In January, in the Jerusalem area, the war was rapidly moving in favor of the Arabs. Near Hebron, south of the capital, the four kibbutzim of the Kfar Etzion bloc were under pressure from 1,000 Arabs. A rescue platoon of thirty-five men set out on foot to help the defenders but was massacred on the way. (One was an American volunteer, Moshe Pearlstein, son of Ella, a prominent Hadassah member in Borough Park, Brooklyn.) The Kfar Etzion fighters held out until mid-May and by so doing relieved the pressure on Jerusalem.

In Jerusalem itself, the Arabs doggedly tried to stop the flow of traffic to Scopus. Davis reported to Yassky early in January that the staff no longer had confidence in British assurances of security. While Davis was writing a report to Yassky, he had to stop to read an urgent communication. Then he went back to writing: "We have just been informed…that a car with bullet-proof sides, with 25 of our personnel, an ambulance and a police escort going to Hadassah were attacked near St. George's Road. A bomb was thrown. Shots were fired and a bullet pierced the roof. A student nurse, class of '48, Hannah Gardi, was killed."

Hannah's death was followed by a three-hour battle between the Arabs and the Haganah during which all eight phone lines to the hospital went dead. Morale on Scopus plummeted. After prolonged pleading by Davis and Magnes, the British finally replaced the police with army units on the road. Spirits rose, but not for long.

Rationing went into effect at the Medical center. Nurses pitched in to carry out menial tasks because of the larger number of persons remaining on the hill. As the gravity of the situation became evident, Magnes brought up the possibility, for the first time, of moving off Scopus to downtown Jerusalem. The fainthearted had begun whispering that it might be best to abandon Scopus. But the hospital's management committee at the time firmly decided to stand fast "even though absolute security is no longer possible." They anticipated Jewish Agency Chairman Ben-Gurion who, one month later, appointed David Shaltiel as commander of Jerusalem and gave him orders not to surrender one inch of ground anywhere in Jerusalem. The possibility that the Arabs would launch a frontal attack to capture Scopus was real. With more than 700 persons, mostly civilians, on the hill, the decision to stay put was not a light one. But there is no doubt that it was the right one, since it was instrumental in helping save most of Jerusalem for Israel. Wrote Davis to Hadassah Medical Organization Chairman Etta Rosensohn on January 20:

> The most important fact of all is that the hospital remains open, is carrying on much as usual...Were Mount Scopus cut off, the Arabs would have a very much smaller Jewish area to besiege and against which to deploy their forces.

The Mandate administration was interested only in safeguarding British interests until evacuation. The British stoutly turned down pleas from the Hebrew University to remove an Arab Legion camp stationed a few hundred yards from the Medical center or even to install a "hotline" to the camp from the University. Even less comprehensible was the British refusal to permit the Jews to build a short $88,000 ring road — at Hadassah's expense — that would bypass the Sheikh Jarrah Quarter and Nashashibi Bend.

By the end of January the war in Jerusalem accounted for 300 Jewish casualties. Nearly all were treated at Hadassah. On the night of February 1, Hadassah itself became a casualty. Early in the day Eli Davis escorted a Red Cross delegation through the clinic in Hasolel Street (now Hahavatzelet) and through the Scopus hospital. They parted in high spirits; the delegation complimented Davis on the high level of excellence he had achieved under battle conditions. At 10:58 that night, a stolen British police truck that was parked outside the offices of *The Palestine Post*, the country's English-language daily, exploded with tremendous force and laid waste to the building. The explosion rattled windows two miles away. The Hadassah clinic across the street was badly damaged as was the entire street. Two British deserters hired by the Mufti and an Arab accomplice were implicated. Three persons were killed and fifty were injured.

By February 3, Yassky had returned from America and was again at his post. Upset that his beautiful medical center had to be turned into an army base hospital, he recalled in a letter to Etta Rosensohn how British medical personnel had benefited from the hospital during the Second World War and how British personnel "were now forced by a treacherous policy of their Government to take the road of treason." However, he added, "Mount Scopus should not be abandoned." He gave orders to brick up operating theaters and halls, fortify windows, build blast walls, dig wells for water reservoirs and build storage huts for food stocks. Yassky was preparing for a siege — and none too soon. The Arabs intensified their attacks. No one was spared; they even exploded a mine under a truck escorting a funeral.

The Trojan Horse trick used against *The Palestine Post* was to be used twice more inside Jewish Jerusalem, with devastating effect. Shortly after dawn on February 22, the British deserters were back with more Mufti agents. This time they planted three trucks, each loaded with one ton of TNT, in the middle of Ben Yehuda Street, the city's main shopping district. The resulting detonation smashed the thoroughfare along its entire length, crumbled six-story buildings, killed at least fifty-two and wounded 123. Hadassah took the seventy most serious cases and while they were being treated, the hospital itself came under attack. A guard on the hospital roof was killed and a bullet narrowly missed Yassky's head as he worked at his desk.

In the home of *The Palestine Post* editor Gershon Agron, who thirty years earlier had greeted the AZMU in London, a secret Haganah listening post had been set up to monitor British police traffic.[1] Among those on duty on the morning of the Ben Yehuda bombing were two members of Junior Hadassah. One, Betty Schoffman Levin, recorded the conversation between a patrol and headquarters in the wake of the Ben Yehuda bombing. When the officer at the scene asked for instructions, British Headquarters ordered, "Leave the scene."

On March 11, the World Zionist Organization headquarters in the center of Jerusalem was blown up when a car bomb exploded in the compound. The Arab driver of the US Consulate had parked it there. Among the thirteen killed was Leib Jaffe, a founder of Keren Hayesod, the financial arm of the WZO.

Mines on the roads and twenty-five-pound shells causing heavy casualties moved Magnes and Davis to ask the Board in New York to request State Department intervention. The University's David Werner Senator addressed a confidential memo to Magnes saying that since the British were unwilling to provide adequate security, the presence of the attackers "makes active Jewish defense unfeasible." Magnes turned to the British commander of Jerusalem, Brigadier C.P. Jones, with a new plea for help. Jones replied through a subordinate that nothing could be done about the Sheikh Jarrah Quarter and fatuously suggested that the Arab and Jewish medical associations should work out a deal. By the end of February, Magnes cabled the National Board, "Road impassable." Hadassah replied, "Preparing memorandum to present to State Department."

By February the road was virtually closed. Occasionally a convoy from Tel Aviv managed to reach Jerusalem with supplies, albeit with heavy casualties. On March 27, a convoy that tried to break through was

---

1 Agron, who had emigrated from the US, often hosted top British officials. The British never discovered the Haganah monitoring room located next to the luxurious living room where they sat drinking cocktails and discussing politics. Ethel Agron, Gershon's wife, was Hadassah Council in Israel chairman in Jerusalem.

decimated. With some exceptions the British, who were ostensibly responsible for security, gave the Arabs a free hand, while restricting the Haganah.

A four-week truce saved the Jewish population on June 11 when only several days' food and water remained. Had it not been for the truce the 70,000 Jews of Jerusalem would have capitulated. Jerusalem had a higher ratio of casualties than anywhere else in the country, proportionately five times higher than the casualties suffered by London during the World War II blitz, although the injuries were similar: multiple bullet damage to chest and abdomen and ruptured organs. Nearly 10 percent of the city's Jewish population suffered casualties.

In makeshift facilities, Hadassah cared for 2,800 wounded up to May 15, 1948. Most were saved only because Hadassah was well-equipped with the latest antibiotics, had excellent operating theaters and specially-trained physicians and nurses to staff them around the clock.

In his detailed account of Jerusalem during the War of Independence, "The Faithful City," Military Governor Dov Joseph wrote, "At the center of the whole (health) effort was Hadassah...Hadassah's doctors, nurses and staff workers served Jerusalem with selfless devotion."

Zionist fortunes elsewhere had reached their nadir. At Lake Success, New York, the United Nations grappled unsuccessfully with the Palestine problem. Now that partition was decided upon, the UN was at a loss to find a way to ensure its implementation. The US State Department, never happy with the resolution, tried to convince the UN to retreat on partition. US delegate Warren Austin declared in February that the UN Charter did not empower the Security Council to enforce the resolution. One month later he suggested that statehood for Jews and Arabs be postponed and replaced by a temporary UN trusteeship. Twice the United States would reverse its position on the question of trusteeship. In Palestine, the fighting *yishuv* looked with disbelief over its shoulder at America's acrobatics.

Fearing a political disaster at the very moment of triumph, Chaim Weizmann rushed to New York on February 4 hoping to see President

Truman. But Truman, weary from constant pressure by Zionists, held Weizmann at bay. Then, in what is now a well-told tale, the latter finally got to the White House through the intervention of Truman's gutsy former haberdashery partner, Eddie Jacobson. On March 18, Weizmann, in the greatest performance of his career, convinced Truman of the urgent need for a Jewish State. The overriding argument was humanitarian. Multitudes in Europe were heading for Zion's gate and would go nowhere else, he said. The following day Austin put forth his trusteeship proposal. The State Department simply had not informed Truman of the change. In retrospect the State Department's action was fortunate, apparently sealing Truman's decision to take his own independent course. Spitting fire at the "striped-pants boys," Truman asked an aide how this could have happened after his assurance to Weizmann that he was for partition. The following month, during Passover, Weizmann was told secretly by the White House that Truman would stand by his promise. The elder statesman kept it to himself but advised the *yishuv's* leaders to go on with the planned declaration of the State come what may. Within eleven minutes after the State of Israel was established on May 14, the White House startled Washington and the world by announcing *de facto* recognition. The US thus became the first nation to grant status to the Jewish nation.

THE CONVOY

At 2:05 pm on March 2, 1948 the operator at the Hadassah exchange in Jerusalem heard an Arab voice warn that the hospital would be blown up within 90 minutes. The explosion did not happen but it was a clear giveaway of Arab intentions. Two days later, Hadassah President Rose Halprin and Denise Tourover called on the State Department and the British embassy in Washington to secure Scopus, then followed up with strong protests to UN Secretary-General Trygve Lie and the International Red Cross. Shortly afterward, commander of Palestine Arab forces Abdul Kader Husseini spoke, on the record, to news correspondents: "Since Jews have been attacking us and blowing up our houses containing women and children from bases in Hadassah Hospital and Hebrew University, I have given orders to occupy or even demolish them." Showing he meant business, he placed a cannon on the roof of the Rockefeller Museum of Archaeology opposite Mount Scopus and began using armor-piercing ammunition and electrically-detonated mines against Scopus traffic. Surgeon Edward Joseph told Yassky that he could no longer take the responsibility of transferring cases to Scopus. Yassky replied sharply: "The time has not yet come to evacuate Mount Scopus...There is no security anywhere."

But reality won out. Yassky carried on negotiations quietly for the use of the Anglican Mission Hospice a few blocks away from the Hasolel Street clinic that Hadassah ran in downtown Jerusalem. On March 15, ten beds were set up for maternity cases and the site became known as Hadassah "A." A century earlier, Jews in Jerusalem were running away from mission hospitals; now they were running back into them.

By mid-March, the Hadassah Emergency Committee resolved that supplies would no longer be concentrated on Scopus but would be dispersed in the center of town. A meeting (held at the home of Myriam Granott, later chairman of the Hadassah Council in Israel,) considered the possibility, never implemented, of returning to the old Rothschild building where Hadassah's vocational school was then located. Magnes noted that the Red Cross had offered to put Scopus under its flag on condition that Hadassah and the University agreed to demilitarize the area. To Hadassah, the Red Cross banner was the white flag of surrender and its leaders persistently refused the proposal.

Yassky asked Bertha Schoolman to take a confidential note to Jewish Agency Treasurer Eliezer Kaplan in Tel Aviv. Unless the Agency did something at once to secure the road to Scopus, the memo said, the hospital would have to cease operations. But Hadassah was determined to remain as long as possible.

In Jewish Jerusalem the supply situation was so bad that Jews were reduced to scrounging in the fields for a weed called *khubeizeh* to supplement their diets, which now consisted of a few slices of bread, an occasional egg, a handful of noodles, some jam and an orange. On Scopus and in the Hasolel clinic, reported Davis, "Our surgeons have been on the job night and day since the end of November, and not one of them has had a weekend off since then." Magnes informed British Chief Secretary Sir Henry Gurney, "I am afraid our devoted doctors, nurses and patients are being subjected to a strain too great to bear."

Yassky prepared an evacuation plan for Scopus. At a joint Hadassah-Hebrew University meeting, he told Golda Meir that unless a minimum of three convoys could safely pass daily, the hospital would close. The only alternative was to accept the Red Cross offer. Meir agreed to raise the subject of Scopus at a Zionist Executive meeting in Tel Aviv. Meanwhile, the Zionist General Council, popularly called the Actions Committee, was in session to debate the proclamation of the Jewish State and to authorize the formation of a cabinet and legislature for the new state's functioning. For that historic session, Hadassah had flown in a delegation from New York: President Rose Halprin, Judith Epstein, Tamar de Sola Pool and Rebecca Shulman. Rose asked Yassky to join them in Tel Aviv, but he was too anxious about Scopus's fate to leave. On April 10, he replied:

> The situation in Jerusalem is very serious and that of Scopus much more so. I do not exaggerate when I say that 100,000 Jews of Jerusalem depend on Hadassah's functioning somehow, somewhere. I am very pessimistic about Scopus...It is our duty to prepare emergency arrangements in the city. We will do our best to hang on.

To Bertha Schoolman, who was to leave for the United States on April 12, he reported, "One convoy is an absurd situation. I am afraid we will not be able to continue to operate the Hospital very much longer...I hope that we will meet again in not a too distant future."

The hope was not to be. Three days later, Dr. Haim Yassky was dead, shot through the liver in an Arab ambush on the road that he and Hadassah's leaders had tried valiantly to make safe.

Five days earlier, on April 8, in the northern outskirts of Jerusalem, the Irgun attacked the Arab village of Deir Yassin, a base for Arab irregulars. As many as 250 Arabs, mostly civilians, were slain. The convoy ambush was not retaliation for the Deir Yassin attack since the Arabs had planned the ambush beforehand, but the Irgun's massacre was cited to justify the Arab attack. The Arab leadership had three goals in attacking the Mount Scopus convoy: to strike a decisive blow that would force the Jews to abandon Scopus and make Jewish Jerusalem more vulnerable, to destroy the will of the Jews to resist an Arab invasion of the city proper and to deprive the Jews of their largest medical facility. And there was a fourth factor. On April 8, in hand-to-hand fighting for control of Qastel Hill, which dominated the Tel Aviv-Jerusalem highway, the Arab hero and ace military commander, Abdul Kader Husseini, was killed by Meir Carmiel, a mobilized Hadassah worker. Shortly thereafter, Carmiel himself died in action.

Conditions for an ambush were ideal in the Sheikh Jarrah Quarter. Over a stretch of a few hundred yards between Nashashibi Bend and Antonius House, there were stone walls on either side of the narrow road. The convoy would be traveling slowly uphill at that point; ahead at Antonius House there was a ninety-degree bend. Caught in that stretch of road, the vehicles would be tin ducks in a shooting gallery. Intervention could come only from the Haganah escort and from a small unit of Scots' Highland Light Infantry stationed in Antonius House. But the British would not shoot unless they received orders to do so, a possibility that was remote.

On April 11, the British military commander in Jerusalem assured questioners that the road was safe but, because of the Deir Yassin attack, the area was tense. Even as he spoke, the Arabs were consulting expert British officer friends on the logistics of the operation. Subsequent events indicate that the Arabs had an understanding whereby they would not be disturbed in their mission so long as they did not shoot at British soldiers. The Arabs could not — and would not — lose this one.

On April 12, Deputy Medical Director Eli Davis returned to town from Scopus. Wryly he commented, "It was not comfortable on the way down." Customarily Yassky and he took turns up on the hill, but on the evening of the 12th, Yassky had a social engagement and did not go up that morning. Gynecologist Yehuda Bromberg was with him that evening. "I was struck by the great depression which had overcome Dr. Yassky," Bromberg wrote three days later. "It was clear that his depression arose from his deep concern over the fate of our hospital. The dangers confronting the hospital because of the difficulties of transport were clear to him, as was the fear of the destruction of the hospital to which he dedicated his life."

On Tuesday, April 13, the largest Scopus convoy yet assembled was to take personnel, patients, visitors, workers and supplies up to the hospital and university. At 8:00 am people began converging on the clinic in Hasolel Street where a University bus and a Hadassah bus, both lightly armored, waited. Three blocks away, outside Hadassah "A," two armored ambulances were parked. Haim and Fanny Yassky entered one of the ambulances, a converted Dodge truck, which only the day before had been painted a glaring white with a big red Star of David on the body.

Back at the clinic the buses quickly filled. Hadassah Social Director Esther Passman Epstein, her arms brimming over with magazines and sweets for the patients, was so determined to get to her wards that she left behind her beloved son, David, who had been injured while carrying out a school experiment. At the clinic, Esther met noted cancer specialist Leonid Doljansky who urged Esther to sit beside him. Three weeks previously, she had become his "mascot" when she moved next to him on a bus and a bullet pierced her hat. Had he, the much taller of the two, been sitting in her place he would have died. But this day Esther was not permitted to board the bus and the ill-fated doctor rode without his lucky mascot. Swearing under her breath, Esther ran three blocks to find a seat on one of the ambulances; but she would live to tell about it.

Dr. Moshe Ben-David, administrator of the planned medical school, got a late start from home, hailed a cab, finally caught one of the buses, sealing his own fate. Shelev Truck Company manager Moshe Lazar had a safe seat in the six-ton Brockway truck of veteran driver Benjamin Adin, but in a move that cost him his life, Lazar changed at the last moment to one of the buses.

By 9:00 am the vehicles were on their way. Three trucks filled with supplies for the hospital and for fortifications joined the two Haganah escort cars, two ambulances and two buses. The exact number of people in the vehicles is not known because precise lists were not kept, but there were well over 100.

At the final checkpost outside Hadassah's Tipat Halav station, which served as a Haganah outpost, the convoy halted to await the customary order from the Haganah to proceed. British inspector Robert J. Webb, chief of the Mea Shearim police station, said the road was safe. Webb was known as a friend to both Arabs and Jews and was said to be well-rewarded by both. One job Webb did for the Jews outside his official duties was to drive over the road to Scopus before a convoy left. Webb would stop at Nashashibi Bend, look around and sometimes wait there till the convoy passed. On this day, Hillman said, he called Webb as usual and Webb answered that the way was clear. But Webb did not station himself at Nashashibi Bend on April 13 and all efforts made by the Haganah to contact him throughout the rest of the day were fruitless.

Commander of the convoy was Jerusalem-born Lieutenant Asher "Zizi" Rahav, a British army sergeant during World War II. Now in Company Noam of the Jerusalem Haganah, the city's only Jewish unit that wore uniforms and black berets, Rahav's assignment was to escort convoys in the Jerusalem area in an armored Ford truck.

It was 9:30 am. Rahav was in the lead in his escort vehicle with ten men and two young Haganah hitchhikers. "When we proceeded a short way through Arab territory on Nablus Road, near a mosque, I had an odd feeling that something was wrong, because there was no traffic. I thought of turning back but instead I told my men to load their weapons and keep their eyes open."

The car had peepholes through which the gunners could shoot and a winged roof of meshed steel covered by canvas.

"Step on it," Rahav told his civilian driver. At the first turn in the road the Arab grocery shop was shuttered — another bad omen. The cars began to climb. Ahead Zizi saw Nashashibi Bend curving like a snake. Rahav held his breath. Through his peephole, he spied the movements of Arabs wearing green Iraqi uniforms with bandoliers. To his left, Rahav noticed that the road was broken. The driver had to swing slightly right. It was 9:45 on Rahav's watch. Suddenly the Ford truck shook violently, throwing the men forward. A mine was electrically detonated five feet in front of them, creating a narrow four-foot-deep ditch. The car's front wheels nosed into the hole and the car settled at a steep angle. The mesh roof and canvas slid back, partly off the vehicle, obscuring the view of the rest of the convoy. "Bullets came through the armor like bees swarming around us," Rahav recalled later. Zizi shot holes in the canvas to see what was happening to the convoy behind. He saw the last vehicles trying to turn around. At Nashashibi Bend, two British armored cars blocked the retreat. Rahav gave orders to his armorer, Baruch Nussbaum, to fire a few bursts at the British cars to get them to move out of the way. He did not know that in one of those cars, sitting as a spectator, was Lieutenant-General G.H.A. MacMillan, commander of all British forces in Palestine. MacMillan ordered his driver to move away from the convoy. Two days later, MacMillan would reply to a protest by University Chancellor Magnes in words that unintentionally admitted British lack of assistance to the beleaguered Hadassah staff in the convoy tragedy:

> I myself motored through the area, passing under the fire of an automatic weapon in a Jewish armored car at 9:45 on my way to Kalandia [Jerusalem's airport]…I assumed that the situation was clearing up and my inference at the time was that it would have cleared up much quicker, had the Jewish armored car stopped firing.

Five vehicles managed to extricate themselves and return to Jewish quarters. The Haganah escort car in the rear, its tires punctured, inexplicably turned tail and returned to Jerusalem. Driving blindly with only a crack to see through, Benjamin Adin reversed, advanced, reversed, backed into the wall of the Nashashibi House and finally turned his six-ton Brockway toward the city. His foot brakes were gone, his tires were flat, the steering wheel worked only partially. On the floor of the cabin was a weeping male passenger who had hopped on at the last moment in an effort to see his wife and newborn son on Scopus. "I never shall see them again," he cried repeatedly. Adin pushed his pedal to the floor and arrived safely at Mandelbaum Gate where his passenger fell out of the cab in a deep faint.

The driver of the larger of the two ambulances, Yosef Levy, was wounded in the head. Surgeon Edward Joseph took a quick look, found it was only superficial and urged him to get moving toward Scopus. Reported Joseph, "We thought the driver was going on but instead he wisely turned the car around and returned. It was the first to get back." Dr. Joseph crawled to join the Haganah men who were trying to edge close to the besieged convoy:

> We were being attacked by a tremendous amount of shooting. It was impossible to lift one's head. The bullets were whizzing everywhere. I asked the soldier nearest me, 'Are these Arabs shooting at us?' He replied, 'No. They are English soldiers.' I knew it had to be true because it was the kind of shooting that only a proper army could do. They were shooting at the Haganah boys. If they had not, we could have reached the convoy.

The surgeon then joined a few men who had been in the Haganah vehicle that retreated and ran to the roof of the Tipat Halav station. Esther Passman Epstein, who had been in Joseph's ambulance, joined the men. With his old pistol, Joseph ran from roof to roof trying to get close enough to get a clear shot. It was a hopeless attempt. As the ambush appeared to be succeeding, Arab volunteers from the region ran to the scene to get in on the kill. Esther could only sob at the end of the day, "It was horrible to see."

Blood was beginning to flow in Zizi Rahav's thinly-armored escort car. Private Shlomo Mizrahi got two bullets in the stomach and fell. Rahav himself caught a steel splinter in the temple; his eye swelled and blood gushed. He kept shooting, aiming with his one good eye. Around noontime one of the hitchhiking Haganah young women, Shoshana Ben-

Ari of Kibbutz Yagur, rose from the floor to help a wounded man, was hit in the mouth by a bullet and died shortly thereafter. At 12:15, Zizi dispatched his armorer, Baruch Nussbaum, to Antonius House about 200 yards farther on to get help from the Highland Light Infantry officers who were observing the battle, their heavy weapons silent. Baruch, who had a slight limp from a case of childhood polio, jumped into the deep ditch made by the mine and crawled along the wall. His body was later found in a wadi in Arab territory.

Back in Jerusalem proper at Haganah headquarters, Commander David Shaltiel called twenty-one-year old Baruch Gilboa, who had arrived in Jerusalem early that morning from Tel Aviv. Gilboa was a commander of an armored unit that had escorted over 150 trucks of supplies to the city, following the capture of Qastel Hill on the city's outskirts. Shaltiel ordered him to take some men in his armored car to the Sheikh Jarrah Quarter and try to tow out the four vehicles under Arab fire.

It was obvious that Shaltiel's intelligence from the scene of battle was faulty; otherwise he would not have ordered a lone escort car into that trap. Gilboa and his men were fatigued from fourteen hours on the road. His civilian driver, apparently shocked by the battle, saw the ditch made by the mine across the road, decided to try to drive over it. He put on speed as he came up to the left of Zizi Rahav's embattled vehicle and landed with a thud in the ditch, injuring some of the passengers. Had he gone to the right of Rahav, he would have missed the ditch, gone on to Antonius House and the men could then have engaged Arabs who were firing at the convoy from a house across the street. Now the two Haganah cars were stuck at the head of the convoy.

Close behind was Yassky's ambulance, its tires shot out, standing breadthwise across the road where it was protected by the two Haganah cars just ahead. About fifty yards behind were the two buses. They were the most open to attack from both sides of the road.

One attempt to extricate the buses was made by a British friend of the Haganah. Major Jack Churchill, of the Highland Light Infantry, drove an open-fronted armored car to the scene on his own initiative and was about to put a tow-line on one of the buses when his driver was killed by a bullet in the neck. Churchill pulled in the tow and drove out of the area, but before doing so, banged on one bus and shouted to the occupants to risk getting out and returning with him. He later reported they had refused to do so.

By early afternoon the two buses were sieves. Only one man from each vehicle survived. Shalom Nissan, a university student, jumped when the Arabs began lobbing grenades at his stricken bus. Miraculously, he dodged the rain of fire and ran all the way to Mount Scopus where he was to provide the first on-scene account of events.

In the other bus was a guard, Nathan Sandowsky, who told a ghastly story that has since been verified. Nathan said that the driver was wounded from the initial fire and lost control. The second driver was lightly wounded but froze from fear and could not function. The bus had three lookouts inside. One was Nathan. Another was Dr. Avraham Freiman, lecturer in Jewish Law, and a third was university employee Zev Mariasin.

> From the rear opening I saw that all the time the British army passed in large convoys. They continued on their way. We shouted 'Help! We have wounded women and men!' But they did not stop. Armored cars of the police arrived and stood for a time without extending any help whatever and without even communicating with us. We were sure that at least they would not let the Arabs approach so close as to burn the vehicles.

From inside the buses, Arabs shouting, "*Minshan Deir Yassin*" (For Deir Yassin) could be heard clearly over and over again. Nathan reported that the arrival of Gilboa's armored car caused rejoicing in the bus. "We saw that our people were at last coming. But the Arabs derived courage from the fact that the police and army cars which passed did not raise a finger."

From the early hours on, bullets found their marks. Gas fumes began to seep in as the Arabs made ready to burn the bus. Molotov cocktails were being thrown. Some of the unhurt passengers tried to make a dash to safety. But the Arabs, only a few yards away, picked them off as they jumped out. As four men ran, a girl in the bus cried, "They are being killed." Nathan deliberated:

> I sat at the side of the opening of the bus with a scalpel — my only weapon. Fire started from the rear of the bus. There were cries, 'We are burning alive.' I dived. The blade of the scalpel broke. I ran the length of the road zigzag. I passed the ambulance and approached an escort car, waving the broken knife in my hand. I pounded on the door shouting, 'I am one of you.' The door opened. Inside all the men were dead or wounded.

It was now about 2:30 pm. Inside Gilboa's armored car, Sandowsky saw Safed-born David Bar-Ner with a grenade in his hand. The pin was out and the grenade primed to explode. Recalls Bar-Ner:

> When Sandowsky climbed in we were waiting for the final assault. It was now a tradition in the Haganah not to be caught alive. We had five dead. Gilboa was paralyzed by a head wound. I had three bullets in my arm. I piled up the six grenades left in the car and pulled the pin on one to blow us up if the Arabs tried to take us prisoner. We had plenty of ammunition left but there was no one left to fire it. Then Sandowsky appeared. His face was blackened from the fire in his bus. He grabbed the grenade from my hand and threw it outside where it went off. Then he took one of our two machine-guns and kept shooting short bursts. That kept the Arabs at bay since they knew we could still shoot back. He saved our lives, for soon after, the British picked us up.

One further feeble and futile attempt to save the convoy was made in the afternoon by the Haganah. Squad Sergeant Haim Kimron took an armored car to Sheikh Jarrah to tow out the vehicles. As Kimron entered the ambush he saw the buses burning. His vehicle stalled in a ditch. Almost immediately, two occupants were killed and three wounded from the fire overhead. He wrote, "Hysterically, I ordered my driver to get the hell out of the ditch. He reversed and we went around to the right of the road, past the two armored cars and beat it up to Mount Scopus. My tires were shot full of holes."

No one knew yet what was happening in the white ambulance with the big red Magen David. Because its armor was the thickest of all the vehicles, this wagon was the safest place to be in that corridor of hell. Next to driver Zecharya Levitan sat Yassky. Behind him on the benches were Fanny Yassky, six doctors, a nurse and a wounded soldier. The ambulance, behind the two armored cars, was a poor target for the Arabs and so it absorbed the least punishment. Yassky, who sat by the driver because he had a revolver and could more easily use it, concerned himself with appraising the situation by looking through the tiny window in the vehicle.

"Every time he opened the window," Yehuda Bromberg reported later, "a rain of shots was fired at him. At 2:00 pm, Yassky informed us that everyone had been killed in the burning buses."

After the buses turned into pyres, Yassky announced, "Now our time has come. No escape from our fate is left. We must bid one another farewell."

He took leave of his wife, thanking her for the happy life that they had lived. At 2:30, Yassky was wounded in the liver by a bullet that must have ricocheted through the ambulance's engine.

"I'm hit," he said and then after a few minutes of continuous chatter, he whispered to Fanny, "*Shalom*, my beloved." Pediatrician Yehuda Mattot, who sat on a bench behind Yassky, recalls: "Fanny Yassky took off her blouse and with it I bandaged Yassky. Only an immediate blood transfusion and an operation could have saved him." Yassky lost consciousness and was dead five minutes later. There was nothing the six physicians and one nurse in the ambulance could do. Ironically, there was not even a first aid kit in the vehicle.

Fanny remained strong. Someone else began to weep. Fanny asked, "Why do you cry? Soon we shall follow him."

Zecharya the driver suddenly got up, opened the door and jumped out. He was shot dead a few yards away.

Dermatologist Haim Cohen asked gynecologist Bruno Berkovitz to join him in an attempt to run for it. But Dr. Ullmann said firmly, "Cohen, we have survived this together from nine o'clock. You can wait another few hours."

Mattot, who missed certain death by changing at the last minute from a bus to the ambulance, tried his luck a second time. He recalled:

> I thought that if I stayed put it would be the end. My wife later thought I did it because I could not stand to be without a cigarette. I jumped into the ditch and I began to crawl. The Arabs spotted me and began shooting. I got one bullet next to my spine. I kept going and got to Antonius House where the British troops welcomed me. Just opposite on the other side of the road were Arabs, apparently the leaders of the whole thing. The British took me in and bandaged me. They were apologetic. They said they were a small unit and they could not do anything. They had been asking for reinforcements but could not get any. I was not able to convince the British to do anything for the convoy.

Throughout the day, pleas to intercede were directed to the British by the Jewish Agency, the Haganah, Magnes, Davis and others. The British authorities suggested a truce to both sides and waited. The few troops at Antonius House were consistently refused permission to use their heavy machine gun and bazookas; a few bursts from these weapons could have smothered the Arab initiative. Hadassah volunteers monitored the British radio conversations throughout the day. This exchange was noted at a critical point:

> Forward British observer: "The buses are burning. Someone has put out a white flag. Request permission to intercede."
>
> British headquarters: "Reinforcements are on the way. Keep everything steady."

But reinforcements, only a few minutes away, took seven hours to get to the site.

Lieutenant-General MacMillan returned to the site at 4:30 pm. Incredibly, he admitted to Magnes by letter that he had been uninformed all day about events in Sheikh Jarrah. Wrote MacMillan:

> I was surprised…to find heavy firing in progress on the spot and my own car, which had been back to barracks and returned again to meet me, had been pierced by a bullet. On arrival once more on the spot, I found that Brigadier Jones had got the matter in hand and had persuaded the Arabs to stop firing but had not been able to achieve this until after he had been forced to fire heavily upon them and kill fifteen.

At about 4:00 pm, Brigadier Jones had finally been given permission to open fire with bazookas. Another army post fired off a few mortars. Then under a smokescreen, half-tracks were sent in to pick up the survivors. A British Intelligence captain who had befriended the Jews arrived under his own steam from military headquarters at the King David Hotel. A wounded Zizi Rahav was already in Antonius House. When the captain asked Zizi what he could do to help, Zizi requested that the captain return to the scene to bring back the weapons and secret operational papers on the body of one of the men. The captain did just that.

The captain would never forget the scene.

> It was grotesque. People were standing over the body of Dr. Yassky, screaming and yelling, while a little farther back beside the two burned-out buses the dead were piled in heaps. The corpses were burning and it was at least 20 minutes after the shooting finally stopped that someone thought to douse them with water.

Precisely how many were killed or wounded in the convoy? It is unlikely that anyone will ever know. A marble memorial bearing seventy-six names stands near Nashashibi Bend. A seventy-seventh is listed as "Unknown." Later, the number was set at seventy-eight. The bodies were so badly burned that the remains were buried in a common grave in Jerusalem's Sanhedria Cemetery.

Three days after the attack, Hadassah handed the Red Cross a list of thirty persons whose bodies were identified and a list of forty-seven "still unaccounted for." In the mid-1970s an inquiry commission reportedly determined that only twenty-five of the bodies were buried in Sanhedria. Later, Yehoshua Levanon, son of victim Zvi Levanon,[1] located an Arab who claimed to have participated in the ambush. The Arab reportedly said that remains of the twenty-two were buried in an Arab cemetery outside the Old City wall, but officials doubt the veracity of the Arab's statement.

Late in 1996, the Israel Defense Ministry announced it was creating a genetic database as a means of identifying the remains of those buried in Sanhedria. Whether the Ministry could inspect the alleged site in the Arab graveyard was questionable given the prevailing political antagonisms.

The night before the massacre, Rose Halprin and Bertha Schoolman had flown home and heard the news on arrival in New York. Judith Epstein and Rebecca Shulman, who remained in Tel Aviv, were having dinner at

---

1 Palmach veteran Zvi Levanon, 25, the deputy commander of Mount Scopus, was employed by Hadassah in the technical department. He was returning to his post after going home to celebrate Yehoshua's second birthday.

their hotel when a newspaperman came up to their table: "I have terrible news for you. Yassky was killed today."

On her return to New York Rebecca told the Board in New York, "I doubt whether we will be able to use Scopus again soon. I recommend that we start building somewhere else."

To Ethel Agron and Eli Davis the Board cabled in May: "We dedicate ourselves to the task of maintaining services and rebuilding Hadassah."

The British reinforced Antonius House and warned both Jews and Arabs that they could countenance no further military activity in Sheikh Jarrah. Nevertheless, on April 25, the Haganah under a young Palmach officer named Yitzhak Rabin, occupied Nashashibi House. But the next day he was shelled out by the British. The Israelis would not return for good until nineteen years later when, under Chief of Staff Yitzhak Rabin, they occupied the entire Arab sector of Jerusalem.

Shelling and sniping made life on Scopus impossible and the road impassable despite the British presence. Fresh food and water were scarce. Davis had to find a way to get the more than 700 people down and contacted Major Jack Churchill:

> Major Churchill told me there was a slight chance of getting through to Mount Scopus, because the Arabs saw the British meant business. He agreed to make the trip up to Scopus and invited me along. The Major took a jeep and his driver. I sat while he stood in the jeep twirling his stick. He looked as though he were on parade in London. Nothing happened as we went through Sheikh Jarrah. On Scopus we were embraced. We had shown it was possible to get through.

Davis decided on the spot to risk a major evacuation because of the low morale. Ben-Gurion had told Hadassah and University representatives several days before the disaster that the hill was to be held at all costs. But Ahron Brezinsky, who was acting as medical director of the hospital, told Davis, "You cannot hold a front-line with sick people who do not want to stay. The atmosphere here is that of a refugee camp. With all the strategic importance of this place, we must get out with what we can."

Davis returned to town to organize the evacuation. A decision was taken to retain a 50-bed hospital on Scopus, demonstrating that the hospital was not being abandoned.

Davis scrounged the impoverished city for fuel for the partial evacuation. So empty was the city that he was reduced to collecting gasoline from private homes, institutions, friends — bottle by bottle. Four convoys made it. Brought into town were 200 patients, 100 student nurses and 300 staff members, as well as 600 tons of equipment and supplies. Not a shot was fired. Left behind were 150 persons, including eight student nurses who ran the kitchen and forty patients. In the university buildings were another 150 men.

Now in charge of Hadassah's destiny were Davis and Ethel Agron, as chair of the Hadassah Council in Israel. Magnes, broken and sick, shattered by British nonchalance over the convoy ("This happened not out in the desert but in plain sight of Jerusalem," he wrote indignantly to General MacMillan), left Jerusalem for the United States where he died in October 1948.

On May 6, Haim Halevy, who administered Scopus, reported, "The hospital no longer exists for all practical purposes." Water and flour were sufficient for two weeks, power was rationed to only four hours daily and "soon there won't be refrigeration." Compounding the problem were intelligence reports that King Abdullah was about to shell Scopus before making a full-scale assault.

By the beginning of May, Davis and members of the Hadassah Council had managed to set up reasonably good facilities in Jerusalem's Hadassah "A" and two blocks down the street in St. Joseph's Convent, now known as Hadassah "B," but the accommodations were hardly luxurious. St. Joseph's, leased on April 29, had been a school for 600 Arab girls run by French nuns. After shells hit the converted hospital, the top floor was evacuated and patients were moved to the dank basements where there was neither water nor electricity. Shelves that stored potatoes were cleaned and became emergency beds. Nurses knelt on the stone floor to change bandages and physicians sat on the floor to examine patients. Together with "A" and "B," the Straus Health Center and the Hasolel Street Clinic, Hadassah improvised 300 beds, nearly as many as it had on Scopus. Heroic volunteer work temporarily made up the difference. Nurse Madeline Lewin-Epstein, who had come with the AZMU in 1918, turned her large apartment into a twenty-bed hospital. She often braved sniper's bullets and mortars to pick up the wounded in the streets and pull them into her home. Hers was the first military hospital in Jerusalem; many of her patients were wounded underground soldiers who could go nowhere else. British police officials would be sitting in a chair in the dental clinic of her popular husband, Sam Lewin-Epstein, while in the living room, only a few yards away, were the men they were hunting.

At the height of Hadassah's problems, the Old City of Jerusalem fell to the Arabs on May 28. Hadassah had staffed the hospital in the Old City's Jewish Quarter early in the fighting, but the position of the Jews was hopeless against overwhelming numbers of Arabs. They fought until they were too few, too starved, too fatigued to go on. Avraham Laufer, one of the surgeons who was sent into the Jewish Quarter, reported that the top floors of the hospital had been shelled and seventy patients had to share mattresses and wooden benches in a synagogue and in basements. Laufer told of one young soldier who had shrapnel in an eye but refused to wait fifteen minutes for an operation to remove it because the situation at his post was desperate. "An hour later they carried him back. His handsome face was blown away by a shell."

About 1,300 women and children were evacuated to the Jewish side of the city, while the men were taken to a prison camp in the Jordanian desert. Three among the POW's were Hadassah physicians: Egon Rys, Eli Peiser and Laufer. Two weeks later, while Rys was in the prison camp, his wife, Hava, a Hadassah nurse, was killed in the last pre-truce shelling of the city.

The Old City refugees were put up in the abandoned houses of the

Katamon quarter, a large neighborhood of Arab villas that had been conquered in bloody fighting by the Haganah. There, Jerusalem's meager food supplies were tightly rationed by volunteers, who themselves were now on starvation diets. Under the supervision of Sara Bavli, head of Hadassah Nutrition, these 1,300 and twenty thousand others were given frugal daily meals in what was known as a "battle of the calories."

One of the Hadassah volunteers who cared for the Old City refugee mothers and children was Betty Levin. She was given charge of a three-room abandoned apartment in which each corner served as "home" for ten refugees — 120 in all. Recalls Betty:

> They told me that at the end of the fighting in the Old City they fled to a synagogue where they huddled together until the Arab Legion found them. The Legion expelled them with only the nightgowns and slippers they wore. My job was to feed them. In the morning, they got two slices of bread each and, for the children, four teaspoons of jam. One day, a distraught mother threw the bread down and cried, 'My children are filthy: their heads are full of lice. I need soap.'

But there was no soap. Betty remembered that before the siege began, her absentee landlady had locked ten large blocks of laundry soap in a room. Disregarding the mortars exploding around her, she walked back to her apartment, a kilometer distant, broke into the locked room and took the soap back to Katamon. There she sliced each block into sixteen squares. The lice were subdued and peace was restored to the apartment.

In the turbulence of siege, Friday, May 14, 1948 was no more than just another day of hunger and death in Jerusalem. No street celebrations marked David Ben-Gurion's proclamation of the State of Israel in the Tel Aviv Museum. Hardly anyone knew about it until the following day, for few in Jerusalem had electricity and news was passed by word of mouth. Only on Sunday, May 16, did *The Palestine Post* appear with its headline: STATE OF ISRAEL BORN.

The highway to Tel Aviv had been sealed again by the Arab armies. Daily rations were down to starvation levels. The Holy City's only link with the outside world was a small one-engine plane that landed under fire in the Valley of the Cross. While great military advances were being made in the rest of the country, at the end of May, Jerusalem appeared to be doomed. The last of the British had left Jerusalem on May 14 — except for those officers who remained behind to command Abdullah's Arab Legion. Residents of the city knew these officers were in command because the merciless shelling would stop precisely at 4:00 pm daily, so British officers could enjoy their tea. It was during that hour that most Israelis dared to go outside for their rations. Scopus was no exception to the bombardment. The buildings suffered badly, but casualties were few because the underground tunnel between the nursing school and the hospital served as a perfect shelter.

Born under fire was a new Hadassah service for Israel — orthopedic surgery. One of its pioneers was British-born Myer Makin, who had been a medical officer at Normandy in 1944 during the Allied invasion of Nazi Europe. Soon after demobilization in 1946, he joined Hadassah as a surgeon. Battle casualties were nothing new to him. He recalled:

> We worked 24 hours on and 24 hours off. The main trouble was getting to work through the shelling. I would borrow my neighbor's bicycle and dash like hell through the streets. The shelling of Jerusalem was much worse than any I had gone through in France. In France we were at the front for three or four days and then were taken for a week's rest. Here it went on constantly. No let-up.

In mid-April, after a British peace effort was rejected by the Mufti, the UN Security Council authorized the Consuls-General of the United States, France and Belgium to try to arrange a truce in Jerusalem. At the same time, American Consul-General Thomas Wasson, the most congenial and effective diplomat in the city, worked to secure Mount Scopus from attack. At the end of the month he was killed by Arab fire near his consulate. Hadassah doctors fought twelve hours in vain to save his life.

Immediately after May 15, the British established a consulate in Jerusalem proper and appointed two consuls to handle Arab and Israeli affairs. Consul John Guy Tempest Sheringham applied himself to the Scopus problem and on May 31, in a phone conversation with Hebrew University Administrator Dr. Werner Senator, he advised Israel to surrender Scopus. Senator left a record of the talk:

> Sheringham: 'The best way to safeguard the University and Hadassah buildings would be to accept King Abdullah's offer to put them under the protection of the Arab Legion.'

> Senator: 'The best way it seems to me would be to advise King Abdullah not to shell the University and Hadassah.'

> Sheringham: 'Your military situation is not very bright. You have not succeeded in driving the Arabs out of Jerusalem.'

> Senator: 'The responsibility for the Legion's acts against the University and Hadassah lay with the British Government.'

In Washington, innumerable pleas were made to every imaginable source to help relieve Scopus. The State Department was helpful in one respect: Secretary of State George Marshall agreed that cables from the National Board could be relayed through the consulate in Jerusalem to Davis and Ethel Agron.

In the end, an agreement was worked out whereby the United Nations would assume control of Scopus, over which it would fly its flag and provide observers to maintain the area as a demilitarized zone. Eighty-four Jewish police would guard installations at Hadassah and the Hebrew University while 40 Arabs would guard Arab property on Scopus. The UN agreed to supply and exchange the Jewish police in regular fortnightly convoys through the Arab Sheikh Jarrah Quarter. Hadassah and the University were evacuated on July 6 and demilitarization was completed on July 7 when the first police, Israeli soldiers in police uniform, went up.

Out of tragedy and fortitude had come triumph. While the price — an entire medical center and university — had been high, Mount Scopus had not fallen into Arab hands and it would serve as a base for Israeli forces to win the entire city in 1967. On balance, Scopus was the pawn that Hadassah sacrificed to save the queen.

Jewish Jerusalem was rescued at the eleventh hour by a month-long truce that began on June 11. In another twenty four hours not another scrap of food would have been available. Battered and bloody, the city stood — most of it in Israeli hands. Looking back, Davis hardly knew how he had made it. Tetanus antitoxin was near the vanishing point and could no longer be given routinely; two wounded died for lack of the drug. X-ray film was short, morphine low, hypodermic needles, alcohol, adhesive plaster and catgut silk practically gone. "We were forced to keep one eye on stocks and one eye on the patient," Davis reported. He pleaded for help from the Red Cross but aid first came dramatically from New York due to the frantic efforts of the National Board.

Hadassah's Margaret Doniger set up blood plasma collection centers on America's east and west coasts. But more immediate first aid came from an airlift of 15,675 pounds of medicines and supplies, organized under the direction of Purchasing Committee Chairman Miriam Handler. These supplies were only a drop compared to the more than two million pounds of supplies sent by Hadassah that year, but they arrived at a critical time.

On the plane was Lola Kramarsky who was to become the first European-born leader elected Hadassah president (1960). Lola and her husband Siegfried Kramarsky, both committed Zionists and close friends of the Weizmanns, arrived in the United States in 1940 as refugees from Hitler's Europe. Lola had been active in the Youth Aliyah movement and was present when Henrietta Szold greeted the first group of Youth Aliyah children to reach Palestine. With Lola on the plane was Jeanette Leibel Lourie, Hadassah's meticulous executive director.

It was now the beginning of July 1948, and the one-month truce was about to end. The chartered craft landed in Amsterdam where the supplies had to be reloaded on a C-54 cargo plane. At that time, Israel had no airfield that could take a larger craft. After long and harrowing hours in flight, during which the pilot of the plane had to radio several times for landing instructions, Lola, Jeanette and the supplies bumped down at Ein Shemer, south of Haifa. Appropriately the date was July 4. Forty Israeli soldiers rushed to the craft and began unloading. The scene was one of great relief and hilarity. Arthur Lourie, a South African-born diplomat, ran out in underwear to greet his wife; he had been bathing when he heard the plane land. Next day, the convoy of trucks arrived in Jerusalem, only four days before the resumption of war.

The next phase of the fighting lasted only ten days but it was sufficient for the Army of Israel, resupplied during the 30-day truce, to take the initiative. Jerusalem was no longer in danger although it was again being continuously shelled. Twenty-four hours before the war was renewed on July 9, Davis had completed a fully equipped underground operating theater in St. Joseph's Convent — the first of its kind in the country. Forty-six direct hits were suffered by St. Joseph's. On the third day, Dr. Shlomo Gorfunkel, a Hadassah X-ray specialist who had organized the Vilna Ghetto uprising and served with the partisans in the Vilna forests during the Holocaust, was killed by Arab fire in the streets of Jerusalem.

The fighting finally ended in Jerusalem on July 19, although sniping and occasional shelling would continue for several years. From the beginning of the shooting in December, Hadassah had treated most of the Jewish casualties in the city — a total of 3,550.

At the time, United Nations peace mediator Count Folke Bernadotte[2] was in Jerusalem offering compromise solutions — among them a considerable withdrawal by Israeli forces. On September 17 he and his French aide were fatally shot by members of LEHI. On arrival at Hadassah there was no hope for their lives. The provisional government of Israel under David Ben-Gurion condemned the act. Three days after the assassination, the Mufti proclaimed a Palestine Arab state — one he could have had less than a year earlier without bloodshed — but now it was too late. King Abdullah outfoxed him and in October mobilized 5,000 notables to accept his sovereignty over all Arab Palestine. In another year he would annex the West Bank and East Jerusalem to his newly-named Hashemite Kingdom of Jordan.

But the war was still not over. In mid-October, Israeli forces, now an organized army, moved south to take the Bedouin village of Beersheba. Hadassah would soon follow the troops to open a hospital there — Hadassah's first in the Negev — as a memorial to Haim Yassky. At October's end, the Israelis consolidated their gains in Galilee.

The final campaign of Israel's War of Independence occurred as the year ended. Forces moved deep into the Negev and Sinai and on January 19, 1949, the shooting war came to an ironic end. Hours before the cease-fire went into effect, five British-piloted Spitfires flew from Egypt to determine whether the Israelis had, as agreed, withdrawn from the Sinai. Mistaking the planes for Egyptians, the Israelis brought four of them down in air-to-air combat and one by ground fire. The word flashed around the world and for a few days it seemed as though the triumphant Israelis might have to fight the British. President Truman and others, including friendly British leaders, scolded the Royal Air Force for having stuck its nose where it did

---

2   Bernadotte, who had arranged the month-long truce in June, proposed a peace settlement that would have given all of Jerusalem and the Negev to Jordan in exchange for western Galilee. Later fighting would, in any case, win all of Galilee for Israel.

not belong and the crisis subsided. In the Rehovot home of Chaim Weizmann, the soon-to-be President informed a British friend and Member of Parliament, Richard Crossman, of the incident. Crossman is said to have replied, "Don't worry. This means that you are now a state. Britain will recognize you within the month." On January 30, 1949, a chastised and humiliated British Foreign Secretary Bevin accorded *de facto* recognition to the State of Israel.

Succeeding Count Bernadotte, American mediator Ralph Bunche negotiated armistice agreements with Egypt, Lebanon, Jordan and Syria in the months of February, March, April and July. Iraq refused to negotiate and removed its troops from the West Bank. While the armistice lines would be the frontiers of Israel for the next nineteen years, the agreements were flimsy and did not, as hoped, lead to peace pacts. But they were a measure of the state's permanence and no one who had gone through the War of Independence in Israel now doubted that the infant state would survive.

Hadassah had been a midwife to the state all through its difficult birth. In recognition of that service, David Ben-Gurion, after becoming Prime Minister in Israel's first elections held on January 25, 1949, said:

> The achievements of Hadassah in Zionism generally; its invaluable contribution to our war of liberation and independence; the work of its people here under fire on Mount Scopus and on the fronts, will live in the history of our nation forever.

THE WEB AND THE WOOF

Israel, the State of the Jews, appeared so abruptly that it left the world breathless. Zionists and most other Jews could not immediately rationalize the event and, for years thereafter, would speak of the State in metaphysical terms — as the miraculous rebirth of the Jewish commonwealth or as the advent of the Messianic Age. Even some Christians greeted Israel as prophecy fulfilled and prepared for the coming of the Messiah.

World Zionists could therefore be forgiven for not having realized that their political mission had now terminated. Worse, they were confounded by abuse emanating from Israel. Angry that Zionist leaders did not rush to settle in Israel, Prime Minister Ben-Gurion belittled those who remained abroad, referring to them merely as "friends of Israel." Great names in the movement gave up their roles like actors on closing night. Chaim Weizmann was elected president, a post with no political power, and died in 1952, almost thirty-five years to the day after the issuance of the Balfour Declaration. Others, like Abba Hillel Silver, who waited in Cleveland for a summons from Jerusalem to join the cabinet; Stephen Wise, who died within a year of statehood; and Louis Lipsky, the once powerful head of the

Zionist Organization of America, would play no part in the political affairs of the state for which they had so valiantly fought.

To all this, Hadassah was an exception — and with good reason. Hadassah had been on the scene from the beginning even thriving through wars and plagues. Henrietta Szold said in 1929, "Hadassah entered into the fabric of Palestinian life, into its web and woof." While other Zionist groups decreased in size or importance after 1948, Hadassah would flourish. By the end of Israel's first quarter-century, the membership of Hadassah would number 325,000 organized in 692 chapters.

None of this was yet evident on a searing August morning in 1948 when three board members — President Rose Halprin, Rebecca Shulman and Anna Tulin — met in Jerusalem with the Hadassah Council and the hospital administration to map a new course for the organization's work in Israel. The task was not easy since Israel itself, still taking form in the crucible of war, was also embarked on an uncharted course.

For five days, under the chairmanship of Ethel Agron who headed Hadassah's Council in Israel, they tried to plan for an unpredictable future. Ethel posed some of the alternatives:

> Will we return to Scopus? Should Hadassah take over the health department of Jerusalem if the city is to be internationalized or should it now limit its work to preventive services? Should Hadassah expand outside Jerusalem? Does the Medical School have an absolute priority?

With the political destiny of the state uncertain, and with masses of poor, ill, uneducated immigrants crowding into the country, Hadassah once again faced an old problem — everything had to be done at once.

Some of the leaders meeting in Jerusalem insisted that Hadassah should concentrate on immigrant care. But Eli Davis spoke against Hadassah's providing across-the-board care for newcomers. That was now the Israeli government's task. Hadassah should do only what it knew best — provide service in specialized fields.

"Hadassah's duty is to administer the medical services for immigrants," retorted Rose Halprin.

"Whatever we do, we must not desert Jerusalem," said Rebecca Shulman.

A compromise solution came from Davis. "The best way to become a factor in Jerusalem and in the State is through the Medical School. The Medical School must get priority." And so it did.

The concept of a school of medicine in Palestine was almost as old as political Zionism itself. In 1913, the Zionist Congress accepted "as a matter of urgency" the establishment of a medical faculty at the projected Hebrew University. After World War I, the American Jewish Physicians Committee was organized to raise funds for the future school. In the 1920s, a parasitology department under British-born Saul Adler and other medical research facilities opened at the University, but no serious thought of a school could be entertained until Hadassah built the hospital center on Mount Scopus. Preparing for that moment, a postgraduate teaching and research center for doctors developed, serving physicians attached to the Allied armies during World War II. Clinical departments formed and the University granted status to heads of Hadassah departments. In December 1945, a $4,000,000 building fund took shape and as the exhausted world laid down its arms, the University and Hadassah finally looked forward to accepting the first students in 1947 or 1948. But these were crisis years. The new generation of physicians would wear uniforms of khaki rather than white.

Soon after World War II, Medical Director Haim Yassky, aware that a successful school depended on a corps of bright young physicians, initiated a fellowship program. He chose his best and sent them to the finest medical institutions in the United States. The first was Polish-born neurosurgeon Aharon Beller. He left on a troopship in April 1946 and returned to Jerusalem two years later because the country was without a neurosurgeon.

In the United States, Hadassah took counsel from its Medical Reference Board headed by Dr. E. M. Bluestone, who had gathered together some of the best-known physicians in American medicine: Duke University's William Perlzweig, the US Public Health Service's Harry Eagle and Henry Makover, educator and author Abraham Wilinsky and Johns Hopkins's Abel Wolman. In Israel, there were Bernhard Zondek, Arieh Dostrovsky, Leonid Doljansky, Moshe Ben-David, Saul Adler, Arieh Feigenbaum. But above all there was Haim Yassky, of whom Eli Davis would say, "He had the vision of a great modern healing-teaching center. For that he worked always. Before his death he had been working on the blueprints of the school. It was the most natural thing in the world, when he had come down from Scopus, to carry on with the healing-teaching hospital idea."

But there was also one other key figure who was only a distant relative of the Hadassah family; the first surgeon-general of the Israel Defense Forces. Haim Sheba served as a catalyst. As head of the Haganah medical services in January 1948, Sheba wrote to all Palestinian Jewish students studying medicine abroad to return home. About fifty answered the call and immediately went into uniform. They were joined by medical students from Russia, Lithuania and Romania who left their schools and emigrated to Israel. Recalled Sheba:

> I suggested that we ask Hadassah not to wait with the medical school until they could begin with the first year but take the boys and girls who had already completed three years, give them a refresher course and proceed with the fourth year. Those who did not respond to the call to return would have to serve an extra year in uniform before they could receive their licenses so as not to give them an unfair advantage.

On September 10, 1948, Sheba formalized his suggestion in writing to Medical Director Davis. "I felt when I wrote that letter," Sheba recalled later, "we would not only be creating a Medical School but we would also be saving Hadassah from losing some of its most valuable senior staff members who might not have had the stamina to remain in Jerusalem while the city was under fire. A few of them had made it clear that they could no longer continue after five months of continual siege."

Davis approved — the students could begin in April 1949. But the students did not want to wait that long. Taking matters into their own hands, they went to Jerusalem to protest. They started a rumor that the army was about to begin a medical school since Hadassah and the University were dragging their feet. Sheba himself gave some credence to the rumor by forming a medical school preparatory unit in the army hospital in Jerusalem. He had ordered four senior officers to begin screening prospective students, but he had no intention of opening a school. The result was that Hadassah and University representatives quickly cooperated. One hundred and twenty candidates passed before the committee, a third were accepted and by November 1948, a three-month preparatory course had begun. In the meantime, Sheba had difficulty with the army. The Ministry of Defense only learned much later that Sheba, at his own initiative, had excused soldiers from regular duties to start studies. Not surprisingly, Sheba was soon in civilian clothes. He organized Israel's Ministry of Health, set the foundations of the state's health services and co-opted three Hadassah senior administrators to assist him.

In February 1949, studies started informally. The scene for the official opening of the school on May 17, 1949 — the holiday of Lag b'Omer in the Hebrew calendar — was foreboding. Claps of thunder and occasional streaks of lighting in an overcast sky interrupted the proceedings. Only a few hundred yards away, across the coils of barbed wire that delineated the divided city, King Abdullah's Arab Legion shot off a few rounds at the thick-walled, shell-pocked building, which a year earlier served as the base for attacks against Arab positions. In one respect, this was a homecoming. Three decades previously, the building had been the Hotel de France — Hadassah's first official home in Jerusalem. In the municipal garden facing the school sat 2,000 guests. The forty-four members of the first class were all in army uniform. Principal speaker David Ben-Gurion spoke of a far-off day when the nation would be at peace. No medical school ever had an inauguration quite like it. At the end of 1949, a second class of sixty-three was formed with many Zionist medical students from Bulgaria, who needed only one year to receive their degrees. Thus, on a hostile border, with students in military dress using texts in English, Polish, Russian and Bulgarian and listening to lectures in Hebrew, the Medical School began.

While most of the professors were European-trained, the influence of American medicine was strong because of the Hadassah Medical Reference Board. Polish-born Moshe Prywes, who spent five years as a prisoner-of-war in a Russian concentration camp in Siberia before emigrating to Israel, served as associate dean of the school until 1965. He considered the American-European synthesis beneficial and wrote:

> The American system brought a new informal approach that gave the students more freedom and produced better teamwork. Our curriculum was European — a six-year course which includes pre-medical sciences — but we applied the American system of pre-selection. We did not, as did the Europeans, allow everyone to enter and then permit only the best to continue.

One innovation was wholly Israeli. The first graduating class on May 13, 1952, took the Oath of the Hebrew Physician. It had been written for the occasion by neurologist Lipmann Halpern, the school's fifth dean. Addressed as "New Men of Medicine in Israel," the graduates were blessed "to enhance the heritage of medicine in Israel." While the best of the traditional Hippocratic oath was retained, the Greek gods played no part in the Israeli doctor's obligation to his or her patients and profession.

After the graduation of the first class, undergraduate studies began. Since then Hadassah's Medical School has provided the State of Israel with 3,500 physicians, one eighth of the total number of its doctors. Recalled dermatologist Arieh Dostrovsky, first dean of the Medical School: "At the beginning we felt that the Medical School could only have been established by Hadassah in Israel, for it was the only hospital that had a standard of any significance."

The logical consequence of a functioning medical school was the appearance soon thereafter of a school of dentistry. Veteran dental surgeon Samuel Lewin-Epstein, who arrived with the American Medical Zionist Unit, urged the creation of a school in the early 1930s. Finding little interest, he contacted professional fraternities in the United States for support. His determination won the backing of Alpha Omega, a large American dental society. The first class of fifteen students enrolled in 1953. Two years later, the faculty opened a clinic in the crowded Straus Health Center where Hadassah ran a dental service for Jerusalem's schoolchildren. It was then that Hadassah gave the school its own home and equipment and joined hands with the Hebrew University to provide a budget for staff and teaching facilities. Later on, Alpha Omega would top its original contributions with a fund of $1,000,000 for a permanent site in the new medical center complex at Ein Kerem.

In that same year, an old dream of Akiva Kosviner came true. Akiva was born in Galilee in 1892, studied pharmacology in Beirut and after practicing briefly in Egypt, settled down on the eve of war in the Rothschild Hospital in Safed as pharmacist. When his Egyptian employer asked him why he was returning to "that desert" in Palestine, Kosviner replied, "Even though I will be making only half the salary, I feel I must contribute something of myself to that desert now."

During World War I, Kosviner spent much of his service at a small Turkish army hospital in a death hole called Tabuk in northern Saudi Arabia. After the war, thankful to be back in Palestine, Kosviner moved his family to Jerusalem and opened a pharmacy, the first in the city outside the ancient walls. Soon, Kosviner became Hadassah's chief pharmacist and began teaching at the Nursing School. But always he dreamed of a school of pharmacology. The school finally began in 1953 with Kosviner as executive secretary. Strictly speaking, it was not the first. Kosviner himself had rented a room in a hotel in the early 1920s and there gave a one-year course to Jews, Arabs and Christians.

Hadassah served as teacher and healer not only in Israel but also in lands far beyond, providing experts in many fields for other nations' foreign-aid programs. Two of the most successful were in the fields of eye care and mental health. In 1959, many Africans living in the bush had no modern medical care. Hadassah's chief ophthalmologist, Scottish-born Isaac Chesar Michaelson, toured Africa's oldest republic, Liberia, and some emerging nations. In the early 1960s, Michaelson sent twenty-five eye doctors to Africa to set up hospitals in urban areas and to organize clinics in the bush.

In October 1961, Hadassah psychiatrist Dan Hertz arrived in Monrovia to direct the continent's first modern psychiatric hospital. He lived in Africa for three years, introducing therapeutic methods in four countries. For his work in mental health, the Liberian president awarded Hertz the Star of Africa.

The Medical School's associate dean, Moshe Prywes, traveled widely advising on teaching programs — to Guatemala in 1959, to Singapore, Ceylon and India in 1960, to Argentina in 1961, to Ghana in 1964. Between 1960 and 1964 the Medical School brought French- and English-speaking Africans to Israel to study; seventy-three of them graduated as physicians in Israel's capital. They returned to their home countries to teach other physicians. These Jerusalem alumni developed a fluency in the Hebrew language, which they used to communicate with each other. Few medical schools have had such alumni.

The Dental School's first dean, Ino Sciaky, was called to the island republic of Malagasy in 1964 and later to Senegal and Congo (Brazzaville), to teach his profession. His successor, Jacob Lewin-Epstein, would make numerous visits to Iran.

One unplanned visit of a Hadassah physician to Africa had an immediate political reward. In October 1961, heart specialist Moshe

Rachmilewitz was on his way home from South Africa when his plane made an unscheduled stop at Addis Ababa, Ethiopia. Israel's consul was there waiting for him and rushed the doctor to the palace of Emperor Haile Selassie, Lion of Judah, where the Empress lay ill. She was being treated by Jordanian and Yugoslav doctors but the medical complications were difficult. After Rachmilewitz put the Empress on the road to recovery, he was given a formal dinner at the palace. Rachmilewitz noted:

> The Emperor emphasized that the Jews and his people were related. On the floor I noticed a huge carpet with a large Magen David. We talked about many things, including politics, and after an hour's conversation he said to me, "I want to tell you something that will please you. Your country was not recognized *de jure* by us. You are leaving tomorrow. On your way to Israel, recognition by Ethiopia of Israel will be announced — this will be in appreciation of the service you gave my wife.

At home, there were tens of thousands of disadvantaged and culturally deprived persons to care for. The immigrants brought with them poverty and sicknesses, superstitions and illiteracy. First they came from the camps in Cyprus and from the displaced persons camps in Europe. Then from Poland and Romania. After that, they came from Yemen on the wings of chartered eagles and from Iraq in an airlift named "Operation Ezra and Nehemia" — 800,000 in all by the end of 1952.

Strict rationing went into effect throughout the country. So poor was the nation that food and goods unloaded from ships went straight from the docks to empty market stalls and shop counters. *Tzena* was the byword — "austerity." In the first years after independence, Israelis were painfully hungry. Hadassah worried about getting large amounts of emergency staples into the larders of the poorest of the poor; it provided healing to the sickest of the sick immigrant children; it offered teenagers an opportunity to take up a dignified vocation. It even arranged large loans for the government. In Washington, Hadassah representative Denise Tourover was put to work to get food from US government warehouses to the Israeli people. By virtue of its membership on the President's Advisory Committee on Voluntary Foreign Aid, Hadassah had the right to receive government surplus foods for free distribution. Denise learned that tons of potatoes stored at Presque Isle, Maine, were available. Israel's embassy in Washington announced that it would gladly accept them provided they were fumigated against the red potato bug. Hadassah had them fumigated and sent shipload after shipload to Haifa harbor. Meat followed. In 1953, Hadassah undertook "Operation Reindeer" — a one-time project that provided $12,000,000 of kosher meat, dried fruits and staples. They were placed into bags inscribed with American and Hadassah insignia and distributed free. The US government sent the rations as a Christmas gift, hence the project's name. Among the recipients were both Israeli Arabs and Jews. The project was something to ponder: an American Christmas gift distributed by a Zionist organization to Palestinian Christian and Muslim Arabs.

No less a problem for Israel was the lack of shelter. The government was determined that no one would sleep on the beaches under the open skies as immigrants did in the mid-1930s. The answer, provided by Jewish Agency official Levi Eshkol, was to set up transit camps. By the end of 1952, 250,000 persons were living in tent and shantytowns up and down the country. One of the largest, and in winter the muddiest, was set up for the Yemenite immigrants east of Tel Aviv at Rosh Ha-ayin. It was there in 1950 that Hadassah pediatricians Yehuda Mattot and Zvi Shamir headed a children's hospital, set up in an abandoned army camp. Shamir reported: "We were dealing with terribly ill children. Almost everyone who came to the hospital suffered badly from malnutrition and acute intestinal infection."

Hadassah staffed that children's hospital for two years. Then, the state's health service was sufficiently organized to move in.

Talpiot camp, on the other side of the railroad tracks in southern

Jerusalem, was even larger than Rosh Ha-ayin. Ten thousand would crowd into the wooded area. There, Hadassah was to do a job it knew well from start to finish — mother and child care. It was in Talpiot that an energetic young Jerusalem-born physician, Kalman Mann, medical deputy to Eli Davis, spoke up for a different approach to medicine:

> We usually emphasize disease in our hospital but as a medical organization we should emphasize health. Because we cater to disease, the emphasis is on diagnosis and treatment. It should be on prevention and promotion of health. Most of the illnesses we meet are really emotional and social — particularly among immigrant communities.

Mann urged the creation of a community health center to monitor all the families in the neighborhood. The family, not the individual, was to be considered the unit of care, and all problems — not only medical — would come under the trained staff in the center. Thus in 1953, in Jerusalem's immigrant suburb of Kiryat Yovel, a unique experiment in social medicine began. A five-year study, carried out by Mann and the center's South African-born director, Jack Medalie, would show that the immigrant community — representing newcomers from thirty countries — had achieved one of the lowest mortality rates in the country.

Other community health centers developed under Hadassah's planning. The community idea worked to such an extent that it spread to Arab communities and even to South America.

The newcomers needed only training and direction to become productive. Because Hadassah had faced the problem of vocational education nearly two decades earlier, it was ready for that task. In the early 1930s, Henrietta Szold worried over the problem of wayward Jewish children sent by the British courts to dubious institutions housing delinquents of all communities. She believed that delinquent Jewish children should be cared for in Jewish homes. She was especially concerned about young Jewish prostitutes and the fact that many Middle Eastern girls became child brides or servants. In 1940, she received $25,000 as an eightieth birthday gift from Hadassah. With it she established the highly-successful home for disturbed, delinquent girls at Ein Vered, east of Tel Aviv. In her search for the right kind of institution, she also developed the idea of training girls for such vocations as preventive therapy.

On one of her Youth Aliyah trips to Haifa she met a robust, energetic home economics school principal named "Doctor" Helen Kittner. At the time Henrietta felt that Youth Aliyah children needed not only to be sent to farms but could also be integrated into urban life, provided they had a vocation. After consulting the Hadassah Council's first vocational education chairman, Rose Viteles, Henrietta dispatched a fifteen-page memo to the National Board suggesting the establishment of a vocational girls' school in Jerusalem. By coincidence the Board was then considering a memorial project for Henrietta's closest friend, Alice Seligsberg. The Board accepted the idea and Henrietta asked Helen Kittner to head the school. The official opening took place in two converted wards of the old Rothschild Hospital on October 14, 1942, the same day that Hadassah met in national convention in New York City.

Helen Kittner, who at the age of four was skilled at knitting stockings for her family, was forward-thinking in later life too. In 1949, when Jerusalem had no tourist trade, she opened a school to train hotel personnel. But in the early 1950s hotels were closing and the school was transferred to the government. Likewise, in 1949, when the country could not feed its burgeoning population properly, much less dress them in haute couture, Helen started a fashion school. It was discontinued after the graduation of the first class. Nevertheless, the Alice Seligsberg School was responsible for highly successful fashion shows that Hadassah sent to the United States to raise funds.

The Seligsberg School outgrew its converted wards and sixteen years later had a $1,000,000, five-story edifice. During its first twenty-five years the school graduated 2,200 girls. Henrietta Szold had said, "I see the school as a big school with every girl in a blue dress and every girl in a white apron…bringing honor to an apron." Helen Kittner fulfilled Henrietta's wish.

In 1944, the hospital compound also housed not only the Seligsberg School but a new vocational center named for Justice Brandeis and workshops for 160 boys and girls under the direction of an unsung pioneer of progressive education in Jerusalem, Deborah Kallen. But within eight years, Helen Kittner had taken over the entire building. The workshops were moved and Miss Kallen was retired.

Also in 1944, three teenage boys were taken into a hut in the Rothschild Hospital compound under Hadassah's sponsorship and taught precision mechanics by German-born, Czech-trained Tunia Gladstein. Within three years, the Brandeis Training Center's 15 students and their teachers were turning out weapons and ammunition for the Haganah. They produced heads for the Haganah's secret weapon — a heavy, noisy mortar called the Davidka. They made hand grenades and mechanisms to set off mines. During the fighting early in 1948, Arab agents learned that Brandeis was the center of an arms workshop and directed shells against it from positions in the Old City. The Rothschild building's thick stone walls provided good protection and no one inside was hurt, but one student was killed on the street on the way to his bench. Conditions became impossible and the workshops moved first to a nearby cellar cafe, then farther away to the Bezalel Art School where the boys had their own electricity generator and could work in two 12-hour shifts.

Brandeis's technical designer Yitzhak Schneider invented a flame-thrower for which the boys made most of the parts. They also turned out muzzles for smoke bombs used to screen Jerusalem's lone landing strip from Arab gunners. With the battle raging around them, the school went on to produce more and more complicated products as the Haganah, cut off from supplies outside Jerusalem, made more and more demands. Schneider, together with handwork technician Yitzhak Moshieff, even put together binocular telescopes. When materials were difficult to obtain, one of the Brandeis men endangered his life by going to the Jerusalem railroad station under fire to rip up tracks for metal. The school, only a few years old, thus played a key part in the battle for Jerusalem.

Brandeis taught more than precision instruments. In 1949, the country's first printing school began there. The school's director was French-born Henry Friedlander, who distinguished himself by designing the first original Hebrew type of modern times, the result of thirty years' research. He named the script "Hadassah." Beautiful in its classic design, yet uncomplicated, Hadassah fonts were adopted for the Swiss-made Hermes typewriter and were widely used by the Israeli government printers and by public institutions.

With bequests from the Brandeis family, new school quarters were built in northern Jerusalem in 1951. Then it became possible to introduce such sophisticated courses as industrial electronics under director Edgar Freund. On the eve of the Six-Day War, Brandeis could convert immediately to the production of complicated components for the Israel Defense Forces, among them vital parts used in the bombing of Egypt on June 5, 1967.

But by no means was the school a war factory. Characteristically Israeli, it was civilian but was subject to call-up for military service at short notice. In civilian life Brandeis would not only teach but it would build instruments to measure avocado peels and sections of the heart-lung machine used by HMO for its first open-heart operations.

In 1969, Seligsberg and Brandeis amalgamated into a comprehensive high school for boys and girls. At the same time, Esther Gottesman, chairman of Hadassah's Israel Education Services, developed the idea of a Hadassah junior college. Precisely three decades after the Seligsberg School was founded, in November 1972, the nation's first junior college students were graduated. Hadassah College expanded rapidly. In 1977, a top-notch education administrator, Dr. Ya'acov Amidi, took over and two years later the name of the institution was changed to the Hadassah College of Technology (HCT). By 1996, having been accredited with academic status in some fields, the College of 900 students was offering four-year courses in selected departments.

While it was good that Hadassah provided vocational education to students who had no talent or desire to become scholars, it was another matter when young people could not decide what they wanted to do or what they could do. Research carried out among Jerusalem's high school seniors revealed that only 25 percent knew their own inclinations regarding their education and future occupation. The others were in a state of indecision.

To test, to counsel and to direct students became the function of Hadassah's Vocational Guidance Bureau, founded in 1944. Its first director was Haim Ormian, one of the country's pioneer educators. Dr. Erwin Arnstein assumed the post soon afterwards and served with distinction for fifteen years. Under Director Zev Sardi, the Bureau branched out into counseling, teaching and research, and its name was then changed to the Hadassah Career Counseling Institute (HCCI).

Testing and therapy for emotionally disturbed schoolchildren required an institution of its own. That need was filled in 1949 with the opening of the Lasker Mental Hygiene Clinic. During the past fifty years, the Institute has had 535,000 clients. More than half were high school graduates for whom the Institute determined the most suitable occupation. Psychometric tests — 420 of them — are conducted in twelve languages.

Not merely a testing organization, the Institute has carried out 850 research projects and serves as a management consultant to Government and to hi-tech companies.

Director Dr. Itzhak Garty, who has led the Institute since 1984, now serves over 40,000 people annually. The Bureau began with 600. The number has grown, he believes, partly because young people have a harder time than ever making up their minds. "Never before have so many opportunities and specialties been open to them nor the competition so great," says Dr. Garty.

Important as its educational function was in the 1950s, Hadassah's main preoccupation was with HMO. With the end of the War of Independence, hospital facilities expanded in a makeshift way utilizing alphabetical names. Hadassah "A" and "B" were war-born, as we have seen. They were soon followed by "C" for tuberculosis patients; "D," located in a derelict building that once housed the harem of the Turkish governor, served internal medicine patients; "E," in an old German Lutheran Hospital, took in surgical cases. One unlettered institution that Hadassah inherited as a result of the war was an Arab leprosarium. When the Arabs abandoned it, the dermatology department assumed responsibility and did notable work there in alleviating the pains of leprosy. By 1951, Hadassah had spread out in at least a dozen buildings over the face of the city.

All told, Hadassah had put together places for 452 beds in Jerusalem in the 1950s, but if one included the hospitals in Beersheba, Safed and Rosh Ha-ayin, they numbered 700. Occupancy at one point, reported the statisticians, was an unbelievable 298.4 percent.

Without Scopus, however, Hadassah was bereft of its crown. Rebecca Shulman had said at the August 1948 meeting in Jerusalem, "We will have to build anew." The loss of Scopus was too fresh to begin rebuilding immediately, but by 1951 the shock had eased and Hadassah leaders began to plan for a new medical center.

One had only to visit the scattered premises to appreciate the need. Working conditions were almost laughable. So cramped were the facilities at the mission, now Hadassah "A," that they expanded into the private quarters of Canon Jones, the mission's director. The delivery room was put into his bathroom and an expensive cobalt unit for cancer therapy was set up in a room the Reverend had formerly used for prayer meetings. In a small kitchen next door, Hadassah opened Israel's first medical isotope center. Down in the damp basements, the walls covered with fungi, were the X-ray labs.

The time had now come not only for a new medical center but for new management. Eli Davis had gone to Jerusalem on a promise from Yassky that he would be able to keep in touch with world medicine while serving as deputy administrator. He found that administration at Hadassah was a twenty-hour-a-day job. Eli Davis had worn Yassky's mantle with great fortitude at Hadassah's most trying hour. Davis spoke directly, plainly and rarely wavered. If these characteristics sometimes brought him into head-on collision with the Hadassah leadership, they also brought him the Board's deep respect; so much so that when in 1950 he decided that, the war being over, he could now return to his first love — medicine — Hadassah dispatched President Rose Halprin and incoming President Etta Rosensohn to Jerusalem to change his mind. Throughout a snowy night in the winter of 1950, even their considerable powers of persuasion failed. Davis, fortified by his wife's resolution and support, had made up his mind, and that was that.

Hadassah was now left without Scopus and without a director. The task at that moment looked impossible. Few qualified men in American medicine would entertain moving to poverty-stricken Israel to take over a hospital dispersed in dilapidated buildings. And so the directorship fell to Davis's deputy Kalman Jacob Mann, son of the city's first Jewish building contractor, seventh generation Jerusalemite, born the year Hadassah was founded. The house he lived in as a child also served Ray Landy and Rose Kaplan as an eye care station in 1914. Mann himself had been treated for trachoma. He was graduated from a teachers' college at 19, went off to England to study medicine with the aim of entering psychiatry. Instead, he took four degrees in medicine, a diploma in tropical medicine and specialized in chest diseases. During the second World War he served as a resuscitation officer at Hendon airfield in charge of chest cases. It was an experience that would prove useful in the Six-Day War.

Mann returned to Jerusalem in 1948 on the promise of a position at Hadassah. But by the time he arrived, Scopus was lost and Eli Davis told him, "It's a shame you came. We have no job for you now." Mann was about to leave Jerusalem to establish a group practice when one day, as he crossed the Street of the Prophets, he met Rebecca Shulman who spent much of Israel's first year in Jerusalem and Haifa.

"How are you getting along at Hadassah?" she asked.

"I'm not."

Under St. Joseph's galvanized roof they sat and they talked. A week later Kalman Mann began as Davis's deputy. Mann explained: "My mother thought it was an honor and Rebecca Shulman kept after me. Dr. Davis was a good teacher and I felt a partnership growing in the building of Hadassah."

Hadassah sent Mann to the United States under its fellowship program to study hospital administration with former Hadassah medical director Dr. E. M. Bluestone. In 1950, while he was in Rochester, New York, Mann received word from Davis that he was about to resign. So it was that at thirty-eight years of age, Kalman Mann became Hadassah's eighth medical director. He was the first to come from native soil and he would serve much longer than any of his predecessors. Under Kalman Mann's steady hand, the Hadassah Medical Organization would build a new home, and keep faith with an old one.

EIN KEREM

"You are crazy, Mann!"

With that, the distinguished rector of the Hebrew University turned on his heels and tramped down the slope to the parked jeep. He had been invited to the top of the mountain by Hadassah's enthusiastic medical director. Before them in a majestic panorama was the Valley of Sorek, the lair where Delilah had snared Samson. Not far away was where the youthful David had foiled the Philistines by slaying Goliath. Peaceful, even primeval, the blue-tinted Judean Hills were ideal for quiet study and research. Kalman Mann had explained to the rector that Jerusalem, a few miles to the north, had nowhere to grow but southward. A broad highway from Tel Aviv would one day cut through the valley; this spot would be the city's grand new entrance. What could be more fitting, he suggested, than to build fortresses of healing and teaching on opposite hills, guarding the gateway to the City of Peace?

The realistic rector was unimpressed. This place was good for goats or Philistines or even for prophets but definitely not for serious students who had to rush to jobs in the city after classes or for sick people in urgent need of a specialist.

Disconsolate, Mann began feeling a little silly that he had supported this site as the successor to Mount Scopus. But he was determined to get one last opinion from a latter-day prophet.

The year was 1951. By then the loss of Scopus lay as heavy as a dirge on the soul of Jerusalem's physicians, nurses and professors. No one doubted any longer that the Hebrew University and Hadassah must build anew. The problem was where. Jerusalem offered no easy locations. Fashioned by nature in the shape of an outstretched hand — of ridges and valleys — the city was further limited for reasons of security. Jewish Jerusalem was the end of a salient that began in the Judean foothills to the west and stuck out like a thumb, in the gut of the heavily populated sections of Arab Palestine that had recently been annexed by Jordan. Arab military positions dominated the city from high points to the south and north. On the eastern border, which cut through the middle of Jerusalem's commercial section, Jordanian sentries sat perched on rooftops. Few sites anywhere were at that time beyond the effective range of Arab guns. Ein Kerem was one.

Hadassah and the University were considering four sites. For Hadassah each had its disadvantage: one was too small for expansion, another was out of the mainstream of the developing city and a third was needed for an airport. That left Ein Kerem — distant but enticing. Ein Kerem — the Well of the Vineyard — a quaint village snugly held in the Valley of Sorek, an artist's dream of statuesque cypresses, crooked lanes and stone-walled churches. Tradition has it that St. John the Baptist was born there.

Long, hard-fought sessions between Hadassah and Hebrew University representatives over sharing the new site came to naught. Always before the University was the specter of the ill-fated Scopus convoy, trapped on hostile ground between the city and the campus. Hadassah was torn between the desire to remain with the University inside urban Jerusalem and to strike out independently on the edge of a wilderness where it could expand without limit. The final decision was put in the hands of David Ben-Gurion, Israel's political seer. At the site, the security-minded prime minister turned to his Hadassah escort and said, "Magnificent! Build here."

From that moment, Hadassah and Hebrew University went their

separate ways. Not even a compromise worked out later by Defense Minister Pinhas Lavon, who suggested that the University's science faculties remain with Hadassah at Ein Kerem, could bridge the gap. In the end, the Medical School and the schools of Dentistry and Pharmacy as well as the Microbiology and Biochemistry departments voted to stay with Hadassah. The University itself built its campus on the Givat Ram ridge, which soon became the geographical center of Jerusalem.

The issue having been decided, Hadassah received 315 acres above the village of Ein Kerem through the Jewish National Fund. Working with primitive equipment, the state's Public Works Department set out bravely to carve a road to the site. But on the way the workers ran into a political barrier that could not be budged with TNT. Part of the land belonged to the Russian Orthodox Church, which took its orders from vicars in the Kremlin. Israel could not then afford diplomatic crises with major powers, so it agreed to stop work while lawyers fought the issue.

In the autumn of 1956, most people expected Israel to launch an attack against Jordan. Repeated Arab raids against Israeli towns and farms on the frontiers had made life unbearable. The crisis peaked on October 25 when Jordan joined Syria and Egypt in a military alliance against Israel. On October 29, the Israeli army struck deep into the Sinai peninsula in an attack coordinated with Britain and France. In 100 hours, Israel occupied the entire peninsula, broke Egyptian President Nasser's blockade of Eilat and smashed his army. Militarily, Israel's operation was a resounding success. Politically, it was a failure. US President Eisenhower condemned the action, forcing Israel to withdraw.

Hadassah had prepared for heavy military casualties in Jerusalem, but when the front opened in Sinai rather than in Jordan, most of the wounded were taken to Beersheba where Hadassah organized and staffed a field hospital.

Golda Meir was then Israel's foreign minister. After the Russians broke off relations with Israel because of the war, Mrs. Meir told Hadassah, "Finish the road quickly. Our relations with the Russians could hardly be worse." Before Moscow could return to Israel, the Henrietta Szold Road was completed to the plateau. And there, four years later, at the southernmost limit of Jerusalem, the medical center complex stood.

The Ein Kerem site inspired grandiose plans among department chiefs that would have required an 800-bed hospital, a 450-student medical school, a 120-student dental school, four acres of space to teach basic sciences and an outpatient clinic to handle 1,000 patients a day. In New York, the National Board was stunned by these proposals. To build a medical center of such proportions went beyond anything Hadassah had ever attempted. The shock was not so much over the expanse as over the expense. The original building budget amounted to nearly $8,000,000 with an additional $2,500,000 to be provided by the University for the professional schools. What Jerusalem was requesting would have amounted to three times that sum. As it developed, soaring costs and needs did force Hadassah to spend an astronomical $30,000,000 by 1971, a decade after the medical center was opened, in addition to $6,000,000 provided by the University.

The medical center finally opened with 420 beds. Yet within a decade the number had risen to 690, the maximum licensed by the Health Ministry. But because of the heavy demand for Hadassah's services, some departments were working at 120 percent capacity. Four-bed wards often had to accommodate five. When they were filled, the corridors were used. At any one time the hospital might have as many as 750 beds occupied.

In New York, a vigorous building fund campaign began. To raise the money for the single largest project in Hadassah's history, the medical center was "sold" in bits and pieces. Donors could buy a brick or square foot in the Center or could be listed as a Founder for $10,000. Out of the Founder's program emerged Hadassah's Major Gifts project ($5,000 and up) which became an important source of funds. The largest single gift until then, $1,000,000, came from Siegfried and Irma Ullmann of New York, for the establishment of Hadassah's 60-bed oncology institute. Named for Moshe Sharett, Israel's second prime minister who had died of cancer, the Institute, under Avraham Hochman, was designed to launch a new era of medical science for Hadassah. Built in 1980, it stocked an arsenal of cancer-fighting weapons: fifty cytotoxic drugs, two supra-modern accelerators, units for psycho-oncology and adolescent oncology. By the end of the 1990s the Institute, under Director Tamar Peretz, was treating 10,000 patients yearly, 45 percent of whom were disease-free after five years.

From the cornerstone laying of the Ein Kerem center on June 5, 1952, to the projected completion of the Sharett Institute in 1975, Hadassah leaped into a new age of medical care.

To design the Center, Hadassah chose Vienna-educated architect Joseph Neufeld. It had long been realized that the accepted shoebox form of most hospitals was inefficient, dismal and hard on nurses' feet. Neufeld substituted a semicircular shape which he called "radial." Thus, the distinguishing feature of the medical center became an eleven-floor radial unit. Inside, the nurses' station was located in the center of the half-circle on each floor and from there, nurses and attendants were within easy reach of the wards. To eliminate the gloom of an ordinary hospital, Neufeld put the corridors in the adjoining recovery wings on the outside — one facing north and one facing south. In summer, the north corridor, opposite the picturesque Sorek Valley and the village of Ein Kerem, became a lounge. In winter, when the north side was buffeted by wind and rain, the sunlit south corridor became the lounge. Neufeld prescribed red and white bricks and pink Jerusalem stone for the building's exterior to blend with the constantly changing colors of Jerusalem's landscape. The overall cheerful effect and the awesome view caused Rebecca Shulman, then Hadassah President, to remark, "This center has been designed so that people will be able to enjoy their bad health."

Neufeld was beset with unusual problems. One was to secure the building against war damage. Surgery, for example, had to be located two floors above ground — high enough to minimize the impact of shrapnel and low enough to be insulated from a direct hit by a shell or a bomb.

Three floors, built underground with connecting tunnels, could be converted into emergency wards.

Inevitably, mistakes were made in the planning. Large windows facing east and south were sun collectors. In the Mediterranean, where the light is blinding during hot, dry summers, planners have learned to use small windows. Neufeld assumed that the hospital would be air-conditioned, but in 1957 a decision was taken to save $1,000,000 by eliminating artificial cooling. Until air conditioners were finally installed, staff and patients suffered during hot spells.

But no problem was so ticklish as the conflict between pathologists and rabbis. Religious law forbids *kohanim* (men belonging to the priestly class) from entering a building in which a corpse is lying. Pathology was an integral part of the Center and Hadassah was the only hospital in Jerusalem to dare open a pathology department. Director Mann took the problem to Chief Rabbi of Israel Isaac Nissim and received a facile reply, "Erect a separate building for pathology." Mann blanched; he did not have the extra $5,000,000. Like a patient seeking a more effective cure, he went off to consult another sage, this time the Chief Rabbi of Jerusalem. He suggested that if the post-mortem room had electronic doors that opened when one approached and closed before others opened, then the pathology department would be sealed off as though it were not part of the rest of the building.

Happily, Mann went back and ordered electronic doors for the hospital. But the cure failed. Staff and visitors who did not have the patience to wait until one door closed as the other opened broke the equipment. Mann was left with the problem of how to make the hospital on-bounds for observant *kohanim*. The solution was deceptively simple — revolving doors were installed.

Problems notwithstanding, the medical center slowly took shape as the 1950s ended. When it was completed, even the critics could agree that no similar institution existed in the Middle East.

One day in the spring of 1959 as construction moved forward,

Hadassah President Miriam Freund sat with Neufeld in her New York office discussing the shape of a small synagogue to be built at the Center. She commented that just that week she had read a newspaper item that Marc Chagall had designed some windows for a French cathedral. "Both Neufeld and I had the thought at once that it would be a wonderful thing if Chagall would do windows for our synagogue."

On the plane to Paris to negotiate with Chagall, Miriam met violinist Isaac Stern and asked him to accompany Neufeld and herself. In Chagall's apartment near Notre Dame the trio tried to convince Chagall in Yiddish, Russian and French. Miriam related:

> While the men were studying the plans for the synagogue, I spoke with Marc's wife. She said, 'Chagall is unhappy that the whole world has come to him but not the Jewish people.' In my broken Yiddish I went over to Chagall and said, 'I have come on behalf of the Jewish people.' I took a deep breath and plunged on, 'We could never repay you enough for doing these windows. I cannot even ask you what your price is since all I can spend is $100,000. That has to cover everything. I know this is no fee for you…but you will be shaping the art history of a new country. All young Israelis are interested in art. You will be their lodestar.' He listened intently, but his only reply was, 'I shall see.'

That was in June 1959. The following December, Miriam and Neufeld flew to Chagall's home in Vence. There they saw completed drawings for twelve windows; each bore the name of an ancient tribe of Israel and its symbol. Subsequently, the windows were painted in striking blues, greens, yellows and reds. The glass was made at the Simone atelier of Charles and Brigitte Marq in Rheims. "When the windows were finished, it was much more than we had ever bargained for. They were so beautiful that France's Minister of Culture André Malraux insisted on showing them in the garden of the Louvre. After that we put them on display at the Museum of Modern Art," Miriam said.

In November 1961, hundreds of thousands packed the museum to see the hit art show of the season. Then the windows were packed and flown on three planes to Israel for security. The windows arrived in Jerusalem in perfect shape; its replacement pieces were shattered. They became one of Israel's most valuable art treasures and one of its greatest tourist attractions, drawing several million tourists to the medical center.

The Abbell synagogue that houses them is a small structure and critics carped that it was much too modest to wear so priceless a diadem. Chagall himself was patently disturbed when he attended the dedication ceremony in 1962. The artist from Vitebsk should have remembered that some of Italy's greatest artworks repose in far shabbier churches, but he suggested that they be transferred to the Israel Museum. Chagall promised to replace them with other windows. He had a few supporters, Miriam Freund among them, but the National Board rejected the idea and they remained at the synagogue.

The dedication of the Hadassah-Hebrew University Medical Center at Ein Kerem took place on August 3, 1960. The day began routinely for Hadassah's 254 physicians, 514 nurses and 1,352 other staff. In ophthalmology, Professor Walter Kornblueth operated on three crosseyed children. A housewife from Athens began to receive massive doses of steroids in dermatology to fight an advanced case of pemphigus, which had been a fatal disease until the early 1950s. "Cancer patients who are incurable are never hopeless," Oncology Department Chief Hochman told his students that day. "We can always add time to their lives." Then carrying his pipe, which he had stopped filling with tobacco for the last month, he went on to check patients whose tumors were being bombarded by cobalt. Orthopedic surgeon Myer Makin removed a torn cartilage from the knee of a football player. Green-uniformed nurse Haya Dorit, a 35-year veteran who directed one of Hadassah's fourteen Tipat Halav mother and infant welfare stations, reassured Hassida Frumkin. Hassida was eight months pregnant with her first child and suffered from swollen legs. In the Kiryat Yovel Community Health Center, Dr. Charlotte Hopp spent part of the morning reviewing the case of fifteen-year old Rahamim, a hemophiliac who had lately developed asthma.

In the late afternoon nearly all workers left their stations to troop out to the plateau above Ein Kerem. There, they joined Israeli notables and 400 overseas guests on the red flagstone plaza. President Miriam Freund began with a prayer in which she noted that Hadassah had entered into "a partnership with Him in the healing of the sick, in the rescuing of the homeless and in the mothering of the motherless." A Freedom Bell, shaped like the Liberty Bell, on which was inscribed "Proclaim Ye Healing Throughout the Land," was ceremoniously rung by Fanny Cohen, former medical center chairman. US Ambassador Ogden Reid began speaking in correct, if halting, Hebrew, then switched to English so the American guests could understand him. He noted that $100,000 had been provided by the US government to build the premature baby wards.

Prime Minister Ben-Gurion, the featured speaker, complained that he was asked to speak English whereas the non-Jewish ambassador could get away with Hebrew. "I have two wishes," said Ben-Gurion. "One is that I hope we go back to Scopus. And the other is that I hope Hadassah women learn the Hebrew language." He went on to chide American Jews for not sending their children to settle in Israel, but, more to the point, he paid tribute to Hadassah's founder:

> Henrietta Szold, who was not only the greatest woman America has yet produced, but undoubtedly one of the noblest personalities of our generation, had two great qualities: her profound knowledge of the Hebrew language and culture and her great desire to work in Israel...May the memory and life's work of Henrietta Szold be a light to guide your path. She gave herself to our country.

Ben-Gurion sat down to polite applause. The dedication was over.

In May 1961, advance parties had transferred the administration and 250,000 individual records, the huge cobalt therapy unit and medical stores. Moving Day followed on June 6. The army provided twenty ambulances to shuttle 300 patients. Director Mann remembered the day with something less than glee:

> I knew we were not completely ready. I was asked to postpone the operation but Hadassah chapters were celebrating the day. We simply had to go. Top administrative people actually shook me and if others had not interfered I might have been mauled. I was accused of 'killing them,' of 'sucking blood' from them. This was a great psychological crisis in the life of our people because so many changes were involved.

When the day was over, Mann cabled New York:

> Proudly report superbly successful completion Operation M-Day. 6:00 am, nurses prepared patients transfer. 7:30, Hadassah flags unfurled at Medical Center; Mrs. Perlman cut ribbon to admit first convoy of army ambulances bedecked with chapter flags. First came worst cases to avoid the midday heat. Medical corpsmen closing in tenderly to transfer stretcher and transfusion cases to previously designated beds under supervision of doctors and nurses. Next came children, some jumping with excitement; babies in arms of girl soldiers, Ya'al volunteers. 45 minutes after leaving town, patients comfortably settled in flower-decked wards, admiring breath-taking view, reciting benedictions.
>
> As convoy followed convoy, department after department resumed normal working, treatments, x-rays, examinations — as kitchen prosaically prepared meatballs. 1:00 pm, army had transferred 300 patients, half stretcher

cases, completing this stage of move. Impossible express boundless joy, gratitude of staff, patients to every member of Hadassah who made this great day possible.

In Hadassah's first half-century this event had made such an indelible imprint that in the ensuing years, the name "Hadassah" became associated in the public mind mainly with the Ein Kerem Medical Center, to the neglect of its many other activities and achievements.

Three hundred thousand members had been preparing for Moving Day by raising an additional $300,000 to meet the extra cost. Each chapter undertook to contribute a share of the total. This effort was symbolized by a blue satin pennant on which the name of the chapter was stamped in gold. A duplicate of each banner had been sent to Jerusalem to be affixed to the army trucks transporting the patients. At the 1961 national convention in Denver, the hall was darkened and the pennants distributed to the achieving chapters. As the lights went on, the hall was a sea of pennants.

For the chapters there was an additional reward. The film *Fifty Miracle Minutes* picturing the move was shown at the evening meeting and there, projected on the screen, they saw the flags flying atop the army trucks as they moved from the town of Jerusalem to the hills. Arthur Goldberg, then US Secretary of Labor, was a guest of the convention. He watched in the darkened room and caught something electric, unique, from the assemblage in that hall. When the lights went up and the women cheered and wept, he too was visibly moved.

In Jerusalem, once the jitters of moving passed and everyone became accustomed to the elephantine elevators, the intercom systems and the push buttons, Ein Kerem settled down to its primary tasks of healing, teaching and research.

The years to mid-1967 were relatively calm and richly productive. Hadassah physicians were doing 90 percent of all medical research carried out in Israel. Gynecologist Bernhard Zondek worked toward the development of a new contraceptive. He had already produced a series of pregnancy tests, a urinalysis to determine whether a fetus was alive and a test to determine sex in hermaphrodites. Now he and his associates had found that when an alarm clock was rung regularly within the hearing of mice during their mating sessions, they became temporarily sterile. Zondek achieved the same results with a supersonic device. The obvious continuation was to develop an audio-contraceptive for humans, but Zondek died before achieving his aim.

Heart surgeon Joseph Borman's cardiac surgery unit developed an electronic defibrillator that controlled irregular heartbeats during open chest operations.

The result of a blow on the head or sclerosis, a rare disease which neurologist Lipman Halpern called unilateral disequilibrium, made patients stumble while walking or see pictures tilting on walls. Halpern found that red-colored glasses aggravated the symptoms while green or blue glasses corrected them.

Orthopedic surgeon Myer Makin, who won a British medical medal for introducing bone formation through bladder transplants, developed a procedure to lengthen shortened legs by as much as two and one-half inches.

Dental School Dean Jacob Lewin-Epstein, together with pharmacologist Edward Superstine, pioneered the use of a pre-anaesthetic suppository for children undergoing dental surgery. Now children fall asleep and wake up without any recollection of undergoing an unhappy experience.

Dermatologist Jacob Sheskin prescribed the drug Thalidomide, which had been responsible for causing deformed babies, to help lepers. He found that while Thalidomide did not cure leprosy it did alleviate pain, skin eruptions and fevers to such an extent that at least half of the patients could be released from the hospital.

Former Medical Director Eli Davis and ophthalmologist Jacob Landau reported on a method to diagnose such ills as arteriosclerosis, hypertension, diabetes and rheumatic fever by placing a patient's fingertip under a microscope. Called clinical capillary microscopy, the test became routine at Hadassah for the first time anywhere.

In the chest disease department, Professor Joseph Rakower reported that if one had to smoke, the safest of all was an old-fashioned narghileh, the water pipe of the Arabs.

Hadassah was back on the job and ready for the new challenges that were sure to come.

SIX DAYS IN JUNE

In June 1967, Israel was again at war and, as usual, the unexpected happened. The most bitter fighting and the heaviest casualties occurred in the City of Peace. Until the latter part of May, Hadassah did not anticipate a war in Jerusalem any more than anyone else, but, like the entire nation, it was prepared for what it did not expect.

As early as December 1964, in conjunction with the army, Hadassah administrators drew up a confidential manual that detailed Hadassah's aid requirements in time of national emergency down to the last safety pin. Periodic drills tested the manual's instructions. Unexpectedly, hospital chiefs would receive a call from an army officer: "In a few minutes you will be receiving 50 wounded soldiers." A short while later, 50 serious-faced schoolchildren would be brought up in ambulances, each wearing a tag describing his imaginary wounds. Medical Deputy Director Jack Karpas, satisfied with the lessons of the drill would say, "We are ready."

On May 15, 1967, Israel celebrated its 19th anniversary with a military show in Jerusalem. In Egypt, soldiers began to march too, but not in parade. They were headed for Sinai. By May 26, war appeared inevitable. On that day the Hadassah hospital pharmacy, under the direction of

Detroit-born Edward Superstine, began preparing massive amounts of sterile solutions, analgesics and antibiotics.

Military intelligence reported that the Egyptians might use gas as they had done before in Yemen. (Gas installations later captured in Sinai justified the report.) Superstine had quantities of one antidote, atropin, on hand, but it was useless against nerve gas. Cables were sent to Gladys Zales, in charge of purchasing supplies for Hadassah in New York, to buy large quantities of the effective antidote. Gladys said, "We were told everywhere it simply was not available. The Red Cross told us to try the military. We called the Pentagon, but they said that we must first get permission from the inventor in Paris. We got a call from the FBI wanting to know why we wanted this antigas medicine. In the end we failed." But on June 4, one day before war began, a supply sufficient for about 5,000 casualties arrived at Ein Kerem. The supposedly secret formula was produced by scientists of the Weizmann Institute of Science in Rehovot. Fortunately it was never needed.

The weekend before the storm broke was unusually quiet. In synagogues the weekly Torah portion that Sabbath was the beginning of the Book of Numbers wherein Moses is commanded by God to take a census of all military-aged men fit to fight for the Promised Land. Not everyone was in synagogue. Large numbers of soldiers, who had been given leave to confuse the enemy, spent their time on Mediterranean beaches. In Tel Aviv, Prime Minister Levi Eshkol's cabinet determined that Big Power intervention against Nasser's blockade of Israeli shipping through the Tiran Straits was not in the cards and that the 100,000 battle-ready Egyptians poised in the Sinai Desert were a death threat to the State of Israel. It authorized Eshkol and the new defense minister, Moshe Dayan, to resolve the problem at their own discretion. In effect, that was the green light for a preemptive attack against Egypt.

In Jerusalem on Sunday, June 4, some householders busied themselves filling sandbags, preparing air-raid shelters and taping up windows. At Ein Kerem, Director Mann and Deputy Director Karpas had 2,000 window panes to worry about. Workers and student volunteers labored throughout the day and night filling sacks and hanging blackout material.

Of particular concern were the Chagall windows. Extricating them without damaging the glass was difficult. Mann cabled Charles Marq in Rheims to fly to Israel to remove them. He arrived on Saturday night, June 3. On Sunday, Marq and Jerusalem architect Dan Ben-Dor studied the problem. Each of the twelve windows was divided into twelve sections. Each section was made up of between forty and fifty individual pieces of glass. The glass in the center was held fast by putty but around the frames, where the glass was set in concrete, they were reinforced with cement. Ben-Dor carefully tried a dentist's drill with no success. He tried other types of saws with little result. That night, Mann visited Marq at the King David Hotel. The only other tourist in the city's largest hotel was former Hadassah president Rebecca Shulman. She had been on her way to the airport to fly home when her son Paul informed her that war was imminent. She turned back on the spot.

Mann recalls, "Marq felt we were all doomed. I tried to assure him that we would survive but he did not believe me. I left the hotel with a heavy heart and he departed next morning on the last plane. Rebecca remained throughout the war."

This same sense of doom pervaded the Western world. Marc Chagall cabled Hadassah, "I am not worried about the windows, only about the safety of Israel. Let Israel be safe and I will make you better windows."

To some extent the threat to Israel's survival was illusory for the nation was sufficiently strong militarily to withstand the onslaught of all its hostile neighbors. The unanswerable question for Israelis on June 4, 1967, was not whether they would fall but how badly they would bleed.

In New York, Hadassah reacted to the crisis on two levels — the political and the material. President Charlotte Jacobson set up an operations room at National Hadassah headquarters on 52nd Street. Says Charlotte:

We went to Washington at the end of May and we came away with a sense of frustration. We saw every senator and congressman. Everyone said that he would never let Israel down. They all made beautiful speeches. When we pressed them, they admitted that the United States would not act alone but in concert with the United Nations. We came away with a terrible feeling. Although no one doubted American friendship, nothing moved. This gave us the sense of urgency. We had to see to it that everything was well-prepared in Israel.

If Washington could do nothing to prevent the war, the alerted American citizens did everything to ensure its outcome. Staff and volunteers at Hadassah's New York headquarters worked 24-hour days for two weeks. Medical institutions and personnel throughout the country called Hadassah to offer supplies and volunteer. An additional switchboard operating night and day at Hadassah headquarters was swamped with calls. During the crisis National Treasurer Faye Schenk did not have to spend an extra cent from the normal budget. "Everything," she said, "was contributed." One morning during the war, Gladys was startled by a call from the executive director of the International Eye Foundation in Washington.

"Mrs. Zales," he said, "I have two fresh eyes to send to Jerusalem. They must be there within 24 hours."

A National Board member was assigned to meet an Eastern Airlines flight from Washington, pick up the seven-pound vacuum jug containing the eyes and put it on an El Al flight. The transfer was accomplished and the eyes were in ophthalmologist Michaelson's hands with little time to spare.

Like many other firms, pharmaceuticals company Johnson & Johnson donated supplies. Upon receiving Hadassah's thanks for the 1,200 cases of surgical dressings, the firm said it planned to make a gift for Israel a yearly event. (True to its word, America's largest medical supply company continued the donation until 1988). An El Al spokesman assured Hadassah that next to ammunition, Hadassah had top priority to move its supplies. TWA and KLM topped that by taking freight free of charge.

The stories of giving and helping during the 1967 war are now part of American-Jewish folklore. Some Jews signed their Social Security checks over to Hadassah. One man said: "If Israel loses, I won't need it. If Israel wins, I am sure to get it back." Treasurer and future President Faye Schenk received a total of $1,200,000 in cash. One envelope arrived with a $100 bill and an ad from *The New York Times* advertising the opening of Peter Ustinov's play, *An Unknown Soldier and His Wife*. A check for $250 was sent by the Fifth Avenue Presbyterian Church with a simple message: "We want to help." From Chicago, an eight-year-old girl sent in several dollars with an apologetic note, "This is all the cash I have on hand."

One late afternoon toward the end of the war, Gladys received a call from S. Klein, a New York department store.

"I understand you need linens," said the Klein official.

Wearily, Gladys replied, "Yes, yes. Send them right over."

"They will be there in one hour," he replied blandly.

An hour later a truck driver interrupted Gladys. "Ma'am, I have some linens for you."

"Fine," she smiled mechanically. "Just put them there on the right of the receiving area."

The driver looked perturbed. "Lady, I don't want to bother you but I think maybe you better come outside and have a look."

Gladys, somewhat annoyed at the interruption, stepped outside. "I nearly fainted," she said. There before her was parked a 50-foot trailer filled to the roof with 7,500 sheets, 4,500 pillowcases and 1,200 blankets. She asked the driver to take them to a garage and the following week they were on a ship to Israel.

In Israel, three weeks of escalating tensions broke in a crescendo of violence on June 5. At 8:10 am, Radio *Kol Yisrael* (the Voice of Israel) gave a terse report that fighting had broken out on the southern front. At that very moment the first wave of Israeli jets screeching precariously low over the Mediterranean had surprised the Egyptian air force and by the end of the morning smashed it out of existence. At about 9:00 am, the Israeli Army chief medical officer called Deputy Director Karpas: "Fighting has broken out in the Negev. Prepare to receive wounded." This time it was no exercise. Hadassah was put immediately into a Phase IV emergency, the highest state of preparedness provided for in its manual.

Outside the synagogue, Dan Ben-Dor and an assistant had been busy with buzzsaws carefully grinding away at the cement. Slowly they lifted the small pieces of glass comprising the Chagall windows and placed them in the original packing cases, which had been brought up from the storerooms. Dan began work on the north side because he feared that the first shelling would come from Jordanian positions on Nebi Samwil in the north. Director Mann also arrived at the hospital early that morning.

> I gazed from my window and could see the sandbags being filled. I heard the bells pealing from the churches of Ein Kerem. The picture seemed serene. When I saw tanks crossing the road in the distance, I gave the order to bring the patients down. Then I saw shells begin to fall in the valley, first near the Agricultural School and then inching toward the hospital. I could not believe my eyes. It was as though I was watching a movie. I could not believe they were aiming at us. But they were.

As Ben-Dor buzzed away with the saw out in the open, a tremendous blast shook the synagogue on the east side. The shells — probably mortars — had come not from Nebi Samwil but from Beit Jala to the southeast of Jerusalem, near Bethlehem. "If I had started on the windows on the east side I would not have been here today," Ben-Dor said later. Fragments of shells ricocheted from the paving stones and punctured five of Chagall's windows. Altogether six shells hit the medical center. But the damage was not serious. Ben-Dor took cover till the shelling stopped, then returned to his work. By Wednesday, working night and day, he removed nine whole windows. At that point, he realized there was no longer need to continue. All Jerusalem was in Israeli hands.

In Pediatrics, department chief Alex Russell was sitting in his chair by the window when a mortar shell burst outside. Shrapnel sprayed through the aluminum blind. "Over my desk," he recalled, "a beam of light shone. That was the window crashing through." Russell rushed off to the maternity pavilion. He reported:

> Windows were shattered on both sides. The last of the babies had been evacuated within minutes before we were hit. Their empty cots were full of splintered glass. All the children were taken to shelters just in time, except for three children having blood transfusions. None was hurt.

In that long day at Hadassah, five normal births would be registered and three circumcisions performed.

After the sixth shell had fallen, all was quiet. The Jordanians were now concentrating on the center of the city. Mann and his emergency staff had to determine whether to evacuate civilian patients. War casualties would soon be arriving. But with the shelling going on in the city, could Mann risk sending other patients away? He did. The time chosen, mid-afternoon, could not have been better. A lull in the firing had occurred as the buses and private cars moved out of the Ein Kerem compound. Not one of the 300 evacuees was hurt. About 150 who could not be moved were left behind.

Nine teams of surgeons were ready when the first war casualties from the fighting in southern Jerusalem were hurried in. All told, 1,200 beds were available at Hadassah and 17 operating theaters stood by, eight of them underground. During peacetime, the hospital had room for fewer than 700 patients and ran nine operating theaters. Pediatricians, psychiatrists, dentists, biochemists, all not normally needed for casualty work, were pressed into service as assistants to surgeons and as anesthetists. All had taken special courses for emergency care.

The casualties were rushed to the outpatient department, which had been turned into a receiving station. There, two of Hadassah's most senior surgeons — Nathan Saltz and Nathan Rabinowitz — personally examined them and made the basic decisions for their care while they were registered.

What concerned the surgeons most was shock. Physical shock is the result of severe tissue injury or heavy loss of blood and can be fatal. During shock, blood pressure falls and because of the insufficiency of blood to carry oxygen to the tissue, it dies. Physicians were hard put to know clinically when shock was no longer reversible or what caused the condition to be halted.

But they did know that in many cases of shock, infusions of blood plasma could make a difference. At Hadassah during the Six-Day War, surgeons made much greater use of another fluid called Hartman's Solution. Says chief surgeon Saltz: "Before the war we learned that tissue destruction resulted from the contraction of a certain amount of the actual tissue fluids in the spaces of the body, not in the bloodstream. In addition to the bloodstream there was a contraction of fluid that surrounds the cells."

Twelve thousand bottles of Hartman's Solution, a modified salt formula containing lactate, had been prepared in the hospital's pharmacy. Ten thousand bottles were used on the 927 cases who were admitted within three days. On the other hand, only 1,000 bottles of blood were used. The result was phenomenal. Says Saltz, "No patient who came to our hospital without an absolute mortal wound was lost in shock."

In the first day of fighting, Hadassah received 86 casualties. They were well-spaced and Saltz thought that the hospital would have no trouble coping from then on. But he did not know that the troops in the Jerusalem area were only organizing for the big confrontation.

Jordan had four full brigades ready to do battle. Facing them in Jerusalem, Israel had a brigade of reservists, many of them middle-aged, with orders not to shoot unless they were shot at and not to escalate the firing. The big action was expected in the south; Sinai was the objective.

Jordan was not thought likely to become involved and so Jerusalem, lightly held, became a calculated risk. Prime Minister Eshkol made repeated attempts to assure King Hussein that he need not worry about an Israeli attack on the Jordanian front. But Hussein, who had signed a defense pact with Nasser and had put his forces under an Egyptian commander, was receiving enthusiastic messages from Nasser that the Egyptians were bombing Israel into submission. Thus, Hussein agreed to open the front in the east; the Jordanian shelling of Jerusalem began at about 10:15 on the morning of June 5. A brigade of Israeli paratroopers under Colonel Mordecai "Motta" Gur was hastily brought up from the Southern Command and thrown into the battle which did not begin in earnest until early on the morning of June 6. That day was a grievously memorable one. Savage hand-to-hand fighting at such places as Ammunition Hill, Mivtar Hill and the Police School were among the most bitter actions in Israeli history. Companies of men were decimated on both sides. At the end of the day, however, Sheikh Jarrah was taken and the road up to Mount Scopus was reopened. Fate gave the victory to Jerusalem-born Chief of Staff Yitzhak Rabin, who nineteen years earlier had been forced by the British to abandon Sheikh Jarrah and Scopus. Recalls Saltz:

> On that Tuesday morning, the wounded suddenly started pouring in and by afternoon we had every single hall of the first and second floors filled with casualties — Jordanians among them. I remember looking over some that I had not managed to get to and I was in despair. I wondered how we were ever going to manage. But we did and everything was ready. No one was lost.

Operations went on around the clock — 310 in three days. And some lasted four hours. Says Saltz, "I never believed it was possible to go three days without sleep but I proved it to myself."

Neurosurgeon Aharon Beller was abroad when the wars began in 1948 and 1956. He was in Madrid for a meeting of neurosurgeons when the

Tiran Straits were closed. "I packed up and returned fast this time and arrived less than two weeks before it broke out. We did not have as much work as in 1948 but it was so concentrated we had to work day and night. I operated non-stop for 50 hours. We had 40 head and 10 spinal cases."

Good as the results were at Ein Kerem, bottlenecks developed. One of the most difficult to handle was the appearance of about 1,200 volunteers. Karpas reported, "All our well-prepared plans were nearly spoiled because there were so many volunteers. We had to put a special person on duty to direct them." *Ya'al* (Hebrew acronym for "A Helping Hand to the Ill"), an organization of white-smocked Israeli women, cleaned floors and cupboards, made bandages, assisted mothers in the maternity hospital to move into shelter, worked in the emergency wards and ran the cafeterias. Over 500 members were registered at Hadassah. Other hospitals adopted the idea and now there are altogether more than 3,000 Ya'al volunteers throughout Israel.

On Wednesday, June 7, heavy fighting ended in Jerusalem. Israeli troops crashed through the Lions Gate of the ancient walled city and ran toward the Western Wall as Jordan's troops fled back across the Jordan River. When the battle-weary Israelis reached the Wall, they wept. Some prayed for the first time in their lives. Later, they had difficulty explaining their reactions. But they did acknowledge that their arrival at the Wall was for them a transcendental moment that bridged two millennia of Jewish history.

With the dwindling of fighting in the Jerusalem theater of operations, the inflow of wounded slackened. By the end of the sixth day, Hadassah had treated one-third of the nation's casualties.

On the seventh day, Israelis rejoiced and much of the world rejoiced with them. In Washington, recalls Hadassah's 15th president, Rose Matzkin, "Jews from every walk of life — from the *hasidim* to the most assimilated — felt very much involved. It was a kind of spontaneous uproar of joy, of dancing and praying, all outbursts of great emotion and relief."

The Six-Day War offered Hadassah and the Hebrew University a special prize — Mount Scopus. After 19 years in limbo, the mount was once again part of Jewish Jerusalem. Until more Arab hospitals could be built and staffed in Judea, Samaria and the Gaza Strip, Arabs would crowd to Ein Kerem for medical care. That meant that the first order of Hadassah's priorities in Israel would be to revive Mount Scopus.

The astounding victory of June 1967 had finally convinced a skeptical world that Israel was a permanent geopolitical fact. On the home front, the pre-war economic depression ended abruptly as the nation prospered. Israelis moved into the territories to found new settlements on barren soil. Within the neighboring Arab world, revolutionary forces formed as the Palestine Liberation Organization (PLO) and under the leadership of Yasser Arafat, Palestinian Arabs went on the rampage for liberation from Israeli occupation.

Still, the euphoric Israelis were hoping for peace. Prime Minister Eshkol offered a treaty based on the return of captured lands. But the revolutionary groups turned to acts of terror. The Egyptians resumed hostilities even though they held only one bank of the Suez Canal and the Israeli hinterland was well beyond the range of their artillery. For its part, Israel felt more secure and invincible than ever.

Nasser retained faith in ultimate victory through a combination of massive retaliation and Big Power politics. Negotiation with Israel was for him tantamount to surrender. In answer to Eshkol's offer, Nasser declared at an Arab summit in Khartoum that there would be no negotiation, no peace and no recognition. Israel replied: no negotiation — no peace.

The result was deadlock and more fighting. Concurrent with vain attempts by Arab irregulars to terrorize Israel into submission, Nasser declared war along the Suez Canal in 1969 with the aim of exhausting Israeli forces through constant shelling and eventually taking back Sinai by direct assault. Against these threats, Israel built an electronic fence on the eastern and northern borders. In the south, it constructed a massive earth fortification: the Bar-Lev line, named for Chief of Staff Haim Bar-Lev.

For eighteen months the line withstood murderous night-and-day cannonading that came to be known as the War of Attrition.

No attempt was made to conceal the bloodletting from the Israeli public. Hourly, the state radio broadcast names of the fallen soldiers. Citizens worked with transistors held to their ears. In shops, restaurants and parlors, conversation stopped every hour on the hour. In Jerusalem, all eyes lifted skyward when a military helicopter appeared heading southward toward Hadassah. The city then knew a battle was in progress. On Yom Kippur 1969, the service in one synagogue was halted when a helicopter was heard overhead, so that prayers for the wounded it bore could be recited. The military established a liaison office in the hospital at Ein Kerem to alert the staff of incoming casualties. A helicopter pad was built on the western flank to receive them. Half of all the wounded were taken to Hadassah. Fifteen teams of physicians and nurses remained constantly prepared as the hospital built up its capacity to treat as many as 1,800 in case of total emergency. Partly because of the wars, Hadassah built up its orthopedic and rehabilitation departments and instituted units for intensive care.

During the War of Attrition in 1970, the Russians began to intervene directly on Egypt's side, prompting the Americans to step in and force a cease-fire. This was the most enervating of all of Israel's wars to date. Casualties were higher than those in the Six-Day War: 552 dead and 1,761 wounded.

Still smarting from their humiliating defeats, Egypt and Syria quietly trained to take revenge. It came when Israel least expected — on Yom Kippur, Saturday, October 6, 1973. The unprepared, overconfident Israeli forces were taken by surprise and suffered heavily. But in the end they scored a military triumph that would lead to peace with Egypt. At the same time the "victory" created political upheaval at home and sent the population into a long, deep depression.

These wars, interlaced with acts of terrorism, would place heavy burdens on Hadassah and the entire medical establishment. It was some comfort, however, that the "daughter of my people" was on hand to provide a reply to the 2,600-year-old lament of the Prophet Jeremiah:

> Is there no balm in Gilead?
> Is there no physician there?
> Why then is not the health
> Of the daughter of my people restored?[1]

---

1   Jeremiah 8:22.

SCOPUS REVIVED

O n the morning of Sunday, April 25, 1976, eight freshly-painted blue and white ambulances from Hadassah, Ein Kerem moved in single file toward Mount Scopus. In the ambulances sat the first contingent of patients to be transferred to the rebuilt and refurbished building that had lain desolate for 28 years.

As the convoy approached Sheikh Jarrah, the site of the 1948 ambush, the vehicles halted. Those patients who were mobile joined staff to stand by the modest stone memorial. Wearing roses on their hospital gowns, they laid a wreath on the monument and then continued their journey to the top of the mountain.

Scopus had been rededicated six months earlier on October 21, 1975, well before it was finished. In the presence of political leaders and 2,000 Hadassah members, Benjamin Adin, the truck driver who had survived the convoy massacre, now 74, hoisted the flag.

Prime Minister Yitzhak Rabin, who fought for Mount Scopus as a soldier in 1948 and as IDF Chief of Staff in 1967, remembered how for nineteen years Israelis would look across the hills "and recall the majesty of this great hospital and the tragedy that had befallen it. Its name will forever be linked with the agonizing battles for freedom and for the reunification of Jerusalem."

Nine years earlier during the Six Day War, soldiers fighting their way to the Old City of Jerusalem and the Western Wall overran Mount Scopus. They found the hospital and the University campus derelict. Moving in the wake of the troops, the city's intrepid mayor Teddy Kollek stopped at an Arab hotel in the eastern part of the city to put a call through to HMO Director-General Dr. Kalman Mann.

"If you want your hospital," Teddy called in his typically direct manner, "Come and get it."

Mann knew the day before that Scopus had fallen into Israeli hands and he sent a cable to Hadassah headquarters in New York: "Scopus Regained."

On the morning of June 9, 1967, Hebrew University President Eliahu Elath and Mann set off with their parties for Scopus in seven cars. With Mann were Hadassah's former President Rebecca Shulman and his predecessor, Dr. Eli Davis.[1] Despite occasional Arab sniper fire, the vehicles paused in the Sheikh Jarrah quarter to stand at the site of the 1948 convoy ambush while Mann recited *kaddish* for the victims.

They then traveled the extra mile to the crest of Scopus where they were welcomed by 120 guards who, a few days earlier, withstood a 36-hour Jordanian Army bombardment. While Israeli jets circled the sky, flags were raised on the roofs of the Hospital and the University. Inside the buildings of both institutions the bulletin boards still bore notices dating to 1948.

On his return to Ein Kerem workers hoisted Mann on their shoulders as though he were the groom at a traditional Jewish wedding. Tears of joy flowed when he reported that Hadassah's flag again flew over Scopus. Speaking over an intercom to those assembled in the dining room of the

---

1   Shulman, who in the early 1950s pledged that Hadassah would return to Scopus, was present during all of Israel's early wars. During the 1948 War of Independence she was Hadassah's representative in Israel. Her son Paul, a volunteer with the Israel Defense Forces, was the first chief of the Israel Navy.

hospital at Ein Kerem, Mann said, "This flag symbolizes an unusual type of war — the war against disease and ignorance. It is a flag of peace."

Later, Mann would write in his *Reflections*: "It was an example of the general state of elation, relief and almost hysterical happiness that gripped the entire nation."

President Charlotte Jacobson arrived in Israel shortly after the war. Together with former president Lola Kramarsky, she had received special permission from the State Department to fly into the forbidden zone. At his office, Prime Minister Eshkol told her that it was essential for Hadassah to reopen the hospital because it would help reunify the city.

Charlotte went with Kalman Mann to the Mount of Olives and there, with the help of several rabbis, searched for the grave of Henrietta Szold. They found that the Jordanians had built a road over the graves in Judaism's oldest cemetery, Henrietta's included. Some stone markers were obliterated, others were reported to have been used as flooring for Jordanian military barracks. Using a cemetery chart, counting the indentations in the ground, they identified the site. The grave was rebuilt and in a formal ceremony a new stone was put up.

Israeli soldiers escorted Charlotte's party to Scopus[2] past minefields and the debris of war. When Charlotte entered the building it immediately became clear to her that Hadassah was not returning to a hospital but to a ruin.

"I'll never forget the weed-choked paths, the areas of waste and loneliness," Charlotte later recalled.

Walls were broken and damaged by shell holes. Woodwork was rotted. Medical equipment and beds were rusted. Winds tore through shattered windows, howling down corridors in what had once been wards and nurses

---

2   The Jordan-Israel Armistice Agreement that ended the 1948-49 war provided free access to the Western Wall, Hospital and University even though the Arab Legion controlled the area. Jordan ignored these provisions even though Scopus was supposedly demilitarized. Every two weeks, a UN-supervised convoy supplied and relieved the Israeli guards at the Hospital and the University buildings.

stations. Henrietta Szold's carefully tended garden was overgrown with weeds. Weeping, the visitors read a message scribbled on a wall by an Israeli guard who had stood lonely watch under the UN flag: "If the day comes and this building is filled again with patients, let them remember those who watched over this place during difficult years."

Charlotte Jacobson returned to her quarters and, overcome with emotion, addressed a letter to Hadassah leaders throughout the US. She related what she saw on Scopus and described her first pilgrimage to the Western Wall where, like thousands of others, she could hardly believe she was not dreaming.

"Verily," she wrote, "the age of miracles is not over. This is indeed an age of renaissance for the Jewish people."

On the national level, Israel's leadership had learned from the siege of 1948 and the war of 1967 that to protect its capital, it must build well in the north, east and south where the city faced Arab armies. In the north, as the Romans had known 2,000 years earlier, Scopus was the key to the city. And on that hill the Hospital and the University would be rebuilt as fortresses both above and below ground — institutions for both peace and war.

For the government it was politically vital to have the hospital in operation quickly because satellite communities were rising nearby. Planned in a semicircle around what was then the border of Jerusalem, new townships such as Ramot, French Hill, Ramat Eshkol, Neve Ya'acov, Talpiot East and Gilo formed a *cordon sanitaire* (safety zone) for Jerusalem's Jewish population.

Jerusalem's mayor had plans of his own. In 28 years in office, Teddy Kollek outdid Herod the Great, garbing the city with gardens and parks. He initiated museums and a fine center for the performing arts. He provided the Arab population with new housing, schools and cultural institutions. The city received a reliable water supply; sewage disappeared from the streets; tourists flocked to artistically-lit sites. In municipal elections held after the war, unprecedented numbers of non-Israeli Arabs flocked to the polls to vote for "Teddy." Jerusalem had never been so grand or so expansive.

Now that the hulk of Scopus was in Hadassah's hands, what was to be done with it? Doubts were at first expressed about the necessity of reopening the hospital. Hadassah now had the larger medical center at Ein Kerem and the expense of rebuilding Scopus would be enormous. The late President Faye Schenk, who oversaw the building campaign, laid any doubts to rest. She wrote: "When Hadassah descended from Mount Scopus in 1948, a silent vow was made that some day we would return." And for Hadassah, a vow could not be broken.

The Hadassah National Board Mid-Winter Conference of 1968 was the first to be held in Jerusalem and a pilgrimage was made to Scopus. Relates former President Ruth Popkin: "We gathered on a cold, miserable day. We literally froze but we were standing on the mosaic floor with Hadassah's symbol still there. We were warmed because we were back on our 'Hill of Healing.'"

The controversy over the purpose and character of the restored hospital absorbed the leadership for more than a year. Kalman Mann wanted a general hospital built to serve the surrounding mixed community of Jews and Arabs. Others were more interested in specialist medical centers, among them a cancer center, a Mayo-type clinic, a psychiatric hospital and institutes for brain research and tropical diseases. A gift of one million pounds sterling was received from a Swiss Jew whose child was disabled. But there was a string attached to the money: build a children's hospital. The gift was returned.

While Hadassah debated, cadres of young Israeli volunteers joined by youth from countries as distant as Australia, India and the US, began cleaning up. They cleared debris, painted walls, laid floors, removed rust from plumbing and built internal walls. Then, the builders could begin.

Charlotte Jacobson, who as HMO chairperson presided over the reconstruction after completing her tenure as President in 1968, favored reopening the hospital immediately. Dr. Mann suggested that in view of the many war injuries, a physical rehabilitation department with 120 beds should be the first priority. Working its way through a maze of complications, the National Board decided in August 1968 to reopen Scopus as a general community hospital to serve both Arabs and Jews. It would have one of the finest rehabilitation centers in the region.

The population in the vicinity of Scopus was reaching 150,000 toward the end of the century. It was that population that the hospital was expected to serve. In the end, its reputation as a fine, clean, quiet institution grew rapidly and attracted Jewish and Arab patients from the entire Jerusalem region.

Politically, a community hospital was the right way to go. Mount Scopus lay at a strategic juncture between Arab and Jewish sides of the city. There were no general hospitals of Hadassah's caliber serving the Arabs. In a major sense, opening an all-purpose hospital was a goodwill gesture for the entire community. Prime Minister Eshkol assured Charlotte Jacobson, "It will help ensure the unification of Jerusalem."

In America, Hadassah's largest fund-raising drive ever was launched. Practically everything that would go into rebuilding Scopus was made available for naming, whether it be a bed or a brick, a ward or a washroom. In the end more than $30,000,000 was raised.[3]

Tel Aviv architect Ya'akov Rechter was chosen to plot the new layout. He would retain Eric Mendelsohn's external "design-for-the ages" Bauhaus architecture. Commented Rechter, "It would have been easier to raze the site and start again but the original building was classical and had been declared a national monument."

The exterior was saved but the interior was reconstructed from scratch.

---

3   The US government contributed an initial grant of $5,000,000 toward reconstruction. Yearly, Hadassah has applied for and received grants under the American Schools and Hospitals Abroad assistance program (ASHA). Grants ranging between $300,000 and $3,000,000 have been used for everything from buying equipment in America to training African doctors. Today, total ASHA grants for Hadassah have amounted to more then $40 million.

The revived hospital's first medical director, Uri Khassis, described the scene as construction got underway: "A labyrinth of wires, pipes, ducts and cables was built to bring air conditioning, gas, demineralized water, soft water, sterile water, oxygen and monitoring units for intensive care."

Over the years, the Scopus hospital became a melting pot. At few other sites in the mixed city would Jew and Arab meet in such accepting conditions.[4] In the pediatric departments alone, Arabs made up about 50 percent of the patients. "While there are two Arab hospitals in the immediate area," says former Scopus Medical Director Jacques Michel, "they [the patients] come to us probably because of Hadassah's name and tradition."

Staffs were integrated with Arabs employed at every level from medicine to maintenance. Dr. Najah Husseini, a relative of the late Grand Mufti of Jerusalem, was hired as an orthopedic surgeon in 1976 at the age of thirty-four. He recalls that when he decided to go to work at Hadassah his father cautioned, "Take the job but remember that there are people who won't like it. You may be endangering your life."

The threats did not materialize. Says Husseini:

> On the contrary, the Arab community respects me because I work at Hadassah. As a member of an old and prominent family stretching back 700 years, it [working at Hadassah] was not an easy decision because of its Zionist enterprise. As an orthopedic surgeon, I need a big hospital to work in and Hadassah is quite simply the best. I'm not a political man, I am a doctor. My interest is in the physical health of my patients, not their souls.

Apart from the usual hospital departments, Scopus boasts the only 35-bed

---

4   One poignant example: in 1989 HMO surgeons at Ein Kerem transplanted the heart of an Israeli soldier killed by Palestinians in Gaza to save the life of a 54-year-old Jerusalem Arab.

rehabilitation center in Israel. "There's nothing that is not done here," says Prof. Michel, "from road accidents to burns, children to the elderly." Its neonatal intensive care unit serves both Hadassah hospitals, as does its hospice for terminal patients.

Death is not a favorite subject of conversation in hospitals. Much less so in the Ina and Jack Kay Hospice for the terminally ill. With its panoramic view of the Judean Hills, the scenic hospice is a serene spot in which to live out one's last days.

Ruth Shahal Gassner, who became the institution's first director at thirty-two, is a nurse by training. She maintains that the occasional unorthodox treatment is beneficial and that a break from conventional treatment does a patient more good than drugs.

The fourteen-bed Scopus hospice, unique in Jerusalem, has a staff of forty-five nurses, social workers, physical and occupational therapists working in an integrated system. Thirty volunteers from half a dozen countries help out. About ten applicants are available for every bed. But not every dying person is admitted. A patient must be conscious, within months of dying and must have come to terms with his or her fate.

Despite its 100 percent mortality rate, the hospice has successfully escaped the air of a morgue. The decor of the carpeted, curtained lounge is one of tranquillity with its enormous oil painting of golden Jerusalem, book-lined shelves and classical music. On Friday nights, candles are lit. Patients have access to the kitchen for a snack and visitors are never restricted. "The hospice is a home, not a hospital," says Shahal.

Says former HMO Director-General Professor Shmuel Penchas, "Pain is an unnecessary curse. We can ensure that patients in the last stages of incurable disease do not suffer dehumanizing pain." For that alone the hospice fulfills the words of Dame Cicely Saunders who founded modern hospice care in London in 1977: "We'll do all we can not only to help you die peacefully but also to help you live until you die."

Adam Friedmann stands at the beginning of the life cycle, among those at Hadassah who are plumbing the mysteries of life's source — the gene. It is a promising field of research seeking *inter alia* to ensure that embryos will grow into healthy humans and live long lives insulated from today's life-threatening diseases.

In 1985, the Israeli-born Friedmann was a professor of neurology at Stanford University when Shmuel Penchas invited him to begin work on gene therapy. In 1988, Friedmann established the Middle East's first department in Molecular Diagnostics on Mount Scopus. "It is much easier to correct the gene in an embryo than in the whole body," says Friedmann.

This revolutionary technology has been used to remove a fertile egg from a woman's ovary, fertilize it in a test tube and then return it to the womb. On November 1, 1983, Hadassah doctors succeeded in inducing a normal birth in a 35-year old 'high risk' woman after they had developed an embryonic cell in a test tube and implanted it in her womb. It was the first "test tube" baby born in Israel.

Research has produced results. Using molecular diagnostics, Friedmann's Department of Genetics identified the chromosome that carries the gene for inclusion body myopathy, a crippling degenerative disease of muscles common among Persian Jews. Tests were established to determine in advance whether families carry the chromosome. Similar type testing can be made for some types of breast and colon cancer, cystic fibrosis and Gaucher's disease.

Hadassah's gene therapy unit is interdisciplinary and includes virologists, molecular biologists and physicians from hematology, neurology, surgery and the liver group.

"The ultimate thing we all want is immortality," observes Dr. Friedmann. "And genes that cause death are known. We carry a lot of genes that mutate during our lives. We could repair all that."

Small as it is, Scopus carries an exceptional number of research programs and researchers. Internists Drori Ben-Yishay and Michael Brusztyn are studying the relationship between insulin resistance and the development of high blood pressure; nephrologist Meir Brezis is examining the causes, prevention and treatment of kidney failure; and neurologist Menachem Hanani is concentrating on the physiology of the autonomic nervous system and of the smooth muscle system.

As the renewal of Scopus reaches its third decade, the hospital's managers feel as though they are in a compression chamber. The number of beds permitted by the Ministry of Health is less than 300 (compared with Ein Kerem's 750), but they are occupied 100 percent year-round. "From time to time our occupancy rate is over 200 percent. We have 50,000 visits to our emergency room every year," says former Scopus Medical Director Michel.[5]

With Jerusalem's population bursting at the seams, Michel worries about Scopus's future. "I'm concerned about what will happen to this hospital in the next ten years when there will be a major increase in population. We will not be able to cope for long with the same number of beds."

Should Scopus expand? Being small has its advantages, admits Michel:

> I know about the behavior of every physician. A proper doctor-patient relationship is a very important asset in this hospital and I don't want to give it up. My principal concern is the patient and his family. For me, treatment isn't only the technical aspect. It's also the environment, the human relationships, the way you address people. And for that I feel we have a tremendous advantage on Mount Scopus, because this is a very congenial hospital. There is a tradition of good humane behavior here.

---

5   Prof. Jacques Michel retired as Scopus Medical Director in 2000 but continues to serve Hadassah as a professor at HMO. He frequently addresses Hadassah International groups in Europe.

WAR AND PEACE

Israelis were returning home from synagogue on the afternoon of October 6, 1973, when across the nation, sirens wailed. A startled public had never heard an alert on a Saturday, certainly not on Yom Kippur, the holiest day of the year.

In Jerusalem, residents were equally shocked to see heavy vehicles rolling through the streets on the only day when traffic usually came to a standstill. The radio, usually silent on the Day of Atonement, broadcasted coded phrases that sent reservists racing to join their units.

The War of Atonement was underway. Israel's leaders had been caught off-guard and the nation would pay dearly. At the Suez Canal, Egyptian forces broke through the lightly defended Bar-Lev line and quickly overran the bunkers. On the Golan Heights, brigades of Syrian tanks ruptured Israel's defenses and nearly forced their way into populated areas of Galilee. Only a small force of Israeli tanks heroically held them at bay until reinforcements could arrive.

It would be 18 days before the Israeli forces surrounded an entire Egyptian army and headed toward Cairo. In the north on the Golan Heights, they threatened to march to Damascus, visible in the distance.

Jerusalem was deceptively quiet that fateful Yom Kippur morning. In the absence of Professor Mann, his deputy director was startled by a red alert: war would break out within a matter of hours. He set the hospital's battle emergency plan into motion. Immediately, 270 patients were sent home. Another 220 were transferred to the top floors. The hospital was ready for 700 military cases and, if need be, could treat 1,200.

Within an hour, 95 of Hadassah's 250 staff physicians joined other reservist staff members rushing to their units.

Nearly 2,000 local volunteers took their places while others from overseas joined them later. In New York alone, about 100 physicians called the Hadassah office to offer their services.

On October 8, President Rose Matzkin hastily summoned a National Board meeting. Rose reported that the national office switchboard was inundated with phone calls. Members wanted to know how they could help. Chapters around the country collected cash and held blood drives.

In Israel, 80 percent of the doctors in military field hospitals were Hadassah graduates. Not only were their trained skills needed but so were their inventiveness and their nerve. In one reported case, a Hadassah physician serving in the Sinai improvised a collar from local sand and water to provide traction for a spinal injury, saving the soldier from total paralysis. Another MD, working under fire, successfully grafted a soldier's severed arm — a delicate procedure even under optimal conditions.

Hadassah-Ein Kerem did not come under fire as it had in the Six-Day War. Fortunately for Israel, this time King Hussein kept Jordan out of the fray. Three years earlier in September 1970, Israel had saved him by sending tanks to the Syrian border when the Syrians and the Palestinians threatened to overthrow his regime. Although the king may not have consciously thought he was returning the favor, in actual fact, he was.

Hadassah's role during this war was to handle the most difficult cases, especially surgery and rehabilitation. All told, 527 critically wounded soldiers were treated. Half were orthopedic cases.

Using porcine skin and silver sulfadiazene, Hadassah's plastic surgeons could save most severe burns patients from horrible disfigurement and loss of limb. Ophthalmologists used a new radiation detector to search out metal splinters lodged in eyes. For the first time, the psychiatric and social services units treated the men and their families simultaneously. Mobile battery-operated X-ray machines had pictures ready in minutes.

The Arab armies had achieved complete tactical surprise. Despite threats from Arab capitals and hostile maneuvering, the Sinai and the Golan Heights were being defended as though Israel were at peace: small and ineffective formations were in position when the Arab forces moved. Shortages of ammunition and faulty equipment hindered the defense; Israeli planes and tanks fell easy prey to Egypt's Russian-supplied rockets and missiles.

It was 1967 in reverse. As Egyptian forces moved dangerously close to Israel's border and the Syrians reached the entrance to Galilee, panic-stricken Defense Minister Moshe Dayan observed to Golda Meir that the Arabs were about to destroy the Jewish State.

Prime Minister Golda Meir repeatedly appealed to US President Richard M. Nixon and Secretary of State Henry Kissinger to restock Israel's depleted armories. Should the Arab forces threaten Israel's existence, she said, Israel would use every means at its disposal to defend itself. The possible use of Israel's undeclared atomic resources could not be ignored. Nixon lost no time ordering supplies rushed to Israel from America's European warehouses. They arrived none too soon. The Russians were reported to have dispatched a nuclear ship in the direction of Alexandria harbor. Little did the world know how close it was to nuclear war.

Despite heavy casualties and the loss of enormous quantities of materials, the Israeli forces turned the tide in less than three weeks. But the price was high: 2,600 dead, 7,300 wounded. Despite their trouncing, Egyptians under Anwar el-Sadat claimed a moral victory, believing that their national honor was restored.

Although Israel could justifiably celebrate its military achievement, the "victory" had deep traumatic repercussions. The Six-Day War had led the nation to believe in its invincibility. But the tragic number of casualties and the diplomatic isolation of 1973 destroyed that illusion.

By 1974, Israel agreed to pull back from the Suez Canal in Sinai and from its forward positions on the Golan. A depressed Golda Meir left office in April 1974, after encouraging her ambassador to the US, former Chief of Staff Yitzhak Rabin, to replace her. He would be Israel's first *sabra* (Israeli-born) prime minister.

In the national elections of 1977, disaffection with Labor Party rule became evident. The public called on veteran right-wing statesman Menachem Begin to run its affairs. Dayan, who escaped official responsibility for the 1973 war's initial failures, became foreign minister in a national unity government.

Begin was in power only five months when, on November 15, 1977, he sent an invitation to Egyptian President Anwar el-Sadat to visit Israel. Five evenings later, Sadat thrilled the entire world by flying into Israel. In an address to the Knesset the following afternoon he declared, "No more war."

Sixteen months of arduous negotiations followed, capped by talks between the principals at Camp David, Maryland, where US President Jimmy Carter took charge. Begin agreed to hand back all of the Sinai to Egypt, uproot the existing Jewish settlements there and offer the Palestinian Arabs autonomy in lands occupied since 1967. Ransom having been paid, Egypt, the world's largest Arab nation, became the first to make peace with Israel.

In Washington, on March 26, 1979, a distinguished crowd of 1,200 gathered on the north lawn of the White House to watch a smiling Sadat and Begin sign the peace documents, with President Carter as witness.[1] In

---

1   For their efforts, Anwar el-Sadat and Menachem Begin shared the 1978 Nobel Peace Prize. But the treaty cost Sadat his life. He was assassinated on October 6, 1981, while watching a military parade in Cairo. His successor, former Air Force Chief Hosni Mubarak, honored the peace accord.

Tel Aviv, 100,000 people gathered to celebrate. In the capitals of extremist Muslim nations, crowds mourned and demonstrated.

Hadassah National President Bernice S. Tannenbaum was present for the historic event, as she was in 1977 when Sadat made his precedent-shattering visit to Jerusalem. At a peace banquet in a striped tent on the White House lawn, Bernice met Sadat and his wife Jehan and was welcomed by Menachem Begin and his wife Aliza. Subsequently, Bernice headed a six-member group of Hadassah leaders, including former President Rose Matzkin, to Cairo where they and Jehan Sadat considered how special education in Egypt could benefit from Hadassah's services, notably in vocational training. Nothing concrete emerged from the meeting because of the cold peace that followed Sadat's initiative. Nevertheless, with this tentative proposal Hadassah entered the field of international affairs.

"The peace opened a new vista of possibilities for Israel and for Hadassah," Bernice says.

Thirty-one years had passed since Israel was founded. But the bloodshed, displacement of peoples and squandered resources could have been avoided if the Arabs had accepted the 1947 UN decision to partition Palestine into Jewish and Arab states.

The Arab world had in the meantime created the Palestine Liberation Organization under Yasser Arafat. The stated aim was to regain all of Mandate Palestine and set up a "democratic" Arab state in which Jews would have "minority rights." No match for the Israeli army in battle, the PLO chose terror as the weapon to achieve its ends.

Airplanes and civilian buses were hijacked, schools raided and children killed, bombs were sent through the mail and settlements in Galilee were attacked with rockets. Headquartered in Beirut and the refugee camps of Lebanon, the PLO targeted Israeli and Jewish institutions overseas.[2] In

---

2   Israel unilaterally withdrew all of its forces from southern Lebanon in May 2000.

London, Israeli ambassador Shlomo Argov was gunned down by a terrorist.

Shortly thereafter, on June 6, 1982, Prime Minister Begin launched "Operation Peace for Galilee," ostensibly to protect Israel's northern frontier. In reality, the objective was to destroy the PLO's infrastructure in Lebanon. Eighty-five thousand Israeli troops invaded PLO strongholds in Lebanon, a nation already torn apart by civil war and controlled by Syria. The Israeli forces temporarily occupied Beirut and destroyed the PLO's ability to operate. After the ground forces left, the air force carried out heavy bombings of the city and finally forced Arafat and his cadres to leave the country. They continued fighting Israel from Tunisia and elsewhere in the Arab world.

Israel evacuated most of its troops from Lebanon by August 1985, but set up an 860-square-kilometer security zone in the south of the country to prevent the Iranian-backed Hezbollah and other fundamentalist groups from attacking settlements in Galilee. The fighting on Lebanese soil, in which Israel also engaged Syrian troops, was costly. From the beginning of the Peace for Galilee campaign until the end of 1996, 713 young Israeli men were killed on Lebanese soil and at least 2,300 more were wounded.

While Israel was simultaneously making both peace and war with its neighbors, Hadassah became engaged on a completely different front. In the US, women were demanding entitlements long denied them. As it began to question its relevance to the assertive American woman, Hadassah saw that its "new vista" was at hand. It had to take up women's issues.

THE JEWISH WOMAN

975-1985 was the United Nations "Decade of Women." Although Hadassah under Henrietta Szold had shown the way in the 1920s, it was only in the latter half of the twentieth century that the feminist movement gathered enough momentum to move women out of their homes into careers. In the 1960s and 1970s, American women were challenging a male-dominated world, marching out of their homes to battle for their rightful place in society. They were joining the army, founding corporations, directing banks, preaching from pulpits, running for office.

Many Jewish women were in the vanguard of the Women's Liberation Movement. A Hadassah-sponsored study of the period showed that 46 percent worked full-time outside the home. This fact had serious implications. More than ever, marriage as a formal religious rite was put on hold and single parenthood became respectable. Marriage between Jews and non-Jews was no longer an oddity. Increasing numbers of Jewish women were working as volunteers for non-Jewish organizations.

With all these changes, Hadassah began a period of soul-searching. Says former Hadassah President Marlene Post, "We continued with all our projects but we asked ourselves whether we really were relevant to people in America, in Israel. We got down into the trenches."

Surveys conducted by Hadassah showed that half of its 300,000-plus membership belonged to 100 of the organization's 1,374 chapters. Most members were age 55 or over. New York and California, America's largest Jewish centers, were under-represented. The typical member was married and led a traditional, conservative lifestyle. It was easy to get new members but difficult to retain them. Young women joined the ranks when they had time, quit when they took up careers.

National Board Member Leah Silverstein, former president of the 4,000-member Chicago Chapter, describes the Jewish community as "more apathetic. Young people never knew a world where Israel did not exist. Even though we included Israel and Zionism in most of our programs, young women were looking for something to do in their own communities."

Former Hadassah President Carmela Kalmanson painted the picture more starkly: "We faced the danger of eroding knowledge of and commitment to Jewish life and Israel."

It became obvious that if Hadassah were to remain afloat on a Zionist keel in American waters, it would have to change course to one closer to that set by the feminist movement. Hadassah fixed its bearings on two parallel directions: "action" and "issues." "Restructuring" and "strategic planning" were the compass points by which Hadassah would find its way. Greater emphasis was placed on issues not necessarily connected with Judaism, Zionism or Israel. Studies were commissioned.

In 1987, President Kalmanson ordered a five-year restructuring plan and set up a strategic planning committee under the leadership of Sue Mizrahi and Jane Zolot. In 1993, it was followed by a second committee, headed by Karen Venezky, that was to extend its reach to the year 2000.

Professionals were called in to guide the volunteer leadership. By the mid-1990s, the staff of Hadassah House in New York numbered 229, half of them in executive or managerial positions. The Executive Committee allocated $2,500,000 to revitalize Hadassah chapters in many communities. Enhancement grants were given out. The result was larger membership, better fundraising, new ventures. Clearly, Hadassah was moving in new directions and updating its management practices.[1]

Essential for any big business is a consistent, determined drive to raise new capital. So it was for the National Board of Hadassah. "We changed the way we do business," says former HMO chair Bonnie Lipton (now National President). "In days gone by, our major funds came from the grass roots. We would wait until funds came to us. Now we aggressively look for gifts, bequests and annuities. We set up special task forces, make appointments to see prospective donors, explain our work and try to provide them with the opportunity to be recognized while they are still alive."

Still, some donations drop into Hadassah's lap.

One such largesse appeared in the wake of a phone call to Hadassah House in 1992. On the line was an aged resident of Los Angeles.

Her question was simply put: "What can I get if I leave money to Hadassah?"

"Like many others," says Bonnie, "this lady was shopping for a project, and many proposals were sent to her." Time passed, until four years later in the spring of 1996, out of the blue, another phone call came from Los Angeles. An attorney representing this same woman declared that he had a prospective donor with a considerable amount of money. Bonnie recalls that the lawyer described the donor as a secretary who retired in 1947 and had never married. In a matter-of-fact tone, the attorney went on, "She wants to leave Hadassah $5,000,000."

Bonnie flew to Los Angeles in June 1996 to suggest several projects that could bear the donor's name. Out of that meeting came approval of a new concept, suggested by HMO Director-General Shmuel Penchas — the Goldyne Savad Institute for Gene Therapy.

---

1 With 271 women currently on its National Board, Hadassah has one of the largest boards of directors of any institution or corporation in the US.

Hadassah is also receiving millions of dollars in wills from its members. Says Bonnie, "A large percentage of these funds also come from non-members who have heard or read about our state-of-the art medical facilities."

Hadassah receives gifts in the form of bequests, stocks and works of art. A male chemist who had been blinded in a factory accident and subsequently collected a large sum of money for his injury, offered $5,000,000 on condition that a hospital be built in the Negev in his name. He was told, "We do not plan on building another hospital in the Negev, but until such time as we do, if you approve, we can use the interest for our hospital in Jerusalem."

Another woman walked into the New York office with a gift of $1,500,000 for the Orthopedics Department at Ein Kerem. She had traveled by bus and refused to take a cab home. Later, Bonnie held a luncheon for her at Hadassah House. The grateful donor admitted to Bonnie, "This is the first time I've had a meal with company in twenty years." Bonnie said, "It broke my heart."

On another occasion, an altruistic angel dropped into Hadassah House in connection with an estate of which she was a trustee. She wanted to commemorate her husband's first wife, with whom she had had a warm friendship. Bonnie responded with a dramatic concept to which the donor readily agreed. Thus, the Jula Goldwurm Maternity Pavilion was born, with the donor selflessly refusing any public recognition for her own efforts.

Despite her present overwhelming presidential schedule, Bonnie Lipton still devotes countless hours and her creative skills to secure major gifts for Hadassah. As a knowledgeable interpreter of the Hadassah medical scene, she is usually successful!

Hadassah's full-fledged entry into the women's movement came during the UN Decade of Women, and on an issue that challenged its Zionist identity. The subject was the "Zionism equals Racism" equation. It was first brought up by Palestine Liberation Organization delegates at the

First International UN Decade of Women Conference held in Mexico City in 1975. "Until that time we were not actively involved in women's issues," says Bernice Tannenbaum. "The UN resolution thrust us into the women's movement."

Helplessly, Israel and Diaspora delegates watched the PLO resolution equating Zionism with racism pass. Only the US and Denmark joined Israel in opposition. Hadassah had sent a delegation to help in the fight, but could do little to change the general anti-Israel attitude.

Later that year, seventy-five nations were mustered by the PLO from among the Arab, Russian and Afro-Asian blocs to steer a similar resolution through the UN General Assembly. Many nations, the 1973 war and the 1974 oil embargo still in their minds, abstained out of fear of retribution by the Arab states.

United Nations Resolution #3379 equating Zionism with racism was the PLO's greatest political victory. Israel's Ambassador to the UN Chaim Herzog tore up the resolution in front of the members of the Security Council and the Australian Parliament condemned the UN's action, but the resolution remained on the books as a tool for vilification of Israel for 16 years.

That put Hadassah, along with world Jewry, into a fighting mood.

What followed was more outreach to other women's organizations and more awareness of its potential strength as America's largest Jewish women's organization.

A large delegation went to the 1980 UN-sponsored mid-Decade of Women conference in Copenhagen to struggle, in vain, against the anti-Zionist resolution.[2] And in 1985 Hadassah leaders faced the critical meeting in Nairobi ending the UN Decade of Women.

What started out in Mexico City as a disaster for Zionism turned into a triumph in Nairobi. But the victory did not come easily. Bernice

---

2 In Copenhagen, former National President Bernice S. Tannenbaum attended as a journalist representing *Hadassah Magazine*. With her press card, she slipped into a PLO meeting, but once recognized, was ejected.

Tannenbaum, then head of the American section of the World Zionist Organization, joined forces with Uzi Narkiss, information head of the WZO in Jerusalem, to initiate a campaign to nullify the UN resolution.

Their first goal was to expunge the Mexico City resolution from a document the Nairobi conference planned to adopt to sum up a decade of women's accomplishments. Toward that end a women's caucus was created. The WZO enlisted the support of the World Jewish Congress and B'nai Brith International.

Once the anti-resolution forces were mobilized, a delegation of five women leaders, led by Bernice, headed for the White House on the morning of August 16, 1984.[3] A smiling, charming President Ronald Reagan sat next to Bernice as the group was served tea, coffee and cookies. For forty minutes he listened as they articulated the case. Unbenownst to them at the time, Reagan's daughter, Maureen Reagen, had been chosen to head the US delegation to the Nairobi meetings.

At the end of the meeting, Reagan's advisor Ed Meese told him, "You should do something to please these women." Before leaving the White House, Bernice asked Reagan to repudiate the UN resolution publicly. He agreed. In addition, he promised that the US delegation would walk out of the Nairobi conference if the "Zionism Equals Racism" resolution was included in the final conference declaration. The president's statement bristled with four strongly-worded paragraphs stating that the United States would "oppose any agenda item at the Nairobi Conference which associates Zionism with Racism."

A year-long campaign followed. AIPAC's Esther Kurtz, Bernice and others lobbied US senators to support a resolution of condemnation that would call on the UN to repeal the invidious Resolution #3379.

---

3   The five-member delegation included three former Hadassah Presidents: Bernice, Charlotte Jacobson, President of JNF, and Frieda Lewis, Chairman, World Jewish Congress, American Section. The other two were Barbara Mandel, President, National Council of Women, and Midge Decter, Director, Committee for the Free World.

Tannenbaum remained in the US as the preliminary women's forum began in Nairobi. After the Senate passed resolution #98 calling for the revocation of #3379, Bernice rushed to the airport where she hopped on a plane to Nairobi. With the issue about to be raised there, she did not wait for the final text of the Senate resolution.

With only the draft in hand, Bernice went straight from Nairobi airport to call on Ambassador Alan Keyes, State Department adviser to the American delegation. When she informed him that the resolution had passed the Senate he replied, "If that's so, our course of action is clear." He indicated publicly that the United States delegation, the largest at the conference, would walk out if a Zionism as Racism motion was adopted. Until the last day the matter was touch and go.

At the conference PLO speakers received wild ovations. Eritrean women demanded independence for Eritrea but challenged Israel's right to statehood. With the exception of Egypt and Jordan, Arab representatives staged a noisy walkout when Israeli delegation head Sara Doron rose to speak.

The US held the key. Each time an anti-Zionist proposal was made, Maureen Reagan spoke up loud and strong. The threat to make good on her father's pledge straightened the backs of Western European and Latin American countries. After all-night deliberation, a compromise proposal by Kenya was finally accepted by the USSR, the PLO and then the conference delegates: Zionism would be omitted from the final document. That rang the death knell for the entire issue.

A few months following Nairobi, the House of Representatives joined the Senate in overwhelmingly repudiating the resolution. Six years later, US President George Bush, following Reagan's lead, admonished the UN General Assembly: "Zionism is not a policy, it is the idea that led to the creation of a home for the Jewish People…To equate Zionism with racism is to reject Israel itself, a member of good standing." On December 16, 1991, the United Nations finally cleansed its books of the canard by a vote of 111 to 25, with 13 abstentions. Egypt, ostensibly at peace with Israel, was one of the twenty-five against.

At the next world conference of women held near Beijing in 1995, Hadassah addressed other critical problems. Zionism no longer appeared to be anyone's scapegoat.

Hadassah volunteers have always been active in Washington, DC, particularly during both World Wars. But then its concerns were narrowly focused on Zionist problems. It was not until the 1980s that the organization began to shoulder a breathtaking spectrum of American social issues ranging from welfare reform to religious freedom.

"I am a professional volunteer," says Hadassah veteran Shirley Blumberg. Like Denise Tourover before her, Shirley pounded the pavement from 1983 to 1991 as Hadassah's Washington Representative. For the next five years she ran "Washington Programs," a project that yearly brought 800 members to the nation's capital for briefings in the Pentagon, State, Justice and Health Departments, in Congress and at the Israel Embassy. By the time they went home, says Shirley, "They were changed women, ready to campaign on behalf of Hadassah's concerns." Local legislators, the media and the public received clear messages from them on where Hadassah stood on the issues.

To get the message out to its members, Hadassah created and sold multicolored, nine-by-four inch "issue cards" for a penny each.[4] Each one of these cards, still being used, navigates members into action. One card, appropriately colored grass green, proclaims "Protect the Earth." Black cards declare "Stop Terrorism," yellow "Stop Domestic Violence," purple "Promote Voter Registration and Participation." A bookmark informs the membership that more than 40,000,000 Americans aged sixteen and over

---

4   Hadassah has had other penny campaigns. Seven decades earlier it asked American schoolchildren to donate a penny to provide lunches for needy children in Jerusalem. Pennies arrived at the Hadassah National office by the basketful.

do not have a high school degree and urges, "Support nationwide reading and writing initiatives with coalition partners." One card addresses a specific concern of Jewish women: "Free the *Agunah*."[5]

As an issue, women's health was a natural for Hadassah. In 1992, National President Deborah Kaplan took nearly 1,500 members to Washington to participate in the "March for Women's Lives." Their banners proclaimed a woman's right to have control over her own body. While eschewing the term "abortion" out of consideration for the views of the Orthodox community, Hadassah is clearly pro-choice; outside the Republican and Democratic presidential conventions of 1996, Hadassah members held placards proclaiming "Pro-Faith, Pro-Family, Pro-Choice."

One of Hadassah's pressing initiatives is its attempt to stop insurance companies from discriminating against women who are genetically predisposed to certain cancers. Nearly 10 percent of all cases of breast and ovarian cancers are genetically linked. Insurance firms use genetic information to limit, deny or even cancel coverage — or to increase premiums. The result is that many women avoid being tested.

In Washington, after US Representative Louise Slaughter (D-NY) co-sponsored legislation in the 104th Session of Congress to forbid this discrimination, a Hadassah task force began an information campaign among legislators. The campaign was partially successful: the bill passed the House but was roadblocked in the Senate. In the 105th Session of 1997, Hadassah's task force again stumped for the legislation.[6]

---

5   An *agunah* (a "chained woman") is one whose husband refuses to grant her a Jewish bill of divorcement (a get) without which she cannot remarry under Jewish law. Women whose husbands abandoned them or disappeared without witnesses likewise are agunot. In Israel, some men who refuse court orders to give their wives divorces are jailed until they do.

6   After being introduced in three successive sessions of Congress, comprehensive legislation prohibiting genetic discrimination still has not been passed at the federal level. Rep. Connie Morella (R-MD), Rep. Louise Slaughter and Sen. Tom Daschle (D-SD) have reintroduced the "Genetic Nondiscrimination in Health Insurance

Probably the best example of Hadassah's recent health work centers on illnesses specific to women, notably osteoporosis,[7] breast cancer and afflictions such as heart disease, not generally considered "women's diseases."

During a recent New York convention, curbside mammography examinations were made available to passersby outside the national office on West 58th Street; mobile testing units were supervised by technicians from New York's Memorial Sloan-Kettering cancer institute. The practice was later adopted by chapters throughout the United States. In the mid-1990s, Hadassah's Women's Health Department developed "Hadassah Cares" cancer awareness programs including "Check It Out" for high school girls and "Buddy Check" for adult women. It later instituted a testicular cancer "Check It Out" program for men and boys.

Heart disease — America's #1 killer — rises among postmenopausal women faster than among men. Yet it is probably the most neglected of all women's illnesses. Says one American heart specialist, "Women go to the doctor less frequently than men; they complain less but they do die of heart disease. Research, however, concentrates on men." To overcome the problem, Hadassah went to Washington in 1995 to help push legislation that established a women's health division at the National Institutes of Health.

Other initiatives occupied other task forces: domestic violence against women ("That legislation was immediately accepted by Senators and Representatives," comments Board member Shirley Blumberg); rape as a hate crime; and foreign aid and continuing support for Hadassah medical

---

and Employment Act" (H.R. 602/S. 318). As of January 2002 there were over 250 bipartisan co-sponsors of H.R. 602 in the House of Representatives and 26 co-sponsors of S. 318 in the Senate. Hadassah remains a tireless advocate for this legislation.

7   Twenty-five million American women and more than half of all women over 65 suffer from the bone-thinning disease. In Jerusalem, Hadassah helped finance the Osteoporosis Center and undertook studies into causes and cures at its Minerva Bone & Calcium Research Center.

and educational institutions in Israel through the American Schools and Hospitals Abroad program (ASHA). A nonpartisan campaign to get Hadassah members to register to vote was launched during the 1996 presidential campaign and continues to this day.

Hadassah has made its voice heard on other issues:

- Immigration reform. Working with the Council of Jewish Federations, Hadassah helped tone down harsher aspects before the recent bill was passed.
- A balanced budget. The organization spoke in opposition because it objected to anticipated cuts in human services.
- Funding private religious schools. Hadassah remains firmly opposed. "We think it's wrong because it weakens the public school system. Jewish communities should support Jewish day schools," says Blumberg.
- The environment. Hadassah has joined a Jewish consortium of organizations to preserve nature.

"These projects enabled us to involve many young women whose primary interests may not necessarily be Israel but who want to give service in the US," says former President Deborah Kaplan.

Hadassah states emphatically that it is in Washington to educate and to inform but not to lobby for any party. The Washington Action Office (WAO) is directed by the American Affairs office in New York which constantly watches political events, and is currently chaired by National Secretary Judith Palkovitz.

Hadassah does not labor alone. It builds or joins coalitions for each new campaign. On laws to restore religious freedom to individuals Hadassah worked with groups as diverse as Baptist and Orthodox Jewish action agencies (for Jewish men, the coalition secured the right to wear a skullcap in the US Army). Washington Action Office Director Marla Gilson and her six-member volunteer task force frequently labor twelve-hour days out of their one-room office in Silver Spring, Maryland.

Hadassah participated in a group of 1,200 Jewish leaders who went to Washington in September 1991 to support Israel's request for the Bush Administration's guarantees of $10 billion in bank loans. An angry President Bush attacked the "powerful political forces" arrayed against him. He characterized himself as "one lonely little guy down here" who, by objecting to the loan guarantees, was presumably protecting the peace process. After Jewish leaders expressed indignation at the remarks, Bush hurried to mend fences. He called in a small select circle of Jewish leaders to assure them of his support for Israel and his desire to avoid confrontation. Deborah Kaplan was one of two women in the group. In the end, Israel received the loan guarantees.

For all its other concerns, it was not until late in the century that Hadassah targeted problems specific to the Jewish woman. For far too long, Jewish females had been denigrated as "ladies" who go to or hold luncheons, matriarchs or Jewish American Princesses. Henrietta Szold and Golda Meir were exceptions in a society where the image of the Jewish woman had become fixed in literature and in men's minds as a specialist in cooking chicken soup, matchmaking and spoiling her children.

One of the first attempts to tackle problems facing the Jewish woman arose during the 72nd national convention held in Miami Beach in August, 1986. Projects were initiated to address the increase in nontraditional family units. Hadassah began to reach out to young singles, single parents and career women.

In 1989, Hadassah provided its members with *Jewish Marital Status*, a collection of forty-three essays on marriage and the family, edited by National Director of Education, Dr. Carol Diament. It revealed that one-third of Jews in the latter part of the twentieth century were single, divorced, widowed, childless or homosexual. The traditional Jewish family as an underpinning of Jewish survival was obviously in trouble.

In 1994, Hadassah created the twenty-three-member National Commission on American Jewish Women to study their problems and to determine ways to bring greater Jewish meaning into their lives. One year later, the NCAJW published *Voices for Change: Future Directions for American Jewish Women*. Largely based on existing individual studies, it brought to light some upsetting revelations:

- Jewish families were having fewer than two children on average.
- More than one-fourth of young Jewish women were intermarried.
- Many younger Jewish women support humanitarian causes, yet the number of those supporting Jewish organizations was decreasing.
- Most Jewish women were not affiliated with synagogues or Jewish organizations.

The picture was not completely bleak, *Voices* reported. "This generation of Jewish women is the most educated in history and perhaps the most thirsty for a richer, deeper engagement with Jewish tradition."

Voices also indicated that insufficient research existed on the American Jewish woman. One outcome was the joint funding by Hadassah and Brandeis University in 1996 of the Hadassah International Research Institute on Jewish Women (HIRIJW). The Institute was set up at Brandeis University under the leadership of Dr. Shulamit Reinharz, Director of Women's Studies at Brandeis. Brandeis, a non-denominational university in Waltham, Massachusetts, is an ideal location for the Institute since it is the only university in the world with a PhD program in Jewish Women's Studies.

Remodeling Hadassah was not confined to the United States. In 1996, a new HMO Medical Board, composed of lay leaders and medical experts, was assembled to direct its medical centers. At the same time, an Israel projects task force, headed by National Treasurer Barbara Tirschwell and Bernice Tannenbaum, was established to see whether Hadassah's projects in Israel were answering Israel's — and Hadassah's — present-day needs.

A study of existing projects by Dr. Daniel Elazar's Jerusalem Center for Public Affairs found that on a national scale Hadassah could best serve the Jewish State by enhancing research and development. For Jerusalem, he suggested an education program to give job training to the *haredi* (ultra-Orthodox) community. Elazar predicted that by Hadassah's centennial year of 2012, the ultra-Orthodox would account for 38 percent of the city's Jewish population. He believed that this fact had implications for Hadassah.

The monopoly of the Orthodox community on matters of personal status such as marriage and divorce is one of the most sensitive Israeli issues facing Diaspora Jewry and Jewish organizations. On advocating religious pluralism, Hadassah has maintained a consistently positive policy.

In 1980, Orthodox and secular Jews in the Knesset debated an amendment to the Law of Return.[8] The proposed amendment would have recognized only Orthodox conversions to Judaism. Some American Jews considered withholding financial support for Israel. Hadassah never considered withholding funds, but did respond.

"Our position was unequivocal," says Carmela Kalmanson. "We expressed strong feelings to the President of Israel and Members of the Knesset. We stood with the majority of Israelis in rejecting the amendment and the National Board of Hadassah passed several statements in support of pluralism." Hadassah spans the spectrum, with members in all religious wings of Judaism. The majority are affiliated with the Conservative and Reform movements, both of which advocate pluralism in Israel.

No matter how the city's demographic character changes, Hadassah

---

8   Israel has no written constitution but it does pass basic laws which are, in effect, the same. The Law of Return (1950), one of the first and the most important to be adopted in Israel, gives all Jews — whether born to a Jewish mother or converted — the automatic right to immigrate to Israel and to citizenship.

and Jerusalem are firmly linked. The National Board made this clear at festivities marking the organization's 85th birthday year, held in the Knesset in January 1997. It gave former Mayor Teddy Kollek a standing ovation when he remarked:

"Nobody has been as faithful to Jerusalem as Hadassah."

UNIVERSITY WITHOUT WALLS

It was 8:00 on a hot Monday morning in July 1996, when nearly 2,000 Hadassah women attending the 82nd Hadassah National Convention gathered in the ballroom of Miami's Fontainebleau Hotel.

Fourteen feet above the stage of the grand ballroom hung the longest prayer shawl ever made. Composed of 48 embroidered, hand-painted patches, the quilted *tallit* measured 123 by 95 inches.[1] Its fringes (*tzitzit*) were six feet long.

The setting was ready for America's largest *Bat Mitzvah* ceremony. One hundred and twenty-two women, ranging in age from Sara Leah Schuval's 12, to Gertrude Kussner's 86, recited the blessings over the Torah scrolls that lay open on four tables. At the four lecterns, 12 celebrants took turns reading the portion of the week, Deuteronomy 1 ("…'Go in and possess the land…' Moses exhorted").

The ceremony was a far cry from the first held in America. In 1922, Judith Kaplan, daughter of rabbi and philosopher Mordecai Kaplan, celebrated her *bat mitzvah* in a modest Friday night service at the Society

---

1   The numerical equivalent in Hebrew letters (*gematria*) of 123 and 95 spelled the words *oneg malka* or "a queen's delight."

for the Advancement of Judaism in New York, which her father had founded.[2]

In 1982, Hadassah conducted a small *Bat Mitzvah* ceremony at the Western Wall in Jerusalem to the hisses and boos of ultra-Orthodox women. At the Miami convention, some women wore phylacteries (*tefillin*) during the morning service. Nearly half wrapped themselves in prayer shawls (*tallitot*). Convention Chairman Barbara Goldstein officiated. A yeshiva graduate, Barbara says, "Women can do everything men can do in synagogue."

"It used to be that boys got bar mitzvahs and girls had a sweet sixteen party," added celebrant Fern Baum, 38, of Sunrise, Florida. "No more."

"The idea behind the *Bat Mitzvah*,[3]" said Barbara Spack, National Jewish Education Chairman who served as cantor, "is to empower women with a knowledge of Judaism so they can teach others. It will deepen their spiritual involvement and their connection to the Jewish community."

Says Leah Reicin, co-chairman of the convention, who conceived this program, "It has changed the lives of 122 women."

Each woman who was called to the Torah had completed a six-month course in Judaism, Hebrew language and observance. At the end of the courses, they were required to write a *drash* (commentary). All 122 did, some in verse. Hadassah later published them in a blue bound volume.

The scope of Hadassah's education effort would do justice to the curriculum of any fine American university. Consider some of the subjects available: medicine and health, religion and ethics, Bible study, Hebrew language and culture, Middle East politics and American affairs, Jewish

---

2   In 1936, Rabbi Kaplan spoke to Hadassah leaders, urging them to start a movement that would establish women's equality under Jewish law. Judith, an artist, teacher, and the spouse of Reconstructionist leader Rabbi Ira Eisenstein, died in 1996.

3   As of Convention 2001, the program has been renamed *Eishet Mitzvah*, as most participants are already full adults, rather than girls entering womanhood.

history, literature, family relations, social advocacy, feminism, technology, and vocations from computers to cooking.

The roots of Hadassah's education efforts are deep, going back to the end of the nineteenth century when Henrietta Szold and her mother initiated study groups solely for women. Many American universities began similar study groups in the late 1800s, but for men only. From its beginnings, Hadassah has never neglected educating its members. In 1916, a School for Zionism was founded by Henrietta's friend Jessie Sampter. She saw Zionist literacy as a prerequisite for the founding of a Hadassah group. The School, imitated by many chapters, was later transformed into an education department headed by a professional educator.

"By educating women," says Jewish Education Director Dr. Carol Diament, "we create leadership and, by doing so, we interest them in Israel."[4] Says Carmela Kalmanson, "The more we know and the richer we are Jewishly, the more we can enrich the Jewish family."

In the search for their Jewishness, Hadassah chapters have made education a priority. One of Hadassah's publications was a book indispensable for teaching: Leo Schwartz's *Great Ages and Ideas of the Jewish People*. Adopted by universities, it was the brainchild of Esther Gottesman, then Education Chairman.

In the late 1950s, Hadassah joined the World Jewish Bible Society. Hadassah's Education Department, then chaired by Rose Goldman, promoted self-led Bible study groups with guides prepared by notable Jewish scholars. Because of the guides' comprehensive approach to the Book of Books, after four years more than 350 groups existed throughout the country. The guides were used by a diverse group of educators and institutions, and by WIZO in Switzerland and Australia. A request even arrived from the librarian of Alcatraz. When former President Judith

---

4 Dr. Carol Diament, Hadassah's National Director of Jewish Education, is the first woman to receive a PhD in Jewish Studies from New York's Yeshiva University.

Epstein heard that inmates of the California state prison were interested, she remarked, "Of course. They have time to study."

In the 1960s Education Chairman Frieda Lewis integrated Bible study and Hebrew language into the department's program. One of Hadassah's more erudite leaders, she later served as its 17th National President.

In the 1980s, the eroding commitments to Jewish life and Israel spurred new efforts. When Carol Diament took over the Jewish Education Department in 1985, she sought to raise Jewish education to a high academic level as a remedy for the serious demographic problems affecting Jewish women. On a trip to Kimberly, Texas, Carol visited a Hadassah weekend retreat where the topic centered on the issues discussed in *Jewish Marital Status*. The president of the group, a divorcée, related to Carol how she rescued her self-image by climbing to the top of the local leadership ladder. "I now feel better about myself. Hadassah has really given me back my life."

Out of that experience, Hadassah developed Vanguard, a singles' project, to bring together single Jewish men and women.

One of the more invidious threats poised at all Jews comes from Christian evangelists who wear the mantle of Jewishness but refer to themselves as "Jews for Jesus" or "Messianic Jews."[5] Some disciples joined Hadassah.

On the national level Hadassah was slow in coming to grips with the situation since its constitution has no religious restrictions. "A national policy is being developed," says former President Marlene Post. "To be a Hadassah member you must accept Jewish values and Zionist principles."

Assimilation, intermarriage and apathy are other perils to Jewish life. The

---

5   Israel's Supreme Court ruled on a 1962 petition submitted by a Jewish-born priest that a person could not at the same time claim to be a Jew and practice another religion. The priest, Oswald Rufeisen, had claimed Israeli citizenship as a born Jew under the Law of Return. His petition was denied.

reply, proclaimed American Jewish educators, is "Jewish continuity." To help stem the downhill slide, Hadassah developed a family learning program.

In the spring of 1993, Hadassah invited the Whizin Institute for Jewish Family Life at the University of Judaism in Los Angeles to help develop a project that would tune in to the need. The result was "Training Wheels: Cycling Through the Jewish Year with Hadassah," geared for children ages two to eight. In 1996, the project published a 484-page canary-yellow, looseleaf manual that had as its logo a teddy bear riding a tricycle emblazoned with the Star of David on the wheels. It was meant for use by Hadassah volunteer teachers and guides.

Popularly referred to in Hebrew as *Al Galgalim*, the aim is to reach the young Jewish family by teaching children how to celebrate the Sabbath, Jewish holidays and customs. "Training Wheels," a metaphor for learning, offered parents, grandparents and their young children a series of educational play experiences, while the adults discuss parenting.

On an academic level, courses and seminars were initiated on college campuses. So far, 2,500 women have participated in one of these seminars billed as "a university without walls."

In 1994, Carole Curtis, then president of the New Rochelle group, convinced the State University at Purchase (New York) to sponsor a joint program with Hadassah. Professors from the university staff volunteered to teach twenty-eight workshops. So successful was the symposium that fourteen more were begun on such campuses as Yale, Brandeis, Stanford and Memphis.

In Richmond, Virginia, Roberta Neblett, a retired comparative languages professor, began teaching a group of sixty women twice monthly. With her daughter she created a young study group that met with the older women and named the joint group "Bubbies and Babes." They used as their text *Ribcage*, a collection of 17 fictional short stories written by Israeli women and published by Hadassah. The title is a reference to Adam's rib, because, as editor Dr. Carol Diament puts it, "The writers came out of their inner world to write about their lives."

The group spawned five others in the area. By the end of 1996, there were 400 throughout the country. Today, enrolled in Hadassah's education programs are an estimated 30,000 women led by a cadre of 4,000 peers.

In Israel, the Hadassah College of Technology,[6] on the premises of the former Rothschild Hospital in downtown Jerusalem, is a success story by any standard. For one, it has the highest ratio of immediate graduate employment in Israel — 92 percent. "That is because we teach and train those skills the country needs," says Ya'acov Amidi, director since 1978.

A PhD in Education Management, Amidi braved critical educators when he insisted that applied courses be taught by professionals in the field rather than by licensed instructors. "People worried that the standard of teaching would drop," says Amidi. "Here the pros get brief teaching courses before they enter a classroom."

Out of the College and into the marketplace flow a steady supply of optometrists, printers, chefs and concierges, computer programmers and engineers, dental technicians, video and X-ray technologists, aerial and underwater photographers.

HCT runs special courses in computers for the legally blind. Seven of the 850 students in 1997 were sightless. One graduate became so proficient at his work that he was put in charge of computers at a police headquarters.

A special one-year course was created for Ethiopian immigrant students who had attended high school in Addis Ababa, but were unable to pass Israel's matriculation tests, required for university entrance. When all

---

6   In 1988, Hadassah's Alice L. Seligsberg High School was transferred to the Jerusalem municipality. The following year, the name of Hadassah College was changed to the Hadassah College of Technology so as not to be confused with community colleges and preparatory schools in the US.

passed the rigorous examinations after the first year, the course became a fixture.

Among the student body are Israelis, Arabs, Druse and Europeans. More than half are women.

HCT is so popular it can only accept one-quarter of the applicants. Still, only 15 percent of the running budget is derived from fees. Hadassah covers 70 percent and certain Government Ministries the remaining 15 percent. "Gradually," says Amidi, "we will upgrade our programs to grant a bachelor's degree and we will be introducing courses to help women return to the work force."

Since 1957, Hadassah has financed another "university without walls" in Jerusalem. Founded in 1909 by Jewish students to further the goals of Zionism and foster traditional Jewish values, Young Judaea was sponsored by the Zionist Organization of America. Henrietta Szold edited its first journal, the *Young Judaean*. Among the first American Zionists to settle in Palestine during World War I were Judaeans. In 1927, it became affiliated with the scout movement in Palestine and many of its clubs thereafter took on the name *Tsofim* (Scouts).

In 1941, Hadassah joined the ZOA to set up a youth commission to take responsibility for Young Judaea. Its first venture was an experimental summer Zionist Camp Institute held in July 1941 outside Amherst, New Hampshire. Hadassah-ZOA scholarships brought together 50 outstanding Young Judaeans from 16 states. For one month the campers, who were known as the *Rishonim* (the First), attended seminars conducted by leading Zionists in the US and Palestine, among them former Hadassah presidents. At the close of the Institute, they voted unanimously to make the camp project a permanent feature of Zionist life in America. Out of this experiment developed the popular Brandeis camps.

Seven years later Young Judaea membership hit its all-time peak of 30,000, but then began slowly to decline along with that of other Zionist groups in the US. No longer able to bear its half of the budget, the ZOA opted out in 1967. Hadassah, under Charlotte Jacobson, assumed complete responsibility, and built a headquarters for Young Judaea on the Hebrew University campus, sharing it with Hadassah's School for Occupational Therapy. On Mount Scopus, the building resonated with Zionist nostalgia; during World War II it was the residence for Hadassah nurses. Henrietta Szold had an office and lived her last years there.

Named for Judith Riklis by corporate magnate Meshulam Riklis who financed the building's reconstruction, Beit Riklis opened in 1969. Young Judaea had wandered from place to place around the city, running one-year courses for overseas youth since 1956. Now it had a home in an academic environment. Today, Beit Riklis serves as dormitory, dining room, library and classrooms.

With new vitality injected by Hadassah, Young Judaea's membership gradually increased and its programs expanded.

In 1967 a group of Young Judaean graduates in the US joined to form a cooperative settlement in Israel. President Faye Schenk made sure the group had a "Hadassah flavor." Aliyah Chairman Rose Goldman "kicked the doors open for us," says founding member Hinda Gross, who later became the President of Hadassah-Israel. In 1970, sixty-two families arrived to spend four years in an integration center outside Jerusalem while negotiating with the Jewish Agency for land.

At Passover 1974, thirty-three families from the original group moved to their new home — Neve Ilan, located on a strategically-located Judean Hills prominence above the village of Abu Ghosh at the entrance to Jerusalem. Unlike other settlements, Neve Ilan was based on light industry — electronics and computers — and social services rather than on agriculture. Later, the settlement included kiwi and citrus culture as well as the raising of turkeys. Most successful of all has been a resort hotel that opened in 1977. Neve Ilan's population today: fifty-five families.

In 1973, Young Judaeans established a kibbutz at Ketura, achieving one of the supreme goals of Zionism. Charlotte Jacobson assisted in negotiating for the land as she had done for Neve Ilan. The kibbutz (pop. 300), located in the Rift Valley (Arava) north of Eilat, specialized in introducing exotic fruits to Israel. Its open society within a traditionally religious community is unusual for Israel, so unusual that the Knesset awarded Ketura a prize for tolerance.

In 1997, the number of young people participating in one of five Young Judaea programs in Israel approached 550. American and British high school students attend a summer leadership training course or join Israel Discovery groups for what Beit Riklis Director Dan Krakow calls "a positive exposure to Israel." A third group is comprised of young people sent by their home communities. On returning home they are engaged in local Jewish community work.

High school graduates join *Hamagshimim* ("the Fulfillers") for continued study and travel in Israel. Often some are age thirty and over. In 1996, Hadassah transformed one of its old buildings in Jerusalem's German Colony to serve Hamagshimim as a community and integration center for new immigrants from English-speaking countries. Among the Hamagshimim was a group of talented US and South African actors whose first production was *Steel Magnolias* by Robert Harling.

Most scholastic of all Young Judaean activities is the ten-month Israel program for high school graduates. Accredited through the University of Judaism in Los Angeles, it focuses on Jewish studies, the Hebrew language and Israel. The year of study is enriched by months of work on a kibbutz.

"That's what makes the program special," says Doron Krakow, Director of Young Judaea. "The living experiences really connect our students to the people and to the country. Every other year we have a Young Judaea contingent joining the March of the Living. They go to Auschwitz and other Nazi camps and ghettos in Europe. Those who go on the March must make a commitment to attend the year-long program. For us, the visit to Poland is part of an educational process."

In the US, Young Judaea conducts six camps — five are junior camps for ages eight to 15. The sixth, Tel Yehudah, is Hadassah's flagship camp, located in Barryville, N.Y. It serves as a national leadership center for those who return from their summers in Jerusalem and for those no longer eligible for one of the junior camps. All told, 1,200 children and teens attend every summer.

The benefits of these programs are evident. Krakow estimates that about 20 percent of the youth who attend the all-year program eventually settle in Israel. "The second end product," he adds, "is that they become actively committed Jews. We know that the rate of intermarriage among them is lower — 20 percent vs. 52 percent for the general Jewish population. At the same time they show a higher rate of affiliation with Jewish and Zionist institutions."

They also have a stronger attachment to Jewish ritual. A 1993 continuity study of Young Judaean graduates was revealing:[7]

- 92 percent of graduates regularly attend a Passover seder (vs. 62 percent of adult Jews overall).
- 85 percent light Chanukah candles (vs. 60 percent).
- 64 percent are involved in a Jewish organization.
- 41 percent have done volunteer work.
- 59 percent have taught in religious schools.
- 66 percent demonstrate a strong affinity for Israel (25 percent higher than their peers).

In 1996, fourteen motivated Hamagshimim graduates enlisted in the Israel Defense Forces. Before that, Young Judaeans on programs in Israel showed their true mettle by remaining during one of the State's most threatening crises — the Gulf War of 1991.

---

7   The telephone study was made of 200 parents and Young Judaea graduates in August-September 1993 by Alan Ganapol of marketQuest, Inc.

THE EXPLOSIVE NINETIES

"Operation Desert Storm," the Allied attack against Iraq, began at 2:40 am on January 17, 1991. Since the previous July, Iraq had occupied the oil emirate of Kuwait. Fearing that the vast oil wealth of Saudi Arabia was next on Iraqi dictator Saddam Hussein's list of conquests, the US marched at the head of a coalition of nations to stifle the threat.

Located at the western side of the Middle East land mass that bridged Asia and Africa, Israel expected the worst from Iraq, and with good reason: Saddam had publicly threatened that he would char half of Israel with chemical weapons, should the US attack Iraq.

Dread of unconventional warfare enveloped Israel. The fright was exacerbated when the Shamir government, at the insistence of the US, kept Israel's mighty air force out of battle. It was well known that Hussein had large stores of poison gas and bacteriological weapons that he could deliver in the warheads of Soviet-made Scud missiles. As a precaution, every Israeli resident received a protective kit containing a gas mask and a syringe to inject atropine, an antidote.[1]

---

1   Israel was nonetheless at the Iraqi front by proxy. The US Navy in the Gulf used Israeli-made drones — remotely guided aircraft — to pinpoint Iraqi targets.

To reassure the Israelis, the US sent teams with Patriot missiles to intercept the Scuds. Never before had Israel depended on foreign soldiers for its defense. Over Iraq, the US Air Force hunted down Scud launching pads. But the Patriots did not effectively stop the missiles and many of the launching pads that the Air Force bombed were dummies.

In anticipation of gas attacks, Hadassah-Ein Kerem installed a triage unit to treat victims on the plaza outside the hospital. With an emergency Hadassah appropriation of $1,000,000, the unit provided doctors with protective suits, arranged long rows of showers and tents and stocked up on anti-gas inoculations.

As military weapons, the Scuds were duds. To reach Israel, the Iraqis had doubled the range of the original Soviet-made weapon to 300 miles. In so doing, they halved its payload to 160 pounds, a mosquito bite by military standards. Without accurate guidance systems, the Scuds often fell within several miles of their planned targets, but still created havoc among the civilian population. Believing correctly that Saddam Hussein would aim his missiles at the Tel Aviv and Haifa areas, tens of thousands of residents fled their homes. Many went to Eilat, thereby saving the resort town from a disastrous tourist season.

The first missile crashed into the Tel Aviv area before dawn on January 17. Six missiles followed within 24 hours. The army calculated that 32 more hit in the 37 days that followed, most of them aiming for vital installations in Tel Aviv, and at the port and refineries of Haifa. Some missiles fell into the Mediterranean, others near Arab villages.

In February 1997, the official Baghdad newspaper *Qadissiya* reported that of a total of ninety-three Iraqi missiles fired during the war, forty-three were aimed at Israel, five of which were targeting the Dimona atomic reactor. Israel refused to confirm it but a map published in the Israeli press at war's end pointed to three missile hits in the general area of the reactor.

Early on, Israel's military leaders determined that Saddam Hussein was not arming the missiles with gas or germs. But as a cautionary measure, Israelis were warned to remain in sealed rooms rather than move to underground shelters during attacks. Israelis went about their daily affairs with anti-gas kits slung over their shoulders like Londoners had during the World War II blitz. Fashion-minded women in Tel Aviv made carrying cases for the kits to match their clothes. At the sound of a siren, everyone rushed to a sealed room, donned masks and waited anxiously for the all-clear signal or watched TV for word that the threat was over.

On the evening of February 23, sirens interrupted an Israel Philharmonic Orchestra concert in Jerusalem conducted by Zubin Mehta. Violinist Isaac Stern stopped in the middle of a Mozart concerto and walked off the stage with the orchestra as 3,300 members of the audience put on their masks. Seconds later Stern walked back on stage, smiled at his ghostly-looking audience and began playing a Bach adagio — without his mask. He received a standing ovation.

Wholesale cancellation of tours by American-Jewish groups created a strong feeling of annoyance among Israelis. The continued presence of German and Japanese tourists only heightened that feeling.

Hadassah snubbed the Scud threat and changed the location of its Mid-Winter Board meeting from Washington, DC, to Jerusalem. Forty members arrived, a relatively large turnout for such meetings even in peaceful times. The timing was exquisite — it was the first day of the war.

Says Board member Ruth Cole, "We voted to go in order to show our solidarity." Apart from a group of French Jews, the Board members were the only guests in their Jerusalem hotel. Earlier that week, Bernice Tannenbaum had been one of two Americans who attended a Jewish Agency Executive meeting where participants deliberated in gas masks.

The war had its lighter side for the Hadassah leaders. Deborah Kaplan remembers that when the first Scuds fell, she was dining in a Chinese restaurant in Tel Aviv with a few Hadassah companions. "A Chinese waiter calmly escorted us to a shelter where we were helped on with our gas masks. But one of the women in the group had a problem. "She could not put on the mask without removing her wig. After a brief moment of hesitation she good-naturedly went about doing so, to everyone's approval," she recalls.

Non-Hadassah youth groups suffered a high rate of attrition with many leaving for home at the first opportunity. But on Mount Scopus, most Young Judaeans stayed. One Young Judaean said that the entreaties of his parents in the US to return were more difficult to face than the Scuds.

Says Director of Young Judaea in Israel Dan Krakow, "There was a feeling that the Diaspora was not really with us during the war. That is why the fact that most of our students remained made a big impact."

Amazingly, the 39 Scuds killed only two Israelis, one a volunteer in the defense effort. They wounded 223, most of them lightly. More than 4,000 buildings were damaged and 1,644 families were evacuated.

Finally, at the end of February, the terror was over. It was Purim and, across the country, children could safely go to parties. Some used masks of Saddam Hussein as the modern-day Haman.

While American forces were mobilizing for war in the Gulf region, a buildup for peace in the Middle East was likewise moving along. In October and November 1991, Israel and its Arab neighbors were brought together by the US and the Soviet Union for a six-day meeting in the Spanish Royal Palace in Madrid.[2]

At the Conference's opening, President Bush pressed for "a real peace." But that was not going to be easy to achieve. Arabs and Israelis used the presence of the world's TV cameras to trade verbal blows and make impossible demands. Syria's foreign minister called Prime Minister Yitzhak Shamir a "terrorist" and Shamir denounced Syria as tyrannical. The Palestinians called for a two-state solution that they knew Israel would not even consider.

Behind closed doors, Israel and the Palestinians outlined principles for a five-year period of autonomy in the West Bank and Gaza to be followed by

---

2   The Madrid Conference was the last major diplomatic move made by the Soviet Union before it broke into fifteen nations in 1991.

a final settlement. Syria foreclosed on a quick agreement by demanding that Israel agree to give up the Golan Heights even before talks began. Lebanon parroted Syria.

Beyond Israel's neighborhood, there was a noticeable relaxation of tensions. The Gulf War had temporarily put Israel in the same camp with all anti-Iraqi forces, including Saudi Arabia. The fact that Israel had refrained from joining the battle played well in Riyadh. That, together with the Madrid Conference, signaled the countries in the Third World that they could now end diplomatic isolation of the Jewish State.

In 1992, Israel was officially recognized by nearly one-half of the world's population when China and India established full diplomatic relations. In a gush of enthusiasm, other nations followed suit, including African nations and the Vatican. In the ensuing years, Gulf state potentates traded visits with Israeli leaders and, together with Morocco and Tunisia, opened offices in Tel Aviv.

The Madrid Conference brought former enemies together to talk face to face, something that Israeli governments had sought for decades. Secret Israel-PLO talks followed in 1993 in Oslo, Norway, where a program was drawn up for Israel's gradual withdrawal from urban areas of the Gaza Strip and the West Bank.

Oslo I, as it became known, was signed on the White House lawn as the world watched. Prime Minister Yitzhak Rabin, who had succeeded Shamir after the 1992 elections, reluctantly shook hands with PLO Chairman Yasser Arafat, but only after considerable nudging by US President Bill Clinton. The picture of the handshake became a journalistic icon.

In September 1995, a second agreement, Oslo 2, continued the peace process. By the beginning of 1997, Israeli troops had redeployed out of the Gaza Strip and West Bank cities after making security arrangements for Jewish settlements.

While peace with the newly established Palestinian Authority crawled forward, insurgent activities continued unabated. In December 1987, a traffic accident in Gaza involving an Israeli and a Palestinian had sparked a six-year uprising. Known as the *Intifada*,[3] the Arabs refined and improved on the methods they used in the 1936-39 riots. Demonstrations led by Arab women and children were supplemented by youngsters throwing rocks at Israeli vehicles traveling on West Bank roads and at Israeli soldiers trying to contain the rioters. Nails and oil slicks placed on highways, tire-burning, Molotov cocktails, hostage-taking, shooting, bus bombings and finally suicide bombs on public transport and in public places in Israel proper, became commonplace. For protection, civilians traveling in the administered territories carried firearms and installed plastic windows in their vehicles.

With the signing of the first Oslo agreement the PLO no longer participated in the intifada. The extreme Islamic fundamentalist group, Hamas, fearing peace was at hand, continued with greater intensity to try to rid the area of the Jewish State.

Throughout this period, Hezbollah attacks from Lebanon rapidly increased. Most often hit was Galilee and, in particular, the border town of Kiryat Shemona. Ultimately, as residents threatened to leave Galilee, the Israeli military was forced to carry out two major operations into Lebanon.

In July 1993, Yitzhak Rabin ordered the armed forces to launch "Operation Accountability." Declared an angry Rabin, "If there is no quiet here, it will not be quiet for residents in southern Lebanon." With that, Israel bombarded seventy [Lebanese] villages from land, sea and air, forcing 300,000 to flee toward Beirut. On the Israeli side, half the residents of Galilee moved south, including hundreds of children. The operation ended after US Secretary of State Warren Christopher brokered a verbal agreement between Israel and Hezbollah to limit clashes. But the

---

3   The Arabic word *intifada*, literally translated as "shaking off," is taken from the shaking of a camel after sexual intercourse. The Palestinians wanted to "shake off" the Israeli occupation.

agreement was often violated and, in the latter part of April 1996, the Israeli army was back in Lebanon with greater force to punish Hezbollah and Lebanon.

"This is war," Chief of Staff Amnon Lipkin-Shahak told a reporter. For seventeen days Israeli guns, planes and ships rained terror on Lebanon in "Operation Grapes of Wrath." The objective was to make attacks on Galilee too painful and costly to repeat.

During the fighting, Hezbollah fired 700 Katyusha rockets into Galilee, nearly twenty times the number of missiles fired at all of Israel by Iraq in the Gulf War. Kiryat Shemona residents spent most of their days and nights in stifling shelters but no one was killed, although 127 were wounded. Nearly all the 1,400 homes destroyed or damaged in Galilee from the rockets were in Kiryat Shemona. More than half of the population of 20,000 fled for the duration.

Lebanon suffered as 400,000 residents in the south fled from their homes. Most of Beirut was blacked out when Israeli planes hit a power station. On one sorrowful day Israeli artillery, responding to a Hezbollah mortar attack, fired back at the source. Less than 350 yards away was a UN post where, unknown to the Israeli unit, Arab civilians had sought refuge. Several shells overshot the mark and killed ninety-six of the refugees.

"It is no accident that Hezbollah fires close to UN posts, knowing that we will be cautious about replying," commented General Lipkin-Shahak.

The end of the fighting came after a week-long effort by US Secretary of State Warren Christopher to arrange a cease-fire — this time, via a written agreement. To ensure that no further attacks would be launched against civilians, a monitoring group was set up consisting of Israeli, Syrian, Lebanese, American and French military personnel. Few believed that the agreement would endure for long.

The Hashemite Kingdom of Jordan had warily maintained friendly relations with Israel since 1970. In July 1994, the two countries began to formalize their cordial relationship. After three years of quiet negotiation,

King Hussein and Prime Minister Rabin signed a declaration at a White House lawn ceremony ending their forty-six-year state of war. The two men had become personal friends and when they shook hands at the White House, it was sincere. Four months later, with President Clinton again in attendance, the two met on the barren border in the Arava between Eilat and Akaba to sign a formal peace treaty.[4] Those two acts brought peace officially to Israel's longest border.

Six months later, tragedy struck. On Saturday night, November 4, as he left a peace rally in front of Tel Aviv city hall, Prime Minister Rabin was assassinated by an Israeli law student, Yigal Amir.[5] The murderer's stated motive was to stop what he regarded as the surrender of Israel's birthright to the Arabs. Thus came to a violent end the life of an Israeli who was respected around the world as a patriot, soldier and statesman. His funeral on Mount Herzl in Jerusalem was attended by world leaders, among them President Clinton, who ended an emotional eulogy with the words, "*Shalom, haver*" (Goodbye, friend).

Rabin was succeeded by Foreign Minister Shimon Peres, who stepped up the peace process much to the chagrin of a large segment of the population. A majority of the electorate was in no mood for what it began to regard as Israel's surrendering of Jewish territories to the Palestinians without reciprocal reductions in tension. If anything, violence increased in ferocity as both sides came closer to a final settlement. In one macabre week at the beginning of 1996, Arab terrorists carried out five bloody onslaughts against civilians. Suicide killers blew up two buses in Jerusalem and a shopping center in Tel Aviv, and drove cars into queues at bus stops in Ashkelon and Jerusalem. Total Israeli dead were 58, injured 222.

Despite the sharp tensions between Israelis and Arabs during these hostilities, physicians at Hadassah hospitals treated victims from both sides

---

4   At the White House ceremonies and in the Arava, Hadassah delegates were present.

5   Amir was sentenced to life imprisonment by the Tel Aviv District Court. An accomplice received a similar sentence.

with dispassionate devotion to duty. One doctor reported to Hadassah at the height of the uprising:

> Our Palestinian physicians, nurses and auxiliary staff are continuing in their jobs. Our Palestinian patients continue seeking Hadassah's help, sitting side by side with Israelis in clinics, lying side by side with them in our wards. We are treating badly burned soldiers and civilians, trapped in the flames of vehicles set alight by Molotov cocktails and bombs. We are operating on gunshot wounds and on people with serious orthopedic and neurological injuries caused by hurled stones.

Angry at the Arab response to Israel's peace moves, the country went to the polls in May 1994. The results were close but when the final ballots were counted, the electorate had sent Peres into opposition with a clear message: the Labor Party had given the Arabs too much, too fast, for too little. Into office came Massachusetts Institute of Technology alumnus and former UN Ambassador Binyamin Netanyahu, a popular spokesman for conservative causes. President Bill Clinton's transparent support for Peres during the campaign had been of no help.

Netanyahu, as leader of the right-wing Likud Bloc, slowed down, but did not stop, the peace process. The PLO understood the electorate's message and began to crack down on its extremist wings. During Netanyahu's first year of leadership, Israelis no longer feared to step on a bus.

In that same month of May, talks began on the final status between Israel and the Palestinians. As the PLO under Arafat established a shadow government to run the Palestinian Authority, there was good reason for Israelis to believe that by the time the negotiations on the final status of the Palestine political entity were scheduled to end in 1999, the Palestinians would declare an independent state in the West Bank and Gaza. The most sensitive and divisive question was the sovereignty of Jerusalem, with Israel adamant against its division and the Palestinians demanding the eastern section for their intended capital. Over Jerusalem there would be acrimonious debate and bloodshed, before an agreement, if any, would be reached.

These momentous events were paralleled by population explosions. Both the Soviet Union and Ethiopia, poles apart geographically and culturally, inundated Israel with immigrants. The Soviet Union was by far the larger of the two sources and its captive Jews were more in the public eye.

Sympathy and support for the Jews of the Soviet Union began to organize on a worldwide scale in the early 1960s. Among the most active in the US on their behalf was Hadassah. In 1966, a delegation of twenty-five Hadassah leaders had traveled to the USSR where they met the "Jews of Silence."

"We all wore large Magen David pins on our lapels so people would know who we were," says Charlotte Jacobson who as National President led the group. "And we were the first to visit Babi Yar."[6]

"The Hadassah women were like an army," said Nobel Laureate Elie Wiesel, who was in Moscow at the time.

In the early 1970s when Charlotte was chairman of the American Section of the World Zionist Organization, the Israeli government asked her to publicize the plight of Russian Jewry, trapped in a country that would not recognize them as a nationality but would not let them leave. The issue was then being handled, without too much enthusiasm, by the Conference of Presidents of Major Jewish Organizations. Charlotte was instrumental in urging the recalcitrant Conference to support a separate organization. Thus was born the National Conference for Soviet Jewry.

From the beginning, Hadassah worked energetically within the NCSJ.

---

6   Babi Yar, commemorated in a poem by Yevgeni Yevtushenko, is the ravine near Kiev where in two days in September 1941, a Nazi *Sonderkommando* (SS unit), supported by Ukrainian militia, murdered 33,771 Jews with machine guns.

It sponsored and participated in demonstrations, published literature, retrained and hired immigrant Soviet doctors and nurses in Israel as waves of mass immigration in the 1970s brought nearly 100,000 to Israel. But in a few short years the flow was stopped by the Soviet dictatorship.

Then followed years of repression. Jews who applied for visas to emigrate to Israel immediately lost their jobs even though their chances of being permitted to leave were slim. A few brave men and women defied the Soviet authorities to campaign for free emigration. They quickly found themselves in gulags or incarcerated in KGB prisons.

In August 1984, on the eve of the Hadassah convention in San Francisco, President Frieda Lewis addressed a message on behalf of Soviet Jews to the Kremlin through the local consul-general. Requesting a renewal of exit visas she said: "We only ask that what has been done for other ethnic groups be done for Jews…We ask that you grant the Jews the full nurture of their cultural and religious heritage." She appealed especially on behalf of Ida Nudel, "a lonely, isolated person, to join her sister in Israel." Ida was released three years later.

During the regime of Mikhail Gorbachev, the gates began to open. In 1989, a tidal wave of nearly 700,000 Russians engulfed Israel. Including the immigration of the 1970s, Israel became the recipient of nearly 800,000 Soviet Jews — the largest single ethnic group in Israel. Prisoner of Zion Natan Sharansky, who had spent 3,255 days in prison, arrived in 1986. Ten years later, he returned to Moscow on an official visit as a member of Israel's cabinet.

Organizing a smooth flow of immigrants to Israel was a logistical headache. Under Jewish Agency direction, immigrants would travel by train from Moscow to Vienna or Rome where they would remain in transit centers and choose their final destinations. Most opted for Israel, but much to the chagrin of the Israeli government a significant number went to the US and other countries. Hadassah pressed for a system that would encourage immigrants to decide their destinations in Moscow and then fly directly to Tel Aviv if that was their choice. "Transit camps were eating up the resources that could be used for integrating immigrants in Israel," said President Carmela Kalmanson. "The primary focus of Jewish communal efforts and funding should be for resettlement in Israel."

In 1990, Hadassah allocated $1,000,000 to train newly-arrived Soviet Jews in Israel. The Hadassah College of Technology was the first institution to propose a program of training and retraining. Hadassah retrained more than 1,000 doctors, dentists, dental assistants, nurses and radiology therapists, raising their skills to Western standards. Two hundred and fifty physicians arrived in one two-week period. So many doctors, nurses, dentists and technologists flooded the hospitals that Russian became the second language heard in the corridors of HMO. In a few years, about one-seventh of all employees working at Hadassah were recent arrivals from the former Soviet Union, including more than 200 nurses and 100 physicians.

In the US, Hadassah sent Soviet Jewish children to Young Judaea camps. In Israel, Young Judaeans formed welcoming committees to greet the Russians with flowers as they stepped off the planes. Hadassah-Israel members successfully tutored Russian students at the Hadassah-Neurim youth village near Netanya. Their students received the highest marks in the state matriculation exams.

Russian immigration provided Israel with rich human resources. Engineers, mathematicians, surveyors, scientists, musicians, researchers in a myriad of specialties were among them. Athletes with Russian names represented Israel on scoreboards the world over — Smashnova (tennis), Krasnov (swimming), Shmerkin (ice-skating). Cities never before endowed with symphony orchestras found themselves enhanced by virtuoso music played by artists from the best conservatories in the Soviet Union. A popular quip at the time had it that whoever stepped off the plane from Russia not carrying a violin case must be a pianist.

No less rich culturally, but totally different, were the 25,000 Ethiopian Jewish immigrants who arrived in two large waves. Israelis were impressed by these beautiful brown-skinned men and women with delicate features and lithe figures. They spoke a native language called Ge'ez as well as Amharic and — those from the cities — English. Some knew Hebrew.

Their lineage extended back to the First Temple period in the ancient kingdom of Kush, homeland of the biblical Queen of Sheba. Legend relates that Sheba's son, Menelik, fathered by Solomon, took Judaic customs to Ethiopia. Judaism was widespread in Ethiopia until the country was converted to Christianity in the fourth century.

Persecuted, many Jews retreated into the mountainous area around Lake Tana on the Blue Nile and into the Gondar region. They lived in their own communities isolated from their fellow Jews, but retained a traditional way of life linked closely to the laws in the Torah. But although they strictly followed the Mosaic laws of purity, the Sabbath and marriage, their Judaism was questioned in Israel and in the West.

After much deliberation in the 1970s, the Chief Rabbinate declared that the *Falashas*, a derogatory name by which the Ethiopians were then commonly known, were indeed Jews. In 1984, the government of Menachem Begin began the unpublicized and complex mission of taking the Ethiopians to Israel from under the noses of a hostile regime. Secretly, an Israeli airlift flew 10,000 of them into Israel during "Operation Moses" at the end of 1984.

When they arrived, they told stories of great adversity. Their families had been torn asunder, they had endured illness, brigands and murderers as they walked, for weeks on end, to transit camps set up in Sudan. Traveling only at night, hiding during the day, they stuffed rags into their children's mouths to keep them from crying as strangers approached. The story of Moshe Beruk, 38, is typical:

> When people began to die we were too afraid to stop to bury
> them. In February 1984, after walking twenty-five days, we
> reached the Sudanese border. We told the authorities we
> were Christians fleeing the famine and they let us into a

refugee camp — a crowded, hungry place where dozens
died every day.

In the camp, Moshe found out that fifty-nine members of his family had
been caught five days from the village and sent back. They were
dispossessed of their land, cows and donkeys, and imprisoned for one
month. Nine months later in November 1984, Moshe and his family were
taken to Khartoum and flown to Israel as part of "Operation Moses."

In Israel, says Moshe, "Every aspect of life had changed for us and we
needed help to relearn it." After three months in an integration center, they
received an apartment and Moshe began his training as a social service
worker.

By 1991, a government friendly to Israel ruled in Addis Ababa. At the
urging of the Bush Administration in Washington, the government
permitted its Jews to emigrate. In a record 33-hour airlift, "Operation
Solomon" took 14,000 Ethiopians from Addis Ababa on the last leg of
their journey.

A difficult period of re-education quickly began for most. As Moshe
Beruk described it:

> We were weakened by the journey and very confused. We
> found that 'home' was an unfamiliar place. Everything
> about it had to be learned — its culture, customs, language,
> shops, food, services and opportunities.

Of the thousands of children who arrived in Israel during "Operation
Moses," 60 percent had lost one or both parents. Many had diseases no
longer seen in the West. Some were HIV positive. Youth Aliyah Director
Eli Amir recalls one child who told him, "Before I came to Israel, I thought
God was black. Now, I think maybe he is white."

Says Amir, "Ninety percent of those we took in had never been to
school and could neither read nor write any language. None of our
textbooks was appropriate."

The Education Ministry could not help Eli. It did not have the necessary $1,000,000 for new books. So he called Hadassah President Ruth Popkin. Only one week before convention, Ruth managed to squeeze the issue into the already completed agenda.

Pleading for eight minutes in a hoarse voice before the pre-convention Board meeting in Miami, Eli convinced the members. The Board voted to give him two-thirds of the sum. After the meeting, Ruth Popkin asked him, "How did you do it? We have a budget deficit of $2,500,000 and you just increased it."

Replied Eli, "What the Board saw was not the Youth Aliyah director but the 14-year-old boy that I was when I went to Israel and was taken in by Youth Aliyah. That was who convinced them."

One of Hadassah's more innovative programs to help the Ethiopians was initiated by the School of Dentistry. When requested by the Joint Distribution Committee to help the community integrate, Community Dentistry Department head Jonathan Mann met with young Ethiopian women. To help them, the dental faculty opened a one-year dental assistant course in 1985 for twenty female students. Says Mann:

> There were vast cultural gaps that we didn't know how to bridge. We felt inadequate trying to explain things that were so simple for us. A filling, for example, is not something that needs explaining to Israelis but the Ethiopians never heard of it. Language was a barrier. Cut off from families, almost all the students had traumatic pasts and overwhelming personal problems.

Educators were brought in to devise new ways to teach. The staff had to reduce the teaching pace and become more aware of cultural differences. The one-year program was expanded to two years and in 1987, eighteen of the students received Israel National Board licenses. After "Operation Solomon," a second course was begun and in 1994, eighteen more students completed it. By 1995, Ethiopians could join Israelis in a mixed course, and study was reduced to 16 months. Says Mann, "It was a major challenge for both the Ethiopians and for us. Both of us profited."

As the historic events of the 1990s unfolded, Hadassah played a supporting role both in the US and in Israel. When the National Board decided in 1990 to hold its Mid-Winter conference and later its national convention in Israel in the wake of the Gulf War, a grateful Mayor Teddy Kollek wrote President Carmela Kalmanson, "The economic damage to our Jerusalem [from the absence of tourists] is great but beyond that it is terribly demoralizing. With this hanging over us, your announcement was a silver lining."

A tradition of periodically assembling in convention more than 6,000 miles from home base was begun by Hadassah in 1978, the year that Begin and Sadat were locked in negotiations with President Jimmy Carter at Camp David. Hadassah took its 66th annual convention to Israel. Chairman Rose Goldman and Co-Chairman Ruth Popkin worked out the logistics of transporting 2,600 delegates and guests. The largest group of visitors to arrive at one time, they occupied every hotel room in Jerusalem and the surrounding area.

"The ruby red tail lights of sixty-five buses winding through the desert," recalls Ruth Popkin, "is one image that will always stay with me. You couldn't miss us."

On Purim 1987, Hadassah assembled 2,500 people in Jerusalem for its 75th birthday party. Then National President, Popkin decided to include the entire city in the celebration by staging a parade. Her story:

> I wanted marchers and floats. Mayor Teddy Kollek agreed to close the streets. Kibbutzim made floats. The regions brought their banners with them. It was cold and bright when we set out and I rode down King George Street with Teddy in a flower-covered, horse-drawn carriage pulled by two horses. We had a ball. When the parade finished, the rain

resumed. Next day's *Jerusalem Post* commented, 'We knew Hadassah had clout; we did not know it had that much clout!'

Former President Deborah Kaplan, the first Hadassah president to be elected in Jerusalem, states, "Our coming to Jerusalem demonstrated that Hadassah's heart is in Jerusalem — the place where Presidents take office." Adds Carmela Kalmanson, "We had something to say about Hadassah's proper place, and the best way to say it was to go to Jerusalem."

Four years later, in 1995, at the 81st national convention, Marlene Edith Post was also elected President in Jerusalem.

During this same dynamic decade, the Hadassah Medical Organization was marching forward. A long list of "firsts" was achieved, among them state-of-the-art radio beam surgery, simultaneous transplanting of five human organs, a heart-lung transplant (on an Arab mother of ten) and a liver transplant (on an Ethiopian child). A rapid response trauma unit and a regional AIDS testing center were established. But of all the impressive accomplishments nothing on the Ein Kerem campus caught the eye or captured the heart as much as the child-friendly new Mother and Child Center.

In the meantime, Hadassah's reach had become global. From its very beginning the organization had not seen the oceans as a barrier to its creativity. Until the establishment of the State of Israel it had concentrated on the Jewish community in Palestine. As the young State extended its help to the Third World under Foreign Minister Golda Meir, Hadassah sent its experts from Jerusalem to remote places in Asia and Africa. Their aid saved many lives and improved the quality of life of many unfortunates, but their presence was only temporary.

HADASSAH GOES GLOBAL

The 1970s had been a decade of dedications for Hadassah. Some Hadassah veterans called President Rose Matzkin "the President of Dedications" because few periods in Hadassah's history had seen so many.

In Israel, Hadassah reopened the Scopus Medical Center with its unique rehabilitation pavilion, helped in the establishment of Kibbutz Ketura, opened the state-of-the-art Sharett Institute of Oncology, graduated its first college class, and began a professional retraining program for Russian immigrants.

In the US, Rose moved Hadassah House from its cramped quarters into a new home on New York's 58th Street and congratulated Hadassah's 100,000th Life Member. There was much more, not the least of which was a Tel Aviv Youth Aliyah Day Center opened in 1976 in the name of Rose Matzkin.

This decade of "do" was, appropriately, capped by the birth of a totally new concept: Hadassah as a universal organization. New projects and demands for high technology equipment created a need for bigger budgets within the Hadassah Medical Organization. In 1983, acting on an inspiration from its HMO chair Bernice Tannenbaum, Hadassah gave birth to a worldwide organization that would become known as Hadassah International.

At about the same time, large numbers of Jews, among them members of the World International Zionist Organization, began moving from Canada to the United States.[1] WIZO members formed study groups in Florida, Texas and other states, causing unrest among local Hadassah leaders. A clash between the world's two largest Zionist organizations seemed unavoidable.

The question of WIZO's infiltration into Hadassah territory was put on the agenda by President Frieda Lewis at the pre-convention National Board meeting on August 6, 1981. "Snowbirds are a phenomenon of Canada as well as the United States," she said with a touch of irony. "These women come to Florida and other sun belt areas and do not understand that they are not part of our organization and demand service from our chapters. They even bear the name Hadassah in their title...Canadian Hadassah WIZO."

WIZO, she said, was advertising in the Florida press, recruiting "people of great means" among immigrants from South America and Iran. Frieda also recalled that WIZO was not bound by any formal contract but "there has been an understanding for many years that they would not organize in the United States and we would not organize outside of the United States."

She asked her Board, "How shall we deal with this?"

The answer came quickly. Hadassah would go global.

No longer bound by the unwritten understanding with WIZO, Hadassah felt freed of its obligation to remain within the borders of the fifty states. HMO chair Bernice Tannenbaum set objectives that would, within little more than a decade, put Hadassah into global orbit and establish it

---

1   Henrietta Szold created WIZO in Canada in 1929. An unwritten, long-honored agreement with Hadassah held that WIZO would not canvas for membership in the US while Hadassah would organize only in the US.

permanently with medical relief associations on five continents. Members overseas would include men and women, Jews and non-Jews.

"I felt that overseas there could be a role for non-Jews," says Bernice. "Medicine has universal appeal and instead of creating little Zionist or Jewish groups which would compete with existing organizations, we would appeal to everyone. This organization would be the international arm of Hadassah, organized as a separate corporation."

The green light to move abroad was given at the August 1983 national convention in Washington, DC. The delegates, by acclamation, formally established the new body under the corporate structure of the Hadassah Medical Relief Association (HMRA), later known as Hadassah International.

Hadassah abroad would be different. For one thing, men would be accepted as members to raise money for medical work.[2] Furthermore, members did not have to subscribe to Zionist ideology. Functions would solely benefit the work of the Hadassah Medical Organization and build relationships between the members and Israel.

To test the waters, Israel would be the first site for Hadassah International. There, Hadassah members who had gone on aliyah had already organized themselves.

Hadassah Council in Israel Chairman Vera Tzur called on one of the American immigrants, former Upper Midwest Region President Barbara Schermer, to form an organization that would give a home to Hadassah alumnae.[3] Barbara had arrived on aliyah in 1969 and by 1970 had put together *Olot Hadassah* (Hadassah immigrants). Around a nucleus of HCI

---

2   In the US, men can only be Hadassah Associates; more than 30,000 have done so. To grant men equal status even in an associate organization such as HMRA was revolutionary. This may well serve as a precedent for the US organization in the 21st century.

3   The HCI served as a liaison to the National Board in New York. It was dissolved in 1996. The HMO Israel Committee, a public advisory body, is still functioning.

members she gathered 200 members in Jerusalem. Later, Olot was extended to Tel Aviv.

Unrecognized by Hadassah in New York, Olot nevertheless kept busy. The members welcomed tourist groups, sponsored symposia, held luncheons and assisted with the 1978 and 1982 national conventions in Jerusalem. But without formal backing and support from New York, Olot eventually collapsed.

A few years later, Hadassah Council President Sylvia Shapiro, a National Board member living in Israel, moved into the vacuum. She was convinced that with the Hadassah-WIZO agreement on its way out, the time had come to form a group in Israel with national support. Rose Joshua, a former region president from Minneapolis, and Sylvia recruited former Olot members as the nucleus and started a unit at the conclusion of the 1982 national convention. Recalls Rose, "We decided to give it six months to see whether we could convince New York headquarters during that time."

In January 1983, the ruling came through from the National Board: the understanding with WIZO was no longer in effect. It was during this period that Hadassah was studying the feasibility of establishing its new international arm.

In February, although not yet a recognized group, Hadassah-Israel began its activities with a Mediscope meeting at Hadassah-Ein Kerem. The turnout of 150 members was larger than expected. With that conference they indicated that the incipient Hadassah-Israel would be much more than a fund-raising organization. Thus, a pattern was set.

On Purim 1983, Hadassah-Israel was officially established. It was Hadassah's 71st birthday. The founding meeting was held around an oval table in Rose Joshua's living room in Jerusalem. Bernice Tannenbaum was there to witness and advise at the birth of the first group within this new international movement. In the fall, Hadassah-Israel held its first membership meeting, electing Rose Joshua as President.

Although the beginning was not easy, Hadassah-Israel passed the test for the leadership in New York. The already-existing natural constituency was American and their language was English, not Hebrew. At first, says Rose Joshua, "We made the error of working like Americans. What we had to do was adapt."

Rose initiated annual Mediscope programs where members gathered for an entire day to be briefed by Hadassah staff on a specific subject, such as medical ethics or new developments.

During the term of office of Rose's successor, Annabelle Bienenfeld Yuval,[4] the organization began a nationwide health awareness program targeted at women, with emphasis on cancer prevention.

The third President, former Baltimore chapter vice-president Sylvia Mehlman, bridged the language gap by introducing simultaneous Hebrew-English translations both at Mediscope meetings and at the national conferences. "At the beginning we were mainly English speakers, but the translations served to bring in more Hebrew-speaking Israelis and united us." During Sylvia's tenure Hadassah-Israel's fund-raising reached major proportions. Its gift to HMO, an echo doppler for cardiograms, was purchased for $200,000.

In 1992, Hadassah-Israel elected Ora Sela, the first native-born Israeli to hold the position of President. She made it a priority to attract non-American Israelis. Hebrew-speaking groups were founded and with that the adaptation to the Israeli scene had succeeded.

Under the dynamic leadership of Hinda Gross, a Gratz College graduate from Philadelphia,[5] Hadassah-Israel's membership by the end of 1997 grew to 2,000, organized in 16 chapters, representing women from forty cities, kibbutzim and moshavim. Half the units spoke English; half spoke Hebrew.

---

4 Annabelle, who has held many leadership positions in Hadassah, emigrated to Israel in 1952, and married David Yuval, who from 1980 to 1989 served as HMO internal auditor and the HWZOA Representative in Israel.

5 After Hinda completed her term, Shoshanna Israeli, a sabra, followed. Hadassah-Israel's current president is Phyllis Levinson, a former president of the Pacific Northwest Region.

Says Hinda, "We are women who do not want to sit at meetings. We want to do things." And they did. The cancer detection campaign expanded, saving lives and improving the quality of life for many Israeli women. Apart from fund-raising events, Hadassah-Israel has instituted health workshops and campaigns to encourage safety devices (the use of bicycle helmets, car seats, etc.).

With the first Hadassah group outside the United States now established in Israel, it was time to mobilize in the rest of the world.

The second nation to join the Hadassah family was France. Instrumental in its beginning was Beatrice Birnbaum, formerly of Baltimore, now resident in Paris. Bea was vice-president of the new entity. After serving as a volunteer for several years, she became the International Director, based in Paris but serving all Europe. In Paris, the first cooperation agreement was concluded in 1989 between the Ein Kerem Medical Center in Jerusalem and Paris' Institute Curie, making expertise from the noted Institute's advanced research on cancer therapy available to Hadassah. It also opened the door to future agreements with other scientific institutions throughout the world. Later cooperative ventures included Turkey's Baskent University Medical School and Hacettepe University Faculty of Medicine.

After France, Hadassah set up shop in Argentina. It began when a Jewish businessman offered his chalet on the snow-covered Andes at San Carlos de Bariloche for a medical conference for public health practitioners. Twenty-five Hadassah-Argentina members attended together with about 100 physicians from Brazil and Argentina.

Bernice exclaimed, "We were not yet viable in Argentina, but we dared to mount a medical conference in a world new to us. For many of those who attended it served as an introduction to the name Hadassah. [HMO Director-General] Shmuel Penchas came to lecture and he was wonderful. From that little beginning we created a strong group of men and women, Jews and non-Jews, who became a force for Hadassah in the country."

Dr. Enrique Pener served first as Head of the Scientific Committee of Hadassah-Argentina, later as its President.[6] In 1996, the group held a symposium on trauma nursing organized by Barbara Sabin, Hadassah-International liaison, in which Hadassah nurses participated, and a medical symposium at the prestigious National Academy of Medicine. Until 1995, with few exceptions, the Academy had been closed to Jewish physicians, according to Beatriz Wolf Cheja, secretary of the group.

With Argentina established, Hadassah spread to other countries in South and Central America. Two groups were founded in Brazil and others in Chile, Colombia, Ecuador, Honduras, Uruguay, Venezuela and Mexico.

In Havana, Dr. Rosa Behar Hasday organized 60 Jews and non-Jews under the banner of Hadassah-Cuba. The group provides dental and ophthalmological services to schools. The Hadassah Pharmacy sorts and distributes donated medications to the community and to children in summer camps. Rosa, who founded the Gastroenterology Department at General Calixto Garcia University Hospital, conducted a medical census of Havana's Jewish community of 500 families. She discovered that Jews were living in all of Cuba's fourteen provinces.

Hadassah-Cuba has alerted the women of Havana to the dangers of breast cancer. At one meeting on prevention, a woman in the audience stood up and said, "I am alive today because of what you taught me." Over and beyond the medical objectives of the group, there is a bond that ties the Cuban Jewish community to Hadassah.

Says Rosa, "Hadassah has helped us bring Cuba's Jews together. We not only learn about Israel and Israeli medicine, but it makes us more conscious of our Judaism."

Dr. Sergio Daniel Simon, president of Hadassah-Brazil, organized Hadassah-São Paulo in 1994. An oncologist with the Albert Einstein

---

6   The organization is now headed by Debora Manassen de Lang.

Hospital in São Paulo, his objective was to "disseminate the work of Hadassah among the whole Brazilian population (population: 160,737,489) in order to counteract Arab propaganda."

After a visit to Vienna by Bernice, Suzi Shaked, retired fashion shop proprietor, mobilized fifty professionals and lay people to form Hadassah-Austria. She organized a project to raise funds for the adolescent psycho-oncology unit at Hadassah Ein Kerem. During an earlier visit to Vienna, Bernice met with a prospective contributor whose interest was improving relations with the Arabs. Over lunch, she suggested that he meet HMO's Director-General. The result of the meeting with "Sami" Penchas was a substantial annual gift for scholarships for the training of Arab physicians at Hadassah.[7]

On the other side of the globe, Hadassah has targeted the two geographical extremities.

In Beijing, the Jewish community is made up of expatriates who are there on business, like Elyse Beth Silverberg, who has been in China since 1982. During the International Women's Conference in August 1996, Hadassah International's Eva Silberman invited Elyse to create a unit. Elyse agreed, hoping to direct the community's young couples to develop joint medical projects between institutions in China and the HMO.

On the North American continent, Hadassah and WIZO have joined hands in Canada. There, Canadian Hadassah WIZO now represents Hadassah International in Canada and has supported many initiatives within HMO, including HMO's Scandiplan, a system that permits pinpointing of body areas for radiation therapy. In 1995, Hadassah-WIZO hosted Hadassah International's Ninth Annual Congress in Montreal.

---

7   Young Hadassah groups have been organized in Paris, Lyon, Luxembourg, Dusseldorf, Vienna and London, and groups in other countries are underway for men and women ages 25-45.

Apart from its scientific and cultural activities, Hadassah International has succeeded in its goal to raise significant amounts of money for HMO. The largest gift to date was a total of $7,000,000 for the PET and Cyclotron unit given after a visit to Paris by Bernice and Professor Henri Atlan, head of the Nuclear Medicine Department. These funds created the Human Biology Research Center on the Ein Kerem campus. Hadassah-France also contributed $250,000 to buy a lithotripter, large additional sums for the Mother and Child Center and for the dialysis day care unit.

For fund-raising, the groups around the world use various techniques: concerts, dinners, galas and special events like a debutante's ball in Italy; an antiques furniture sale in Venezuela; a "Jerusalem Grand Prix" at the racetrack in Vincennes, France that harvested a sizable sum, donating the "lost" bets to the Mother and Child Center; an art sale and classical music concerts organized in Sweden to support pediatric oncologist residents training at Ein Kerem.

Hadassah International has gone beyond its goals of raising funds for HMO, building ties between its members and Israel and creating medical relationships between HMO and scientific institutions in its member countries. It has also created a place which embraces Jews and non-Jews, men and women, lay and professional. On the local level, they work together in harmony and with flexibility. Each group can make its own choices as to its structure, composition of its membership and which medical disciplines will receive the funds they raise. Despite some differences in procedure, there is surety of purpose and complete support of the vision and mission of Hadassah International.

Vienna's Suzi Shaked reports that a non-Jewish member of her Board recently told her that she knew nothing about Jewish customs and ceremonies. "I took her to the Jewish community center," Suzi says. "There I explained Jewish ceremonies, like Havdalah [ceremony that marks the end of the Sabbath]. It took away a little of the strangeness of working with people of other religions."

During its second decade, Hadassah International was in the hands of former President Deborah Kaplan as Coordinator. Deborah and a team of talented volunteers have kept up the momentum with new groups and new relationships with medical institutions. For the first time a European conference was held in Paris and a Pan-American conference in Buenos Aires.

Hadassah's grasp of the globe, excluding Israel, began decades ago when it shared its expertise with health care workers from abroad and began sending its people on temporary missions to Asia and Africa. Since then, more than 10,000 Hadassah experts have visited over 100 countries. More than 28,000 trainees from 112 nations have come to Hadassah for courses. A map of the world where Hadassah has a presence or made an impact would extend from Fiji to Canada and from Denmark to Chile — seventy-eight states in all.

A few of their exploits bear retelling.

As Hadassah sent Rose Kaplan and Rachel Landy to Palestine in 1912, HMO sent nurses into Bosnia and Herzegovina in 1995 and 1996.

When Board Member Nancy Falchuk[8], initiator of Hadassah's Nurses Councils, paid a visit to St. Louis, she was approached by local Nurses Council president Elsie Shemin-Roth, R.N., who asked that something be done for the innocent victims of ravaged Bosnia and Herzegovina. In August 1994, Elsie, supported by Hadassah, went to Sarajevo to assess the needs of two hospitals. With her went Kathryn Bauschard of St. Louis, Deanna Perlmutter of Boston, and Charlotte Franklin of Santa Barbara, California, all registered nurses.[9]

---

8   Now a vice president, Nancy Falchuk is also Hadassah International Coordinator.

9   Elsie was a homemaker before she began to study nursing. At age 54 she became the oldest North American to receive a nursing degree. A mother of five and a grandmother of three, she has worked with immigrants in Israel and cared for Jews in Ethiopia. For her courage, weekly news magazine *Time* cited Elsie as a local hero (*Time* Special Report, June 17, 1996).

"The two hospitals we visited have been bombed and shelled, and anti-aircraft weaponry are currently pointed directly at the hospitals," Elsie reported. "Electricity to run the generators is limited and there is running water for two hours a day."

The hospitals needed everything from dialysis and I.V. solutions to cereal for babies and backpacks for public health nurses. The result: a five-month campaign, launched by the Nurses Councils, amassing 33 tons of supplies valued at $3,500,000.

On February 22, 1995, Elsie and fellow nurse Sherry Hahn of Arlington, Massachusetts, arrived in Sarajevo. They "sneaked in," according to Elsie, under the banner of the UN High Commissioner for Refugees. For the following seven days they distributed supplies, among them a defibrillator and over 100 prosthetics to replace feet, legs and knees. They were assisted by La Benevolencija, the 102-year-old Jewish aid society.

In July 1995, Elsie was back in Sarajevo, this time to help transfer four children and two adults to Hadassah-Ein Kerem in Jerusalem. Some suffered from severe phosphorous grenade burns and could not be treated in the war zone. "These people had no future without Hadassah's help," Elsie said. On the way to Jerusalem the patients were attended by Hadassah surgeon Ahmed Eid and a surgical nurse.

By early 1996, the condition in war-torn Sarajevo had become desperate and Elsie, age 65, returned for a fourth time. In March, she left for the war zone accompanied by Sherry Hahn and a Bosnian anesthesiology nurse, Safeta (Sada) Ovcina. Through the intervention of US Defense Secretary William Perry and US Democratic Party leader Richard Gephardt, the supplies were shipped on the *S.S. Inspiration* to Rotterdam. From there they went by rail to Lublijana, Slovenia, and then by truck to Split, Croatia. Each of the 8,000 cartons had to clear customs before they were allowed to continue to Sarajevo.

Elsie reported on arrival in the Bosnian capital:

> It has been 43 months since the war began and the people are freezing, hungry and emotionally exhausted. We are bringing the tools to help them survive, build a sense of self, and gain the confidence to start living again.

Hadassah's second shipment to Bosnia amounted to seventy-five tons, valued at $10,000,000. Contributed by more than 100 communities across the US, it included thrty-five hand-made quilts from California and hand-knitted hats and mittens from senior citizens in Florida. A *bar mitzvah* boy from upstate New York spent $500.00 of his gift money to contribute a package of medicines.

Some of the supplies were given to children in the Isak Samokovlija elementary school. Named for a Jewish physician and poet, the non-sectarian school of 1,200 pupils was hit by 5,000 shells. Thirty-three pupils were killed outside the school, eighty-four orphaned.

"There are no words in my language to say how grateful I am to Hadassah for giving me the chance to return to Bosnia to help my people," said Sada. The mission meant that she could be reunited with her family.

The team spent Passover in Sarajevo where La Benevolencija arranged seders. In attendance at the ecumenical seder on the second night, aside from Jews of a Sarajevo suburb, were the Archbishop of Bosnia, leaders of the Serbian Orthodox church, representatives of the Moslem community and three American soldiers.

The saga of Elsie and her team was duly registered in the Congressional Record by Senator Barbara Mikulski, Democrat of Maryland, a life member of Hadassah.

Then there is the tale of the earthquake of December 7, 1988 in northwest Armenia that took the lives of more than 55,000, entombed three cities, destroyed scores of villages and made tens of thousands homeless. Four days later, a call from Prof. Jacques Michel, medical director of Mount

Scopus, came through to Yoel Donchin, head of the Critical Care Transport Unit at Ein Kerem. CCTU is a medical rapid response squad that answers emergency calls for help anywhere in the world.

CCTU had its beginnings with the Armenian earthquake. Michel asked Donchin whether he would go. Donchin was the right man; he eagerly accepted, enlisted nephrologist Ze'ev Katzir, pediatrician Yaron Dagani, neurologist Alexander Lussus and emergency services chief Samuel Hyman. Supplies and equipment for two weeks were packed and sent to the airport labeled, "A Gift to the Russian People."

Part of a nineteen-person medical team under the supervision of the Israeli army, the four Hadassah doctors did not arrive in Tbilisi, Georgia, until nine days after the quake hit. Bad weather had delayed them. From the Georgian capital, their mobile hospital was transported in a convoy of trucks 100 miles through treacherous snow-covered mountains to Kirovakan, twenty miles from the epicenter.

The quake had left Kirovakan in the dead of winter without hospital facilities. Donchin's team was set up in a covered sports stadium that they divided with plastic sheets. They set up trauma and general medicine in one area and hospitalization in another. A tent became an operating theater. "We saw about 350 patients a day for two weeks," Donchin recalls:

> The first patients arrived in great pain from unset fractures and untreated infections. When word got about that the Israelis had arrived with a hospital, the doctors were inundated with Armenians complaining of everything from chronic ailments to headaches…People came from all over when they heard an Israeli hospital was available. Nobody was turned away. Our presence gave the people moral support. Some patients cried when they left us. They gave us fresh fruit to supplement our combat rations.

All told, the MDs handled 2,400 cases, including non-quake-related illnesses like tonsillitis and appendicitis.

So appreciative were the townspeople that shopkeepers refused to take money from the doctors. They were invited to private homes. Dressed in Israeli army uniforms they walked arm in arm with Red Army soldiers. "Everywhere we turned, we were welcomed with outstretched arms," reports Donchin. Once hospitals became operative, they picked up their equipment and returned home. They had been away fourteen days.

For Yoel Donchin, flying out of the country to save lives is a common occurrence. His team of doctors makes up to 100 trips abroad yearly. "We can leave at a moment's notice." Donchin says he likes the work although he is frequently on duty around the clock. "I am restless and I need quick rewards. Saving a life is my profession."

In the mid-80s, HMO Director-General Shmuel Penchas and the National Board considered projects to help African nations. One of the proposals was to staff a hospital in Sudan to serve Ethiopian Jews who had reached Sudan on their way to Israel.

Hadassah, however, was committed to helping Africa. On a suggestion from the USAID department of the US government, it was agreed that the women's organization would oversee the construction in Kinshasa, Zaïre, of a "model hospital," as then-President Ruth Popkin put it. Prof. Penchas turned over direct responsibility for the project to his deputy at Ein Kerem, Zvi Stern. The two went to Kinshasa in 1984 and 1985 to see the site and work out the overall project with the government.

Stern told *Hadassah Magazine*, "The US government selected Hadassah for this project because it knows from experience that without the involvement of a private voluntary organization, AID money disappears and the project will fail. It did not fail and only one-third of the allocated money was spent."

Egyptian-born Eli Mor, administrator of the Scopus hospital, arrived in Kinshasa in January 1987. He remained for thirty months, supervising the construction of the hospital, which consisted of eight single-story buildings. The site chosen was the poor Kimbanseke suburb of the capital, Kinshasa, the locality of a Christian sect known as the Kimbangists.[10]

A five-member team came next. It included Moshe Harel, head of the Scopus medical supply department, and Eli's twenty-six-year-old daughter Astar, a designer, who laid out the interior. By serving as architect and contractor, Eli spent only $500,000 of the estimated $1,500,000 allotment.

Once the buildings were up, the first of Hadassah's specialists arrived for a two-month period to train the Zairean staffs. There was pediatrician Dan Engelhard, specialist in infectious diseases and immunology who had already worked in the refugee camps of Cambodia. There was head ophthalmological operating theater nurse Zippora Sharon who set up sterilization rooms and guided the nurses. Also in the group was veteran housekeeping services head Sema Levy, who was part of the team that supervised the cleaning of the Scopus hospital after its return in 1967. Now with a team of nine she was cleaning up the mess the builders left behind. Working in heat that reached 120 degrees, Sema introduced cleaning routines and taught the Zaireans how to use mechanical scrubbers. Before she left, the appreciative locals presented her with a gift — a monkey. Sema politely declined.

In 1989, the local staff took over and Hadassah retired from the scene to the plaudits of the AID administration. Professor Penchas received a letter from Administrator Peter McPherson who called the Kinshasa enterprise the "best project" ever launched by AID in Africa.

HMO has dispatched not only its experts but its ideas as well. One of those is the concept that a community should receive its health services in relation to its measured needs.

---

10 The Kimbangist Christians are followers of Joseph Kimbageh, a Belgian, jailed because of treasonous utterances. After Kimbageh died in prison, millions of his followers regarded him as a prophet. They worked in the hospital as volunteers.

It was in the Kiryat Hayovel suburb of Jerusalem that the idea was formed into a scientific model and tested. The experiment was initiated by Sidney Kark, a public health specialist who trained in Johannesburg and practiced in rural Natal and Durban. He could not test his concept in South Africa because the apartheid government did not approve of many of his South African colleagues. He left South Africa and went to live in and work in Israel.

Kalman Mann had ideas similar to Kark's and lectured on them at an international congress of Jewish physicians held in Jerusalem in 1952. Against considerable professional opposition in Hadassah, he insisted on establishing a public health program and staffing social workers for the hospital. In fact, on taking his position, Mann had made it a condition that he open a community health center. He won, and in 1956 opened the Kiryat Hayovel center, primarily as a comprehensive family medicine practice.

When Mann heard Kark's lecture on a similar subject, he exclaimed, "I was most eager to get the Kiryat Hayovel project started." He lost no time in contacting Kark and his colleagues who worked with him in South Africa. Kark himself began working at Hadassah in 1959 as head of the Social Medicine Department[11] and the Kiryat Hayovel community health project until his retirement in 1981.

When the Jewish Agency began to shut down its immigrant transit camps in the 1960s, large numbers of immigrants with tuberculosis were transferred to the Kiryat Hayovel suburb of Jerusalem. Many were Yemenites who had no immunity to the disease.

"Such a large number of cases is no longer an individual problem, but a problem of the whole community," Mann insisted at the time.

---

11 The Department of Social Medicine was founded in 1949 and headed by Theodore Grushka. In 1962, the Hebrew University combined the Department with Hadassah's Department of Community Health Services into a Department of Social Medicine which offered a Master of Public Health degree. In 1980, the School of Public Health and Community Medicine was founded.

The Kiryat Hayovel community was multi-ethnic, coming from Eastern Europe, North Africa and Yemen, with a small number from Israel. The project found differences in the growth and development of babies from these ethnic groups. There were differences, too, in intellectual achievements that led to variations in health standards.

Teams working out of the community center tailored health programs to fit the community's needs. To determine these needs, Hadassah public health nurses spent two years going from door to door in the suburb. They interviewed 12,000 persons, focusing on mothers and babies while other adults were questioned about heart disease.

Using Kiryat Hayovel as a base, Hadassah's public health staff began a care and prevention program which has continued since 1970, becoming one of the longest running community health projects anywhere.

In 1971, the first international course in social medicine was begun in the department with the support of Israel's Foreign Ministry. More than 500 students from abroad have studied in the year-long course now given at the School. On returning to their native lands, most graduates occupy senior positions in public health.

Many other Third World countries have taken up the concept through students who have studied at the School. They have come from Myanmar and Belize, Canada and West Germany, Japan and Australia — nearly sixty countries.

"Our students have gone back to Africa, Asia, South America with these concepts and are developing programs," says Professor Leon Epstein. "We conducted workshops and seminars in the boondocks of South Africa."

The community health idea was used throughout Israel. In the United Kingdom it was adapted to British general practice.

"The important thing is that something that was developed in Kiryat Hayovel is having an impact in primary healthcare services in many parts of the world," Epstein continues. "South Africans came to Israel to develop the idea and then we went back there with it forty years later."

Hadassah globe-girdling experts have physically gone everywhere except to countries hostile to Israel. Ideas, however, do not need bodies. They merely have to be transmitted and radio is one good way to achieve that. Since 1973, Israel Broadcasting Authority staff member Ilana Basri has been reading medical advice provided by Hadassah physicians to radio listeners throughout the Arabic-speaking world.

Ilana was born in Iraq and made aliyah at the age of eighteen in 1950. Soon afterward, she was employed as assistant director of IBA's Arabic Service. In 1971, she entered Hadassah's new cardiac unit for tests. "I was so impressed, I decided to tell our Arab listeners about it," she recalls. In 1973 she began "Doctor Behind the Microphone" on a regular basis.

So popular was the program that requests came by mail from listeners in Libya and Iraq, with which Israel has no relations and no postal service. Listeners would post their letters through neutral countries. The mail became so heavy that Ilana arranged for an IBA post office box in Switzerland. She would translate the questions into Hebrew and refer them to Hadassah physicians.

"No matter how busy the senior doctors are they always get back to me within two weeks," says Ilana. Ilana would read the replies in Arabic on the radio. On many occasions the patients would ask Ilana whether she could arrange for Israeli visas so that they could be treated at Hadassah. In nearly every case she could.

The flow of Arabs from countries still at war with Israel grew to such proportions that Ilana went to Ben-Gurion Airport to meet the arrivals late at night. One summer day, twelve patients arrived simultaneously, eight of them to be treated for eye problems.

"I am constantly deluged with problems from a dozen Arab countries," says Ilana. One psychosomatic skin problem was raised by a man in an extremely bellicose nation. The ailment required the patient to be seen personally by the physician. The patient, who could not go to Israel for political reasons, asked that the physician, Ya'acov Shanon, meet with him in Europe. Professor Shanon, who at one time headed the unit at Hadassah

Ein Kerem dealing with the problem, agreed to go without a fee but only if Ilana accompanied him as translator.

Ilana and the professor spent ten days abroad. She paid her own expenses and refused to accept the patient's offer of a refund. "The patient went home cured," Ilana reported.

A large number of Ilana's listeners complain of eye problems. Many ask for second opinions. A mother in the oil-rich Arab state of Qatar wrote to Ilana that doctors in Europe refused to treat her three-year-old blind baby because the chance of success was low. Ilana consulted Shaul Merin, Ophthalmology Unit head at Scopus, whose examination confirmed an unusual congenital vitreous disease that had kept the baby sightless since birth. He operated successfully. After a short recovery, the mother and her seeing child went home elated and full of praise for Israel, Hadassah and Professor Merin.[12]

By the time Ilana reached the mandatory retirement age of sixty-five in April 1997, she was doing a five-minute spot six days a week, one live fifty-five-minute call-in program on Sundays, and a half-hour show on Thursdays. When her listeners heard she was about to retire, Ilana was inundated with letters from all over the Arab world to continue. Her bosses agreed and so has Ilana.

"I will go on working even though officially I am retired," Ilana said, and added with a laugh, "There are crazy people in this world, and I am one of them."

---

12 Hadassah ophthalmologist Shmuel Levinger traveled to Tashkent, Uzbekistan, in 1995 to help open an eye hospital. He headed a team of ten local doctors and fifteen nurses. In three weeks, he examined 350 patients, performed 49 operations on patients with cataracts and glaucoma, and gave 40 hours of lectures. In 1996, he returned and in one week operated on sixty-three patients, half of whom were blind. All were able to see afterwards. "I kept busy," he says.

FOR THE LOVE OF PEOPLE

Most people have some natural, inner strength or characteristic that helps express their personality. For me, it has been a love of people.

— *Kalman Jacob Mann, Reflections on a Life in Health Care*

The changing of the Hadassah Medical Organization guard took place in Jerusalem on September 1, 1981.

On that day HMO Director-General Dr. Kalman Jacob Mann, preeminent among the nation's medical managers, retired and made way for Shmuel Penchas, a specialist in internal medicine and health administration. Then Hadassah moved into a new world of medicine where high technology and cost effectiveness took on paramount importance.

Kalman Mann had served as director-general for more than thirty years under ten Hadassah Presidents. No one had ruled the roost longer. Under Mann's guiding hand, the hospital evolved from a fragmented institution improvising to meet critical needs into an imposing university, a teaching medical center of world esteem.

Four of Ein Kerem's five professional schools were founded during Mann's tenure: pharmacology, dentistry, occupational therapy and public health. He opened Ein Kerem, reopened Mount Scopus and multiplied the number of beds at these institutions from 100 to 1,100 and the staff from several hundred to 4,250. During his tenure, the budget increased over 40 times from $2,300,000 to $93,000,000.[1] Specialization began and research programs were organized. Ten services became 75. Acute care units were introduced, as were academic nursing, social service and dentistry for geriatric patients. Hadassah became the first to start family medicine as a specialty.

But more significant than these accomplishments, Mann had impressed the entire organization with the need to put heart and soul into HMO's bricks and mortar. He had brought to Hadassah new generations of physicians and nurses. His most difficult battle was against the explosive health costs that began in the mid-1960s. For Mann, a humanitarian and a healer, costs were secondary to the doctor's need to provide the best medical care to the most who could benefit. If a new building were vital to the community, he would begin, in the spirit of Henrietta Szold, never sure where the money would come from to finish the job. Somehow the price tag would be covered. The economic philosophy underlying the principle was in keeping with the overall expansive, creative spirit of the new Jewish nation.

Kalman Mann's peers and students remember him for his lectures on the overriding importance of people and spirit. A typical Mann lecture to students would contain lines like these:

> If your point of departure is always money, you will destroy the institution in no time. You take millions of dollars to build a hospital, millions of dollars to equip it and millions of dollars to maintain the physical part. If you don't have

---

1 HMO's total budget for the year 2001 was approximately $400,000,000.

millions of dollars to create the people in it who will later on produce the *neshoma* (soul, spirit), then you have done very little.

It was a tribute to his inspired leadership that of the 500 doctors he sent to train in the US and Europe only four did not return. In the end, he did not win the battle of the budget but he did set an example and a standard. After retirement, he continued his humanitarian work, caring for tens of thousands of Israelis by guiding Yad Sarah, a nationwide institution that provides free medical equipment and assistance to patients.

Born in 1912, the same year as Hadassah, Kalman Jacob Mann suffered fatal injuries in a traffic accident and died on March 14, 1997 at the Ein Kerem Medical Center that he had helped to create. The cherubic smile that reassured was gone, except in the memories of hundreds of thousands of men, women and children the world over who had benefited from his care and concern.

Mann's deputy director Shmuel Penchas was the first Director General to have graduated from the Hebrew University-Hadassah School of Medicine. He took the helm at a time when fast-changing, sophisticated technology was rocketing western medicine into astronomical costs. Fortunately for Hadassah, he was well trained for the battle to contain costs.

Penchas had been the army's medical director in Jerusalem during the Yom Kippur War. One of Mann's specialists in family medicine, he prepared himself for the new age that was dawning in the world of computers and high technology. He joined the world cybernetics revolution, first by studying electrical engineering at the Haifa Technion and then by two years' postgraduate work in medical engineering at London University. That was followed by computer science research in medicine at Harvard University and Massachusetts General Hospital. On his return from Harvard, he was appointed second-in-command. He took up the title of

HMO Director-General in 1981. Mann's successor was well-trained to cope with the new age.

Penchas began by streamlining management and instituting strict control procedures. His operating style was new. No longer was the director-general's door open to all. Where once department heads burst unannounced into Kalman Mann's office, now they went through channels, reporting to their hospital director who, in turn, reported to Penchas.

Penchas went after costs with a vengeance. His eye rarely left the budget or the bottom line. Cost-cutting and cost-effectiveness became his guideposts. He would oppose accepting an endowment for a building unless maintenance money came with it. With the purchase of a big piece of expensive machinery, he demanded that an additional 12 percent be set aside for future maintenance.

His efforts sometimes reaped bitter fruit. In April 1997 the Israel Medical Association authorized rare work sanctions by Hadassah's 700 physicians. They protested, *inter alia*, against Hadassah management's cost-cutting measures, calling for either a 4 percent reduction in pay or the dismissal of eighty doctors.

Then Penchas's deputy, Shlomo Mor-Yosef, explained that neither Hadassah management nor the physicians were responsible for the HMO's accumulated deficit. The blame for the strike was to be laid at the door of the government which took upon itself the responsibility for running a nationalized health system it would not, or could not, finance. Besides, the government fixed fees and growth rates unrealistically. Hadassah is reimbursed for some services by as much as six or seven times less than the actual cost, noted Mor-Yosef.

The most dramatic changes in healthcare during the last quarter of a century are the soaring cost of medicine and rapidly changing technology. Costs have run so high that even wealthy nations find it difficult to cover the health bill. For medical practitioners, the emerging ethical and moral problems can be horrendous. Doctors and nurses at Ein Kerem's general intensive care unit[2] face these questions daily.

At Ein Kerem, general intensive care is a losing proposition financially. Each of the unit's beds costs the hospital $1,000 a day to run. One nurse is assigned to each patient; a doctor can tend to no more than three or four. Patients need frequent blood infusions and expensive antibiotics. Normally they remain in the intensive care unit (ICU) three to four days, although there have been exceptions. One patient remained 110 days.

In few other areas of the hospital does cost-effectiveness play so vital a role as in intensive care. Says Dr. Yoel Donchin, "If I have ten beds and fifteen patients, some patients cannot be accommodated. Every day we have to choose who is to be treated and who not." Donchin believes the answer to the economic dilemma lies in prevention. But there is a cost effectiveness to prevention as well.

"Not all prevention comes without costs," says Leon Epstein, Director of the Social Medicine Department in the Braun School of Public Health. "No country in the world can provide everything that everybody needs. In the US, that concept is accepted at the governmental level but there are 40,000,000 Americans without health insurance. Many people in the US believe that health is a private commodity that people can buy if they have the money."

To provide the best possible care, a tertiary care hospital like Hadassah must acquire state-of-the-art technology. The new equipment in turn creates more sub-specializations, which require numerous and expensive tests.

For example, in the field of imaging, Hadassah has progressed from simple X-rays to CT scans, MRI's and the $4,000,000 Positron Emission

---

2   The Ein Kerem medical center has special intensive care units for anesthesiology, neurology, burns, pediatrics, cardiology, cardiothoracic surgery, neonatology, and special diseases. Surgical cases are directed to general intensive care.

Tomography (PET)[3] and isotope-producing Cyclotron. Lasers, nuclear medicine, cobalt guns, linear accelerators, automated labs and a lithotripter are part of Hadassah's inventory of equipment valued at $45,000,000.

Because of the cost, more medicine is practiced outside the hospital than in the past. Says Penchas, "Hospitals are slowly being transformed into huge intensive care units. Most non-intensive care is ambulatory or done in day-care units." And hospitalization periods have been cut. Once mothers remained in the hospital for up to a week after giving birth; they are now released from Hadassah within 48 hours.

At the same time, specialization has brought Hadassah an impressive list of Israeli "firsts": a bone bank, a skin bank to treat burns, a trauma unit. Shimon Slavin's Bone Marrow Transplantation Department was one of the first to carry out the procedure successfully. Like saplings from mother trees, new departments have sprouted from sub-specialties such as hematology, gastroenterology, nephrology and vascular surgery.

Not everything about the Ein Kerem campus is cost containment, miracle-making machines or sophisticated specialties. It is also a world where pink kangaroos and yellow elephants exist with red rabbits and blue lions. This wonderland, a delight to the child's eye, is located on the main plaza of the Ein Kerem campus and is referred to by adults as the Mother and Child Center.

Dedicated during national convention in Jerusalem in August, 1995 as "child-friendly," the six-story building was tied like a gift with 745 feet of cherry-red, polyester ribbon. "A gift from Hadassah to the people of Jerusalem," said President Deborah Kaplan. A donkey with milk cans suspended from its side grazed the grounds during the ceremony, a symbol

---

3   PET is a research and diagnostic tool that goes one step beyond the images of a CT Scan and an MRI. It identifies the metabolism of a tissue, which is especially useful in treating tumors. It can show functioning of the brain in real time. Hadassah was first in the Middle East, and among the first anywhere, to use it. A French friend of Hadassah donated the PET and his foundation maintains it.

of the donkeys who carried Hadassah's Donkey Milk Express some eight decades previously. The Center's Jula Goldwurm Maternity Pavilion opened the following June. On June 16th, the Center's first baby was born to Devorah Asulin by Caesarean section. He was named Israel. The Wolfson Children's Pavilion received its first patients on September 9, 1996.

The Center's entrance is an invitation to play. Architect Arthur Spector[4] designed an arched gateway for this $27,000,000 building with a decorative green cube on the corner of either side and a blue ball balancing a red triangle in the center. On the triangle, a smiling yellow kangaroo with an infant in her pouch greets everyone into the miracle building where sick children become well and mothers have babies. The marsupial and its infant became the Center's logo.

Director-General Penchas had set the tone for the building when he approached the National Board with a request that "we do something for the children." The concept of providing a "Road to Recovery" was that of the late Blanche Shukow, a national Vice-President known for her imagination and creativity. Says Bonnie Lipton, then HMO Chair, "It was her idea that everything — sheets, towels, pajamas, ceilings, walls — be adorned with children's figures."

"To help a child find its way around," says Spector, "we identified each floor with its own color and an animal as well as a number." Cars, trucks, boats, computer games, music room, kindergarten, glass elevator framed by towers and turrets — here is a world familiar to children.

Wherever the kids turn, there is fantasy land. Smiling, green-faced trash cans with round yellow tummies open to accept chewing gum wrappers when young patients grab the trash man's nose. *Mezuzot* are shaped like rockets with blue bodies and red-pointed tops. Two white hands clasp them. "Children like to grab," explains a guide escorting visitors. Says

---

4   Arthur Spector's late mother, Dorothy, of Brookline, Massachusetts, was a member of the National Board and, a life member of Hadassah's Honorary Council.

Bonnie, "If someone gives us a $1,000,000 gift, their enamel plaque is designed with turrets and towers and magic hands. The motif is carried throughout."

The fifty maternity and seventy-eight pediatric beds are in semi-private rooms, each equipped with futon beds for parents to sleep overnight. Thirty-six cradles hold newborn infants. Designed to serve Jerusalem's 200,000 children, the Center was so crowded during its first week that women had their babies in the corridors. Six delivery rooms[5] were insufficient.

Teachers tutor hospitalized schoolchildren, who stay in touch with their schools via e-mail. Anorexia and bulimia patients attend cooking classes under the direction of a dietitian. A child recovering from brain surgery kneads dough. Choice of menu makes the hospital stay a happier experience when a junior patient can choose lunch from a menu of hamburgers, schnitzel and hot dogs or pizza and French fries with cake and chocolate milk for dessert.

Spector says confidently, "This building speaks a different language to a different generation."

But does it speed the healing? Some parents are certain that it does. Says Ahuva Shachar, mother of 18-month-old Rivka, who was moved to the new pavilion when it first opened, "We'd been hearing about the move for a long time. I can't say I was particularly interested in luxury. All I wanted was for Rivka to be well again. But better conditions help us all."

But some prospective parents had to battle infertility. Next door to the Center, Dr. Aby Lewin has taken on the heartbreaking problem of infertility in both men and women, and pre-implantation diagnosis. As a result of Dr. Lewin's lab's successes, people who previously had no chance of having biological offspring can be more hopeful. One anxious, childless man who had been married thirteen years was aided through the lab's work and, in time, his wife gave birth to a boy through test-tube fertilization.

---

5   Referred to euphemistically at the Center as "birthing rooms."

Says Aby, "The couple could hardly believe the miracle and, to tell the truth, it was hard for me to believe it as well. Since then, we have performed the new treatment many times."

Research projects are part of the fabric of Hadassah. To jump-start investigations of ailments that have stumped the medical profession, the research and development department provides researchers with leads to funding and help in writing proposals.

A procedure is being developed at Hadassah to cure thalassemia, a crippling and ultimately fatal disease genetically transmitted. The procedure involves transplanting blood cells from the umbilical cord of newborn infants. There are only six umbilical cord blood banks in the world, one of them at Ein Kerem.

Dermatology has one of the more active research programs at Ein Kerem. The original studies of Zvi Even-Paz, who formerly headed the department, showed that extensive sun exposure[6] and bathing in the mineral-rich waters in the Dead Sea region cleared skin eruptions brought on by psoriasis. The relief brought to patients with much less risk than from the side effects of other therapies led to the creation of a spa center that attracts thousands of sufferers to the area from abroad. The economic by-product has been the creation of a countrywide health industry based on the Dead Sea's unique natural resources. In 1996 it earned $132,000,000 and attracted 200,000 patients. Ten percent of those were from abroad.

Textbooks had long claimed that young children are not affected by fungal infections. After examining 1,200 children aged six to fourteen, Hadassah dermatologist Vera Leibovici and her team found that fungus develops between toes and in nails, and that unless treated early, the disease can become nearly impossible to cure.

---

6   Long exposure to the sun at the Dead Sea is possible because nature filters out most of the harmful rays. The mineral content of the Sea and adjacent springs are the richest in the world.

David Enk, a specialist in immunological reactions, has studied melanomas, one of the most dangerous of all cancers. With financing from an Israeli cosmetic firm, he has been investigating how a pigment produced from tomatoes may have a positive effect on the skin.

In orthopedics, Charles Howard has experimented on mending fractures, especially among the aged. In geriatric medicine, Dan Dannenberg has collaborated with Arieh Ben-Yehuda to see whether a particular molecule improved the immune system in the elderly, and whether it improved the effect of anti-flu vaccines.

Neurologist Oded Abramsky carried out the first trials on a drug developed in Israel that is effective against the early stages of multiple sclerosis.[7]

Research has benefited every branch of medicine. Noteworthy is the unremitting struggle against homo sapiens's greatest natural enemy — heart disease.

In 1967, South African surgeon Christiaan Barnard showed that transplanting the human heart was one realistic solution for a diseased heart. But patients did not survive long because their bodies rejected the new hearts. Transplants only became viable in 1985 with the introduction of cyclosporin, a drug that overcame the rejection problem. Two years later Hadassah cardiothoracic surgeon Joseph "Joe" Borman, a South African like Barnard, would perform the first successful heart transplant in Israel.[8]

But before Borman could proceed, Hadassah first had to obtain rabbinical permission for the procedure. A day-long seminar with thirty doctors took place at the hospital with Israel's two chief rabbis. After the physicians presented their case with slides, statistics and explanations, the

---

7   The drug copaxone was developed by Professor Michael Sela, Professor Ruth Arnon and Dr. Dvora Teitelbaum of the Weizmann Institute of Science, Rehovot. Arnon and Teitelbaum received "Women of Distinction" awards from Hadassah at its 85th anniversary celebrations in Jerusalem in January, 1997.

8   Two transplants in Israel were attempted in 1968 by Tel Aviv surgeons but the patients did not survive one month.

rabbis acknowledged that the overriding principle of *pikuaḥ nefesh* (saving a life) applied.

Borman and his teams had the green light. But organ donors were scarce. Through most of 1987, the two teams were constantly on the alert. Once a heart became available, they had only twelve hours to begin the operation.

Borman takes up the story:

> No teams could have been better prepared than we were. The recipient was a grandfather, Ovadia Matzri, 51. He was given 90 minutes notice to come to the hospital. He and his family arrived at 6:30 and shortly before 10:00 pm the operation had begun. Fifteen doctors worked simultaneously in two operating rooms.
>
> We were in a state of high tension after all the preparations but everything went like clockwork. In a long career in cardiac surgery I've had many exciting moments. But nothing before or since ever compared with that first human heart transplant when we took the clamp off the aorta and blood began flowing into the new heart.
>
> We gave it an electric shock and it started to beat. I felt that heart beating through my entire body. I stood and stared down at it. In place of the huge sick heart we had cut out only a short while before, a young healthy heart was beating vigorously. I watched it and knew that the patient would be well.[9]

Transplants then became a common occurrence at Hadassah. A milestone was reached in 1992, when five human organs — liver, pancreas, heart and

---

9   Matzri survived for three years, then died of a stroke unrelated to the transplant. The survival of transplant patients is now 80 percent for up to one year, 70 percent to five years and 50 percent as long as ten years.

both kidneys — of a twenty-nine-year-old man were used to save the lives of four different patients. The donor's two corneas were put aside for future use.

Despite all the sophisticated machines and wonder drugs available to modern medicine, a physician must frequently tell a patient that there is nothing more that can be done. Too often, the doctor's unhappy verdict is, "You'll just have to learn to live with it."

Well, not necessarily. In the past few decades, great numbers of patients have been exploring alternative therapies. Hadassah's expert in the field is Martine Toledano, head of the unit for complementary medicine. Martine received her medical degree in Paris. At first she thought the idea of complementary medicine was "rubbish." But as she learned more, she says, she became enthusiastic:

> It's clear we need some additional form of medicine, but in 1990 when our unit was established at Ein Kerem, most doctors were unwilling to believe what they could not explain. Things have now changed. Most doctors recognize there are many ways to help a patient. Someone suffering backache can be treated with a course of Voltaren or with Chinese medicine or another approach. In short, complementary medicine adds therapeutic tools to the doctor's arsenal.

The Hadassah physician's armory is formidable: homeopathy, acupuncture, osteopathy, chiropractice, auricular therapy, reflexology, Feldenkreis and hypnosis. In an examination, Dr. Martine Toledano's team will look at a patient's foot or eye or test the body's energy.

"Patients used to come to us as a last resort. Now we will be the first resort. Patients who don't like taking drugs or want to avoid surgery will see first whether complementary medicine has anything to offer them. Usually we have."

Hundreds of patients go to the unit each month. "That is a sign we are succeeding," says Martine. "We treated one woman whose entire body was affected with lesions from psoriasis. Her body is now completely clean. An 80-year-old man came to us because he did not want to undergo surgery for a disc problem. After three treatments, his pain was far less and he no longer feels he needs surgery. We've had particular success in treating pain problems that Hadassah's pain clinic cannot help."

Many cancer patients apply to the unit. Says Martine, "We always encourage them to continue their chemotherapy but we help them cope with it better on an emotional level. With homeopathy and reflexology techniques we can help decrease side effects. "We are a clinic of doctors who simply offer more treatment possibilities."

Hadassah Ein Kerem is a self-contained city devoted to healing, research and teaching. Within its precincts, a visitor can find a bank, a post office, a travel agent, a synagogue or great art. Its halls teem with men and women in white or green rushing about carrying vials, reading charts, answering emergency calls, wheeling beds — all to preseve life or relieve suffering.

All who enter Hadassah, great and small, are given the best treatment that science and compassion can offer. The two medical centers at either pole of Jerusalem resonate with accomplishments that have won worldwide attention.

About to conclude his tenure as HMO Director-General in 1998, Shmuel Penchas could deservedly take pride in having played a major role in orchestrating many of these achievements. The following words, spoken by Penchas before a Hadassah assembly, could well serve as a guide to charter HMO's course into the twenty-first century:

> The Hadassah Medical Organization can be the envy of other nations. I believe in the uniqueness of what HMO must do — this is a brave new world where we shall not treat diseases after they occur, but where we will prevent their

inception. We will be there at the cradle, preventing an early grave.

What Hadassah is now enabling HMO to do is of major importance to humanity, to the Jewish people, to the battle for women's and children's health, and to the glory of the State of Israel.

AFTERWORD

by Teddy Kollek

Hadassah and I were born within months of each other, on opposite sides of the globe. It, of course, was as unaware of the infant struggling into life in pre-World War I Vienna as I was of the group of determined women in New York who sent two nurses to open a health station in Jerusalem — and launched a singular medical phenomenon.

I discovered them sooner than they found out about me. By the time I reached Palestine twenty-two years later, Hadassah had already thrown a network of health stations across the country, one of them within reach of the swampy Kinneret shore where I went to build a new kibbutz.

It was not until the late 1940s and early 1950s, however, when I spent four years in the United States that I made contact with Hadassah on its home ground. It was then I first began to understand the single-minded vigor of these women and their involvement in the health and social services of a country 6,000 miles away.

Five years later, I was chairing the Israel Government Tourist Corporation. Around 45,000 tourists were expected that year — a small figure compared with the numbers who come today, but then as now an important injection into the country's economy.

But with the Sinai Campaign, the United States placed a ban on travel to the Middle East. Tourism plummeted. Israel's hoteliers and everyone else who depended on the tourist trade faced bankruptcy. The isolation was strongly felt not only in the economic field.

Almost naturally I turned to Hadassah. I asked that they schedule a mission in Jerusalem and request State Department permission for its members to attend. Hadassah agreed and marched into action. The tourist blockade was broken and Israel, particularly Jerusalem, was turned into the international convention center it is today.

With this kind of precedent, I was not at all surprised thirty-five years later when Hadassah moved part of its 1991 mid-winter convention to Jerusalem, arriving even as Saddam Hussein's scud missiles were falling. It was a gesture of solidarity and cheer that I and other Jerusalemites appreciated — another link in the bond between Hadassah and Jerusalem.

Part of the reason this bond has endured is that Hadassah holds Jerusalem at the center of its aspirations. It is no mere chance that Hadassah opened its first health station in this most special of cities or built its hospitals and medical schools here.

One of Hadassah's hallmarks has been practical Zionism, the recognition that the road to a dream begins with the possible, building under its feet even if the ultimate goal remains over a distant horizon. For Hadassah the possible has meant providing the best and most advanced in preventive and curative health care and in medical research and education. By establishing centers of medical excellence, the organization contributes not only to the health of Jerusalem's citizens — and to the modern city's prestige — but also makes a vital and massive contribution to Jerusalem's economy, providing thousands of jobs. Indeed, Hadassah is — along with the national government, the city administration and the Hebrew University — one of Jerusalem's four largest employers.

Another vital and potentially explosive area where Hadassah has contributed so much is promoting the ideal of equality. Hadassah has, since the first day, taken in all comers, regardless of how and where they worship.

That Hadassah has credibility among all sectors of the population has been borne out many times. When Jerusalem was divided, Hadassah was cut off from most of the Arab population who had come to know it before 1948, but its reputation survived. In the first days after the city's reunification, the large number of Arabs who showed up at Hadassah demonstrated that its good name was intact even beyond a hostile frontier; this is one of the greatest tributes to Hadassah.

Hadassah has done the seemingly impossible so often that it is now virtually expected of the organization. It has raised phenomenal sums of money to build and maintain high-technology hospitals that practice advanced medicine. It has solved practical and administrative, political and bureaucratic problems along the way because the objective was so clear that obstacles were seen merely as challenges to be overcome.

I'll never forget how Hadassah responded to my phone call in June 1967. Hadassah's original hospital on Mount Scopus had been behind Jordanian lines for nineteen years, during which time the new medical center had risen in Ein Kerem.

It was in the heady week of the Six-Day War; the battle for Jerusalem had just been won. Somewhat euphoric myself, I picked up the phone and called Kalman Mann, then Director-General of the Hadassah-Hebrew University Medical Center. "If you want your hospital, come and get it," I said. And come they did. First Dr. Mann and his colleagues came, renewing acquaintance with the abandoned building on Mount Scopus. Within weeks Hadassah had undertaken a massive fund-raising drive to rebuild its first hospital even though it had been replaced with the Ein Kerem facility. Instead of a single hospital anchoring one end of the city, Hadassah's two hospitals would embrace Jerusalem from opposite sides.

Approaching the close of its first century, Hadassah is visibly full of vigor. Its hospitals are flourishing, its community health center is expanding, its technical college is growing, its career center is busier than ever. As always Hadassah remains flexible and responsive. Today, Soviet and Ethiopian immigrants need help and all Hadassah's multi-faceted institutions are involved. Tomorrow? I don't know as yet, nor do they, but I've no doubt that as soon as they do, they'll play their part.

I am proud to share the year of my birth with Hadassah, though I know that I will not be able to match its record for longevity. But I have no doubt that the city beloved by us all will keep pace with this extraordinary organization. And I hope that some successor of mine, some mayor of Jerusalem a hundred years hence, will be privileged to write a tribute to yet another update of *It Takes a Dream*.

Teddy Kollek

EPILOGUE

"The new world ahead will require an intensification of every strength and every fineness — intellectual vigor, purity of soul, fervent spirit — but also of new outlooks and new vistas. For the task of achieving such ends…may Hadassah fortify you, whether your role in the new era be to follow or to lead."

— *Henrietta Szold*

These words of Hadassah's founder are prophetic. A visionary of biblical scale, Szold understood that an organization is the sum total of its past, its present and — most importantly — its future. It also represents the collective wisdom of those who came before and those who are today charged with moving Hadassah forward.

As we move into the heart of the 21st century, we see that some things remain as they were in Szold's day. There is still a critical need for first rate medical care in Israel. Without advanced education, a nation's and a people's opportunities are limited. And our youth are, quite simply, our future. However, in the 90 years since Hadassah's founding the world has changed in ways that not even Szold could have imagined. In fact, the world is a different place today than it was only 15 years ago. We have learned new words and concepts like "internet," "globalization" and "distance medicine" that would have been meaningless to most of us, even in the mid-1990s.

With our evolution as a society and an organization, we have asked our national presidents, past and present, to imagine how Hadassah will move forward into this brave, new shrinking world of instant communication: what these changes mean to our organization and what our organization means to these changes. What follows is their collective wisdom and vision, or to paraphrase Henrietta Szold: "new outlooks and vistas expressed with intellectual vigor, purity of soul, fervent spirit." May Hadassah fortify you!

MEDICINE AND HEALTH CARE

The present decade shows promise for unprecedented medical breakthroughs in new treatments for our most dreaded diseases — the breakthrough in understanding gene therapy has opened new horizons for potential cures. Cancer treatments, organ and tissue transplantation, and stem cell research will bring new hope for discovery of future treatments and new life-saving modalities. Innovative medical and biotechnological research will be an invaluable tool in the fight against debilitating and once fatal diseases.

Therefore, I envision a vast increase in research grants to our young, talented physicians — those receiving specialized scholarships will study abroad in advanced scientific institutions. Investment in tomorrow's medical leaders is key to Hadassah's future growth and will enable Hadassah and Israel to maintain their renowned and respected reputations in the world of science and medicine.

The Hadassah Medical Organization will take creative steps to reach out to the people of Israel by intensifying its public health information and education seminars and symposia. In Hebrew, Arabic and English, HMO will conduct programs on radio, television and the internet, geared to teach the varied populations of Israel about preventive measures, new treatments, and their own civic responsibility for the health and wellbeing of their families and their communities. Hadassah will go directly to some sectors of the Israeli public by presenting health education lectures in the Ultra-Orthodox communities and in Druze and Arab villages.

— *Charlotte Jacobson*, National President 1964-1968

TECHNOLOGY

Never in their wildest sci-fi predictions did the authors of that literary genre foresee the full extent of our future. And, in that future, I foresee even more developments that can be used for the betterment of us all.

I foresee our technological college geared to the needs of the 21st and 22nd centuries, a world filled with mechanisms and artificial intelligence equipment that will be serviced and equipped by educated and knowledgeable people. Our students will learn how to control the virus that eats information by deletion, how to be of assistance through higher mathematics, how to help fight disease, and protect privacy. The mind staggers at the possibilities, but we know that Israel will produce the physicists, the inventors, the engineers, and the teachers who will lead the world.

What is a school? In the next century, or maybe sooner, that will be a legitimate question. Classrooms and lecturers, books to read and study and enjoy will have almost vanished. The computer will rule. But, in order to use the machines, in order to keep them working, there will be a need for physicists, program writers, mathematicians, etc. The Hadassah College of Technology will be at the heart of such training and teaching through methods as yet only dreams.

There will be a brave new world in which individuals will utilize their best attributes and will achieve spiritual fulfillment according to their abilities and desires. Let us hope that such a time will come — and that our children and their children will learn to use the technological advances with wisdom and in peace.

— *Rose E. Matzkin*, National President 1972-1976*

---

* As we went to press, former National President Rose E. Matzkin died. We are honored to share her last formal statement as President.

THE INTERNATIONAL SCENE

In the coming era of intensified globalization, I foresee a burst of productivity, innovation and growth that will revolutionize the Hadassah landscape in international arenas.

In the United Nations, Hadassah will build boldly upon the milestone victory achieved when it was granted special consultative status in ECOSOC (the UN Economic and Social Council).

Hadassah's passion and powerful voice will earn global respect as its leaders demonstrate their creative talents in groundbreaking international conferences and symposia. Hadassah will bring the expertise and experience of its volunteers and its medical, research and educational personnel to world platforms — thus opening up new avenues of outreach to people and places around the globe.

Hadassah will be in the forefront of the battles to protect human rights, women's rights, and other international issues of concern to us as Americans, Jews and Zionists. When those who convene global conferences dare to equate "Zionism with Racism" and attempt to isolate Israel and define her as a pariah in the world community, accusing her of genocide or crimes against humanity, they will be challenged by forceful and knowledgeable Hadassah leaders. Together with other like-minded delegations, they will fight and finally defeat the inclusion of these canards in any and all United Nations' documents, agendas and debates!

Hadassah will also galvanize its energies to expand the frontiers of its own international family. Hadassah will venture into new areas — planting roots in the Far East, the Pacific Rim Countries and Eastern Europe. I predict that in the first two decades of the 21st century, Hadassah will double the numbers of its units, resulting in a dynamic Hadassah presence in more than 60 countries on all continents. By then, we will also have established a vast network of new cooperative relationships between scientific institutions all over the world and the Hadassah Medical Organization in Jerusalem. --- This is my vision — this is not a dream — and if we will it, we can make it happen!

— *Bernice S. Tannenbaum*, National President 1976-1980

THE NEW CENTURY

I have been involved with Hadassah for over half of the 20th century and a witness to the steadfastness of our purpose and goals. I believe the inevitable changes that will take place in the 21st century will not change Hadassah's mission. Just as Hadassah has, for over fifty years, been in the forefront of Israel's efforts to rescue, mold and educate its youth at risk, I believe Hadassah will have to remain involved in this blessed work in the years ahead.

Family structures will continue to change. Home-centered and residential education will undergo constant re-evaluation. The future will be shaped by computers, new teaching tools and methods not yet invented, but youth will still be at the center of our concerns.

Technology will change, borders may change, but human nature rarely does! There will always be young boys and girls who will need to be rescued from troubled homes or receive special attention and education to ensure their proper development. The richest nations in the world have never been able to solve the problems of youth at risk without the help of voluntary organizations. There will always be a need for Hadassah to help the disadvantaged youth of Israel. The method and means to fulfill these may vary, but the goal will not!

— *Ruth W. Popkin*, National President 1984-1988

THE AMERICAN SCENE

The contours of American national life will depend in no small part on the number of Americans who will shape it. While the American population grows and becomes even more ethnically diverse, sadly the Jewish community will continue to shrink. Therefore, everyone within this smaller community will have a greater responsibility to be proactive because they will be the keepers of our heritage as Jews. The *Power of One* will take on added significance to protect the core values of democracy as well.

Recognizing that the information age will knit the world ever closer together, Hadassah must intensify its efforts to use the most advanced technologies to teach, inform and reach each member directly with the important issues of the moment.

Critical issues will continue to be under attack. Hadassah will have to increase its advocacy of strict separation between church and state, protecting reproductive choice and quality of life and medical initiatives. Continuing foreign aid to Israel will be a major concern. As the largest Zionist organization in the United States, Hadassah believes that Israel is central to the identity and security of the Jewish people, and will maintain, as a priority, its advocacy for Israel and Zionism.

The ultimate power of Hadassah lies in each member participating intelligently and fully as a grassroots activist.

— *Carmela E. Kalmanson*, National President 1988-1991

JEWISH EDUCATION

In the basic field of Jewish education, Hadassah must aspire to raise its organizational sights — not only to engage American Jewish women and men in the study of Jewish texts, both ancient and modern, in English and Hebrew — but to again be the catalyst for intensive Jewish family education and learning.

Hadassah needs and wants our Jewish education leaders to truly be the transmitters of knowledge. Therefore we must inspire, teach and fund them at training seminars that will thoroughly prepare them to become great Jewish leaders as well as family education teachers.

With National's support and encouragement, Hadassah units should be sponsoring educational seminars that explore and analyze the classics of our tradition, even as they grapple with the relevant issues in Jewish life, which will be important in the future. We must provide cutting-edge educational materials that are effective, important and prescient; material that must be delivery-available on the Internet.

Both the *Hadassah Magazine* and our Internet websites should provide a monthly review of our various courses of study.

Every member must want/accept an obligation for personal ongoing study. But it is the National office that must regularly offer a generous Jewish-based curriculum in order that every member at whatever level — will be ensured a deeper and more committed connection to Jewish textual traditions. Whether peripheral or intense, every member should expect to be the recipient of ongoing education for herself as her heritage/right and Hadassah's responsibility.

Because assimilation into contemporary non-Jewish life will soon become the norm rather than the exception — Hadassah leaders must recognize that-individually and organizationally — their vision must be directed to provide Hadassah members with the necessary skills, teachers and materials that will enable them to understand their Jewish heritage on the highest levels and create the continuum for Jewish survival for themselves and their families.

Visionaries and dreamers...this is who we are! Jewish educators and inheritors...this, too, is who we are. This vision reflects both our past history and our hopes and dreams for the future. It is fired by a spark and a passion and an intangible element that makes Hadassah unique and distinct. This is who we are...and we are like no other organization!

— *Deborah B. Kaplan*, National President 1991-1995

YOUTH

Hadassah proudly moved into the new millennium committed to the renaissance of Young Judaea, its pacesetting Zionist Youth Movement that emerged from its most invigorating period of growth in its 92-year history. Young Judaea, deeply rooted in its historical ideals has new innovative and visionary programs, which increased enrollments in camp and Israeli programs to all time heights. Our graduates have a meaningful and significant presence and impact on American and Israeli life and society, nurtured and taught to them through their educational and inspirational learning years in our Zionist Youth Movement.

I believe that peer-led Young Judaea will become the primary vital Zionist and Jewish experiential, educational force for young people. Together with Hadassah, Young Judaea will be known and respected as the visionary creators of Jewish leadership, embracing core values of Judaism, Zionism, education, service and love for our people.

The headlines will reflect Hadassah's nurturing results. Young Judaean elected National Hadassah President! Young Judaeans become heads of each religious stream and vow to work for Jewish peoplehood! A Young Judaean — the Prime Minister of Israel! A Young Judaean — President of the United States! A Young Judaean wins the Noble Peace Prize for bringing lasting peace in the Middle East!

— *Marlene E. Post*, National President 1995-1998

LOOKING TO THE FUTURE

I cannot express my own vision without returning to the prophetic vision of Henrietta Szold whose profound understanding of the needs of Zion was surpassed only by the agenda she set and the legacy she left for the women of Hadassah to follow.

To look to the future, one must thoroughly understand that 90 years after our founding, health, Zionist and Jewish education, child rescue, land reclamation and youth still remain at the heart of our mission.

This continuity is what has strengthened Hadassah and given us the courage and the power to be pioneers and standard setters in our Israel institutions. It is also what makes us strong advocates for Israel on Capitol Hill and strong advocates for issues that are imperatives for us as American Jewish women.

My vision for the future of Hadassah is to continue to be guided by our mission and to continue to find new and creative ways to meet the needs of tomorrow in a complex world of change.

Call it vision or call it dreams —

- To imbue new generations with the spirit, the meaning and the purpose of Zionism.
- To develop a quality membership to whom HWZOA will provide quality tools to build skills and leadership.
- To instill a love of Judaism and Zionism in our members and in the generations to come by providing them with training and the opportunity to assume leadership positions in Hadassah and the Jewish community.
- To enhance Jewish education programs and to encourage fluency in the Hebrew language, so that one day Hadassah Board meetings throughout the US may be conducted in Hebrew.
- To promote the ideals of voluntarism for all people everywhere and to provide incentives for attracting women to choose voluntarism as a career path.
- To serve as role models and to educate other populations of women within Israel and in neighboring countries about issues of women's health, child care, family development and other social needs so they can experience personal growth, develop self esteem, improve parenting skills and even more.

Big dreams? Absolutely. But that is what Henrietta Szold taught us. "Dare to dream, and when you dream, dream big." It takes a dream, a dreamer and a doer to turn the dream into reality. That is our past. That is our future.

— *Bonnie Lipton*, National President 1999-

The dream lives on...

Presidents of Hadassah

Henrietta Szold (Founder)*
1912-1921
1923-1926

Alice Seligsberg*
1921-1923

Irma Lindheim*
1926-1928

Zip Szold*
1928-1930

Rose Jacobs*
1930-1932
1934-1937

Rose L. Halprin*
1932-1934
1947-1952

Judith Epstein*
1937-1939
1943-1947

Tamar de Sola Pool*
1939-1943

Etta Rosensohn*
1952-1953

Rebecca Shulman*
1953-1956

*deceased

Dr. Miriam Freund Rosenthal*
1956-1960

Lola Kramarsky*
1960-1964

Charlotte Jacobson
1964-1968

Faye L. Schenk*
1968-1972

Rose E. Matzkin*
1972-1976

Bernice S. Tannenbaum
1976-1980

Frieda S. Lewis*
1980-1984

Ruth W. Popkin
1984-1988

Carmela E. Kalmanson
1988-1991

Deborah B. Kaplan
1991-1995

Marlene Edith Post
1995-1999

Bonnie Lipton
1999-

INDEX